Business and Politics in India

The Other One Percent

Sanjoy Chakravorty, Devesh Kapur, and Nirvikar Singh

Social Justice through Inclusion

Francesca R. Jensenius

Disposession without Development

Michael Levien

The Man Who Remade India

Vinay Sitapati

Business and Politics in India

Edited by Christophe Jaffrelot, Atul Kohli, and Kanta Murali

Business and Politics in India

EDITED BY CHRISTOPHE JAFFRELOT,
ATUL KOHLI, AND KANTA MURALI

OXFORD
UNIVERSITY PRESS

OXFORD
UNIVERSITY PRESS

Oxford University Press is a department of the University of Oxford. It furthers the University's objective of excellence in research, scholarship, and education by publishing worldwide. Oxford is a registered trade mark of Oxford University Press in the UK and certain other countries.

Published in the United States of America by Oxford University Press
198 Madison Avenue, New York, NY 10016, United States of America.

Library of Congress Cataloging-in-Publication
Data Names: Jaffrelot, Christophe, editor. | Kohli, Atul, editor. | Murali, Kanta, editor.
Title: Business and politics in India / edited by Christophe Jaffrelot,
Atul Kohli and Kanta Murali.
Description: New York : Oxford University Press, [2019]
Identifiers: LCCN 2018017070 | ISBN 9780190912468 (hardcover) |
ISBN 9780190912475 (paperback) | ISBN 9780190912482 (updf) | ISBN 9780190912499 (epub)
Subjects: LCSH: Industrial policy—India. | Business and politics—India.
Classification: LCC HD3616.I43 B87 2019 |
DDC 338.954—dc23 LC record available at https://lccn.loc.gov/2018017070

1 3 5 7 9 8 6 4 2

Paperback printed by WebCom, Inc., Canada
Hardback printed by Bridgeport National Bindery, Inc., United States of America

CONTENTS

ACKNOWLEDGMENTS

This project was conceived over a lunch conversation between Atul Kohli and Christophe Jaffrelot on the Princeton campus. Atul then applied for a grant to the Princeton Institute for International and Regional Studies (PIIRS). This facilitated the conference that led to this volume. Thanks are thus due to the director of PIIRS at that time, Mark Beissinger, for funding this project. Christophe and Atul then invited Kanta Murali to join as the third editor. All three chose the paper writers. In addition to the paper writers, five other scholars joined the small conference at Princeton: Amrita Basu, Kanchan Chandra, Devesh Kapur, Sanjay Ruparelia, and Vinay Sitapati. We would like to thank them for their helpful comments on the early drafts of the papers that appear in this volume. When Atul presented an outline of the project at the meetings of the American Political Science Association in 2016, Ashutosh Varshney was kind enough to invite us to submit the volume for consideration in the book series he edits for Oxford University Press. We thank Ashutosh Varshney for this opportunity. Two anonymous reviewers also need to be acknowledged for their useful suggestions for revisions.

CONTRIBUTORS

Rina Agarwala is Associate Professor in the Department of Sociology at Johns Hopkins University.

John Harriss is Professor in the School for International Studies at Simon Fraser University.

Patrick Heller is the Lyn Crost Professor of Social Sciences and Professor of Sociology and International Studies at Brown University.

Christophe Jaffrelot is Senior Research Fellow at CERI-Sciences Po/CNRS.

Rob Jenkins is Professor of Political Science at Hunter College and the Graduate Center at City University of New York.

Sunila S. Kale is Associate Professor, Henry M. Jackson School of International Studies at the University of Washington.

Atul Kohli is the David Bruce Professor of International Affairs at Princeton University.

Partha Mukhopadhyay is Senior Fellow at the Centre for Policy Research.

Kanta Murali is Assistant Professor in the Department of Political Science at the University of Toronto.

C. Rammanohar Reddy is Readers' Editor at Scroll.in.

Aseema Sinha is the Wagener Chair of South Asian Politics and George R. Roberts Fellow in the Department of Government at Claremont McKenna College.

Michael Walton is Senior Lecturer in Public Policy at Harvard Kennedy School.

Andrew Wyatt is Senior Lecturer in the School of Sociology, Politics and International Studies at the University of Bristol.

Business and Politics in India

Introduction

CHRISTOPHE JAFFRELOT, ATUL KOHLI, AND KANTA MURALI

Over the last few decades politics in India has moved steadily in a probusiness direction. The earlier state commitment to socialism and redistribution has been replaced by the goal of growth promotion via support for private enterprise. Unlike in many other developing or communist countries, this important shift in India has been incremental; it has come about within the frame of democracy and without any dramatic regime change. It has also led to a political strengthening within India of indigenous—instead of foreign—capital. The probusiness shift in India has important implications for both how the world's largest democracy is governed and for the life-chances of the citizens of that democracy. In this volume we seek to analyze the growing power of business groups in the Indian polity.

A study of the role of business in Indian politics is of both normative and scholarly significance. As India's economy modernizes rapidly, with the private sector in the lead, some shift in political power toward business groups is to be expected; to an extent, this change is par for the course. Moreover, business groups in any capitalist economy are central economic actors and legitimate participants in the political process. However, the legitimacy of a democracy rests on a variety of citizens and groups having access to power; veto power held by any narrow group threatens to transform a democracy into an oligarchy. The struggle between the power of wealth and the power of numbers is a perennial one in all capitalist democracies. What is important for democracy to flourish is that this struggle is not won once for all by either side.

The moral argument that might support growing concentration of wealth and power would be that such an arrangement helps create greater wealth that will eventually reach the poor. What this standpoint ignores, however, is an omnipresent political question: once the rich come to control the state, and state power becomes more and more privatized, what political pressures will push the state to undertake tasks that serve the broader good? With an enormous number of poor in India, the Indian state faces giant public responsibilities. Beyond poverty alleviation, these responsibilities include provision of education, health, and infrastructure among others. The more the state caters to narrow, private interests, the greater the danger that the public functions of the state will become a distant second concern. Of course, the "socialist" Indian state of the past hardly proved itself a successful agent of inclusive development; it would thus be unfair to attribute the present failures of the Indian state to the growing power of business. Nevertheless, it is the case that, with growing wealth and public revenues, it becomes possible to imagine effective state intervention, aimed at promoting the public good. It need not be added, but we will, that the Indian state at present is hardly effective enough to initiate such public actions; for a journey in that direction to even begin, what will be needed in the future are political leaders who prioritize broader goals over narrow collaboration with the economic elite.

The Scholarly Context

A long tradition of scholarship has probed the power of business in democracies, especially advanced industrial democracies. This scholarship is concerned both with assessing the extent of business power and with how business groups exercise power. As to the first issue, important liberal scholars have suggested that business groups in democracies often exercise more power than other interest groups. Business groups are thus first among equals, who can come to exercise disproportionate control—or "veto power"—that in turn may endanger the health of democracies (e.g., Dahl 1975; Lindblom 1977; Gilens and Page 2014). Some Marxist scholars describe such disproportionate power of business groups in capitalist democracies as hegemonic power. The concept of hegemony suggests that not only do business groups exercise overwhelming power, but they also help create a cultural context in which such control seems natural and inevitable (e.g., Gramsci 1971).

Beyond assessing the extent of business power, both liberal and Marxist scholars have debated whether capitalists influence the functioning of democracies by direct participation in politics, or if the system of capitalism itself constraints capitalist states. The former can be described as instrumental or direct power, while scholars often label the latter mode of exercising power as structural or indirect power.[1] Examples of instrumental power include: when businessmen finance elections to seek favorable policies, lobby governments to tilt decisions in their own favor, or even come to occupy positions of power directly. Structural power, by contrast, operates via the principle that the powerful in society get what they want whether they actively seek it or not.[2] Because businessmen control key economic levers in any capitalist society, politicians must take into account the preference of business groups, both to maintain the health of the economy and to secure their own political futures. Since investors can readily move their investments to more favorable locations, the threat of capital flight is often enough to pressure leaders to pursue probusiness policies. Though scholars may disagree as to which is more prevalent and important—instrumental or structural power—most scholars are likely to agree that the power of business operates via both pathways. We will discuss these general considerations again in subsequent chapters of this volume.

Beyond advanced industrial democracies, scholars have also begun to analyze the role of business in the politics of developing countries (e.g., Handley 2008; Hundt 2009; Schneider 2004; Winters 2011). India is a prime developing country for such studies because of its robust democracy and because of the shift to probusiness economic policies since the 1980s. It is not surprising, then, that scholars of politics and society in India have disagreed in their assessment of the relative power of business groups within the Indian state, as well as on how this power is exercised. While some scholars have suggested that Indian capitalists exercised disproportionate power in the making of modern India (e.g., Chibber 2003), most have suggested that business groups in "socialist" India—say, prior to the 1980s—competed for influence with other powerful groups, such as landed classes and the state elite (e.g., Bardhan 1984; Raj 1973; Kochanek 1974; Rudolph and Rudolph 1987). Since economic liberalization, however, there is a growing sense among scholars that the power of business groups in India has expanded, maybe even dramatically (e.g., Kohli 2012). This shift in balance of power, in turn, points to new issues that are probed systematically in the studies that are included in this volume.

In this volume we pursue several research questions aimed at focusing attention on the growing role of business in Indian politics. First, we seek to assess the power of business groups: has the power of business achieved a nearly hegemonic status? As one might imagine, this question will be difficult to answer categorically, especially because of the nebulous nature of power. Still, we seek to understand if the power of business in India has expanded from veto power—where business groups in the past could block changes that threatened their interests—to agenda-setting power, that is, power to mold future patterns of political and social change. Moreover, as noted above, hegemony implies something more than acquisition of raw power; it suggests a degree of legitimacy associated with the exercise of that power. So we also seek to understand if business groups in India are increasingly capable of transforming power into authority.

Second, whether business power is becoming hegemonic or not, how do business groups mold Indian politics? Scholars of power have well understood that the powerful do not always need to explicitly demand what they want. This is what is meant by structural power. Producers, bankers, and owners of capital occupy pivotal positions in the structure of any private economy. As the role of private business in India's overall economy has grown, how have politicians responded to such changes in the structural power of business? In addition, business groups consciously seek to influence the political process; we seek to understand these efforts too. Conscious strategies in India vary from well-organized efforts via chambers of commerce to personalistic efforts that many characterize as crony capitalism.

And finally we seek to understand how the power of business groups in India varies along several dimensions.[3] At the national level we probe the capacity of business groups to achieve favorable policies in such critical areas as acquisition of land and control over labor. More diffusely, we explore the manner in which business influences the functioning of Indian media and seeks to mold urban spaces. And, of course, given India's regional diversity, we seek to understand the varying political role of business groups in select Indian states.

In this brief introduction to the volume we provide some historical background that helps situate the role of business in the Indian political economy, first in the pre-1980 period—the so-called socialist phase of the Indian political economy—and then over the last few decades as the role of the private sector has expanded steadily. While the basic factual information is likely to be well known to specialists, the interpretation we provide is just as likely to be distinct; moreover, nonspecialists may want a quick overview before moving to more specialized essays. We then finally lay out the plan of the volume, including brief summaries of the essays that follow.

Historical Background

The socialist Indian state of the past, say, from 1950 to 1980, was never deeply antibusiness. For that matter, this state was also never totally beholden to business interests. The reality of state-business relations in India during the socialist phase lay somewhere between these extreme but popular misconceptions. While the state was very much in the lead, India was also very much a private enterprise economy. The political and economic elite forged a working relationship during much of this period, cozy at times but uneasy at other times. State-business relations during this early phase are thus best thought of as varying along several dimensions: over time, along issue areas, and across regional states of India.

Following independence, the Congress Party inherited a moderately well-functioning colonial state and then modified it in line with its own interests and ideology. If the economic focus of the early British colonial state in India was the collection of land revenues, the late colonial state, say, post-1857, was concerned mainly with keeping the Indian economy open for British manufactured goods. This was a law-and-order state that played a minimal role in fostering economic development. In spite of economic neglect, a number of private industries emerged in India during the late nineteenth and the first half of the twentieth centuries: for example, a jute industry—largely British owned—flourished in eastern India; Parsis, Marwaris, and others pioneered textile industry in western India; Tata initiated steel production prior to World War I; and during the interwar years sugar, paper, glass, and even shipbuilding were initiated by Indian industrialists (for details, see Bagchi 1972; Ray 1979; Tomlinson 1993). While the share of large private industry in India at the time of independence was only 7–8 percent of the national product, a small but significant number of large Indian business houses had already made their appearance; these included Birla, Tata, Dalmia, Walchand, Shri Ram, Thapar, and Singhanias.

Indian business groups were already politically active in the first half of the twentieth century (Low 1988). While early Indian industrialists sought to work with the colonial state, following World War I the relations between these business groups and Congress leaders grew warmer. For example, Indian industry did rather well during World War I but then suffered as British imports resumed. Indian industrialists, especially in textile and steel, then lobbied the colonial state furiously for some protections, but largely in vain.[4] Gandhi and others in the Congress Party then took up the cause of government support for private Indian industry.[5] Indian business groups in turn started providing financial support to the Congress, with Gandhi as a key intermediary. The Left within the Congress was of course suspicious of such links. Nevertheless, the uneasy dance between the Congress and Indian business groups had begun well before World War II (e.g., Markovits 1985). Indian business then became organized as a national chamber of commerce. Anticipating independence—and suspicious of the Left within the Congress, especially Nehru—Indian industrialists produced the so-called Bombay Plan in 1943 to influence economic policy of a Congress-led government of sovereign India. Key elements of this plan—such as planning, a mixed economy, protectionism, and public investment in heavy industry—eventually converged with Nehru's preference for a state-led, "socialist" economy (Rothermund 1986).[6] By mid-century, then, Indian capitalists and nationalists had created a working relationship of sorts that fluctuated between mutual suspicion and mutual cooperation.

State-business relations in Nehru's India need to be understood within the political context of the period (e.g., Naseemullah 2017). After the death of Gandhi and Patel, Nehru emerged as India's unquestioned leader, and his brand of left-leaning nationalism became India's dominant ideology. Simplifying drastically, we can say that Nehru's priority was to build a strong, modern India, with the Indian state in the lead (Gopal 1984). The approach to the economy—and thus to the private sector—was a product of this overarching ambition (Myrdal 1968). Nehru emphasized heavy industry as a hallmark of a strong nation-state and sought to promote it via direct state intervention. It is worth recalling that, following World War II, Nehru's state-oriented inclinations were very much part of a shared global belief in the efficacy of the state in solving pressing problems. Though Nehru's model of state-led development—with import substitution as the core strategy—departed from the logic of free markets,[7] the relationship of the state and businessmen during this period was more complicated; some Indian businessmen resented governmental controls, while others flourished within the frame of a relatively closed economy. On the one hand, there can be no denying that the license-permit raj made the life of Indian private industrialists difficult, expensive, and less productive. On the other hand, however, Nehru's nationalist preference to limit foreign investment and goods in India gave Indian businesses ample opportunity to grow while producing for the domestic market.

Nehru's emphasis on the state occupying the "commanding heights" of the economy and on public ownership of heavy industry can readily be characterized as anti-private enterprise.[8] However, the focus on the public sector during this period should be kept in perspective. While some public investment may indeed have "crowded out" the private sector, it was hardly the case that the Indian private sector was ready to enter fields of heavy industry where the rates of return were low or capricious. Thus, for example, we now know that, wanting to expand India's steel industry, Nehru sent his minister of steel—T. T. Krishnamachari, a successful industrialist in his own right and Nehru's confidant—to approach Indian industrialists. It was only when private business was unwilling to enter the field that Nehru decided that the public sector would have to take the lead in steel (Pinglé 1999). Nehru was thus no antibusiness, socialist ideologue. His primary goal was nation-building in India; he worked with Indian business groups when possible, but put his greater faith in state intervention when it came to his core priority of promoting heavy industry.

There is no denying that Indian business was viewed with suspicion in the left-leaning political milieu of the period.[9] While business groups were already organized in two national and several state-level chambers of commerce, systematic links between the political and economic elite were limited. Business groups funded the political activities of the Congress Party, but this was often viewed as something less than legitimate, a set of activities that were best kept under cover. Major links between business and the state were often personalistic instead, whereby agents of business groups established relationships with select ministries and bureaucrats. Bureaucrats enabled business groups to get around the maze of laws and regulations that existed on paper, and business agents in turn returned the favor by greasing the palms of bureaucrats. The more important business houses—such as the Tata group—often had direct contacts with the executive, including Nehru. While state-business relations during the Nehru period may not have been cozy, they were also far from contentious;[10] they were certainly less contentious then they would become during the next phase, namely, during the reign of Indira Gandhi.

As is well known, Indira Gandhi radicalized Indian politics during the 1960s and the 1970s (Frankel 2005; Guha 2007; Jayakar 1992). Even more than during the Nehru period, Indira Gandhi's economic policies reflected her political need to maintain personal power within the context of a turbulent polity. Following Nehru's death, India's political class was factionalized by the mid-1960s, restlessness among India's poor was growing, and Congress's popularity was in decline. Sensing opportunity, Indian business groups started supporting more right-of-center political forces, both within and outside of the Congress Party. It was in this context that Indira Gandhi embraced the populist slogan of *garibi hatao* and split the Congress Party. During this process she also marginalized the more probusiness factions of the Congress party—led by the likes of Morarji Desai—and turned the Congress Party to the left. Indira Gandhi's popularity soared, both as a result of her charismatic populism and due to such fortuitous circumstances as a war against Pakistan that led to the creation of Bangladesh in 1971. The economic policies that Indira Gandhi pursued, then, have to be understood as efforts to maintain her nationalist and left-of-center political credentials in a populist garb.

Indira Gandhi's rhetoric and policies were a mixed bag, left-leaning enough to put a chill on state-business relations during this period, but also ambiguous enough to leave room for some tacit cooperation between the political and economic elite. On the one side of the political ledger, big business and conservative politicians were increasingly treated as enemies of "progress." Nationalization of private banks put real fear in the business community. Antimonopoly restrictions were strengthened, as were growth and the entry of big business into new ventures. Financial contributions by private companies to political parties were also banned. Taken together, these actions of Indira Gandhi could indeed be interpreted as a sharp, antibusiness turn to the left. However, keen observers could not miss a more mixed message. Adoption of Green Revolution policies in the mid-1960s suggested that, when pressed, Indira Gandhi was willing to cooperate with private producers to promote economic growth. When labor turned militant in the early 1970s, Indira Gandhi was again fully capable of turning the power of the state upon the "proletariat." Restrictions on foreign capital entering India also could not but please major Indian business houses; by now they were quite used to a noncompetitive market. And then during the Emergency (1975–77), when normal democratic politics was suspended, Indira Gandhi used her newfound powers, not to pursue any such radical policies as land reforms, but to curtail labor militancy and to emphasize the need for discipline and efficiency in the economy (Blair 1980; Dasgupta 1978; Kochanek 1976).

Indira Gandhi's apparent radicalism pushed state-business relations under the table. Both the Congress Party and India's business community possessed significant power resources, but each also needed the other. Indira Gandhi was hugely popular with India's poor, but this support was not well organized; she understood this limitation and seldom pushed her radicalism too far. The business community, in turn, used its ultimate weapon: a capital strike. Corporate investment declined during this period; along with the decline in public sector investment, economic growth thus decelerated (Bardhan 1984). These factors threatened to neutralize Indira Gandhi's popularity gains. Moreover, the Congress Party was strapped for cash and often needed the business community to help out. The business community, again in turn, needed to work around the accumulating obstacles to private economic initiative. A vast network of corrupt dealings thus developed during this period—and beyond—that tied agents of business houses to Congress Party functionaries. For example, Indira Gandhi's personal relations with Dhirubhai Ambani are well known (e.g., McDonald 2010). Briefcases full of cash filled the coffers of the Congress Party and eased state restrictions on conducting private business. While not the most effective or efficient mode of organizing state-business relations, "briefcase politics" did facilitate a working relationship of sorts in Indira's India.

The Probusiness Tilt

Over the last three to four decades politics and policy in India have moved steadily in a probusiness direction. This change was initiated by Indira Gandhi herself after she returned to power in 1980, deepened by her son Rajiv Gandhi during the second half of the 1980s, and then accelerated and modified following some basic policy changes in 1991. With Narendra Modi as India's prime minister at present, it would be difficult to deny the slow but definite transformation of India from a socialist political economy to one that sharply prioritizes economic growth and business interests. How this change came about and its consequences are already being studied.[11] Our focus in this volume is state-business relations during this period. Here, as an introduction, we provide only a very brief overview of the political and economic context; detailed studies of state-business relations then follow.

When Indira Gandhi returned to power in 1980, the polity was rather turbulent and economic growth sluggish. She had already begun her rightward shift in economic policy during the Emergency; now she prioritized economic growth over redistributive goals.[12] Her strategy to boost economic growth was a product of the constraints she faced. Opening the Indian economy to foreign capital was never high on her agenda; she was still too much of a nationalist for that. Following the increase in global oil prices, moreover, India faced foreign exchange constraints. For example, after 1982—the year of the Mexican peso crisis—foreign exchange liquidity dried up in the global economy. A public sector-led growth within India might have suited her politically, but this was becoming a less viable option: an increasing share of public revenues were devoted to buying political support, public investments were under pressure, and it was clear to most observers at the time that India's public sector was relatively inefficient. An alternative model was available from the experience with the Green Revolution within India: state-producer cooperation could lead to higher rates of growth. This model attracted Indira Gandhi. She slowly discarded her populist rhetoric and started courting Indian business groups, with the hope that they would take the lead to boost India's economic growth.

New priorities and rhetoric found expression in concrete changes. Indira Gandhi slowly but surely let go of her left-leaning advisers and replaced them instead with those with established probusiness reputations. One of India's main chambers of commerce—the Federation of Indian Chambers of Commerce and Industry, or FICCI—provided a "blueprint" for India's economic growth, identifying key constraints on private sector-led growth. Indira Gandhi more or less accepted this diagnosis of what ailed India's growth, and policy changes followed. She then diluted the restrictions on the growth of big business, creating new opportunities for big business to invest and enter new areas of production. In order to facilitate private financing of new investment, her government provided support for the development of private equity markets. Labor militancy was curtailed. Some imports were liberalized, but were aimed mainly at facilitating inputs for export growth. While these changes were not announced as major changes—a sense of continuity was maintained—and they indeed did not add up to a dramatic transformation, it is also the case that these changes marked the beginning of a shift away from *garibi hatao* to a growth-first model of development.

Rajiv Gandhi then intensified the changes initiated by his mother. Key decisions to abandon populism/socialism in favor of a growth-first strategy had already been taken. From here on it was a matter of what policies were politically feasible and economically successful. Rajiv made a clean ideological break from socialism; instead he started championing efficiency, computer-led modernity, and collaboration with Indian business groups. For a brief moment he even sought to open up the Indian economy to global economic forces. That move, however, was defeated, at least in part due to the opposition by Indian business groups, who had much to lose from foreign competition and investment. Rajiv then focused on growth promotion via encouraging domestic private capital and by providing public support for increased production. Significant policy changes included further elimination of state controls on economic activities of private Indian firms. Corporate taxes were lowered to encourage investment, and taxes on the middle class were lowered to boost demand in the economy. There was some currency devaluation to encourage exports, and some import barriers were lowered. Believing that public sector investment produces growth, the government during this period kept up the pace of such investment, especially in infrastructure. In the face of the shrinking tax base, this strategy was of course a debt crisis in the making, a crisis that came to a head in 1991. Meanwhile, Rajiv Gandhi also embraced something akin to an industrial policy in such select areas as information technology. The government provided direct support for information technology firms to emerge and flourish; within this new probusiness milieu such new firms as Infosys and WIPRO matured. It is not surprising, then, that India's economic growth picked up significantly during these years and relations between the state and business grew rather warm.

A financial crisis in 1991 provided the occasion for a much more significant external opening of the Indian economy. Deeper changes in India's external and internal political context were conducive to these major policy shifts. Among external changes, one may underline the following: the decline of the Soviet Union put pressure on India to reorder its political and economic ties to the West; membership in the World Trade Organization was by now imminent, implying that trade would need to be deregulated; a loan from the International Monetary Fund to deal with the financial crisis imposed the normal pressures of "structural adjustment"; and Indian decision-makers wanted access to foreign capital in the form of portfolio investment that was increasingly available in the world economy. Within India, a budgetary and balance-of-payments crisis was, of course, looming. In addition, the domestic political context was also by now altered. One especially significant change was the changing politics of business groups within India. Not only had internal liberalization helped big business grow during the 1980s but export-oriented business houses—such as information technology—had become politically active. A new chamber of commerce—the Confederation of Indian Industry, or CII—that favored limited global opening of Indian economy came into being; this was in addition to the two older chambers of commerce that often represented business groups that had flourished under the import substitution policy regime.[13] Policy preferences of business groups within India were increasingly divided, providing opportunities for a more proliberalization political elite to push changes. Leaders like Narasimha Rao and Manmohan Singh then used the financial crisis as an occasion to liberalize the Indian economy.[14]

As one might imagine, external opening of the Indian economy was a mixed blessing for Indian business groups. Some of them had opposed any such opening vigorously during the 1990s, even shifting their political support to, what was at that time, the more domestically-oriented, *swadeshi* opposition party, the emerging Bharatiya Janata Party (BJP).[15] For the most part, however, even the Congress-led Indian state did not push economic liberalization too hard. For example, political constraints made it difficult to push privatization of public industry or to tame labor unions in any decisive manner. Moreover, nearly alone in the developing world, the Indian state has privileged the interests of domestic capital over that of foreign capital. Liberalizing changes since 1991 have thus focused most sharply on facilitating the leadership of Indian capital in the growth process. External opening has been calibrated to meet this goal: trade barriers have come down but only slowly; and the role of foreign investment in the growth process in India—while increasing—is still relatively limited. Even after India lost its battles with the WTO, more recent trade liberalization has been accompanied by state intervention aimed at helping Indian business groups cope with a more open economy (Sinha 2016).

As is well known, India's economy over the last few decades has grown at a rather rapid rate. This growth has been steered by an alliance of state and private Indian capital. Such a model of development in India is creating new problems: economic inequalities have grown, and poverty is coming down only at a slow rate. This economic pattern is also creating political problems: leaders puzzle over how to win elections while channeling benefits to the few and how to deal with various demands of the excluded groups. A two-track polity of sorts has emerged. That is, India's probusiness tilt has also meant that there is a separation between the electoral and policy tracks. The poor are needed for elections but then—from the point of view of the holders of power—it is best that they stay away when policies are made. This arrangement is held together by short-term solutions such as cultural/religious nationalism. Unlike parts of East Asia, where a narrow state and business alliance for growth was held together by authoritarian regimes, the Indian model may be more attractive due to its democratic character but also potentially problematic because of its inability to spread economic gains and contain resulting pressures. While a conservative, religious party—which is in power at present—may provide a short-term nationalist "solution" to such conflicting economic pressures, a unavoidable issue remains: are such "solutions" durable? Is a democratic developmental state possible?

Given the growth of the role of private capital in the Indian economy, we seek to understand the political impact of shifts in class power in society. The more dramatic changes are clear even to a casual observer of Indian politics. Thus, for example, Narendra Modi is probably the first Indian prime minister openly anointed by leaders of the business community. In what follows, we probe such shifts in power more deeply. How significant is the power shift? Can business groups mold policies to suit their interests? How do they do so? We also seek to understand how the power of business varies across policy areas at the national level and, of course, across Indian states where levels of development and underlying political configurations vary. And finally, we hope to shed light on a broader issue of great significance: if power at the apex of the political pyramid is indeed getting more concentrated, what does that imply for the functioning of a large democracy with an enormous number of poor citizens? Can a probusiness model of high growth be institutionalized in such a democracy?

The Volume: A Preview

The chapters in the volume are organized thematically. The first two chapters analyze the power of business in contemporary India from two different standpoints. The first discussion, by Kanta Murali, conceptualizes power in structural terms. As noted above, following a long line of scholarship, we conceptualize structural power as power that results from the significance of the private sector in the economy. Understood as such, power by business groups is not always exercised via a self-conscious and well-organized set of demands. This latter and more direct exercise of power—we also noted above—may instead be considered an instrumental use of power. The second chapter, by Aseema Sinha, then analyzes the variety of more direct actions of business groups to influence political outcomes. Taken together, these two analyses provide us with a sense of the growing power of business in India, how this operates, and some of the limits that business groups face as they seek to mold state policies.

The more the Indian economy is dominated by the private sector, the greater is the structural power of private business within the Indian political economy. Murali explicates the mechanisms via which such structural power operates and then demonstrates its operation empirically. The legitimacy of policymakers rests on generating growth and creating prosperity. According to Murali, then, policymakers need to take account of business preferences and to create a business-friendly environment so as to attract investment. Control over investment and the threat of capital flight, in turn, give business owners enormous influence over state decisions. Structural power of this type has grown markedly in postliberalization India. This is because, first, the role of the private sector in the economy has grown considerably, especially when compared to the role of the public sector. And second, economic liberalization in India has freed capital to move into new sectors and given business groups spatial mobility. As a result, politicians now find themselves competing for investment and catering to business demands.

Murali then demonstrates this structural power at work by comparing Gujarat and Punjab. At the onset of liberalization, private industry already played a much more significant role in the economy of Gujarat than in Punjab. Sanguine about such differences, Murali suggests that it is no coincidence that state leaders in Gujarat adopted policies that were friendlier to private industry than those in Punjab. The results are also there for all to see: industry in Gujarat has boomed, but not in Punjab. Such a comparison allows Murali not only to demonstrate structural power at work but also to qualify her argument. In conclusion she notes that the structural power of business in India is not without limits. It often runs up against other forces in the political economy: the importance of noneconomic electoral appeals, the heterogeneous preferences of business groups, the diminished but still significant role of the public sector in the economy, and heavy state intervention that encourages crony capitalism.

Sinha's chapter, in turn, documents the direct links that increasingly connect the political and the business classes. In her view, the Indian state is best thought of as one that is by now quite "porous" to business interests, and the "boundaries" between the state and business are more and more blurred. She demonstrates this political change in a number of institutional settings. First, she provides data to support the claim that more and more businessmen are directly joining legislatures, both at the national level and at the level of states. In a political setting where the state can influence business fortunes and where access to the state via elections costs a lot of money, this direct and growing role of businessmen is comprehensible. Among her notable findings is the extremely high business representation in the BJP-dominated Lok Sabha, on the one hand, and, on the other hand, the near total grip that businessmen have on state legislatures such as Maharashtra. This growing presence of businessmen as political representatives leads to concrete policy change through a variety of pathways, especially through direct influence—if not control—of parliamentary committees within which laws are formulated. Sinha provides a number of important examples of such influence, including the role of a tobacco baron turned BJP politician who argued successfully in a committee that the use of tobacco did not create health risks. "Alternative facts," it turns out, are not the monopoly of American political elites.

Sinha also documents the growing power of businessmen in such other institutions as the Office of the Prime Minister, regulatory agencies, and the new public-private sector partnerships that have sprung up to facilitate new economic activities, especially investment in infrastructure. Her suggestion is that at times this close collaboration may well be developmental—meaning that it leads to better policies, including new investment and growth—but it is just as likely to lead to corruption and crony capitalism. She demonstrates the latter trend via a study of the well-known case of Vijay Mallya, who now owes giant sums of money to a variety of Indian banks, including public sector banks, which are likely never to be paid back.

The two chapters by Murali and Sinha, then, provide us with an overview of the growing power of business in India. It is growing in part because private groups increasingly drive the economy. Political leaders who wish to promote economic growth then feel compelled to create business-friendly policies. Lest this outcome be misunderstood as largely benign—serving the general good, via the generation of economic growth—it should be reiterated that economic growth in India continues to be seriously maldistributed. Business houses and their agents have also begun to exercise power more directly via control of legislatures, parliamentary committees, and access to other significant decision-making bodies. While some of this influence is being used to create probusiness policies, there is also plenty of crony capitalism that facilitates corrupt gains by both the political and the economic elite.

With a macro account of the growing power of business in Indian politics in place, the four chapters that follow analyze its impact across specific issue areas. If the power of business groups has indeed grown, are they able to mold policies in areas of interest to them? Costs of labor and access to cheap land are crucial for business profitability. How have laws governing labor and land altered in the probusiness era? Have policies shifted in a probusiness direction? In addition, one may expect growing power of business to be manifest in areas that go beyond those of direct profitability of a firm. Large business operations, for example, are generally located in major urban centers. Do business groups seek to mold urban spaces and, if so, with what degree of success? And finally, one anticipates growth in the role of business in institutions that mold the values of a society. One of the contributions to this volume analyzes the changing nature of Indian media in the probusiness era.

Given that labor is a key issue for business, Rina Agarwala analyzes how the labor regime in India has been modified during the recent decades. Agarwala documents that the power of organized labor in India is indeed being diluted. The underlying political process, however, is complex. Instead of business actors taking the lead, the Indian state has taken it upon itself to undermine the traditional power of formally employed labor. As Murali notes in her chapter, taming labor is a classic example of the structural power of business at work, where the political elite initiate actions deemed to be of great interest to business groups. Agarwala traces the historical evolution of this element of structural power in India from the early 1900s to the present. On the face of it, Agarwala suggests, organized formal labor in India has successfully resisted reforms to labor regulations that could have undermined labor's hard-won gains of the twentieth century. The deeper reality, however, is that the Indian state has used alternate strategies to tame formal labor; these strategies have helped business groups achieve their goals of cheaper and more "flexible" labor, but without sacrificing the democratic legitimacy of the state, especially among workers.

Agarwala then documents how the Indian state has used a multipronged strategy to weaken the labor regime that dominated India until the 1980s. First, political leaders have channeled the public debate on labor in the direction of what they claim is needed to remain competitive in the 21st century global market economy: labor flexibility. By avoiding direct attacks on wages or job security, the national state has protected its democratic credentials. However, in the name of labor flexibility, national leaders have not only reduced the resources available to labor ministries to implement labor laws, which protect wages and job security but also allowed a variety of regional states to amend national labor laws. The cumulative impact of these strategies has been to undermine "the power of all existing labor labor laws." In addition, the Indian state has promoted informal labor, both as a political category—by sanctioning surveys, counting and cataloging, arguing for their plight—and then, more important, as a substitute to organized labor for business groups. Agarwala thus highlights that informal employment is becoming more male, urban, and more overtly connected to—but working on the margins of—the formal economy than before. These trends normalize informal employment, which, in turn, helps business profitability by keeping wages down and by providing a more flexible labor force. At the same time, by championing informal labor—where the majority of working Indians survive—the Indian state has also protected, if not enhanced, its legitimacy. In conclusion, Agarwala reminds us that such victories on the part of business and state elites may well be challenged in the future. Capital versus labor is a classic battle of modernization; if history offers lessons, it is that working people have seldom accepted their fate lying down. She also documents examples of lower-class activism emerging across various sectors of the economy.

The chapter by Rob Jenkins focuses on state-business relations around the issue of land policy. India is a land-scarce country. New enterprises—industrial or otherwise—require ready access to cheap land. Much of the land in India, however, already helps sustain the livelihood of the rural majority. Access to land for new, large-scale economic activities, then, sets up another classic battle of modernization: cities versus the countryside. In contrast to labor policies, where, in Agarwala's judgment, the old labor protections are being diluted, Jenkins documents that the capacity of business groups to mold land policies is more "ambiguous." The incapacity of business to shape land policy is especially manifest at the national level. For example, new legislation—the Right to Fair Compensation and Transparency in Land Acquisition, Rehabilitation and Resettlement Act (LARRA)—was passed in 2013 to protect agricultural and other land, making it difficult to secure cheap land quickly for economic projects. The failure of businessmen to shape this policy is evidence of the continuing power of the countryside to fight for its core interests. Landowners control economic resources. Even if small and large landowners are not well organized, they—and all those who depend on land for livelihood—constitute a powerful electoral force. The political elite must balance the growing power of business groups against the continuing class and electoral power of agriculturalists. As

Jenkins notes, even the strongly probusiness Modi government has been unable to modify LARRA, at least so far.

The struggle over land policies in India has now shifted down from the national to the state governments. Businessmen have had considerably more success at this level. Jenkins analyzes these efforts in select states. Since authority over land is shared by the national and state governments, LARRA is now being amended successfully in several states in favor of business interests. Business groups are directly involved in writing these new laws, underlining the porosity of the Indian state suggested by Sinha. Why are the constraints of class and electoral power of agriculturalists not as significant at the level of states? They are; that is why the amendments to LARRA have proceeded furthest in those states where probusiness political forces are truly powerful, such as Rajasthan and Gujarat. In conclusion, Jenkins qualifies his discussion by noting that land policy in India continues to evolve; a variety of forces muddy the waters for business groups, even in probusiness states.

Cities are where one might expect the better off city dwellers—the bourgeoisie, or those who reside in the *bourg*, Old French for "market town"—to create urban spaces that are both livable and conducive to further economic development. The fact that business groups in India's major cities are not playing such a constructive—or even self-serving—role is the puzzle investigated by Patrick Heller, Partha Mukhopadhyay, and Michael Walton. Based on a study of Bangalore, Mumbai, and Delhi, they argue that governance in major Indian cities is simply not focused on the development of the city. City-based political and economic elites collude instead to share land rents. Why should this be so? Why should crony capitalism dominate at the expense of a more developmental cooperation between the political and economic elites? Heller et al. suggest that poor governance has to be understood in terms of what is missing in most Indian cities, namely, a city-based ruling coalition that might shape policies to facilitate growth or inclusion or both.

While taking note of some of the variation across Indian cities, Heller et al. probe the deeper causes of poor governance of cities. One important contextual factor is that city governments enjoy limited powers. Limited sovereignty, in turn, creates perverse incentives: in order to secure what they need, businessmen focus their energies on higher levels of government. The main factor of production that cities control is land. Given land scarcity and rising prices, then, local political and economic elites come together to extract rents. This is not to say that local elites do not harbor higher ambitions to create "world-class cities," but such efforts often fail because political and economic power in Indian cities is fractured. These divided elites pursue particular interests at the expense of any broader good, whether growth or inclusion. Other actors that might challenge such narrow, self-serving cabals are also not effective; middle-class civil society is often divided, the organized working class is relatively small, and large segments of informal workers remain unorganized.

And finally, how have the position and the role of media altered in the new probusiness era? Rammanohar Reddy traces elements of both continuity and change in the role of media in contemporary India. Among the notable changes is the enormous growth in both print and television media. While a variety of factors have driven this growth—including rising literacy, incomes, and changing technology—a key background condition tis the rise of a consumer economy that has accompanied economic liberalization. Advertising is central to this consumer economy. The result is that as much as two-thirds of the revenue of print and broadcast media now originates in advertising. In turn, advertising dominance over media has an important impact on the role that the media plays in Indian society.

The more the media is a source of profit via advertising revenues, the more persistent is the search for readers and viewers. This in turn has led to both sensationalism and trivialization in the production and dissemination of news. Corporate ownership of media has also increased. While corporate owners may not directly seek to influence the views expressed in media, only foolish editors will question specific corporations on which they depend for advertising revenue. Media owners and operators—including journalists—also have a vested interest in the process of economic growth that sustains the consumption economy. This biases the perspectives offered in the media, often supportive of economic growth at the expense of social inclusion. More important, media, as a source of profit, is beginning to influence political preferences expressed within the media. During the last election, Reddy suggests, the media favored Modi at the expense of the Congress Party. This reflected the dominant values that the media increasingly embraces: private sector-led growth and nationalism, especially as expressed in issues of national security. Reddy argues that commodification has meant that publishers have struck a Faustian bargain with commerce, resulting in the loss of the uniqueness that is associated with a product of journalism.

The final three chapters in the volume then explore regional variations across Indian states. It is no surprise that in a large country like India, business-government relations vary across states. One dimension of this variation is simply different levels of economic development. In richer states, business groups often represent a sizable corporate sector. One might expect business groups to influence politics in these states systematically, with the purpose of creating a probusiness environment. By contrast, one would expect more personalistic relations to prevail in poorer states, both as a cause and as a consequence of low levels of capitalist development. In addition to the levels of development, how politics is organized in respective states often complicates government-business relations across these states. Even in more industrialized states, business-government relations can be more or less cooperative, depending on the support base and the ideology of the rulers. Caste and other identities that may join or separate the political and economic elites can also alter the dynamics of government-business relations. Some of these diversities are captured well in our three state-level case studies.

Gujarat is one of India's most developed states. Economic development has long been led by a strong private sector rooted in industry. With the BJP now in power, the "Gujarat model" has taken on a new significance because it is this model that Modi hopes to extend to all of India. What exactly is the nature of business-government relations in the Gujarat model? The essay by Christophe Jaffrelot not only explicates this model but also underlines some of its important limits. Political and private sector elites cooperated in Gujarat from a fairly early period, even defying Nehru's efforts to champion state-led industrial development. As business-friendly governments repeatedly supported private sector initiatives, Gujarat became an economic leader in India, well before Modi. As long as the focus within Gujarat was on small and medium industries, say, prior to the 1990s, the business-friendly model did not create serious imbalances. Economic growth was accompanied by job creation, on the one hand, and, on the other hand, public finances were managed so that enough was left to support provision of public goods. While Gujarat was certainly never a model of "inclusive development," steady economic growth and well-managed public interventions made the state a sound economic performer.

By contrast, over the last decade or two, state-business relations in Gujarat have evolved in less desirable directions. First, the Modi government in the state came to champion large corporate houses over small and medium businesses. While this has ensured continuing economic growth and industrialization, the costs are beginning to accumulate. Large subsidies provided to giant corporations have cut into public finances; this pressure, in turn, has led to a decline in investment in education and health. The pattern of investment of big corporate firms has also been more capital intensive, leading to fewer new jobs per unit of investment than in the past. And finally, government-business cooperation has been accompanied by grand corruption. A case study of Modi's relations with the giant Adani business group demonstrates how such connections develop. More importantly, the case study underlines that personalist and corrupt relations continue unabated in the "advanced" state of Gujarat and may even have intensified following "liberalization."

Like Gujarat, Tamil Nadu has experienced high rates of economic growth in recent decades, including industrial growth, but unlike Gujarat, poverty in Tamil Nadu has declined sharply.[16] Thus, it is an enigmatic case that departs from modal Indian tendency that aspires but often fails to achieve inclusive growth. The puzzle of Tamil Nadu is even deeper insofar as these good developmental outcomes have been achieved under the leadership of regional nationalist parties that many would characterize as corrupt and personalistic. So the importance of understanding state-business relations in Tamil Nadu is clear. John Harriss and Andrew Wyatt help us understand this puzzling case in their essay.

While taking account of complex underlying realities, Harriss and Wyatt argue that ruling arrangements in Tamil Nadu are best understood as versions of "Bonapartism"—a concept first formulated by Marx—which ensures that the interests of business classes are served but without undermining the political autonomy of powerful political leaders. Regional leaders have thus secured power on the basis of Tamil nationalism, caste politics, and populism. This has enhanced the political autonomy of leaders from dominant classes and the concentration of power in the hands of charismatic individuals. Leaders, in turn, have used this autonomy to pursue some redistributive programs. However, regional nationalist leaders of Tamil Nadu also never turned against business.

This outcome can be interpreted as a case of the structural power of business groups. One can readily imagine capital flight, had Tamil nationalists turned truly antibusiness. However, Tamil leaders were not all that radical to begin with; they were not moved by ideological commitments. Tamil leaders were instead regional nationalists, who made personal fortunes but also pursued development of their state. Over time, these leaders have become probusiness. State-business relations in Tamil Nadu thus vary from mutual indifference to active state support. One also notices considerable overlap between the political and economic elites in smaller enterprises, as well as state elites explicitly courting big business—often foreign business—for megaprojects to boost economic growth in the state. Reminded of recent trends in Gujarat, one wonders if this approach favoring big business in Tamil Nadu will be able to maintain its inclusive character in the future.

At the other end of the development spectrum within India lie a number of poor but politically important states. These include Uttar Pradesh (UP), Bihar, Madhya Pradesh (MP), and Odisha. Industrial development in these states is relatively rudimentary, as is the corporate sector. There is plenty of close cooperation between business and political elites in these states, but much of it takes the form of crony capitalism. Ruling elites in these states often lack public purpose. They pursue what look like development policies but, on closer scrutiny, turn out to be policies that enrich a select few, without productive gains. Both political and economic elites gain but at the expense of the broader public good. The case of Odisha, discussed below, exemplifies this type of neopatrimonial state-business relationship.

Sunila Kale documents that, over the decades, politics and policy in Odisha have been consistently probusiness. The underlying forces that help explain this continuity are twofold: political and economic elites comprise a narrow group, whose members share caste and class background; and the lower strata remain relatively undermobilized. The irony is that a tight state and business alliance has failed to create sustained economic dynamism. Odisha's economy was and remains an extractive economy, dependent on mines and metallurgy. While economic growth has picked up in recent years, Odisha is one of India's poorest states.

Kale explains this pattern of development by focusing on the personalistic nature of state-business relations. While government policies have often been probusiness, the modal outcome is the creation of crony capitalism. Such arrangements benefit both political and economic elites, without creating any sustained economic transformation. The deeper roots of this pattern of development are that the ruling elite lack any real commitment to the public good and the private sector remains dependent on state support for profitability. The political elites then provide support to business without demanding performance and business groups, in turn, collect subsidized profits that they share with the political elite. State-business relations then become a source of mutual convenience rather than a basis of sustained economic diversification.

We will return in the conclusion to trace some themes that run across these chapters, address the broader questions concerning the growing power of business groups in Indian politics, and situate the Indian experience in a broader comparative perspective.

References

Bagchi, Amiya Kumar. 1972. *Private Investment In India, 1900–1939*. Cambridge: University Press.

Bardhan, P. 1984. *The Political Economy of Development in India*. New Delhi: Oxford University Press.

Basu, Amrita. 2015. *Violent Conjunctures in Democratic India*. New York: Cambridge University Press.

Bhagwati, Jagdish N., and Padma Desai. 1970. *India: Planning for Industrialization*. London: Oxford University Press.

Bhagwati, Jagdish N., and Arvind Panagariya. 2013. *Why Growth Matters: How Economic Growth in India Reduced Poverty and the Lessons for Other Developing Countries*. New York: PublicAffairs.

Birla, G. D. 1953. *In the Shadow of the Mahatma: A Personal Memoir*. Bombay: Orient Longmans.

Blair, H. W. 1980. "Mrs. Gandhi's Emergency, the Indian Elections of 1977, Pluralism and Marxism." *Modern Asian Studies* 14 (2): 237–71.

Chibber, Vivek. 2003. *Locked in Place: State-Building and Late Industrialization in India*. Princeton, NJ: Princeton University Press.

Culpepper, Pepper D. 2015. "Structural Power and Political Science in the Post-crisis Era." *Business and Politics* 17 (3): 391–409.

Dahl, Robert. 1975. "Pluralism Revisited." *Comparative Politics* 10 (2): 191–203.

Dasgupta, Jyotindra. 1978. "An Era of Caesars: Emergency Regimes and Development Politics in Asia." *Asian Survey* 18 (4): 315–49.

Drèze, Jean, and Amartya Sen. 2013. *An Uncertain Glory: India and Its Contradictions*. Princeton, NJ: Princeton University Press.

Erdman, Howard L. 1967. *The Swatantra Party and Indian Conservatism*. New York: Cambridge University Press.

Frankel, Francine. 2005. *India's Political Economy, 1947–2004: The Gradual Revolution*. Princeton, NJ: Princeton University Press.

Gilens, Martin, and Benjamin I. Page. 2014. "Testing Theories of American Politics: Elites, Interest Groups, and Average Citizens." *Perspectives on Politics* 12 (3): 564–81.

Gold, David A., Y. H. Lo, and Erik Ohlin Wright. 1975. "Recent Developments in Marxist Theories of the Capitalist State." *Monthly Review* 27 (5): 36–51.

Gopal, Sarvepalli. 1984. *Jawaharlal Nehru: A Biography*. New Delhi: Oxford University Press.

Gramsci, Antonio. 1971. *Selections from the Prison Notebooks*. Ed. Quintin Hoare and Geoffrey Nowell-Smith, New York: Independent Publishers.

Guha, Ramachandra. 2007. *India after Gandhi: The History of the World's Largest Democracy*. London: Macmillan.

Hacker, Jacob, and Paul Pierson. 2002. "Business Power and Social Policy: Employers and the Formation of the American Welfare State." *Politics & Society* 30 (2): 277–325.

Handley, Antoinette. 2008. *Business and the State in Africa: Economic Policy-Making in the Neo-liberal Era*. New York: Cambridge University Press.

Hundt, David. 2009. *Korea's Developmental Alliance: State, Capital and the Politics of Rapid Development*. New York: Routledge.

Jaffrelot, Christophe. 1996. *The Hindu Nationalist Movement and Indian Politics*. New York: Columbia University Press.

Jalan, Bimal. 1991. *India's Economic Crisis: The Way Ahead*. Delhi: Oxford University Press.

Jayakar, Pupul. 1992. *Indira Gandhi: An Intimate Biography*. New York: Pantheon.

Jenkins, Rob. 1999. *Democratic Politics and Economic Reform in India*. Cambridge: Cambridge University Press.

Kochanek, Stanley A. 1974. *Business and Politics in India*. Berkeley: University of California Press.

———. 1976. "Mrs. Gandhi's Pyramid: The New Congress." In *Indira's India: A Political System Reappraised*, ed. Henry C. Hart, 93–124. Boulder, CO: Westview.

———. 1987. "Briefcase Politics in India: The Congress Party and the Business Elite." *Asian Survey* 27 (12): 1278–301.

Kohli, Atul. 2012. *Poverty amid Plenty in the New India*. Cambridge: Cambridge University Press.

Lindblom, Charles. 1977. *Politics and Markets*. New York: Basic Books.

Low, D. A. 1988. "The Forgotten Bania: Merchant Communities and the Indian National Congress." In *The Indian National Congress: Centenary Hindsights*, ed. D. A. Low, 129–54. Delhi: Oxford University Press.

Lukes, Steven. 2005. *Power: A Radical View*. 2nd ed. Basingstoke: Palgrave Macmillan.

Markovits, Claude. 1985. *Indian Business and Nationalist Politics, 1931–1939: The Indigenous Capitalist Class and the Rise of the Congress Party*. New York: Cambridge University Press.

McDonald, Hamish. 2010. *Ambani and Sons*. New Delhi: Roli Books.

Miliband, Ralph. 1969. *The State in Capitalist Society*. London: Weidenfeld and Nicolson.

Murali, Kanta. 2017. *Caste, Class, and Capital: The Social and Political Origins of Economic Policy in India*. Cambridge: Cambridge University Press.

Myrdal, Gunnar. 1968. *Asian Drama: An Inquiry into the Poverty of Nations*. New York: Pantheon.

Nanda, B. R. 1990. *In Gandhi's Footsteps. The Life and Time of Jamnalal Bajaj*. Delhi: Oxford University Press.

Naseemullah, Adnan. 2017. *Development after Statism: Industrial Firms and the Political Economy of South Asia*. Cambridge: Cambridge University Press.

Panagariya, Arvind. 2008. *India: The Emerging Giant*. New York: Oxford University Press.

Pinglé, Vibha. 1999. *Rethinking the Developmental State: India's Industry in Comparative Perspective*. New Delhi: Oxford University Press.

Poulantzas, Nicos. 1980. *State, Power and Socialism*. New York: Schocken.

Raj, K. N. 1973. "The Politics and Economics of 'Intermediate Regimes.'" *Economic and Political Weekly* 8 (27): 1169–98.

Ray, Rajat Kanta. 1979. *Industrialization in India: Growth and Conflict in the Private Corporate Sector, 1914–47*. Delhi: Oxford University Press.

Rothermund, Dietmar. 1986. *An Economic History of India: From Pre-colonial Times to 1986*. New York: Croom Helm.

Rudolph, Lloyd I., and Susanne Hoeber Rudolph. 1987. *In Pursuit of Lakshmi: The Political Economy of the Indian State*. Chicago: University of Chicago Press.

Ruperalia, Sanjay, Sanjay Reddy, John Harriss, and Stuart Corbridge. 2011. *Understanding India's New Political Economy*. New York: Routledge.

Schneider, B. R. 2004. *Business Politics and the State in Twentieth-Century Latin America*. Cambridge: Cambridge University Press.

Sinha, Aseema. 2016. *Globalizing India: How Global Rules and Markets Are Shaping India's Rise to Power*. New York: Cambridge University Press.

Sitapati, Vinay. 2016. *Half-Lion: How Narasimha Rao Transformed India*. New Delhi: Viking.

Tomlinson, B. R. 1993. *The Economy of Modern INDIA, 1860–1970*. New York: Cambridge University Press.

Winters, Jeffrey A. 2011. *Oligarchy*. New York: Cambridge University Press.

PART I

THE POWER OF BUSINESS
IN CONTEMPORARY INDIA

Economic Liberalization and the Structural Power of Business

KANTA MURALI

Introduction

In 2006, the Tata group announced that it would produce the world's cheapest car—the Nano.[1] Priced at $2,500, the Nano was targeted at a class of consumers who would have otherwise been unlikely to own a car in their lifetime. The announcement was accompanied by considerable media fanfare, with observers hailing it as "icon of Indian ingenuity and entrepreneurialism" and as a prime example of *jugaad*, the type of frugal innovation at which India seems to excel ("A New Home for the Nano" 2008, 85; "Asian Innovation" 2012, 68). For many, there was a much larger symbolism associated with the Nano project—after decades of slow growth, India was finally living up to its economic potential, and the Nano symbolized this very ascent.

When it came to selecting the production location for the Nano project, the Tata group surprisingly chose Communist-run West Bengal. The Left Front had continuously held power in the state since 1977, and the state witnessed a steady decline in industrial growth in that time. Attempting to redress the decline, the Communists in West Bengal, since the 1990s, began to reorient their economic strategy and promote the state as a business-friendly destination, much along the lines of their Chinese counterparts. That the Tatas had chosen Singur as the production site over other competing locations was a major victory for the West Bengal government.

But it was a fleeting victory. To attract the investment of the Tatas, West Bengal offered a generous package that included 997 acres of highly subsidized farmland as well as other substantial, but undisclosed, concessions (Murali 2017). However, land acquisition by the government for the Nano plant proved to be controversial and brought the project to a halt. After two years of regular protests, often violent, from local farmers, activists, and the main opposition party, the Tata group announced in 2008 that the Nano project would move out of West Bengal.

The decision of the Tatas immediately catalyzed responses from numerous states, which began to offer competing packages of concessions and incentives in the hope of bringing the Nano plant to their jurisdictions. In the end, Gujarat beat out rival offers. Like West Bengal, Gujarat offered the Tatas a generous package of incentives; key benefits were said to include 1,100 acres of subsidized government land; a soft loan of Rs. 95,700 million at an interest rate of 0.1 percent payable after twenty years; free water; and exemptions from electricity duty, registration, and transfer of land charges ("Sop Opera on Nano Begins in Gujarat" 2008; "Nano Gets New Home" 2008).[2]

In many ways, the Nano vignette reflects the growth of one central dimension of leverage that business in India today exercises—structural power, or what Kohli (2012) refers to as indirect power. Among other major transformative effects, economic liberalization in India resulted in a greatly increased role for the private sector. Critically, public investment has supplanted private investment as the main catalyst of growth over the last two and a half decades. In turn, governments, whose political fortunes are, in part, tied to economic performance, need to attract private capital to spur growth. Moreover, as the Nano episode highlights, state governments compete to attract private industrial investment. To do so, they have to undertake business-friendly measures. Importantly, the imperative of policymakers to take into account business preferences and to create business-friendly environments arises independently of any instrumental role that capital may play to influence decision-making. In the case of the Nano, the decision to move out of West Bengal automatically prompted favorable packages for the Tatas from other states.

That the structural power of business in India has risen since the onset of the 1991 reforms is obvious even to a casual observer.[3] Yet, given the nature of the variable itself, analytically assessing both the content and effects of business's structural power is a much more challenging task. In broad terms, this chapter is an attempt to understand the broad evolution of business's structural power in India in the era of economic liberalization. Specifically, it tries to address the following questions: How has economic liberalization affected the nature of business's structural power? What effects has this had on policy?

To answer these questions, the chapter is organized as follows. The next section offers a brief review of the comparative literature on the concept of structural power. In doing so, it distinguishes structural power from instrumental power and also highlights the empirical challenges associated with analyzing structural power. The third section discusses the changing role of the private sector in the Indian economy after the onset of market reforms; some basic data at the national level point to business's growing structural power in India. In addition, the third section also links the empirical discussion of structural power here very briefly to the chapters of Reddy and Agarwala in this book.

The growth of structural power is empirically most clearly illustrated at the state level. The fourth section examines policies employed by two Indian states, Gujarat and Punjab, in the competition for industrial investment, which ensued after the onset of market reforms in 1991. For both pluralists and Marxists, the two main strands of the literature analyzing the theme, business's structural power arises primarily through its control of investment. A focus on policies related to industrial investment is therefore worthwhile. Finally, while capital's growing structural power implies that direction of policy in India tends to be biased toward it, this influence is potentially mitigated by certain contextual factors. I conclude by asking what factors potentially constrain and mediate business's structural power in India.

Several conclusions can be drawn from this examination of structural power. The first (and obvious) conclusion is that a marked increase in business's structural power is evident in the postliberalization era.[4] The second main observation is that structural power varies across states (it is also likely to vary across time, though the analysis here does not address that). The importance and composition of the private sector, and levels of capital mobility, differ across state economies, resulting in different levels of structural power. These differences in structural power across states tend to be correlated with the extent to which investment policies are business friendly. Finally, while the general direction of policy in India has been clearly probusiness in the era of liberalization, the extent of business's structural leverage in India is likely to be mitigated by certain factors. I identify four factors that potentially limit structural power of business in India—the importance of noneconomic factors in determining electoral outcomes, internal heterogeneity of capital and varied preferences, the continuing role of the public sector in the Indian economy, and the dependence of business on the state through continued patterns of patronage and cronyism.

Structural Power and Its Implications for the Policy Process

Before proceeding to specific details on India, it is worth highlighting some basic claims on the structural power of business in the comparative political economy literature. These arguments offer a basic framework along which the nature of structural power and its limitations can be analyzed. In broad terms, the power of business in capitalist democracies can be categorized in terms of three different sources of influence—structural, instrumental, and ideational power.

Discussions of structural power in advanced industrial democracies were prominent in both pluralist and Marxist scholarship in the 1960s and 1970s (e.g., Block 1987; Lindblom 1977; Poulantzas 1975). Analyses of structural power fell out of favor by the 1980s, and the literature on business and politics in advanced industrial democracies focused disproportionately on the direct or instrumental role of business in shaping policy outcomes.[5] More recently, there has been renewed interest in analyses of structural power (Culpepper 2015; Culpepper and Reinke 2014; Fairfield 2015; Hacker and Pierson 2002; Smith 1999, 2000; Winters 1996). In the Indian context, Kohli (2012) points to the marked shift in business's structural power after the 1980s.

For both pluralists and Marxists, business's structural power stems from the fact that firms are the primary agents of economic performance in capitalist democracies. The state relies on investment by firms to generate growth, create jobs, and perform a variety of economic functions. In turn, political fortunes of policymakers are, at least in part, tied to economic performance. Firms seek to maximize profits and decide when, where, and how much to invest. Absent expectations of profit, investment will not occur. Through its ability to withhold investment, business can affect economic performance significantly (and subsequently the electoral prospects of policymakers). It is from this aspect that business primarily derives structural power.

The ability to withhold investment means that policymakers in capitalist democracies have an automatic imperative to create business-friendly environments and, more generally, take into account business interests in the policy process. For Lindblom, "In the eyes of government officials, businessmen do not appear simply as the representatives of a special interest, as representatives of interest groups do. They appear as functionaries performing functions that government officials regard as indispensable . . . any government official who understands the requirements of his position and the responsibilities that market-oriented systems throw on businessmen will therefore grant them a privileged position. He does not have to be bribed, duped or pressured to do so. Nor does he have to be an uncritical admirer of businessmen to do so. He simply understands, as is plain to see, that public affairs in market-oriented systems are in the hands of two groups of leaders, government and business, who must collaborate and that to make the system work government leadership must often defer to business leadership" (1977, 175).

Critically, as Lindblom emphasizes, business's structural power means that it influences the policy process in capitalist democracies even when it does not overtly act to do so. Winters (1996, 2) suggests that "outside and in some respects prior to the overt political process, those controlling investment resources 'vote' in a way that nonpropertied citizens in the wider public cannot." It is in this aspect—the lack of overt action—that business's structural power can be contrasted with instrumental power; the latter source of power stems from capital's ability to exert direct influence on politicians through activities such as lobbying and campaign contributions, and by being directly part of the legislative process. As the chapter by Aseema Sinha in this book clearly points out, the legislative influence of business in parliament and state assemblies in India has risen significantly in the postliberalization period.

In addition to this basic logic, several other key implications arise from structural power arguments. Structural power arguments imply that ideological views or affiliations of officeholders play no role in mitigating capital's leverage; structural power places similar pressures on politicians across the ideological divide. Accordingly, the necessity of politicians of all ideological affiliations to take into account business preferences in capitalist democracies is expected to undermine popular control of policy (Smith 2000).

Hacker and Pierson (2002) offer several clarifications that are useful in understanding arguments related to business's structural power. Structural power arguments do not rest on the assumption that business interests are monolithic. Nor will business always get what it wants in the policy process; structural power arguments suggests the direction of policy is *generally biased* toward business, but policymakers will sometimes make decisions that run counter to capital's preferences. As Hacker and Pierson point out, business's structural power is primarily a signaling device and does not dictate policy choices, which are the result of a more complex set of causes. Furthermore, they suggest that the actual *extent* to which business influences specific policy choices is a function of instrumental power rather than structural power. In that sense, structural and instrumental power typically interact to explain policy outcomes.

It is important to note that structural power is a variable and not a constant (Culpepper 2015; Hacker and Pierson 2002; Winters 1996). The structural influence of business is based on a threat of exit, and this, in turn, is affected by several factors. For example, the extent of capital mobility will affect structural power, and firms with more immobile assets will be less capable of exercising structural power than those that can exit more easily. Related to this, Hacker and Pierson suggest that the structural power of capital increases in decentralized federal systems. Because mobility is easier across regions within a country than across countries, pressures to create healthy business climates are particularly likely to be observed within units of a federal system. Among other aspects that mitigate business's structural power, Winters points out that structural leverage decreases as "access to and control over investment resources that can replace those controlled privately increases" (1996, 36). The more the state relies on its own capital, the further the ability of business to constrain policy is diminished. Similarly, the structural power of mobile capital is lower if investment is not concentrated in sectors that employ large numbers of people or are important to access technology or important to the state's revenue base. Winters also points out that certain political characteristics of governments—stability and fragmentation—affect mobility of capital and, in turn, its structural power.

Finally, while, conceptually, structural power arguments are relatively clear in their mechanisms, there are numerous empirical challenges in identifying the impact of structural power. For a start, disentangling instrumental and structural influences on policy outcomes tends to be very difficult in practice. Moreover, one critical aspect related to structural power tends to be unobservable. Structural power arguments expect capital to influence two aspects of the policy process—first, the setting of policy agendas and, second, actual policy decisions on issues that are already on the agenda. The former poses an empirical challenge; while business's structural power may theoretically explain why certain policies never reach the government agenda, this cannot be observed. As such, the agenda setting implications, a central component of structural power arguments, are difficult, if not typically impossible, to analyze.

Despite these challenges, some basic insights from structural power arguments provide a framework along which the changing nature of structural power in India can be empirically analyzed. In the next section, I characterize the shift in the evolution of business-state relations and offer some basic data at the national level on the increased role of the private sector in the economy, which indicate business's rising structural power after liberalization. The fourth section of this chapter continues the empirical discussion but focuses on the state level in India, where capital's increased structural power is clearly evident. In particular, I focus on policy responses of Gujarat and Punjab in the competition for investment, a process that was triggered by the virtual elimination of the licensing system in 1991.

The Evolution of Structural Power after Liberalization

The background and policies that accompanied India's high-growth phase are by now well known. Nevertheless, some brief comments help set the stage for understanding the growth in business's structural power. As Kohli (2012) and Rodrik and Subramanian (2004) argue, India's political economy began moving in a new direction after 1980. Socialist rhetoric was discarded for a probusiness model, and this resulted in India moving to a higher growth path. For Kohli, the Indian state's reconfigured relationship with business—a narrow alliance between the two—after 1980 explains patterns of both dynamism at the apex of the economy and exclusion below.

The liberalization process that accompanied this probusiness tilt occurred in two stages—first in the 1980s under Indira and Rajiv Gandhi, and then through the extensive reforms of 1991. The policy changes in the 1980s were very modest and primarily focused on internal liberalization. Among the key policy changes of the 1980s, twenty-five industries were delicensed, "broad-banding" or diversification into related products was allowed without licenses for certain sectors, and restrictions on large firms covered by the Monopolies and Restrictive Trade Practices (MRTP) Act were eased. There was a general move toward tariffs from quantitative restrictions, and import liberalization of capital goods, electronics, and certain consumer goods took place. Importantly, both Kohli, and Rodrik and Subramanian emphasize the "attitudinal" shift of the state; the state was looking to increase growth and adopted a probusiness model to do so from the 1980s.

Though modest, the reforms of the 1980s paved the way for a much more significant and extensive shift in the form of the 1991 reforms. For the purposes of the analysis on structural power, it is the extensive reforms that began in 1991 that are particularly critical. The reforms of 1991 represented a sea change in the country's development paradigm. They catalyzed India's shift from an archetype of dirigisme to an economy that would come to be driven by the private sector. In contrast to liberalizing measures in the 1980s, the reforms that began in 1991 reconfigured both the internal and the external economic policy framework. The centerpiece of India's postindependence policy regime—the industrial licensing system, the infamous "license-permit raj"—was virtually eliminated, drastically reducing state control of the private sector. Private investment supplanted public investment as the main engine of growth; this in turn had major consequences for the nature and content of policymaking in the country (e.g., Ahluwalia 2000; Jenkins 1999; Kohli 2004, 2006; Rudolph and Rudolph 2001; Singh and Srinivasan 2006; Sinha 2005). The reforms of 1991 also led to the marked decentralization of economic decision-making in India; with the end of licensing, states became key players in the Indian economy. On the external front, the trade and foreign investment regimes were gradually liberalized, representing a sharp break with the principles of self-sufficiency and inward focus that India had stubbornly held onto for almost four and a half decades after independence. Over time, the reforms succeeded in integrating India firmly into the global economy.

Two aspects of the 1991 reforms are particularly central in catalyzing an expanded role for the private sector in the economy and, as a result, increased structural power of capital. First, the private sector was allowed to enter sectors that were previously restricted to the public sector. Second, and more importantly, the virtual elimination of the licensing system increased capital mobility. The elimination of the licensing system meant that the center no longer controlled location decisions on investment. In turn, states began to compete to attract investment and had to formulate business-friendly policy environments to do so.

Over time, private investment in India has supplanted public investment as the primary engine of growth.

Some basic data on investment and employment clearly indicate the expanded role of the private sector and, as a result, a marked rise in business's structural power after 1991. One point that should be noted at the outset is that though its activities were subject to considerable regulation, the role of the private sector, particularly in terms of investment, was not insignificant prior to the 1980s. This can be seen in some of the figures below. However, the shift in the policy framework, particularly the removal of state controls on where private investment could be located as well as allowing the private sector to enter new sectors, resulted in a major expansion of its role.

Figures 2.1, 2.2, 2.3 and 2.4 below highlight some basic investment and employment data on the private sector's material importance in the Indian economy. Several trends can be seen in the figures below. As figure 2.1 indicates, capital formation by the private sector (as a percentage of GDP) increased from the mid-1980s and particularly after 1991. Further, the gap between the private and public sectors on this metric widened in those periods. Figure 2.2, which includes the private corporate sector's share of total paid-up capital, points to rising investment share of the private sector after the mid-1980s and especially after 1991. What can also be seen in figure 2.2 is that the private sector's share of total paid-up capital begins to decline after 1965 and particularly after 1969; the

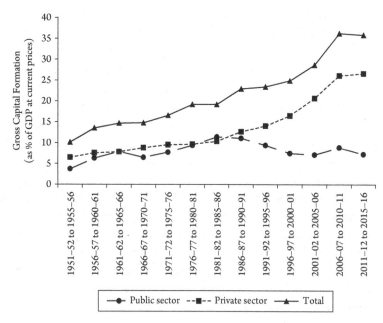

Figure 2.1 Gross Capital Formation by Sector (as percentage of GDP, five-year averages), 1951–52 to 2015–16. Source: Calculated from table 1.9, Economic Survey 2017–18.

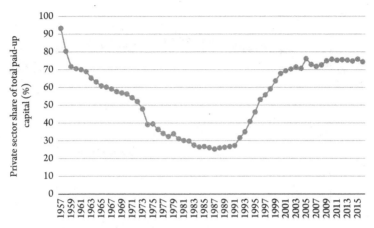

Figure 2.2 Private Companies' Share of Total Paid-Up Capital of Companies at Work, 1957–2016. Source: Statement XI, Companies at Work, 1956–57 to 2013–14 and Statement IX, Active Companies 1956–57 to 2015–16; Annual Report on Working and Administration of Companies Act 1956 and 2013, Ministry of Corporate Affairs.

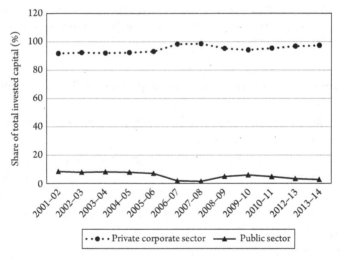

Figure 2.3 Share of Private Corporate Sector and Public Sector Investment from the Annual Survey of Industries. Source: Annual Survey of Industries, 2001–02 to 2013–14.

latter marking the height of Indira Gandhi's left-oriented policy regime (bank nationalization, restrictions on large firms through the MRTP Act, and general tightening of licensing requirements occurred in 1969). Figure 2.3 includes data from a different source—the Annual Survey of Industries—and suggests that the share of the private sector in total invested capital since the 2000s is even higher than that indicated by the share of total paid-up capital collected as part of the administration of the Companies Act in figure 2.2. In short, figures 2.1, 2.2

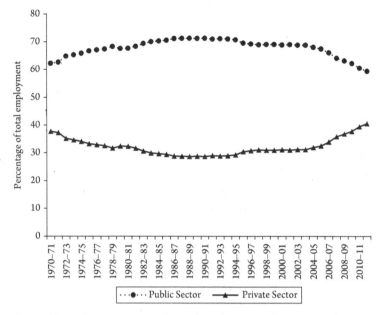

Figure 2.4 Public and Private Sector Share of Total Organized Sector Employment, 1970–71 to 2011–12. Source: Reserve Bank of India Handbook of Statistics on Indian Economy, 2010, 2015, 2016–17.

and 2.3 point to the private sector's rising importance in the Indian economy in terms of investment from the mid-1980s.

While the rising material importance of the private sector clearly evident in its contributions to investment, contribution to employment, however, is much more modest. In fact, one of the key features of India's high-growth era has been the marked lack of employment generation in the organized sector (e.g., Nagaraj 2006). As several authors have noted, India's growth after 1991 has been both capital-intensive and service-sector oriented in a country that remains largely rural and agricultural (e.g., Anant et al. 2006; Subramanian 2008). Almost 93 percent of India's workforce continues to be employed in the informal sector (Agarwala 2013). In that sense, there is a marked disjuncture between the main sources of livelihood in India and the key drivers of growth. The lack of growth in formal sector employment is likely to act as a check on the extent of business power.

As figure 2.4 indicates, the public sector continues to account for a significant portion of total employment in India. Moreover, numerous trends suggest that excluded groups continue to look to the state for economic opportunities. Agitations for reservations by dominant caste groups such as the Patels in Gujarat and Jats in Haryana are one example of this. As Jaffrelot (2015) points out, members of these "neo-middle classes" are aspirational but have not been able to find jobs due to the capital-intensive nature of growth.

Structural Power, Interstate Competition for Investment, and Probusiness Policies

General aggregate trends at the national level in the previous section pointed to rising importance of the private sector over time.[6] In this section, I focus on industrial investment policies at the state level, where the growing structural leverage of capital is even more evident. Among other major changes, the reforms of 1991 led to a sharp decentralization in economic decision-making and brought state governments to the forefront of policymaking. The growing importance of subnational governments in the economic policy process was sharply brought into focus in the context of open competition between states for private industrial investment, which ensued because of the reforms. Under India's federal system, states have jurisdictional authority over several aspects of economic policy.[7] Until 1991, the central government played a dominant role in economic decision-making, and the industrial licensing system allowed the center to maintain formal control over the geographical distribution of investment.

But with the virtual abolition of the industrial licensing system in 1991, New Delhi's role in influencing the spatial distribution of investment was effectively eliminated. This meant that private industrial investment was no longer subject to geographical constraints by the federal government, and Indian states began to compete openly to attract domestic and foreign private investment.[8] According to Rudolph and Rudolph (2001, 1541), "By the end of the 1990s, state chief ministers became the marquee players in India's federal market economy. What has attracted media and policy attention in recent years is the competition among the states for international attention and for domestic and foreign private investment."

Interstate competition for investment is a useful arena in which to examine structural power. In this section, I examine investment promotion policies across two states, Gujarat and Punjab, in the competition for investment between 1991 and 2010. These two states have been among India's richest but have differed significantly in their approach to attracting investment after 1991. To set the context, table 2.1 includes a brief overview of certain key socioeconomic indicators in these two states. Before outlining the nature of variation in investment policy responses of Gujarat and Punjab, I briefly digress to discuss the process of case selection below.

Table 2.1 **An Overview of Key Socioeconomic Indicators in Gujarat and Punjab**

	Gujarat	*Punjab*
Population (in millions)	60.4	27.7
Per capita net state domestic product (in Rs., constant prices), 2015–16	122,502	99,372
Poverty (% below poverty line)	31.6	20.9
Literacy (%), 2011	78.0	75.8
Manufacturing (% of net state value added), 2015–16	25.1	12.7
Agriculture, forestry, and fishing (% of net state value added), 2015–16	17.7	30.9

Source: Population from census of India, 2011; per capita income and net state value added from RBI Handbook of Statistics on Indian Economy, 2016–17; literacy rates from Economic Survey, 2017–18.

Case Selection

The empirical evidence in this section is drawn from Murali (2017). Based on Lieberman (2005), that book relied on a nested research design and combined four in-depth qualitative case studies with a broader time-series cross-section (TSCS) analysis. Gujarat and Punjab were two of the four case studies examined. I relied on the method suggested by Lieberman (2005) to pick the cases. Given the lack of systematic data on policy variation, I selected the cases based on investment outcomes. A preliminary quantitative analysis was first used to examine the explanatory leverage of existing theories in accounting for the variation in investment outcomes observed across Indian states. Specifically, existing studies from neoclassical economics and economic geography predict that certain socioeconomic factors are likely to drive investment location (e.g., Barro 1991; Lucas 1990; Krugman 1998). To determine the adequacy of socioeconomic variables in explaining investment outcomes, a simple cross-section OLS regression was run. Cumulative investment across Indian states between 1991 and 2007 was regressed on proxies of four socioeconomic variables frequently identified as affecting investment location (level of economic development, market size, human capital, and infrastructure). Using results from this regression, figure 2.5 plots actual investment values against values predicted by socioeconomic variables identified in existing theories.

As figure 2.5 suggests, existing theories offer only a partial explanation for outcomes observed. Employing an "off-the-line" strategy, two cases—Gujarat and Punjab—that are not well predicted by socioeconomic factors were chosen

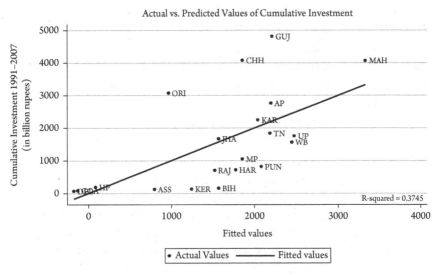

Figure 2.5 Case Selection

(indicated by "GUJ" and "PUN" in figure 2.5). Importantly, socioeconomic variables would have predicted very similar levels of investment in Gujarat and Punjab, but actual outcomes vary considerably, making the comparison a potentially interesting one.

Comparing Policy Responses of Gujarat and Punjab

I compare policies in Gujarat and Punjab along eight dimensions that are central to the investment climate—infrastructure, regulatory environment, concessions and subsidies, land acquisition for industrial use, labor laws, special economic zones, organizational framework, and branding and promotion. These are areas that are typically identified in investment climate surveys as affecting decisions of individual investors. These dimensions have also been identified by international financial institutions as being constitutive of a favorable investment climate (e.g., World Bank 2002, 2005, 2007a, 2007b, 2009; World Bank and International Finance Corporation 2004a, 2004b, 2009, 2012). The data used in this comparison are based on an analysis of state industrial policies, other government documents, and interviews with investors and bureaucrats completed as part of Murali (2017).

Table 2.2 summarizes the policy responses of Gujarat and Punjab along eight different dimensions, but I also discuss three of these dimensions— infrastructure, concessions and subsidies, and regulatory framework—in more detail below. Two main observations on structural power can be drawn from the

Table 2.2 **Varied Policy Responses in Gujarat and Punjab, 1991–2010**

	Gujarat	*Punjab*
Institutional framework for infrastructure building	GID Act in 1999. GIDB, GMB, and GIDC very active. Special initiatives such as port-led industrialization. GMB's port policy in 1995.	PID Act and PIDB in 2002
Infrastructure (electricity)	Captive power policy has facilitated surplus electricity generation. Gujarat Electricity (Reorganization and Regulation) Act in 2003. Average annual state expenditure on energy (as % of total expenditure) between 1991–92 and 2009–10 was 10.4%. Generally eschewed electricity subsidies, unlike other states.	Very slow to undertake process of electricity restructuring reforms. Cabinet approval of unbundling in 2010. Major electricity shortfall. Average annual state expenditure on energy (as % of total expenditure) between 1991–92 and 2009–10 was 8.5%. Free electricity to various groups has had an adverse effect on state finances.
Infrastructure (roads)	Average annual state expenditure on roads and bridges (as % of total expenditure) between 1991–92 and 2009–10 was 3.9%.	Average annual state expenditure on roads and bridges (as % of total expenditure) between 1991–92 and 2009–10 was 1.9%.
Incentives and subsidies	Strong reliance on tax concessions prior to 2003. Over time, focus has shifted to other aspects of investment promotion but continues to offer subsidies comparable to competitors including land, capital investment subsidies, commercial tax concessions, stamp duty. and technology reimbursements. Sizable subsidies continue to large investors.	Poor fiscal situation has meant state not able to provide substantial subsidies, including those promised in policy statements, leading to low credibility with investors.

(*Continued*)

Table 2.2 **Continued**

	Gujarat	*Punjab*
Regulatory environment	Single Window Act in 2000. Functions as initial point of contact. Includes time limits and provisions for deemed clearances. Investor facilitation services offered since 1978 by Indextb. Self-certification in lieu of inspections and consolidated returns under several laws.	Punjab Industrial Facilitation Act in 2005. Self-certification allowed in many areas.
Labor laws/ environment	Labor law flexibility in SEZs and IT sector, particularly with respect to hiring and firing related to Section V of the Industrial Disputes Act. Low man-days lost.	Low man-days lost. Labor law flexibility in SEZs and IT but scope not as wide as Gujarat.
Land acquisition	State has been proactive in creating land banks and then transferring to industry. Active in providing subsidized land for large projects. Amended laws to allow easier conversion from agricultural to industrial use and to acquire land around highways.	Land is major constraint for manufacturing. State reluctant to acquire land.
Special economic zones (SEZs)	SEZ policy in 2004. 53 SEZs approved and 30 have been notified (as of March 30, 2012).	8 approvals and 2 notifications for SEZs (as of March 30, 2012)
Institutional framework for industrialization	State corporations have adapted effectively to postliberalization environment. Indextb, GIDC, GIDB, GIIC, GFC, GMB all active.	Bureaucracy slow to adapt postliberalization environment. Corporations performed poorly. PSIDC defunct.
Branding, promotion, and information activities	Major effort in promoting state as investment destination and information dissemination through Vibrant Gujarat investor summits. Indextb plays an active role in these areas.	Few efforts at promotion and information dissemination

examination of investment promotion policies in Gujarat and Punjab. First, in response to the competition for investment, states have undertaken a variety of policy efforts since 1991 to create business-friendly investment climates. This is consistent with expectations of increasing structural power brought about by capital mobility. The elimination of the licensing system in 1991 meant that the center ceded control over location decisions related to industrial investment. Accordingly, the reforms of 1991 represent an increase in capital mobility. In turn, this mobility and the ensuing competition for investment catalyzed an automatic imperative for states to undertake probusiness policies to attract investment.

The second observation that arises from an examination of investment promotion policies after 1991 is that policy efforts differ across states. Gujarat has been far more proactive and investor-friendly in the competition for investment than Punjab. Indeed, it has, arguably, been the most proactive state in the competition for investment. It has formulated measures that are more business-friendly than its counterparts and has also adopted some policies at an earlier period. The state has offered generous concessions and subsidies to investors, consistently enhanced its infrastructure base, and created a large number of special economic zones. A strong bureaucratic framework for industrialization, which existed even prior to 1991, has been frequently supplemented with new laws and organizations. Gujarat has had fewer problems in transferring land to industry than its counterparts. This is particularly notable; land acquisition has perhaps been the most politically contentious issue surrounding industrialization in India since 1991. Finally, Gujarat has promoted itself vigorously through investor summits and other branding exercises.

In contrast, Punjab has been slow to react to the needs of the postliberalization environment. A vicious cycle of competitive populism since the mid-1990s has weakened the state's finances. As a result, its ability to create new infrastructure and offer subsidies to business has been significantly eroded. Measures such as free electricity to powerful agricultural interests have resulted in shortfalls and acted as major constraints to new projects. It has also been slower than Gujarat to enact regulatory changes. Land acquisition efforts have been limited.

At a very basic level, dissimilar policy efforts of Punjab and Gujarat are correlated with the different role played by industrial capital in the economy of each of the states at the start of the reforms process. Industry has historically enjoyed a more prominent place in Gujarat, while agriculture formed the backbone of the Punjab economy. In 1991, when licensing was eliminated, industry accounted for 36.7 percent of the state's domestic product, while it represented a little less than a quarter of the domestic product in Punjab.[9] In short, it is reasonable to assume that the structural power of industrial capital in Gujarat was greater than that in Punjab at the start of the reforms process. The fact that

Gujarat has been far more proactive in the competition for industrial investment is therefore not surprising and would have been anticipated by structural power arguments.

One point needs to be highlighted here. Policy outcomes are explained by multiple causes, and business power is likely to be one of the many factors that drive policies. Moreover, the extent to which policies are business-friendly will be a function of structural or instrumental power or some combination of both. In addition, this analysis cannot disentangle the effects of structural and instrumental business power. In all likelihood, the two sources of power interact and reinforce each other (Culpepper 2015). As such, I do not claim that Gujarat and Punjab's differing policy environments are solely the result of differences in structural power between these states. I simply suggest that the importance of industrial capital in both states is positively and clearly associated with the level of probusiness policies in each state, which is consistent with structural power arguments.

The policies undertaken by Punjab and Gujarat are summarized in table 2.2. In addition, I discuss three dimensions of investment promotion in detail below to illustrate the imperative of policymakers to attract capital since 1991 and to show that this imperative affects policymakers in different states in a dissimilar manner. This, in turn, suggests that structural power is not a constant but differs across space.

Infrastructure

Gujarat has made infrastructure creation one of the main planks of its investment promotion strategy. It has also been noticeably more aggressive in attempting to attract private sector participation in infrastructure through public-private partnerships. It was among the first states in the country to pass an act, the Gujarat Infrastructure Development Act in 1999, to create a formal institutional framework for infrastructure development. Even prior to the passage of the act, the state created the Gujarat Infrastructure Development Board (GIDB) in 1995 dedicated to identifying new infrastructure projects, reviewing existing infrastructure, and assisting with implementation.

Gujarat was also more extensive in its approach to infrastructure development. Its port policy is one example. To take full advantage of its extensive coastline and spur industrialization away from the developed Ahmedabad-Vadodara belt, the state through the Gujarat Maritime Board (GMB) put in place a port policy in 1995. Among other initiatives, Gujarat's port policy allowed the private sector to set up captive jetties, encouraged joint sector initiatives, and also allowed private players to completely own and operate certain greenfield ports.[10] Some authors suggest that Gujarat's port policies in areas such as Hazira, Dahej, Sikka, Mundra, and Pipavav have reaped considerable rewards in terms of investment (e.g., Aiyar 2008). Two examples—that of Reliance Industries' oil refinery in Jamnagar and Essar Steel's plant in Hazira—lend some support to this view. It is unlikely that either project would have been located in Gujarat if not for benefits arising from well-developed infrastructure facilities.

Punjab's infrastructure in 1991, particularly its road network, was more developed than that of many other states, but the state has failed to supplement this initial base substantially in the postreform period. The Punjab Infrastructure Development and Regulation Act was passed in 2002 and the Punjab Infrastructure Development Board was created the same year. A pattern of competitive populism between the main political parties has adversely affected the state's financial health since the mid-1990s, which limited new infrastructure development and affected maintenance of existing infrastructure.

Aside from noticeable differences in overall approaches to infrastructure development, dissimilarities are also evident when specific areas such as electricity and roads are examined. Electricity is a concurrent subject under India's federal system whereby both the center and regions enjoy responsibilities, but the states have sole jurisdiction over state electricity boards, which are responsible for generation, transmission, and distribution of electricity. By the early 1990s, most Indian states were saddled with dysfunctional state electricity boards. Growing demand, inadequate investment in generation facilities, and major transmission and distribution losses resulting from theft and provision of free power to politically vital interest groups resulted in an adverse situation. At the time, various international agencies as well as the central government actively recommended comprehensive state-level electricity reforms, most notably the unbundling of state electricity boards into separate transmission, generation, and distribution companies.

Authors such as Kochhar et al. (2005) suggest that electricity reforms are a good indicator of the reformist credentials of individual subnational governments. An examination of electricity reforms points to differences. Since the early 1990s, Gujarat encouraged captive (self-)generation by industry, putting in place a captive power policy in 1998, which some observers suggest has enhanced the state's generation capacity (Hansen 2008). In 2003, it passed the Gujarat Electricity Industry (Reorganization and Regulation) Act. This led to the unbundling of the Gujarat Electricity Board into separate companies for transmission, distribution, and generation. Punjab has been reluctant to overhaul its electricity sector. Despite the federal government's recommendations that the process of electricity restructuring take place by 2003, neither state did so. The Punjab cabinet finally approved unbundling of the state electricity board in April 2010.

A comparison of expenditures also makes differences between the two states clear. The average annual expenditure on energy (as a percentage of total state expenditure) between 1991–92 and 2009–10 was 10.4 percent in Gujarat and 8.5 percent in Punjab (calculated from RBI 2010). The average proportion of total expenditure spent on roads and bridges in Punjab between 1991–92 and 2009–10 was 1.86 percent compared to 3.9 percent in Gujarat.

Concessions, Subsidies, and Incentives

In the first decade after liberalization, sales tax concessions were one of the main instruments used by state governments to attract investment.[11] To stem a race to the bottom that was ensuing and as part of a larger attempt at overall tax reforms, the central government pushed for the implementation of a value-added tax (VAT) to replace the archaic sales tax system in 2000.[12] Coordination problems and opposition from the states led to delays in implementation, and the system finally came into force in 2003. The introduction of the VAT system after 2003 meant that sales tax concessions could no longer be used as the primary policy tool to attract investment.[13] Nevertheless, even after the introduction of VAT, states continued to use a variety of concessions and incentives to attract business to their jurisdictions, including exemptions from stamp duty and registration fees, electricity duties, and concessions on other types of taxes.

Gujarat and Punjab differed in their reliance on and ability to offer concessions. After 2000, Gujarat moved toward a more broad-based approach that includes a focus on infrastructure creation and business-friendly regulatory measures (Gujarat 2000, 2003, 2009). However, it continued to use a variety of non-sales tax subsidies liberally, as can be seen in its discretionary packages to "mega investments." The Tata Nano episode, described in the introduction, epitomizes a dynamic that has often characterized subnational competition for investment since 1991—states in India have liberally used concessions and subsidies to attract large projects. At the same time, large investors have demonstrated considerable ability to bargain with state governments to obtain favorable terms. The leverage that business enjoys has been magnified by the fact that concessions to large investors have typically been offered on a discretionary basis. Discretionary concessions have been most starkly evident in certain sectors such as mining and telecom in India, which continue to be substantially regulated by the central government. States also offered a variety of subsidies to a broader group of investors besides large-scale ones after 2000. These included concessions on land, interest, stamp duty, electricity, and technology.

The use of concessions has differed across states. Gujarat continued to offer concessions after the elimination of the sales tax regime but adopted a more broad-based approach to investment promotion. As the Nano case suggested, concessions remained a part of Gujarat's policy toolkit. Punjab's weak financial situation affected its ability to offer concessions even more drastically. A comparison of industrial policies before 2009 showed that Punjab offered fewer subsidies than Gujarat. Moreover, its precarious finances meant that even promises made in industrial policies often remain unfulfilled. Ahluwalia et al. (2008) highlight the fact that these unfulfilled promises led to low credibility of the government with investors.

Regulatory Environment Related to Starting and Operating a Business

In terms of easing procedures to start a business, several Indian states adopted a "single-window system" that, in theory, allows investors to obtain all governmental clearances required to start a business from a single point. In practice, however, the concept of obtaining all clearances from one single government node has not worked. Despite the overall failure of single-window clearance systems to act as a one-stop shop for approvals, some states have been more active in undertaking measures to ease regulations. The scope of the provisions of the single-window system also varies across states. For instance, some states specify time limits that departments must follow in giving clearances and include provisions for "deemed clearances," whereby permission is assumed to be granted if government agencies do not respond within the specified time limit.

Gujarat has been a forerunner in easing regulations to start a business. Formally, its single-window system was put in place in 2000. However, Sinha (2005) clearly outlines that Indextb, a government agency, has acted as a facilitator and initial point of contact for investors since 1978. Apart from differences in timing, the scope of these system and the activities of investment facilitation agency in Gujarat stand out. Gujarat's single-window system includes provisions for time-bound approvals and deemed clearances. Even prior to 1991, Indextb undertook a range of facilitation and information dissemination tasks (Sinha 2005). It continues to be extremely active, particularly with large projects, serving as an initial point of contact for prospective investors, setting up interviews with government departments, and providing a variety of other services related to promotion and information dissemination. In contrast, the scope of Punjab's single-window system is more limited than Gujarat's or AP's. For instance, until 2008, Punjab's system did not have any provisions for time-bound clearances or deemed approvals, as the other two states did.

Unlike single-window systems, attempts at easing some regulatory requirements in terms of inspections of business operations have met with more success. Businesses in India are subject to a variety of state and central laws that require inspections, including a plethora of labor laws, social security laws, and workplace safety acts. Both states adopted self-certification norms and rationalized inspections but did so at different times. Gujarat has allowed self-certification with respect to numerous labor and workplace laws for small and medium enterprises since 2000. Punjab adopted similar measures of self-certification a few years later, in 2005; Bihar did so in 2006.

The empirical evidence in the previous section highlighted the steady growth in business's structural power at the national level since 1991, while the evidence in this section illustrated this change even more clearly at the state level. The analysis at the state level also pointed to the unevenness of business's structural power across Indian states; the indirect and automatic influence business has on policy is evident in some states more than others. In addition to the evidence presented here, other chapters in this book, specifically those of Agarwala and Reddy, also offer evidence that is consistent with the claim of increasing structural leverage of business. Their conclusions are worth highlighting in the context of the discussion in this chapter.

Agarwala points out that despite strong demands of capital and its associations in the period of economic liberalization, formal labor reform has virtually been nonexistent. Yet the state's actions in the realm of labor point to a clear bias toward business. In particular, the state has effectively used subtle, almost subterranean, methods to undermine formal laws and afford business greater labor flexibility without making changes to the actual laws themselves. Accordingly, while more overt actions of business attempting to change formal laws were not effective, the state, nevertheless, ensured that labor policies were consistent with the larger probusiness project.

Similarly, Reddy's analysis of the media similarly has implications for the issue of structural power. According to Reddy, the Indian media landscape has transformed dramatically since the 1990s; in particular, the Indian media became commodified after the 1990s. This commodification was accompanied by a transformation in journalistic practices; as media publishers and owners developed a major stake in a rapid economic growth, the media began to internalize the values of the dominant probusiness paradigm. As in Agarwala's chapter, this shift in journalistic values reflects the indirect nature through which business's structural power works and the implicit influence that capital has in these domains.

Conclusion: Potential Factors That Mitigate Business's Structural Power

A central contention of this book is that the power of business in India has clearly increased in the liberalization era and that this change has had major consequences in numerous policy dimensions. Moreover, capital's power is manifest in both direct and indirect ways. The focus of this chapter was on the indirect pathway through which business exerts influence—its structural power. This chapter documented the heightened role for private capital in the economy, both at the national and the state levels, since 1991 and it illustrated this mechanism through case studies of two Indian states in the competition for investment. Moreover, the chapter outlined the uneven nature of capital's structural power in India. In particular, it demonstrated the spatial variation of this power through the paired comparison of Gujarat and Punjab.

While greater business power has meant that the general direction of policy in India has been significantly biased toward capital, the influence of capital is not hegemonic. Several factors are potentially likely to limit business power. These factors are likely to make the state-business relationship less one-sided than structural power arguments expect. As Kohli (2012, 8) suggests, the nature of India's democracy, particularly the fact that a large section of the electorate is poor, means that "the Indian state can thus never fully be a handmaiden to India business."

I offer brief observations on four factors—the importance of noneconomic factors in determining electoral outcomes, internal heterogeneity of capital and varied preferences, the continuing role of the public sector in the Indian economy, and patterns of cronyism—that are likely to limit business's structural power. First, the "two track" nature of Indian democracy has been a central feature of the high-growth phase after 1980 (Kohli 2006, 2012). This has resulted in the electoral realm remaining relatively separate from the policymaking one. Moreover, clientelistic dynamics, and issues of identity and ethnicity remain central to Indian electoral politics, particularly in linking voters to politicians. Theoretically, the connection between economic performance and electoral outcomes is a central mechanism in the logic of structural power arguments. To win elections, politicians need economic growth and need private sector investment to achieve growth. If the link between electoral outcomes and economic performance is weak, politicians are less likely to be completely biased toward business. In India, while there are some suggestions that economic performance may increasingly matter for electoral outcomes (see Vaishnav and Swanson 2013), evidence for this mechanism remains weak. Issues such as identity, ethnicity, and clientelism continue to be the foundations of the link between voters and politicians. As such, the importance of noneconomic factors, often along the lines of social identity, in electoral dynamics in India weakens a key mechanisms through which business's structural power is expected to work.

Second, business interests are not monolithic. As observers have pointed out, there is a discernible difference in the preferences and interests of the "old economy" firms and newer firms linked to the service sector in areas such as information technology (e.g., Kohli 2012). For example, the latter have typically favored more external engagement of the Indian economy than the former. Business preferences also typically vary by firm size; capital in India is internally heterogeneous and includes small, medium, and large firms. Internal heterogeneity could potentially act as a check on its policy influence. As such, different policies can have varied impacts across firms and sectors. Since structural power is based on a threat of withholding investment, firms with differing preferences on the same issue are likely to send mixed investment signals, which limits policy influence.

Third, the public sector continues to have a notable presence in the Indian economy, and this automatically places limits on capital's influence. As figure 2.4 suggested, a significant portion of employment in the organized sector is in public enterprises. Importantly, India's high-growth era has been non-inclusive in that it has been service sector-oriented and capital intensive and has generated minimal employment in the formal sector (e.g., Subramanian 2008). In that sense, there is a marked disconnect between the livelihoods of a majority of the population, which is employed in the agricultural sector, and sources of growth in India. The fact that the private corporate sector accounts for a small portion of total employment limits its leverage vis-à-vis the state. Moreover, several societal sections have been excluded from the fruits of this high-growth phase. These excluded sections have typically turned toward the state. The public sector also dominates key sectors such as banking. As a result, the state continues to have key instruments that give it some leverage over business.

Finally, while capital's power has clearly grown, it continues to depend on governments for a variety of functions. Moreover, patronage and cronyism remain central features of the link between the state and private sector in India. Indeed, as Chandra (2015) points out, the postliberalization economy has not seen a retreat of the state and patronage. Rather, she suggests that a retreat of patronage in some areas has been accompanied by a relocation to others. In particular, she argues that the state control of resources in the new economy has relocated in three ways: through its control of previously reserved sectors, through its control of inputs such as land, raw materials, and credit, and through the creation of new regulations while old ones have been abolished. As such, a quid pro quo element continues to exist between the state and the private sector in India. Governments also retain considerable discretionary power over various aspects of the policy process. For example, even in the realm of investment promotion, discussed in this chapter, states typically offer discretionary packages to large investors. This discretionary power fragments capital and limits the structural power of business.

References

Agarwala, Rina. 2013. *Informal Labor, Formal Politics, and Dignified Discontent in India.* Cambridge: Cambridge University Press.

Ahluwalia, M. S. 2000. "Economic Performance of States in the Post-reforms Period." *Economic and Political Weekly*, May 6, 1637–48.

Ahluwalia, M. S., Isher Judge, Saumitra Chaudhuri, and Samrat Sidhu. 2008. *Punjab Industrial Review.* Vienna: UNIDO.

Aiyar, Swaminathan S. Ankalesaria. 2008. "The Benefits of Port Liberalization: A Case Study from India." Washington, DC: Cato Institute.

Anant, T. C. A., R. Hasan, R. Mohapatra, R. Nagaraj, and S. K. Sasikumar. 2006. "Labor Markets in India: Issues and Perspectives." In *Labor Markets in Asia: Issues and Perspectives,* ed. J. Felipe and R. Hasan, 205–300. Basingstoke, Hampshire: Palgrave Macmillan.

Barro, R. 1991. "Economic Growth in a Cross Section of Countries." *Quarterly Journal of Economics* 106 (2): 407–43.

Block, Fred L. 1987. *Revising State Theory: Essays in Politics and Postindustrialism.* Philadelphia: Temple University Press.

Chandra, Kanchan. 2015. "The New Indian State: The Relocation of Patronage in the Post-liberalisation Economy." *Economic and Political Weekly* 50 (41): 46–58.

Culpepper, Pepper D. 2015. "Structural Power and Political Science in the Post-crisis Era." *Business and Politics* 17 (3): 391–409.

Culpepper, Pepper D., and Raphael Reinke. 2014. "Structural Power and Bank Bailouts in the United Kingdom and the United States." *Politics & Society* 42 (4): 427–54.

Fairfield, Tasha. 2015. "Structural Power in Comparative Political Economy: Perspectives from Policy Formulation in Latin America." *Business and Politics* 17 (3): 411–41.

Gujarat, Government of. 2000. "Industrial Policy 2000." Gandhinagar: Department of Industries and Mines, Government of Gujarat.

———. 2003. "Industrial Policy 2003." Gandhinagar: Department of Industries and Mines, Government of Gujarat.

———. 2009. "Industrial Policy 2009."Gandhinagar: Department of Industries and Mines, Government of Gujarat.

Hacker, Jacob, and Paul Pierson. 2002. "Business Power and Social Policy: Employers and the Formation of the American Welfare State." *Politics & Society* 30 (2): 277–325.

Hansen, Christopher Joshi. 2008. "Bottom-up Electricity Reform Using Industrial Captive Generation: A Case Study of Gujarat, India." Oxford Institute for Energy Studies.

Jaffrelot, Christophe. 2015. "Patels and the Neo-Middle Class Syndrome." *Indian Express* August 27, 2015.

Jenkins, Rob. 1999. *Democratic Politics and Economic Reform in India.* Cambridge: Cambridge University Press.

Kochhar, K., U. Kumar, R. Rajan, A. Subramanian, and I. Tokatlidis. 2006. "India's Pattern of Development: What Happened? What Follows?." *Journal of Monetary Economics* 53: 981–1019.

Kohli, Atul. 2004. *State-Directed Development: Political Power and Industrialization in the Global Periphery.* Cambridge: Cambridge University Press.

———. 2006. "Politics of Economic Growth in India, 1980–2005, Parts I and II." *Economic and Political Weekly*, April 1 and April 8 41 (13): 1251–9 and 41 (14): 1361–70.

———. 2012. *Poverty amid Plenty in the New India.* Cambridge: Cambridge University Press.

Krugman, P. 1998. "What's New about the New Economic Geography." *Oxford Review of Economic Policy* 14 (2): 7–17.

Lieberman, Evan. 2005. "Nested Analysis as a Mixed-Method Strategy for Comparative Research." *American Political Science Review* 99 (3): 435–52.

Lindblom, Charles Edward. 1977. *Politics and Markets: The World's Political Economic Systems.* New York: Basic Books.

Lucas, R. E. 1990. "Why Doesn't Capital Flow from Rich to Poor Countries?" *American Economic Review* 80 (2): 92–6.

Miliband, Ralph. 1969. *The State in Capitalist Society.* London: Weidenfeld & Nicolson.

Murali, Kanta. 2017. *Caste, Class, and Capital: The Social and Political Origins of Economic Policy in India*. Cambridge: Cambridge University Press.

Nagaraj, R. 2006. *Economic Growth and Reforms: Selected Essays*. Delhi: Academic Foundation.

"Nano Gets a New Home in Gujarat." 2008. *Indian Express*, October 7.

Poulantzas, Nicos A. 1975. *Political Power and Social Classes*. London: NLB; Atlantic Highlands, NJ: Humanities Press.

RBI (Reserve Bank of India). 2010. *Handbook of Statistics on State Government Finances*. Mumbai: RBI.

Rodrik, D., and A. Subramanian. 2004. "From Hindu Growth to Productivity Surge: The Mystery of the Indian Growth Transition." Harvard University.

Rudolph, Lloyd I., and Susanne Hoeber Rudolph. 2001. "Iconisation of Chandrababu: Sharing Sovereignty in India's Federal Market Economy." *Economic and Political Weekly*, 36 (18): 1541–52.

Singh, N., and T. N. Srinivasan. 2006. "Indian Federalism, Economic Reform and Globalization." In *Federalism and Economic Reform*, ed. J. Wallack and T. N. Srinivasan, 301–63. Cambridge: Cambridge University Press.

Sinha, Aseema. 2005. *The Regional Roots of Developmental Politics in India: A Divided Leviathan*. Bloomington: Indiana University Press.

Smith, Mark A. 1999. "Public Opinion, Elections, and Representation within a Market Economy: Does the Structural Power of Business Undermine Popular Sovereignty?" *American Journal of Political Science* 43 (3): 842–63.

———. 2000. *American Business and Political Power: Public Opinion, Elections, and Democracy*. Chicago: University of Chicago Press.

"Sop Opera on Nano Begins in Gujarat." 2008. *Economic Times*, November 12.

Subramanian, Arvind. 2008. *India's Turn: Understanding the Economic Transformation*. New Delhi: Oxford University Press.

Vaishnav, Milan, and Reedy Swanson. 2015. "Does Good Economics Make for Good Politics? Evidence from Indian States." *India Review* 14 (3): 279–311.

Vogel, David. 1983. "The Power of Business: A Re-appraisal." *British Journal of Political Science* 13 (1): 19–43.

Winters, Jeffrey A. 1996. *Power in Motion: Capital Mobility and the Indonesian State*. Ithaca, NY: Cornell University Press.

World Bank. 2002. "Investment Climate Survey in India 2002." World Bank.

———. 2005. *World Development Report 2005: A Better Investment Climate for Everyone*. Washington, DC: World Bank.

———. 2007a. *Doing Business in South Asia in 2007*. Washington, DC: World Bank.

———. 2007b. *The Investment Climate in Brazil, India and South Africa: A Comparison of Approaches for Sustaining Economic Growth in Emerging Economies*. Washington, DC: World Bank Institute.

———. 2009. "Investment Promotion Essentials: What Sets the World's Best Investment Facilitators Apart from the Rest." Washington, DC: World Bank. www.wbginvestmentclimate.org.

World Bank and International Finance Corporation. 2004a. "Doing Business in 2004: Understanding Regulation." Washington, DC: World Bank.

———. 2004b. "India: Investment Climate and Management Industry." Washington, DC: World Bank.

———. 2009. "Doing Business in India 2009." Washington, DC: World Bank.

———. 2012. "Doing Business 2012: Doing Business in a More Transparent World." Washington, DC: World Bank.

India's Porous State

Blurred Boundaries and the Evolving Business-State Relationship

ASEEMA SINHA

Introduction

In order to understand the topography of the business-politics relationships in India, we need a theory and an updated empirical account of the evolving nature of the Indian state. Such a theory must account *both* for the working of a developmental state *and* for the nature of business and its movement *inside* democratic institutions even as India's political actors are beginning to engage in numerous business activities. I argue that public and state institutions are being transformed to incorporate business interests and influence, even as new actors and associations are seeking to take advantage of "pro-business policies" (Kohli 2006a, 2006b) and the state's desire to pursue growth and development in more activist ways; these actors mediate the business-state boundaries, creating new channels of access across the porous state. I present new evidence to show that business interests have moved inside state agencies and that political actors have become businessmen. Interestingly, business movement inside state institutions and public spaces has mixed effects, but irrespective of the types of effects, it will be difficult for India's democratic state to resist business interests because of both a transformation of the state from within and the conversion of political actors into businessmen.

How should we think about the nature of the Indian state after liberalization, the movement of industrial classes inside state agencies, and the diffusion of entrepreneurship among India's political classes? Are these distinct developments or different sides of the same coin? What are the consequences of this compact between business and state actors for public interest and democratic quality? Building on recent writings on the state, I argue that the state in

India is a Janus-faced state that pursues both development and patronage. Most scholars analyze only one face of the state, but this dual nature is its defining feature (Herring 1999; Sinha 2005b; Sud 2009; Sinha 2011; Levien 2013; Gupta 2012; Chandra 2015; Jenkins and Manor 2017). This Janus-faced character of the state allows business actors to infiltrate multiple arenas and access points across institutions of democracy, public institutions, and regulatory bodies.

Three elements affect the current configuration of the business-politics relationship and dynamic: India's democratic structures, increased state capacity demanded by second generation reforms, and changing developmental goals of the state. The democratic character of the Indian state facilitates a porous structure and access points, where multiple interests seek to influence and change government policies.[1] The consolidation of Indian democracy in the last seventy years has made for a plurality of interests and stakeholders, who access varied choice points and seek to modify policy. Over time, and especially after the economic reforms of 1991, state actors have become more open and receptive to business inclusion. The Indian state has taken increasing responsibility for achieving economic growth and development, pushed by rising demands for growth, education, infrastructure, health insurance, jobs, etc. from many sections of society (Sinha 2016b). Thus, the *directive* role of the state, combined with new *developmental* requirements of a liberalized state and its persistent *democratic structure*, facilitates the re-shaping of the porous state. This chapter analyzes how this porous state works, creating a new business-state compact and re-shaping the nature of capitalism as well as India's political economy.

How does this argument enhance the prevailing ways of viewing the business-politics relationship? Modifying and enhancing the structural view,[2] which argues that businesses have a hold over the state on account of their material and exit power, this chapter uses the distinction formulated by Culpepper (2015), to argue that there are "mutual dependencies" between state and capital in India. While business power has grown, although not coherently, "Large holders of capital depend upon finding a regulatory environment in which they can generate a return from their capital" (Culpepper 2015, 398). Paradoxically, the renewal and reassertion of the Indian state has created fresh opportunities and fresh regulations for business infiltration and diverse instrumental strategies of influence and access. In a parallel vein, in 2010, I had observed the then-recent entry of businessmen into the Indian parliament, arguing for the importance of new arenas that had become important for business interests (Sinha 2010a). In this chapter, I show how new instruments of access and influence are being fine-tuned by diverse business actors. Yet the Indian state has also reasserted itself, and "globalized markets and captured states are not the whole story" (Culpepper 2015, 393) of contemporary Indian political economy. The Indian state has put growth and welfare on its agenda and sought to use banks to pursue growth-friendly policies (see PTI 2014). Finance has become the new tool of an activist and trading state, one that creates new opportunities for rent-seeking.[3] The new developmental trading state (Sinha 2016a), where a newly interventionist state helps businesses seek export markets, further solidifies India's emerging business-politics relationships and business movement inside public agencies.

Other scholars have also commented on the paradoxical double-sided nature of the Indian state, where transactions between private and state actors operate in the shadow of the state but legally (Sinha 2010b; Gupta 2012; Chandra 2015; Sud 2009; Levien 2013). Chandra articulates this double view in the following way:

> Further, although there is some overlap between the two concepts, patronage is not synonymous with corruption. Corruption is usually defined as the illegal use of public resource for private gains (Manion 1996). But the patronage transactions described here usually take place within the letter of the law. They exploit and expand the discretion available within the law, rather than breaking it outright (see Sud 2009 on the "blurring" and "skirting" of legal boundaries). And while they certainly provide ample opportunities for rent-seeking on both sides, state officials may also be motivated by business-friendly notions of "development," and business owners may also cultivate relationships with state officials as a necessary evil to get work done in an ambiguous environment. (Chandra 2015, 47)

Herring (1999, 324)'s analysis also put forward the concept of the porous state and embeddedness in the following way to characterize the pre-liberalization state:

> Embeddedness thus worked against the sort of capital-state relationship that empowers the state to act against some in the interests of all. Particularistic embeddedness created in practice a porous state; regulations deterred some, delayed everyone, but in the final analysis only intermittently approached state goals.

These concepts have important implications for the nature of the post-liberalized state in India. First of all, it might be necessary to go beyond the common assumption that economic liberalization amounts to a withdrawal of the state (Strange 1996).[4] What does the current Indian state look like? I suggest that a state with fuzzier boundaries is being re-formed, which includes business representation in more regularized yet invisible ways than anticipated. The "embedded particularistic" (Herring 1999, 321) state has morphed into a porous state with formal inclusion of business representation. The approach of simultaneously looking at the "mutual dependencies" (Culpepper 2015) between the state and business does help us understand recent developments within India. However, the metaphor of mutual dependencies assumes that business and state exist as separate actors and take distinct institutional forms. Building on, but also going beyond, a "mutual dependencies" metaphor, I argue that many political and economic institutions in India incorporate business interests more centrally than before and that business has begun to shape mainstream—both democratic and regulatory—institutions. The state has become more porous as business has moved into diverse institutions. Importantly, political actors—especially politicians from all political parties—are investing in business activities.

Blurred boundaries, I argue, is a more apt metaphor than mutual dependencies.[5] Focusing on blurring boundaries means that we must focus on both the *institutions* and the *agents* that mediate the boundaries of state action and private sector. This theory of blurred boundaries and the porous state should map both the institutional roles of business actors as well as the instrumental strategies adapted by business actors, which may enhance the structural power of business discussed in chapter 2 of this volume. Opening up the black box of "business-state" relations, this chapter explores the workings of key institutions of Indian political life, such as the parliament, independent regulatory agencies, public private partnerships, and bureaucracy, to map the influence of business *inside* institutions.[6] I find that key actors, such as prominent businesspersons from both old and new sectors of the economy, overlapping brokers, and organizations such as business associations, mediate public institutions and private power in multiple ways. Thus, this chapter focuses *both* on the agents that mediate and the institutions within which private power finds a new home— the brokers and mediators—*and* new protagonists and organizations (political parties, associations and individual politicians, for example). India's regulatory institutions work according to democratic and pluralistic mechanisms, adapted for the field of development and regulation; this structure facilitates business movement inside institutions.[7]

To demonstrate my argument, I collected new data on the incorporation of business within new policy spaces created by the government to further second-generation reforms in India. Occupation data for the Lok Sabha, Rajya Sabha (India's legislative bodies), and state-level legislative assemblies, data on politicians' and their families' business links, and data on the PM's Advisory Council and independent agencies allow me to document multiple access points and movements of business across fuzzy boundaries of the state. This new evidence and data reveal a fascinating picture of subtle and invisible ways in which political and business actors are interacting together within institutions of a democratic developmental state. Together, they point to the emergence of porous boundaries (the porous state) that India's democratic structure encourages and engenders.

Mixed Consequences

This movement of business actors within public institutions raises an important question: What are the consequences of business entry into public institutions? It is difficult to trace the effect of such incorporation on some specific policies or policy outputs, although that is needed to make definitive judgments about effects. I offer only a framework of analysis and tentative hypotheses about suggested effects in this chapter. At first glance there may be two possibilities: One, the industrial groups may shape policy to suit their business interests or reorient the public agency toward their interests. This may be deleterious for public interest and even the pursuit of balanced growth, creating a pattern of lopsided growth. A second possibility is that business actors contribute to better policies or allow the state to go after the bad pennies within the business sector and support the work of the state agencies, contributing to the growth of the whole economy. Here, we may see the developmental role of business in support for competition.

An initial, somewhat tentative, conclusion that emerges is that there may be a variable effect of business representation across public institutions. We see a definite negative effect of business on the output of parliamentary committees and the legislative output of the parliament. Serious conflicts of interests are affecting the independence of laws and policies that are produced by parliament. Development finance, especially in the infrastructure sectors, has become the site of rent-seeking and subversion of public interest. In contrast, independent institutions such as the Securities and Exchange Board of India (SEBI) and Telecom Regulatory Authority of India (TRAI) benefit from such business incorporation with better policies and some possibility for competitive rather than oligopolistic practices. Prima facie, the creation of the PM Advisory Council on Trade and Industry could check collusion and introduce some new policy ideas, although it is also the place where business could exercise structural power. How can we explain this variability in effects across policy arenas and public agencies?

In order to understand the variable effect of business on public and consumer interests, I suggest an overlapping typology of different kinds of state activities and different types of business structure. Figure 3.1 highlights that the state pursues growth and trade but also development related functions. Business influence has varying consequences on public interest depending upon the type of policy affected.

Table 3.1 creates a typology of the conditions under which business activities may have positive or negative effects.

Business incorporation is those arenas and policies where considerations of growth and capital accumulation are the dominant considerations—the growth or trading state—may have some beneficial effects. In addition, the structure of business competition and industrial structure—whether it is competitive or

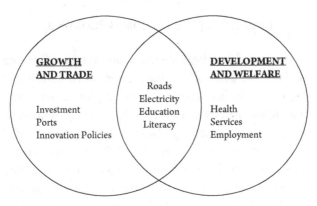

Figure 3.1 Overlapping Functions of the State

monopolistic—may also play a role. In policy arenas where development and quality-of-life issues such as education, literacy, and health—broader issues that affect the public and consumer interests—are dealt with, we may find that the narrow goals of business activities undermine the larger developmental goal of the state. The evidence gathered in this chapter shows that business action and incorporation within legislative institutions, and in matters related to budgetary allocations—finance and public sector banks—has created serious problems for the pursuit of a public or common interest. Business action within regulatory agencies and in giving policy advice to the government can have more positive effects. Future research could explore these hypotheses and tentative conclusions. I provide some selective evidence below about these differential effects.

Table 3.1 **Variable consequences of business incorporation**

Types of policies → Structure of business ↓	Growth and trade policies	Development policies (education, health, public investment in roads and infrastructure)
Narrow and monopolistic	Lopsided or uneven growth. Finance in infrastructure sectors, e.g., nonperforming loans (case study of Vijay Mallya).	Harmful for the common good: consumers and citizens. e.g., legislative decisions about public health
Broad and competitive	Balanced growth, e.g., PM Advisory Council on Trade and Industry	Beneficial for public good (ensures competition), e.g., Telecom TRAI

Source: Author's Typology

Legacies of the License-Quota Raj

Since India's trajectory of post-1991 liberalization has taken place within existing institutions and policy frameworks without a serious rupture, it make sense to explore the legacies of the license-quota-permit raj for current patterns of business infiltration. Most analysts agree that India before liberalization should be categorized as a form of state capitalism, wherein the state regulated and directed private sector and industrial activity. By the 1970s India was a protected and a heavily regulated economy known in common parlance as the "license-quota-permit raj." The government regulated the private sector through many different regulations and provided external controls to prevent international imports.

Despite the ubiquity of the regulatory regime, two distinct views on what this economic structure means for the business-state relationship have emerged. The dominant "junior actor" view holds that the Indian state is a dominant actor that dictates the terms of regulation, provides discretionary policies, and affects business strategies as well as the structure of private sector investment. Most economists and political scientists seem to concur with this view (Rudolph and Rudolph 1987; Sen 2013; Ahluwalia 1985; Bhagwati 1993). Bhagwati (1993), for example, argued that state controls and protectionism resulted in unproductive rent-seeking behavior by firms. In this view businesses were rule-takers, were relatively weak, and lobbied against the opening up of the economy. State actors were distant and dictated the regulatory contract, which they used for both developmental and patronage purposes. In a similar vein, Kanchan Chandra, in a recent article, argues that the state's control over resources has been "relocated" and this has reinforced the state's discretionary authority (Chandra 2015).

A second "agenda setter" account sees the business actors as "invisible but crucial partners." In this view, business actors shaped the government's agenda even when the state was dominant (Chibber 2003). Herring's account of embedded particularism may be consistent with this view (1999). Herring argued that business infiltrated the state albeit in an individualist ways rather than collectively. This view is also consistent with the idea of "blurred boundaries" I argue for in this chapter. In a similar way, Evans (1995) categorized India as an intermediate state where business power and state power were evenly matched. While embedded autonomy was sacrificed, business power was not insignificant.

While there is some overlap between two views—for example, the agreement that business shapes the agenda of the government—these two views still regard the two actors, state and private sector, as separate and distinct, with distinct goals and purposes. For the first, business as a *junior partner*, view, the Indian state thrives by reasserting its boundaries and regulatory authority over rules, policies, and rents. For the agenda-setter view, business is powerful and a distinct class. In contrast, I argue here that what is striking about post-1991 India is the degree to which business actors and interests have become implicated in the texture of prominent institutions and diffused across many layers of Indian social and political life. In the process, the nature of the regulatory agencies has itself been transformed, providing enhanced legitimacy to business strategies. In some policy areas this has taken the form of institutionalized consultation, but in some others it has taken the form of business representation. Crucially, and this is a big change from previous regimes, political actors have begun to delve into business and private sector activity using their resources, regulatory information, and access to the state to benefit their businesses. This can also be called the "joint partner" view of the relationship, but the joint partners idea seems to rely on the boundaries and distinctiveness of each actors, which I argue are being transformed. In the sections below, I document the varied ways in which the boundaries between the Indian state and business have become porous and osmotic.

Mapping the Porous State: The Institutional Basis of a New Business-State Relationship

An important question worth exploring is how the joint and dual-faced nature of India's political economy—both developmental and predatory—evolves and works in practice. What are the specific elements and practices of this dual dynamic? The only way to assess the working relationship between business and state is to open the black box of the Indian state and examine what's happening inside public and democratic institutions. In this section I look at a variety of institutional and policy spaces to assess the current working of the business-state relationship and if both the developmental and the crony faces of the relationship are visible. I examine six distinct institutions:

a. Legislative bodies both at the center and across the states, including parties
b. The Prime Minister's Council on Trade and Industry
c. Independent regulatory bodies
d. Public-private partnerships
e. The role of business associations within multilateral institutions such as the WTO
f. Banks and finance

I also try to identify the actors and agencies that allow for the movement of diverse interests across boundaries. Here, political brokers and business associations emerge as significant mediators of linkage across the boundaries of private activity and state action. Yet the effect of business representation across these varied institutions is differentiated by whether these policies are growth enhancing or development oriented and whether the structure of business organization is competitive or oligopolistic. In some cases the movement of business inside public institutions has negative effects on the public interest (legislatures, for example) while in some other institutions (PM's council and regulatory agencies like TRAI) it checks unilateral and monopoly control by dominant business actors creating a somewhat salutary effect.

Legislative Representation and Business

In March–April 2015, a member of the parliamentary committee on health claimed that there were no health risks associated with tobacco use (Ghosh 2015). The mainstream media laughed at this suggestion. However, his comments were consequential; he was Shyama Charan Gupta, a BJP MP, known as the "bidi baron," with an annual turnover of Rs. 200–250 crore in the bidi business (Ghosh 2015). The health ministry heeded the recommendation of the parliamentary health committee *not* to display a warning covering 85 percent of tobacco products. This example highlights the emerging *instrumental* role of business actors within a national institution: the parliament, where economic policymaking has become more salient. Business's role in parliamentary committees has become especially prominent, even as committees overseeing economic and financial matters have proliferated. Table 3.2 provides a selective list of the large number committees in the parliament related to industry and business subjects, creating many possibilities for conflict of interests to emerge.

The role of business within the Indian parliament is important in three distinct ways. First, it increases the representative power of business in a prominent institution. Such representative power increases the legitimacy of business by giving political space to business actors. Second, it enables business to make policy, apart from affecting how policies are implemented. Many laws are shaped by business presence in the two houses. Third, business's roles in parliamentary committees give it a unique function of criticizing government policy and government departments and shaping policies in more specialized arenas related to business interests. This enhances the instrumental power of business to lobby the concerned officers, ministries, and MPs. As noted by Jairam Ramesh, a Congress Party MP and minister, a seat on the panel gives Vijay Mallya "access to information, and an unfair advantage to influence policy" (Rajshkhar 2016b).

This latter role also creates the potential for conflict of interest of diverse kinds. Conflict of interest has become a serious issue within these committees (National Social Watch 2011). Many examples of such conflicts of interests have come to light. Business members are asking questions that affect their specific

Table 3.2 **Parliamentary committees dealing with economic policy**

Committee name	Date/timeline
Finance	
Estimates	Ongoing; set up each year
Public Accounts	Ongoing
Public Undertakings	Ongoing
Commerce	
Industrial Corridors in India	February 2016
Ease of Doing Business	December 2015
Rubber Industry in India	August 2015
Export Infrastructure in India	June 2015
Rubber Industry in India	November 2014
Investigative committees	
JPC for Telecom	October 2013
JPC on Pesticide Residue and Soft Drinks	February 2004
JPC on Stock market Scams	December 2002
JPC into Securities and Banking Transactions Irregularities	December 1993
JPC into Bofors Contract	April 2008

Source: Collated from website of the Indian parliament.

business interests. In 2009, for example, the Telugu Desam Party (TDP) member from Andhra Pradesh raised a question related to highways. His business group was seeking to do business with the National Highways Authority of India (Rahman. 2009). Such access and questions give policy information to business actors even as policy is taking shape. As a former Congress MP from Karnataka noted: "You can direct policy. When a law is drafted, it is the standing committee which vets it. The government system is under its thumb. It can call any bureaucrat. Even as a MP, you have access to the bureaucracy" (Rajshkhar 2016b). Most of the legislative work takes place within parliamentary committees, where conflicts of interests are pervasive. The Committee on Public Undertakings addressed this issue to all its members in 2009 when it was found that three of its members—T. Subbarami Reddy, Lagadapati Rajagopal, and Nama Nageswara Rao—were "using their position to further their business interests" (Rajshkhar 2016b). Vijay Mallya served on three committees—Consultative Committee on Civil Aviation, Standing Committee on Chemicals and Fertilizer, and Standing

Committee on Commerce—while he was in the Rajya Sabha. He had business interests in all three sectors. Kupendra Reddy, a real estate businessman from Karnataka, served on the select committee to debate and discuss the Real Estate Regulation and Development Bill passed in 2013. In 2009 a newsmagazine story outlined that three committees—the Standing Committee on Health, the Standing Committee on Finance, and the Standing Committee on Industry and the Public Accounts Committee had massive business representation in each of their committees. Shafi Rahman (2009) noted:

> The 31-member Standing Committee on Finance is virtually an industry who's who—venture capitalist Rajeev Chandrasekhar (Independent) from Karnataka, chief-minister hopeful of Andhra Pradesh and business magnate Y. S. Jaganmohan Reddy (Congress), Maharashtra based industrialist Vijay Jawaharlal Darda (Congress), Sambasiva Rayapati and industrialist Magunta Srinivasulu Reddy (Congress) from Andhra Pradesh. The 26-member Standing Committee on Industry has Uttar Pradesh businessman Akhilesh Das (BSP) as its chairperson; perfume baron Badruddin Ajmal (AUDF) and Andhra Pradesh textile manufacturer Gireesh Kumar Sanghi (Congress) are its members. Over a third of the members of the committee on industry—nine out of 26—are from business and industry. The Public Accounts Committee boasts of members like industrialist Navin Jindal (Congress), Andhra Pradesh-based contractor Kavuri Sambasiva Rao (Congress) and Tamil Nadu educationist M. Thambi Durai (AIADMK).

In 2008 a special inquiry committee of parliament that inquired into parliamentary misconduct said: "The committee members are of the view that a provision may be made to the effect that if a member has a personal, pecuniary or direct interest on any subject/matter, he should not be nominated in the first place to the Departmentally Related Standing Committee, which normally examines such subjects/matters" (Second Report 2008). Some of the recommendations of the committee were accepted by the Rajya Sabha but have been ignored by the Lok Sabha.

These facts give us the context to examine the increase in business representation in parliament. Thangam Therarasu, a former education minister in Tamil Nadu, spoke of "a shift in how businessmen approach politics. Before liberalization, India had ministers who were close to industrialists—but thereafter industrialists began entering politics mostly though the Rajya Sabha" (Rajshkhar 2016b). While many businessmen entered the parliament through the Rajya Sabha in the early days after liberalization in 1991 (for example, Anil Ambani and Vijay Mallya), the Lok Sabha also has recently seen a marked increase in business representation. In 1991, 14.2 percent of Lok Sabha MPs belonged to "business" or "trader" professions. By 2014 the number had increased to 26.2 percent (see table 3.3). Rajya Sabha (table 3.4) has also seen a similar increase. Some prominent Rajya Sabha members include Rahul Bajaj, Vijay Mallya, Anil Ambani, Rajkumar Dhoot, and M. A. M. Ramaswamy.

How does this picture look like across states? I collected data on the occupation of members of legislative assemblies (MLAs) in the legislative assemblies of all states from myneta.com. These data pertain to 2014 or 2013, as longitudinal data are not available as yet. Clearly, legislative assemblies have seen the penetration of business occupation categories in much larger proportions than the national parliament, although the northeastern states have negligible business presence.[8] Table 3.5 documents an emerging pattern where many state assemblies (esp. Goa and Maharashtra) have higher representation of business actors than the national parliament, even as business presence is increasing in both houses of the national legislature (Table 3.6).

What about political parties? While most of the business MPs come from the two major parties (BJP and the Congress Party), some regional parties have larger than expected share (given their number of seats). Business representation in smaller, regional, and secondary parties is even more pervasive (see tables 3.7 and 3.8). TDP, the Sikkim Democratic Front, and AIDMK have strong business representation. Why do these parties nominate businessmen? It is clear that parties sponsor business people who support the party and raise money for the party. Smaller regional parties are more dependent upon business funds

Table 3.3 **Business representation in the Lok Sabha (LS)**

	Party in power	Share of business occupations in LS (%)	Number of business members/ Total LS members
2014: 16th Lok Sabha	BJP	26.33	143/543
2009: 15th Lok Sabha	Congress Party	21.60	121/560
2004: 14th Lok Sabha	Congress Party	19.28	113/586
1999: 13th LS	NDA/BJP	17.25	98/568
1998: 12th LS	NDA/BJP	14.46	79/546
1996: 11th LS	United Front	15.94	88/552
1991: 10th LS	Congress Party	14.20	79/556

Source: Author's calculations from data available at Lok Sabha's website.

Table 3.4 **Business representation in the Rajya Sabha (RS)**

	Share of business occupations in RS (%)	Number of business members/ Total RS members
2014	11.90	29/243
2009	15.90	38/239
1998	12.60	31/246
1994	9.88	8/81

Source: Sinha (2010a). The 2014 data were collected from Rajya Sabha's website: http://rajyasabha. nic.in/.

Table 3.5 **Business representation across Indian states**

State	MLAs with business, industry, trading occupations	Total members (MLAs)	Percentage of business in assemblies
Andhra Pradesh	79	174	0.45
Arunachal Pradesh	9	60	0.15
Assam	51	126	0.40
Bihar	57	243	0.23
Chhattisgarh	20	90	0.22
Delhi	30	69	0.43
Goa	28	40	0.70
Gujarat	64	182	0.35
Haryana	36	90	0.40
Himachal Pradesh	19	68	0.28
Jammu and Kashmir	22	87	0.25
Jharkhand	19	81	0.23
Karnataka	73	215	0.34
Kerala	9	140	0.06
Madhya Pradesh	69	230	0.30
Maharashtra	141	283	0.50
Manipur	2	60	0.03
Meghalaya	12	60	0.20

(Continued)

Table 3.5 **Continued**

State	MLAs with business, industry, trading occupations	Total members (MLAs)	Percentage of business in assemblies
Mizoram	11	40	0.28
Nagaland	5	60	0.08
Odisha	20	147	0.14
Puducherry	13	30	0.43
Punjab	38	117	0.32
Rajasthan	59	200	0.30
Sikkim	3	32	0.09
Tamil Nadu	41	119	0.34
Telangana	66	224	0.29
Tripura	2	60	0.03
Uttarakhand	15	70	0.21
Uttar Pradesh	128	403	0.32
West Bengal	55	293	0.19

Source: Author's collection and coding from myneta.com.

Table 3.6 **Grouping states according to proportion of business representation**

States	
States with 50%–70% business representation	Goa and Maharashtra
States with 30%–49% business representation	Andhra Pradesh, Assam, Haryana, Gujarat, Delhi, Madhya Pradesh, Karnataka, Rajasthan, Punjab, Pondicherry, Tamil Nadu, Uttar Pradesh
States with 20%–30%	Uttarkhand, Telengana, Jharkhand, Jammu and Kashmir, Himachal Pradesh, Chattisgarh, Bihar
States with less than 20%	Tripura, Sikkim, Odisha, Nagaland, Mizoram, Meghalaya, Manipur, Kerala, Arunachal Pradesh, West Bengal

Source: Author's analysis based on table 3.5.

Table 3.7 **Business MPs across parties, 2014**

Party name	Number of business MPs
Bharatiya Janata Party	86
Telugu Desam Party	10
Indian National Congress	8
Sikkim Democratic Front	8
All India Anna Dravida Munnetra Kazhagam	7
Yuvajana Sramika Rythu Congress Party	7
Telangana Rashtra Samithi	4
All India United Democratic Front	3
All India Trinamool Congress	2
Biju Janata Dal	2
All India N.R. Congress	1
Apna Dal	1
Indian National Lok Dal	1
Janata Dal (Secular)	1
Nationalist Congress Party	1
Samajwadi Party	1
Independent Candidate	1
Total	**144**

Source: Collated by the author from Lok Sabha website.

for monetary support and sponsor the entry of businessmen in larger numbers. An investigative reporting cited a comment by a senior JD(S) member states: "Senior JD(S) leader MS Narayana Rao said the party supported these businesspeople because they had joined and supported it. If someone says we are selling [Rajya Sabha] seats for a price, that is not correct. . . . They helped the party. If MPs or MLAs contribute to the party, that is not trading. He conceded that the JD(S) was going through a financial crunch" (Rajshekhar 2016a).

Political Brokers: Mediating the Boundaries

An analysis that stresses the blurred boundaries between a fast-expanding private sector and public institutions must also pay attention to the *brokers* who

Table 3.8 **Business MPs across parties, 2009**

Party name	Number of business MPs
Indian National Congress	44
Bharatiya Janata Party	35
Bahujan Samaj Party	8
Dravida Munnetra Kazhagam	8
Shiv Sena	5
All India Trinamool Congress	4
Janata Dal (United)	4
Nationalist Congress Party	4
Samajwadi Party	3
Telugu Desam Party	3
All India United Democratic Front	1
Biju Janata Dal	1
Haryana Janhit Congress	1
Janata Dal (Secular)	1
Sikkim Democratic Front	1
Total	123

Source: Collated by the author from the Lok Sabha website.

enable movement from one arena to another. Here I offer case studies of three such brokers, who belong to both political and business worlds and have played a prominent role: Parimal Nathwani, K. D. Singh, and Rajeev Chandrasekhar. All three are Rajya Sabha members.

Rajeev Chandrasekhar lists his profession as "entrepreneur," and he was the "founder" of BPL Mobile, a mobile phone service provider. His assets are worth around thirty-seven crores.[9] He is proud to have "lent" his views as an entrepreneur within the Rajya Sabha and in many policy forums. He has been active member of the Rajya Sabha with attendance in the range of 80–100 percent attendance.[10] He noted: "Whenever people ask me for my views as an entrepreneur, I have lent my views. . . . I have prepared a national security document as president of FICCI. I do my research . . . that has nothing to do with my political affiliation" (Manoj 2010). He is currently the chairman and chief executive officer, Jupiter Capital, a venture development, management, and investment company, focusing on infrastructure and technology ventures since July 2005.[11] In addition, he holds the directorship of a consultancy company called Vectra

Consultancy Services Private Limited, based in Bangalore. Chandrashekar also owns four "infrastructure companies," a couple of which seem to be real estate companies.[12] Notably, he has served on "Infrastructure Taskforce" of the government of Karnataka, revealing a direct conflict of interest. He also seems to own a media company in Kerala, which includes the *Kochi Post*. Chandrashekar represented Karnataka from an independent party from April 2006 to April 2012 and then again from 2012 to 2018. He was elected to the Rajya Sabha with the support of the BJP and was part of a "Study Group to prepare a document on BJP's vision of national development" (Manoj 2010). In 2016 he was also appointed the vice chairman of the Kerala wing of the BJP. While a member of the Rajya Sabha, Chandrasekhar has played a major in many regulatory reforms and committees. He has been a member of a large number of legislative committees and government bodies, all related to economic and finance-related subjects.[13]

Parimal Nathwai is an MP of Rajya Sabha from Jharkhand and has served two terms in the Rajya Sabha, first in 2008 and then from 2014 to 2020. His nomination was supported by both the BJP and the All Jharkhand Student Union Party. He is the Reliance man in the parliament and serves as the "Group President (Corporate Affairs and projects), Reliance Industries LTD"; he joined Reliance in 1997. He has a prominent website that documents his many achievements and what he calls a "rags-to-riches story."[14] Nathwai suggests that his entry into the Rajya Sabha was serendipitous: "I had never thought about it, really. Reliance had started its operations in retail (Reliance trends) and for a case of land dispute, I was sent to meet Jharkhand's Advocate General. AG asked me to wait for 10 minutes in the same cabin while he was having a conversation with a group of 8–9 MLAs, who were worried about the upcoming Rajya Sabha elections. Once the meeting was over, the advocate general asked me if I was interested. The offer was definitely tempting." He also reflects on Mukesh Ambai's views on the matter: "He [Mukesh Ambani] said—your victory or defeat is now Reliance's and Mukesh Ambani's victory or defeat. He very softly told me to go ahead with this only if I was sure that I would win or it would spoil both his as well as Reliance's reputation. The elections were only 20 days away and he told me not to waste time at Mumbai anymore." He also states: "Reliance has been fully supportive of my work in Jharkhand. Managing my time with my job at Reliance and with my tenure as MP, wouldn't have been possible without Mukeshbhai's support."[15] His attendance in the Rajya Sabha deliberations is quite indifferent and ranges between 15 and 40 percent.[16]

K. D. Singh is a member of Rajya Sabha from West Bengal and belongs to the Trinamool Congress. His political career started as a member of the Jharkhand Mukti Morcha (JMM) in 2010, and he is alleged to have paid his way into the Rajya Sabha. His business activities started in 1988 with Turbo Industries, which was renamed Alchemist in 2004. His business interests are involved with healthcare, pharmaceuticals, food processing, real estate, infrastructure, and retail brands. K. D. Singh has been involved in a number of scandals and is considered to be a key political broker. These brokers are both representative of the ways in which businessmen enter legislative institutions and how they continue to span different realms of public and private life.

Politicians Moving into Business Activity

As business actors have moved closer to legislative, public, and party organizations, politicians have begun to engage in business activities, mostly in small and medium enterprises.[17] As T. N. Ninan, a prominent editor, noted:

> Rajeev Chandrasekhar, who ran a telecom business before selling out to become an investor (including in the media) and a member of Parliament, told James Crabtree of the Financial Times: "We have a completely unique phenomenon in India, which I call political entrepreneurship, that has taken root in the last five to six years.... They [the politicians] are saying: 'We don't want briefcases full of cash and Swiss bank accounts and all that any more. We want to own businesses ourselves. We want equity stakes.'" (Ninan 2015)

Dynastic and professional politicians are now investing in and creating new businesses both at the national level and across India's states.[18] A few examples offer striking evidence of the pervasiveness of this phenomenon. I collated data on the business interests of sixty-eight politicians based on reports published by *LiveMint,* and table 3.A1 in the appendix summarizes that database. The results point to a significant and definite trend: More and more politicians are businessmen across a variety of sectors. The sectoral spread of politicians' investment in the world of private business is striking, although they are engaged in small and medium-sized companies as of now. As Wyatt (2017) notes, real estate and property development are especially attractive to politicians. Media is another important sector, especially in South India. Importantly, there is a massive cross-holding pattern in that members of the same family hold equity stakes in various companies, which then hold stakes in other companies (see table 3.A1 in the appendix). Strikingly, family members of politicians are ubiquitous in the business world. Even where the political head of the family does not hold any equity, his or her family members hold equity stakes in many business companies. A few examples from diverse parties highlight this larger trend, but this phenomenon is by now pervasive across all parties.[19] Overall, the most significant transformation in the last few decades is the movement of politicians into business and private sector activity. A few examples follow.

Nitin Gadkari, the BJP leader who is also India's transportation minister, along with his wife Kanchan and sons Nikhil and Sarang, controls several companies in power, sugar, agriculture, real estate, and infrastructure, including Purti Power and Sugar, Vidarbha Realtors, Yash Agro Energy, Purti Alternative Fuels, Chaitanya Constructions and Builders, Purti Marketing, and GMT Mining and Power (Malik 2014). Milind Deora, a Congress MP, and his family have stakes in energy, entertainment, and media companies. Chandan Mitra, a sitting Rajya Sabha member from the BJP and editor of *The Pioneer* newspaper, has stakes in companies including Pioneer Periodicals, Pioneer Events, Sanchar Holdings, Morningstar Multimedia, and CMYK Printech. His wife, Shobori Ganguli, has stakes in Tin Tin Printech and Vibgyor Travels. His son Kushan Mitra has a stake in Saraswati Lodestar Services. Chandan Mitra is also a director on the boards of Rainbow Productions and Reliable Ventures India. The DMK leader, Dayanidhi Maran, and a former Union minister, has stakes in largely media, cable TV, and publication companies (Malik 2014). Supriya Sule, a member of the NCP, and her family hold business interests in a film company, finance and consultancy, and real estate. Her family members have equity interests in media, aviation, and infrastructure. There is also considerable cross-holding among the companies owned by Sule's family members (Malik 2014). This trend is very widespread across parties, pointing to the larger point stressed in this chapter: the boundaries between politics and business have become permeable, and actors from both realms are freely moving across them.

Business Associations: Overlapping Jurisdictions and Creating Linkages

Kunal Sen, in concurrence with many other scholars, suggests that "with the onset of major economic reforms in 1991, the command and control regime was dismantled, and with this the Indian state shifted away from a hostile relationship with business and toward one that was closer to and more collaborative" (Sen 2013, 9). Who are the business actors that mediate the new business-state compact, and ensure collaboration? Many scholars have noted the role of business associations in mediating India's reform program. Kochanek addressed this issue directly in "The Transformation of Interest Politics in India," arguing that "interest politics has become less individual, patron-client and particularistic and more collective, open, and genuinely pluralistic" (Kochanek 1995–96, 529–30). He further noted:

> Economic, social, and political changes have had a profound impact on
> the transformation of interest politics in India. These changes have been
> especially visible in the case of Indian business, which has witnessed

the decline of established organizations, like FICCI and Assocham, and the rise of CII as the premier apex association representing business in India. These changes have resulted from the rise of new industries and regions, the break-up of elite families, increased competition for status and recognition, the breakdown of consensus, and attempts to preserve the status quo in the midst of rapid economic development and enhanced competition. (Kochanek 1995–96, 549)

Kochanek (1995–96), Sinha (2005b), and Sen (2013) also find some evidence of "effective" business-state interactions mediated by business associations. Pedersen (2000) offers a society-centric explanation for the 1991 reforms wherein new segments of business—"technologically more advanced" or modern medium and small-scale sectors—led to changing patterns of organization and interests in favor of globalization (also see Pedersen 2008). Sinha (2005b) emphasized a more political story, arguing that in response to the rise of CII, FICCI revived itself, creating a disorganized yet state-dominated business system. More recently, Kuldeep Mathur suggests the creation of new policy spaces that incorporate business interests in a more transparent manner (2014).

While each of these accounts notes the enhancement of the role of business associations, we don't know how and why these business associations have become more crucial to the changing business-state relationship. While there are some functional arguments, for example, the fact that organizations such as the CII and FICCI provide information or credible signals (Sen 2013), I suggest that these business organizations also be recognized as intermediating linkage organizations that allow state and political actors to participate across overlapping jurisdictions. Many of India's new regulations are being governed with such a joint-decision model. Such overlapping contexts and the participation of the CII and FICCI in them is the institutional embodiment of the diffusion of business ideas and practices across different elements of the business-state dynamic.

How does this overlapping structure work in practice? I offer some evidence from the field of trade policy and India's engagement with the WTO.[20] While business actors played an important role the dirigiste regime, their role was largely reactive, responding to regulations post facto. This scenario continued even during the 1990s. The government did not feel it necessary to consult with business even when its decisions would affect the workings and strategies that such companies adopted. S. Venkataramanan, a senior government official, similarly noted in 1997: "GOI [government of India] should engage the trade and business community in an intensive dialogue in order to arrive at agreed methods for handling the impending confrontations with WTO. On and off consultations will not do. We should not face WTO without a proper defense strategy. Such a strategy cannot be devised in isolation at New Delhi or Geneva. It has to involve those who are affected."[21] This situation continued until the late 1990s, when the government finally began to consult with business associations in a more proactive way.

Then, in 1999 the government's delegation to the WTO's ministerial meeting in Seattle included two members from India's main business associations. By the new century, the functioning of India's trade ministry—the Ministry of Commerce—had been radically transformed, with the inclusion of business representation in a formal, regular, and direct way since 1998–99 (Sinha 2007, 2016; Mathur 2014). The Ministry of Commerce has consulted heavily with business in preparation for the yearly meetings at the WTO since 1998–99. For example, recently (March 2016), the Ministry of Commerce and Industry revived a board of trade. The reconstituted BOT consists of nineteen members from industry and academia (nonofficial members), thirty-one heads of trade and industry associations (ex officio members), and twenty top officials, including thirteen secretaries to the government of India plus the deputy governor, RBI; chairman, Railway Board, chairman, National Highways Authority of India, chairman and managing director, ECGC; managing director, EXIM Bank; chairman and managing director, SBI; and managing director, Container Corporation of India (official members). Thus, business associations participate in joint or porous institutions in making and shaping policy, especially in the field of trade policy. In addition to the role of collective organizations such as the CII and FICCI, specific and well-reputed businesspersons, especially from new sectors such as pharmaceutical, biotech, and software, have also begun to play a more major role in key national institutions. We turn to the analysis of their role in the next section.

Institutional Incorporation of Business as Advisers: Prime Minister's Council on Trade and Industry

In the late 1990s, prominent business actors began to advise the PM directly. The Prime Minister's Council on Trade and Industry was created on August 28, 1998.[22] It was constituted by the PM as its chairman, with economic ministers and prominent businessmen. Vajpayee, the PM at that time, who set up the body, created eight subject groups to "recommend implementable action points" on such themes as good governance in the private sector, public sector disinvestment, and power-sector reforms. N. K. Singh, secretary to the PMO at that time, observed, "The council was created to develop a lasting partnership and trust with the industry. That, to me, is the more important than any set of recommendations" (Saran 2012). G. P. Goenka, president of FICCI and a member of the advisory body, noted: "Consultations with the industry—which is the real practitioner of economic reforms—helps government fine-tune its policy" (Saran 2012). Table 3.9 outlines the list of businessmen represented in the last four such councils. These councils were the most active during Vajpayee's time. From 1998 to 2013 the council seems to have debated and generated policy recommendations, but we don't have evidence about whether those recommendations have been implemented. There is no record of it having met after Modi's election to power in 2014.

In 2013 there was a revolt of sorts, as twenty business leaders did not attend the meeting of the council. Bharti Group chairman Sunil Bharti Mittal told the Council in 2013, "The recent Rs 650-crore penalty levied on Bharti Airtel by the telecom department seemed unfair and would lead to more litigation between corporates and the government" (Dhoot 2013). Can this be an example of the structural exit-power of business? In terms of effects, the broader representation of the council and its role as an advisory body would suggest that it might play a positive role in shaping India's economic policies.

Independent Regulatory Agencies and Business Incorporation

The second-generation economic reforms (starting in the late 1990s) were marked by a flurry of regulations, the formalization of independent regulatory agencies, and a formal, public consultation with Indian business.[23] The argument in this chapter concurs with Mathur, who observes: "This transformed role for the state in India has created new policy spaces where the government and business jointly develop public policy" (2014, 153–54). However, the notion of "joint partners" ignores the renewal of the role of the state in performing new developmental functions. And it ignores the crony capitalist elements of the "joint" relationship (see next section). This is clear especially in diverse sectors where new rulemaking and state-making—new state agencies—*coevolved* with business participation in the working of these agencies. For example, in 2004, the government of India appointed a three-member commission—the Investment Commission—to enhance and facilitate investment in India. Its members were Ratan Tata, Deepak Parikh, and Ashok Ganguly, all prominent industrialists, and the commission enjoyed significant autonomy and status (Mathur 2014).

Table 3.9 **PM's council on trade and industry, 1998, 2010, 2011, and 2013**

	PM's Council in 1998	*PM's Council in 2010*	*PM's Council in 2011*	*PM's Council in 2013*
	Three meetings under Vajpayee (August 28, 1998; December 11, 1999; April 29, 2000)	**26 May 2010 (PM was Manmohan Singh)**	**31 March 2011 (PM was Manmohan Singh)**	**29 July 2013 (PM was Manmohan Singh)**
1.	Ratan Tata (Tata Sons)	Dr. V. Krishnamurthy (civil servant)	Narayana Murthy (Infosys)	Rahul Bajaj (Bajaj Auto)
2	Mukesh Ambani (Reliance Industries Limited)	Ratan Tata (Tata Sons)	Rahul Bajaj (Bajaj Auto)	Dr. Ashok Ganguly (Hindustan Unilever)
3	R. P. Goenka (RPG Group)	Rahul Bajaj (Bajaj Auto)	Mukesh Ambani (Reliance Industries Ltd.)	Mukesh Ambani (Reliance Industries Ltd.)
4.	P. K. Mittal (Ispat Industries Ltd.)	Dr. Ashok Ganguly (Hindustan Unilever)	Ratan Tata (Tata Sons)	Narayana Murthy (Infosys)
5.	Kumar Mangalam Birla (Aditya Birla Group)	Keshub Mahindra (Mahindra Group)	Dr. Ashok Ganguly (Hindustan Unilever)	Azim Premji (Wipro Ltd.)
6.	Suresh Krishna (TVS Group)	Narayana Murthy (Infosys)	Sunil B. Mittal, (Bharti Enterprises)	Swati Piramal (Piramal Enterprises Ltd.)
7.	Narayana Murthy (Infosys)	Mukesh Ambani (Reliance Industries Ltd.)	Swati Pirmal, (Piramal Enterprises Ltd.)	Deepak Parekh (HDFC)
8.	Nusli Wadia (Wadia)	R. P. Goenka (RPG Group)	Deepak Parekh (HDFC)	Jamshyd N. Godrej (Godrej and Boyce)
9.	A. C. Muthiah (SPIC and SVCE)	Azim Premji (Wipro Ltd.)	Jamshyd N. Godrej (Godrej and Boyce)	Ms. Chanda Kochhar (ICICI Bank)

(Continued)

Table 3.9 **Continued**

	PM's Council in 1998	PM's Council in 2010	PM's Council in 2011	PM's Council in 2013
10	Dr. Parvinder Singh (Ranbaxy)	Sunil Mittal (Bharti Enterprises)	M.S. Banga (Hindustan Unilever)	Venu Srinivasan (Sundaram-Clayton Ltd.)
11		Kumaramangalam Birla (Aditya Birla Group)	Chanda Kochar (ICICI Bank)	Sunil Kant Munjal (Hero Enterprises)
12		Swati Piramal (Piramal Enterprises Ltd.)	Sunil Kant Munjal (Hero Enterprises)	S. Gopala-krishnan (Infosys)
13		Deepak Parekh (HDFC)	Anu Aga (Thermax Ltd.)	Dr. Rana Kapoor (Yes Bank)
14		Jamshyd Godrej (Godrej and Boyce)		Sunil B. Mittal (Bharti Enterprises)
15		Kiran Mazumdar-Shaw (Biocon Ltd.)		Naina Lal Kidwai (HSBC)
16		M. S. Banga (Hindustan Unilever)		
17		Dr. K. Anji Reddy (Dr. Reddy's Laboratories)		
18		Chanda Kochhar (ICICI Bank)		
19		Venu Srinivasan (Sundaram-Clayton Ltd.)		
20		Sunil Kant Munjal (Hero Enterprises)		
21		Anu Aga (Thermax Ltd.)		

Source: Collated from Press Information Bureau, Government of India, PMO, July 29, 2013, http://pib.nic.in/newsite/PrintRelease.aspx?relid=97468.

One can see a "developmental role"—creation of new ordered markets, for example—clearly in many of these agencies. For example, SEBI saw its role to be both regulatory and developmental in 1992 (SEBI, Annual Report, 1992–93, 3):

> Further to the powers of SEBI under the SEBI Act, certain critical sections of the Securities Contracts (Regulation) Act, 1956, can now be administered also by SEBI besides the Central Government. These sections empower SEBI to conduct enquiries into the working of the Stock Exchanges, suo motu amend the rules and byelaws of the Stock Exchanges, approve the rules and byelaws of the Stock Exchanges and license dealers in securities outside the areas of jurisdiction of the Stock Exchanges.
>
> *The regulatory and developmental functions of a regulatory body are strongly interlinked.* The objective of the regulations, particularly in a growing market, is not only to regulate but also to guide its development and that of its participants. The notification of the rules and regulations governing some of the intermediaries, thereby bringing these intermediaries under a regulatory purview for the first time, and the efficient implementation and continuous enforcement of these regulations, are among the important investor protection and developmental measures taken by SEBI during the year under review, which underpin its twin role of regulation and market development envisaged under the Act. (Emphasis added)

Telecom regulation reveals the incorporation of business interests at the creation period of reregulation and new policies. Bureaucrats still steer the process of reregulation, and businessmen have not captured the state, but the role of business actors is frontal, direct, and public (Jacob 2010). Tables 3.10 and 3.11 outline the scope of business representation in what are claimed to be "independent" agencies in regulating telecom, stock and securities markets, electricity, petroleum, and insurance.

A brief review of the creation of some of these agencies reveals how the process of economic liberalization demanded both the creation of new regulations, agencies as well as greater business input for information sharing, and coparticipation. The SEBI was formed in 1988. At that time it had no teeth or power. Around 1992 the powers and authority of the agency were enhanced. It was felt that the economic reforms of 1991 called for capital market reforms with "emphasis on investor service and protection, disclosure and transparency."[24] Even then, the SEBI was essentially a government agency, with officials from the Ministry of Finance and other civil servants. By 1998, a businessperson was included on the executive board. Prominent businesspersons were selected for the position: in 1998, K. M. Birla, chairman of Aditya Birla group, was appointed by the central government, and over the years members from Infosys and Sundaram-Clayton have filled that role. Simultaneously, the SEBI has undertaken numerous oversight actions of specific companies, brokers, and markets, revealing a clear independence and autonomy from business interests. In the case of SEBI, business representation may have helped the organization be a better regulator of the stock markets and India's financial sector.

In telecom, the regulator was created to curtail the monopoly power of the Department of Telecommunication in the Ministry of Communications as well as to allow the possibility of fair competition among private indigenous and foreign capital. In doing so, struggles around telecom regulation reveal the paradoxical and Janus-faced character of the Indian state clearly. India's telecom regulator—TRAI—was set up in 1997 after much struggle (Mukherji 2004), "to promote non-discriminatory completion, enabling private sector participation and promoting universal access" (Doassani 2002, 74). It works with and has some conflict with the Department of Telecommunication (DOT) that sets policy, and allocates licenses. Initially the DOT sought to exert control over policy, and TRAI struggled to establish its authority and space. Business interests traditionally lobbied the bureaucracy—the DOT—until around 2000, when TRAI became powerful and began to be subject to public and more transparent lobbying. Lobbying in the DOT is more invisible and secret. It has contributed to many charges of private influence and corruption, as in the latest 2G scam. However, TRAI has also introduced competitive and transparent practices into the telecom sector precisely on account of its public route of lobbying. Overall, both the PM's Council on Trade and Industry and regulatory agencies have given access to key business actors, as well as the ability to create and shape policy and institutions. These two institutional spaces seem to confirm the "joint partner" model. Their effects on public policy and in reining in crony capitalism seem to be positive, although it is possible that some rent-seeking goes on in the shadow of the legitimate state-business interactions.

The Creation of New Policy Spaces for the Private Sector: Public-Private Partnerships

The structural power of business may have increased in the post-1991 era because of an institutional innovation that transformed the "joint venture" idea in the 1980s (esp. in Gujarat; see Sinha 2005a) into what has come to be called PPP, or public-private partnership. Kuldeep Mathur also notes the significance of the PPP in creating "new policy spaces for business" (Mathur 2014). He argues that the emphasis on PPP changed the pattern of governance and perceptions regarding the roles and responsibilities of different development actors in the context of globalization and liberalization. This institutional innovation was pushed

Table 3.10 **Independent agencies and business incorporation**

	Business presence in organization structure	Business consultation mechanism	Role of business	Created in	Crony capitalist episode
Telecom Regulatory Authority of India (TRAI)	No	Yes, transparent, public	Feedback; Input Information; Policy formulation	1997	2008–10 (2G spectrum scam)
Securities and Exchange Board of India (SEBI)	Business representation started only after 1998 and was inconsistent	Not clear	Code of conduct for conflict of interest exists	Established in 1988 and modified in 1992 by a law	1992 (Harshad Mehta), 2001 (Ketan Parikh)
Insurance Regulatory and Development Authority (IRDA)	Yes; usually LIC and one member from private insurance industry	Yes, but state-owned insurance providers dominate	Policy input[a]	2000	

Central Electricity Regulatory Commission (CERC)	Yes, though the CERC Board consists mostly of experts A separate Central Advisory Committee of 31 members (commerce, industry, transport, agri, labor, NGOs, and academic and research bodies in the electricity sector)	Advisory	Strong but differs across states	1998
Petroleum and Natural gas Regulatory Board (PNGRB)	Yes (one member)	Not sure		2007

Source: Author calculations from Annual Reports of each agency and CAG reports.

[a] The first annual report states: "The Authority [IRDA] has always believed in openness and transparency; it has followed the practice of prior consultation with various interests. It has issued draft regulations and guidelines, generated discussions on the various issues and finalized its regulations in an open manner. This has resulted in an acceptance of the regulations by various constituents of the market. Many of the regulations have also been looked into by international bodies and found to match up to world standards. The Indian insurance market is thus run and regulated on globally acceptable standards" (Annual Report, IDRA, 2000–2001, pp, 2).

Table 3.11 **Specific business presence in regulatory agencies**

	Prominent businessmen
SEBI	K. M Birla, Birla group, 1998–2001
	Venu Srinivasam, Sundaram Clayton, 2005–8
	Mohandas Pai, Infosys, 2010–13
CERC	CEO, Reliance Infrastructure
	MD, Tata Power Company
	President, CII
	President, FICCI
	Adani
TRAI	Not available

Source: Author's calculations.

and formalized by the Ministry of Finance starting in the middle to late 1990s. "The Rakesh Mohan Committee on Infrastructure [Ministry of Finance 1996] noted that the principal problem in India was building the right framework for private participation in infrastructure (Sinha 2010b)." This was the first articulation of the idea of PPPs. As Vinayak Chatterjee notes, there are three different types of PPPs, and all three of them have been used in infrastructure sectors intensively: full private provision, or FPP, where the government facilitates the project but allows full ownership of assets to private players; PPP, where the investment is funded and operated through a partnership with the government and one or more private players; and PFI, or private finance initiative, where the private sector funds public sector units. Vinayak Chatterkee notes: "This differs from privatization since the responsibility of providing essential services to the public is not transferred to the private sector; nor is the asset-ownership transferred. As, for example, in solid waste management, electricity distribution franchising and so on" (Chatterjee 2012).

While the idea of PPP is not new, a new branding of it *as* PPP was made possible by the economic reforms of 1991. It was first started in electricity provision; the government announced private generation of electricity in 1991. The government at that time set up independent power producers, or IPPs. By 1995 the idea began to be popular for the development of roads, and varied models of "build and own" came to dominate the construction of highways under the amended National Highways Act of 1995. In telephone provisions, a competitive bidding process led to provision of licenses in four metro cities and eighteen state circles (Chatterjee 2012). The Expert Group on Commercialization of Infrastructure, or the Rakesh Mohan Committee, in its report concretized and formalized the idea. In Gujarat the PPP framework was first tried in the port sector and was quite successful (Sinha 2010b). On January 20, 1997, an Infrastructure Development Finance company was incorporated in Chennai, encouraged by the then-finance minister, P. Chidamabaran. While PPP amounted to a new philosophy of the state's role in the economy, it also created new opportunities for corruption and crony capitalism. My argument in this chapter is that the new developmental role of the state was a necessary factor in creating spaces for legitimate, growth-enhancing, but also crony capitalist, relationships. Finance is the crucial linchpin of the two sides of the state; I analyze that next.

Finance and New Rent-Seeking Opportunities

The Kingfisher case is an example of collective failure of the system. The banks should have declared it a[n] NPA [nonperforming loan] much earlier. Why did the RBI even clear the restructuring of Kingfisher? Even now, the way banks are going after Mallya, they will not be able to recover any money. A criminal case or money laundering investigation will only focus on prosecution, not on recovery of money. Do you think Mallya will not contest the case? So in all this, how will banks recover their money? Instead, banks should look at one-time settlement of dues," says K C Chakravarty, former deputy governor of the Reserve Bank of India. (Narayan, Johnson, and Vikraman 2016)

Vijay Mallya captured the headlines in early 2016 on account of his massive "non-performing loans" (NPAs) and his flamboyant lifestyle. I argue that his NPAs were the direct result of his taking advantage of varied benefits provided by the new developmental state. Essentially, Vijay Mallya grew in the shadow of the new developmental state. India's banks are the face of the new developmental state and the mutual imbrication of business and developmental goals and functionaries. Vijay Mallya also embodies a classic crony capitalist relationship, which was achieved by his movement inside banking institutions and legislative bodies.

As Indian growth unfolded in the 1990s, policymakers realized a hard constraint generated by the state of India's infrastructure. This led to the Rakesh Mohan Committee report (1996), which spoke of India's needs in infrastructure. By the early 2000s, the government initiated a "paradigm shift" by "creating an enabling policy and regulatory framework for attracting private capital in infrastructure projects. A comprehensive architecture was, therefore, brought into effect for promoting public-private partnerships in sectors such as electricity provision, highways, ports, airports, and railways" (Roy 2015). However, the thorny issue was financing; investors were wary of large projects and long-term gestation periods. Commercial banks, nationalized banks, and nonbanking institutions become the main source for funding given the absence of a bond market, foreign debt instruments, and insurance markets (Roy

2015). By mid-2002 many PPPs were unveiled. Roy notes: "According to the data published by the erstwhile Planning Commission, the total investment in infrastructure over the Eleventh Plan period (2007–12) aggregated US$480 billion, which constituted seven per cent of GDP as compared to five percent during the Tenth Plan (2002–7). In particular, private investment increased from about 22 percent of the total investment in infrastructure during 2002–7 to about 37 percent during 2007–12, which implied a three-fold increase in absolute terms" (Roy 2015). While the government created a dedicated financial instrument to address some of the perceived needs (India Infrastructure Finance Company), many private sector projects also sought loans from the public sector and commercial banks. The late 1990s and middle of the next decade saw a flurry of such activity. Many of these loans have now come undone and have become "nonperforming." The intermingling of a legitimate need to enhance India's infrastructure created a powerful renewal of the state's guidance to provide finance in key sectors. This guidance, then, led to the reinvolvement of banking finance in the development field, which then created the conditions for both legitimate and not-so-legitimate dealings with the private sector. With this in mind, we can analyze the story of Vijay Mallya in greater depth.

We now know that Vijay Mallya owes Rs. 6,955 crores to many banks (see table 3.12). "United Bank of India was the first lender to declare Kingfisher and Mallya a 'willful defaulter' in May 2014. The same year, State Bank of India (SBI) issued a notice to tag Kingfisher Airlines, Mallya and United Breweries Holdings as 'willful defaulters.' The SBI notice of August 19, 2014 alleged diversion of funds by Kingfisher Airlines to UB Group of companies and other firms. Mallya has challenged the decision of United Bank and the SBI in various courts. In February 2016, Punjab National Bank, another lender, declared Mallya and Kingfisher a willful defaulter" (Khushboo Narayan, Johnson, and Vikraman 2016). By then, it was too late.

The corrupt nexus between Vijay Mallya may have begun 2002, when Mallya became a Rajya Sabha member. Vijay Mallya became the chairman of United Breweries Group in 1983 after his father's death. In 1988 United Breweries acquired Paints and Engineering, followed by the takeover of Mangalore Chemicals and Fertilizers in 1990. In 1994 he bought a media company that was renamed Vijay TV, now part of the star alliance. UB, the beer company, became extremely successful, but along the way Vijay Mallya began buying stakes in a football company and RIFA publications. In 2002 he was elected to the Rajya Sabha as an independent candidate but with joint support of the Congress Party and the Janata Dal.[25] What is interesting is that soon after becoming a member of the Rajya Sabha, Mallya become a member of the Committee on Science and Technology and Environment and Forests of the Rajya Sabha. In 2003 he was a member of the Committee on Defense and joined the Janata Party as the national working

Table 3.12 **Kingfisher's loans by banks**

Bank	Rs. Crore
State Bank of India	1874.66
IDBI Bank	885.64
PNB	815.08
Bank of India	666.13
Bank of Baroda	639.89
United Bank of India	415.02
Central Bank of India	448.53
UCO bank	351.2
Corporation Bank	312.98
State Bank of Mysore	169.06
Indian Overseas Bank	157.02
Federal Bank	102.3
Punjab and Sind Bank	62.14
Axis Bank	56.32
Consortium Total	6,955.97

Source: Gokhale (2017, 4).

president. In 2004 he was a member of the Committee on Industry, revealing a direct conflict of interest. In 2005 he moved into the airlines business, and in 2010, while in the Rajya Sabha, he served on the consultative committee for the Ministry of Civil Aviation. Thus, a business magnate in the airlines business was responsible for making and shaping policy for airlines, revealing a direct conflict of interest. In 2012 Malaya served on the Committee on Chemicals and Fertilizers despite being a chairman of Mangalore and Chemicals and Fertilizers; for the first time Justice Khare noted a conflict of interest (Saleem n.d.). By 2010–12 problems had begun to appear in his airline business, and five independent directors resigned from the company in 2011–12 ("Mallya Minister Nexus" 2011).

By then Vijay Mallya's political networks were wide and deep. It is believed that United Progressive Alliance (UPA) government's civil aviation minister, Vylar Ravi, had requested the finance minister Pranab Mukherjee to "ask banks to restructure the loans of Kingfisher Airlines" after Vijay Mallya spoke to Vylar Ravi ("Mallya Minister Nexus" 2011). Praful Patel, the civil airlines minister in the UPA government, regularly issued instructions to Indian Airlines, India's domestic carrier, to withdraw flights from specific sectors or change timings of existing flights so as to benefit Kingfisher Airlines ("Mallya Minister Nexus" 2011). In 2010, the Parliamentary Standing Committee on Public Undertakings noted that Air India had been put at a disadvantage against private competitors, "including its declining route network" ("Mallya Minister Nexus" 2011). Following this, Air India and Indian Airlines merged, but the merger benefited two private players—Kingfisher and Jet Airways. The parliamentary standing committee set up to examine the merger said: "Reasons for going ahead with huge purchases by the civil aviation ministry despite Air India and Indian Airlines not having the capacity to support it, remain unknown to the Committee. It, therefore, recommends that this aspect needs to be further probed to fix the responsibility for taking such an ambitious decision that has become a big financial liability" ("Mallya Minister Nexus" 2011). Praful Patel's disclosed assets grew from 79 crores in April 2009 to 122 crores in April 2011 ("Mallya Minister Nexus" 2011). Clearly, Vijay Mallya used his political networks to benefit his airline business and seek many loans.

As an example of the blurred boundaries, Kingfisher Airlines used retired bureaucrats on its board of directors. India has begun to see some revolving door phenomena more generally, but the empirical mapping of that revolving door is a laborious and painstaking task that is not attempted in this chapter. Some names jump out. G. N. Bajpai was an independent director on the board of Kingfisher from September 2011 to January 9, 2012, when he resigned. Bajpai was a former chairman of LIC and also chairman of the National Stock Exchange. Kingfisher also employed ex-finance secretary Piyush Mankad on its board of directors. This case study highlights the mutual imbrication of banking finance, political connections, and legislative representation. It would not have been possible without the movement of business actors across boundaries of public institutions and the Janus-faced state interested in growth as well as rent-seeking.

Conclusion

We need an integrated account of the evolving business-politics relationship that goes beyond bifurcated views of a crony capitalist or a developmental state. The relationship can no longer be understood as either developmental or crony capitalist; it is both. The developmental state has re-formed itself and is interested in both rapid growth and welfare. In the shadow of the legitimate activities of a new developmental state lie institutional opportunities for corrupt and illegal activities. In fact, the new functions of a renewed developmental state have created *more* opportunities and spaces for corrupt activities.

Overall, the boundaries between business and state action have become fuzzy and porous. Business has been incorporated into many public institutions legally, directly, and formally. We need to understand these blurred boundaries in order to assess the changing nature of Indian democracy, state, and capitalism. As the private sector began to dominate the Indian economy, business moved into public, regulatory institutions, in turn creating new spaces, where business became more invisible and yet powerful. This chapter showed how key brokers and actors mediate the blurred boundaries. The multiple layers of the democratic state create more access and choice points, allowing business actors to move across fuzzier boundaries and giving political actors the motivation and wherewithal to become entrepreneurs. Business associations and key brokers are also crucial to the bridging of the gap between the private and the public sectors of India's new political economy. This chapter provided a fine-grained picture not only of how private power and public institutions interact but of how key agents and brokers move back and forth.

The emergence of a new business-state compact also has serious consequences for public interest, competition, and the overall structure of the economy. Business actors and associations have evolved new instrumental strategies for dealing with reregulation and an increase in public interest in development and welfare. In some policy and industrial sectors, we see the clear consolidation of lopsided growth, made worse by the role of finance in creating new rent-seekers and business beneficiaries, who access and infiltrate political agencies and institutions both for personal and for business interests. In other policy arenas, where broader business representation has emerged, some positive effects of the evolving business-state relationship are apparent. We are at a turning point in terms of the instrumental and institutional role of business within state institutions across diverse policy arenas. Both its contours and its effects need to be understood, carefully, attending to the double-edged nature of state and private activities.

References

Primary and Government Documents

Central Electricity Regulatory Commission. Annual report, various years.
IRDA (Insurance Regulatory and Development Authority). Annual report, various years.
Ministry of Finance. 1996. *The India Infrastructure Report: Policy Imperatives for Growth and Welfare*, Expert Group on the Commercialization of Infrastructure Projects, Rakesh Mohan Committee, vols. 1–3, published on Behalf of the Ministry of Finance, by NCAER, New Delhi, 1996.
SEBI (Securities and Exchange Board of India). Annual report, various years.
Second Report of the Committee to Inquire into Misconduct of Members of Lok Sabha. 2008. March. (Deo Committee report.)
TRAI (Telecom Regulatory Authority of India). Annual report, various years.

Secondary References

Ahulwalia, Isher. 1985. *Industrial Growth in India: Stagnation since the Mid-sixties*. New Delhi: Oxford University Press.

Amsden, Alice H. 1989. *Asia's Next Giant: South Korea and Late Industrialization*. New York: Oxford University Press.

Anand, Utkarsh. 2014. "All Coal Black Licenses since 93 Illegal: Supreme Court." *Indian Express*, August 26.

Bandyopadhyay, Tamal. 2015. *Sahara: The Untold Story*. Mumbai: Jaico Publishing House.

Bhagwati, Jagdish. 1993. *India in Transition: Freeing the Economy*. Oxford: Clarendon Press.

Bhargava, Jitendra. 2013. *The Descent of Air India: An Insider's View of How a Once Globally Cherished Brand Was Grounded by Those Entrusted with the Task of Making It Soar*. Self-published.

Block, Fred. 1980. "Beyond Relative Autonomy: State Managers as Historical Subjects." *Socialist Register* 17: 227–41.

———. 1987. *Revising State Theory: Essays on Politics and Postindustrialism*. Philadelphia: Temple University Press.

———. 2008. "Swimming against the Current: The Rise of a Hidden Developmental State in the United States." *Politics and Society* 36 (2): 169–206.

Chandra, Kanchan. 2015. "The New Indian State: The Relocation of Patronage in the Post-liberalization Economy." *Economic and Political Weekly* 50 (41): 46–58.

Chatterjee, Elizabeth. 2017. "Reinventing State Capitalism in India: A View from the Energy Sector." *Contemporary South Asia* 25 (1): 85–100.

Chatterjee, Vinayak. 2012. "PPP in India: The Story So Far." *Business Standard*, May 14. http://www.business-standard.com/article/opinion/vinayak-chatterjee-ppp-in-india-the-story-so-far-112051400022_1.html.

Chibber, Vivek. 2003. *Locked in Place: State-Building and Late Industrialization in India*. Princeton, NJ: Princeton University Press.

Culpepper, Pepper. 2015. "Structural Power and Political-Science in the Post-crisis Era." *Business and Politics* 17 (3): 391–410.

Dhoot, Vikas. 2013. "India Inc. Runs Out of Patience as UPA Govt. Hits Policy Roadblock." *Economic Times*, August 21. http://articles.economictimes.indiatimes.com/2013-08-21/news/41433323_1_rahul-bajaj-board-meeting-upa-government.

Dossani, Rafiq, ed. 2002. *Telecommunications Reform in India*. Westport, CT: Quorum Books.

Dubey, Abhishek. 2011. *The IPL Story: Cricket, Glamour and Big Money*. New Delhi: Longman.

Evans, Peter. 1995. *Embedded Autonomy: States and Industrial Transformation*. Princeton, NJ: Princeton University Press.

Fairfield, Tasha. 2015. *Private Wealth and Public Revenue in Latin America: Business Power and Tax Politics*. New York: Cambridge University Press.

Ghosh, Abantika. 2015. "MP Shyama Charan Gupta Who Said Nothing Wrong with Beedis Flaunts His Beedi Empire." *Indian Express*, April 2. http://indianexpress.com/article/india/india-others/mp-shyama-charan-gupta-who-said-nothing-wrong-with-beedis-flaunts-his-beedi-empire/.

Gokhale, Nihar. 2017. "Banks May Lose 4300 Crore on Loans to Kingfisher Airlines." *Economic and Political Weekly* 52 (23) (June 10). http://www.epw.in/journal/2017/23/web-exclusives/banks-may-lose-%E2%82%B94300-crore-loans-kingfisher-airlines.html.

Gupta, Akhil. 1995. "Blurred Boundaries: The Discourse of Corruption, the Culture of Politics, and the Imagined State." *American Ethnologist* 22 (2): 375–402.

———. 2012. *Red Tape: Bureaucracy, Structural Violence and Poverty in India*. Durham, NC: Duke University Press.

Herring, Ronald. 1999. "Embedded Particularism: India's Failed Developmental State." In *The Developmental State*, ed. Meredith Woo-Cumings, 306–34. Ithaca, NY: Cornell University Press.

Jenkins, Rob, and James Manor. 2017. *Politics and the Right to Work: India's National Rural Employment Guarantee Act*. New York: Oxford University Press.

Jacob, Anil. 2010. "Steering the State: The Politics of Institutional Change in the Pharmaceutical and Telecom Sectors in Post-reform India," Ph.D. dissertation, submitted to Rutgers University.

Johnson, Chalmers. 1982. *MITI and the Japanese Miracle: The Growth of Industrial Policy, 1925–1975*. Stanford, CA: Stanford University Press.

———. 1999. "The Developmental State: The Odyssey of a Concept." In *The Developmental State*, ed. Meredith Woo-Cumings, 32–60. Ithaca, NY: Cornell University Press.

Kochanek, Stanley. 1995–96. "The Transformation of Interest Politics in India." *Pacific Affairs* 68 (4): 529–51.

Kohli, Atul. 2006a. "Politics of Economic Growth in India, 1980–2005, Part I: The 1980s." *Economic and Political Weekly* 41 (13): 1251–59.

———. 2006b. "Politics of Economic Growth in India, 1980–2005, Part II: The 1990s and Beyond." *Economic and Political Weekly* 41 (14): 1361–70.

Levien, Michael. 2013. "Regimes of Dispossession: From Steel Towns to Special Economic Zones." *Development and Change* 44 (2): 381–407.

Lindblom, Charles E. 1977. *Politics and Markets*. New York: Basic Books.

Malik, Aman. 2014. "The Business Interests of Nitin Gadkari." *LiveMint*, May 12. http://www.livemint.com/Politics/XiA8agO3UPCdodEcQ00RoI/The-business-interests-of-Nitin-Gadkari.html.

"Mallya Minister Nexus: Scams in the Sky, Misery on India." 2011. *IBTL*, November 12. http://www.ibtl.in/news/exclusive/1560/mallya-minister-nexus:-scams-in-the-sky--misery-on-india/.

Manion. Melanie. 1996. "Corruption by Design: Bribery in Chinese Enterprise Licensing." *Journal of Law, Economics and Organization*, 12 (1): 167–95.

———. 2004. *Corruption by Design: Building Clean Government in Mainland China and Hong Kong*. Cambridge, MA: Harvard University Press.

Manoj, C. G. 2010. "Rajeev, Both Independent and BJP." *Indian Express*, December 11. http://archive.indianexpress.com/news/rajeev-both-independent-and-bjp/723134/.

Mathur, Kuldeep. 2014. "Business, Policy Spaces, and Governance in India." In *Linking Global Trade and Human Rights*, ed. Daniel Drache and Lesley A. Jacobs, 153–73. Cambridge: Cambridge University Press.

Mazumdar, Surajit. 2008. "Crony Capitalism and Contemporary India-II." ISID Working Paper, 2008/4, Institute for Studies in Industrial Development, March.

Mukherji, Rahul. 2004. "Managing Competition: Politics and the Building of Independent Regulatory Institutions." *India Review* 3 (4): 278–305.

Narayan, Khushboo, T. A. Johnson, and Shaji Vikraman. 2016. "From Bang to Bust: The Kingfisher Story." *Indian Express*, March 14. http://indianexpress.com/article/india/india-news-india/sunday-story-once-upon-a-time-there-was-a-king-vijay-mallya/.

National Social Watch. 2011. *Citizen's Report on Governance and Development, 2010*. New Delhi: Sage Publications.

Nayar, Baldev Raj. 2009. *The Myth of the Shrinking State: Globalization and the State in India*. New Delhi: Oxford University Press.

Ninan, T. N. 2015. "The Murky Links of Politics, Media and Business." Excerpts from Ninan's *The Turn of the Tortoise. Times of India*, October 11. http://timesofindia.indiatimes.com/home/sunday-times/deep-focus/The-murky-links-of-politics-media-business/articleshow/49304986.cms.

Ó'Riain, Sean, 2004. *The Politics of High-Tech Growth: Developmental Network States in the Global Economy*. Cambridge: Cambridge University Press.

———. 2010. "Addicted to Growth: State, Market and the Difficult Politics of Development in Ireland." In *The Nation-State in Transformation: Economic Globalization, Institutional Mediation and Political Values*, ed. M. Bøss, 163–90 Aarhus: Aarhus University Press.

Parakh, P. C. 2014. *Crusader or Conspirator: Coalgate and Other Truths*. New Delhi: Manas Publications.

Pedersen, Jørgen Dige 2000. "Explaining Economic Liberalization in India: State and Society Perspectives." *World Development* 28 (2): 265–82.

———. 2008. *Globalization, Development and the State: The Performance of India and Brazil since 1990*. Hampshire: Palgrave Macmillan.

PTI (Press Trust of India). 2014. "Government Plans Industrial Corridors, Smart Cities to Boost Manufacturing." *Economic Times*, December 30. http://articles.economictimes.indiatimes.com/2014-12-30/news/57528666_1_delhi-mumbai-industrial-corridor-smart-cities-dmic.

Rahman, Shaffi. 2009. "Business of the Day." *India Today*, November 12. http://indiatoday. intoday.in/story/Business+of+the+day/1/70610.html.

Rajshekhar, M. 2016a. "How Do So Many Industrialists Get into Rajya Sabha." Scroll.in, March 21. http://scroll.in/article/805332/how-do-so-many-industrialists-get-into-the-rajya-sabha.

———. 2016b. "Why India Has So Many Businessmen in Parliament." *Quartz India*, March 23. http://qz.com/645737/why-india-has-so-many-businessmen-in-parliament/.

Roy, Anna. 2015. "Innovative Financing." *World Bank Blog*, July 9. http://blogs.worldbank.org/ ppps/innovative-financing-case-india-infrastructure-finance-company.

Rudolph, Lloyd I., and Susanne Hoeber Rudolph. 1987. *In Pursuit of Lakshmi: The Political Economy of the Indian State*. Chicago: University of Chicago Press.

Saleem, Shaikh. N.d. "Vijay Mallya's Twin Hats Draw Criticism." *Business Standard*. http:// www.sify.com/finance/vijay-mallya-s-twin-hats-draw-criticism-imagegallery-others-mlvlQFejfehsi.html.

Saran, Rohit. 2012. "Tell Me How." *India Today*, July 24. http://indiatoday.intoday.in/story/tell-me-how/1/254464.html.

Schamis, Hector. 2002. *Re-forming the State: The Politics of Privatization in Latin America and Europe*. Ann Arbor: University of Michigan Press.

Sen, Kunal, ed. 2013. *State-Business Relations and Economic Development in Africa and India*. New York: Routledge.

Shaffer, Gregory, ed. 2014. *Transnational Legal Ordering and State Change*. Cambridge: Cambridge University Press.

Shaffer, Gregory, James Nedumpara, and Aseema Sinha. 2015. "State Transformation and the Rise of Lawyers: The WTO, India, and Transnational Legal Ordering." *Law and Society Review* 49 (3): 595–629.

Sinha, Aseema. 2005a. *The Regional Roots of Developmental Politics in India: A Divided Leviathan*. Bloomington: Indiana University Press.

———. 2005b. "Understanding the Rise and Transformation of Business Collective Action in India." *Business and Politics* 7 (2): 1–35.

———. 2007. "Global Linkages and Domestic Politics: Trade Reform and Institution Building in India in Comparative Perspective." *Comparative Political Studies* 40 (10): 1183–210.

———. 2010a. "Business and Politics." In *Oxford Companion to Politics in India*, ed. Niraja Gopal-Jayal and Pratap Bhanu Mehta, 459–76. New Delhi: Oxford University Press.

———. 2010b. "Understanding Economic Reform of Public Services in a High Growth State of India." In *Public Service Delivery in India: Understanding the Reform Process*, ed. Vikram Chand, 126–76. New Delhi: Oxford University Press.

———. 2011. "An Institutional Perspective on the Post-liberalization State in India." In *The State in India after Liberalization: Inter-disciplinary Perspectives*, ed. Akhil Gupta and K. Sivaramakrishnan, 49–68. New York: Routledge.

———. 2016a. *Globalizing India: How Global Rules and Markets Are Shaping India's Rise to Power*. Cambridge: Cambridge University Press.

———. 2016b. "Why Has 'Development' Become a Political Issue in Indian Politics?" *Brown Journal of World Affairs*, Vol. XXIII (1), (15 pages), Fall–Winter.

Snyder, Richard. 1999. "After Neoliberalism: The Politics of Re-regulation in Mexico." *World Politics* 51 (2): 173–204.

Strange, Susan. 1996. *The Retreat of the State: The Diffusion of Power in the Global Economy*. Cambridge: Cambridge University Press.

Sud, Nikita. 2009. "The Indian State in a Liberalizing Landscape." *Development and Change* 40 (4): 645–65.

Thakurta, Paranjoy, with Subit Ghosh and J. Chaudhuri. 2014. *Gas Wars: Crony Capitalism and the Ambanis*. New Delhi: Paranjoy Guha Thakurta.

Trubek, David, Helena Alviar Garcia, Diogo Coutinho, and Alvaro Santos, eds. 2013. *Law and the New Developmental State: The Brazilian Experience in Latin American Context*. New York: Cambridge University Press.

Vogel, David. 2012. *The Politics of Precaution: Regulating Health, Safety and Environmental Risks in Europe and the United States*. Princeton, NJ: Princeton University Press.

Vogel, Steven K. 1998. *Freer Markets, More Rules: Regulatory Reform in Advanced Industrial Countries.* Ithaca, NY: Cornell University Press.

Wade, Robert H. 2003. *Governing the Market: Economic Theory and the Role of Government in East Asian Industrialization.* Princeton, NJ: Princeton University Press.

Weiss, Linda. 2005. "The State-Augmenting Effects of Globalization." *New Political Economy* 10 (3): 345–53.

Winters, Jeffrey. A. 2011. *Oligarchy.* Cambridge: Cambridge University Press.

Wyatt, Andrew. 2017. "India's Entrepreneurial Politicians and their Political Capital." Unpublished paper.

Appendix

Acknowledgments

First of all, I acknowledge comments and feedback from the participants of the workshop on business and politics held May 7–9, 2016. At the Princeton workshop, Kanchan Chandra was the discussant on the paper on which this chapter is based, and her feedback was very useful. In addition, comments from Atul Kohli, Kanta Murali, and Christophe Jaffrelot were very useful for revising the paper. Comments from two reviewers are also gratefully acknowledged. I also presented this paper at the Keck Center for International and Startegic Studies at Claremont McKenna College; comments from its participants were valuable. Mark Schneider's suggestions were very useful. I thank Sara Kazemian, Lisa Piergalini, and Noopur Kore, graduate students from Claremont Graduate University, for helping me collect data for this chapter.

Table 3.A1 **Business Interests of Politicians and Their Families**

Politician Name	State	Number of different companies where the politician has equity stakes plus directorships	Number of companies where family members have equity stakes plus directorships	Sector
Ajay Maken	New Delhi	3	5	Cybersecurity
Ajit Singh and Jayant Choudhary	Uttar Pradesh	3	3	Agriculture
Ajoy Kumar	Jharkhand	7	0	Research, healthcare
Annu Tandon	Uttar Pradesh	8	44	Trading
Anurag Singh Thakur	Himachal Pradesh	8	11	Online systems, cricket
Avtar Singh Bhadana	Haryana	0	16	Real estate, communications, aviation
Chandan Mitra	West Bengal	9	6	Media, journalism
Dayanidhi Maran	Chennai	2	41	Media, radio, cable
Dinesh Trivedi	West Bengal	0	2	N/A
Dushyant Singh	Rajasthan	0	2	Finance
Gaddam Vivekanad	Andhra Pradesh	6	8	Energy, real estate, construction, media
Gopinath Munde	Maharashtra	0	61	Energy, distillery, sugar
H. D. Deve Gowda	Karnataka	3	7	Mining, technology, nursing homes

Harsimrat Kaur Badal	Punjab	3	44	Energy
Hema Malini	Uttar Pradesh	2	8	Entertainment
Jay Panda	Odisha	13	61	Media, finance, legal, aviation, real estate
Jaya Prada & Amar Singh		2	10	Entertainment, energy
Jayant Sinha	Jharkhand	6	69	Consulting, finance
Jyoti Mirdha Gehlaut	Rajasthan	15	171	Real estate, power, media, housing finance
Jyotiradhitya Scindia	Madhya Pradesh	10	10	Finance
Kalikesh Narayan Singh Deo	Odisha	6	9	Finance, real estate
Kamal Nath	Haryana	1	52	Technology, motels, finance, real estate, steel
Kapil Sibal	New Delhi	1	4	Farming, electronics, trading
Karti Chidambaram	Tamil Nadu	15	16	Plantation
Kuldeep Bishnoi	Haryana	7	18	Real estate, exports, trading
L. K. Sudhish	Tamil Nadu	5	13	Energy, entertainment, agriculture
L. K. Advani	Gujarat	0	2	Entertainment
M. M. Pallam Raju	Andhra Pradesh	3	4	Energy, foods

(Continued)

Table 3.A1 **Continued**

Politician Name	State	Number of different companies where the politician has equity stakes plus directorships	Number of companies where family members have equity stakes plus directorships	Sector
Mahabal Mishra	New Dehli	1	26	Trading, real estate, construction, exports
Mallikarjun Kharge	Karnataka	0	14	Finance, technology, real estate
Maneka Gandhi	Uttar Pradesh	1	8	Technology, steel, construction, real estate
Maulana Badruddin Ajmal	Assam	9	24	Retail, finance, distillery, biotech, education
Mausam Benzair & Abu Hasem Khan Chouhury	West Bengal	2	18	Real estate, medical
Meera Sanyal	Maharashtra	4	3	Retail, foods, real estate
Meira Kumar	Bihar	0	1	Agriculture
Mekapati Rajamohan Reddy	Andhra Pradesh	1	75	Construction, real estate, infrastructure
Milind Deora	Maharashtra	5	70	Real estate, investment
Mohammed Azhruddin	Rajasthan	1	1	Entertainment
Nandan Nilekani	Karnataka	3	2	Technology

Name	State			Sector
Nishikant Dubey	Jharkhand	2	1	Entertainment, investment
Nitin Gadkari	Maharashtra	11	61	Energy, sugar, agriculture, real estate, infrastructure
Pa Sangma	Meghalaya	0	1	Technology
Pinaki Misra	Odisha	8	4	Hotels
Pratibha Singh	Himachal Pradesh	2	19	Infrastructure
Preneet Kaur & Amarinder Singh	Punjab	1	6	Technology, real estate, engineering
Priya Dutt	Maharashtra	0	23	Entertainment
Raj Babbar	Uttar Pradesh	0	10	Entertainment, consulting, real estate
Rao Inderjit Singh	New Dehli	3	4	Resorts
Sachin Pilot	Rajasthan	1	17	Foods, energy
Salman Khurshid	Uttar Pradesh	1	5	Storage
Sandeep Dikshit	New Dehli	2	2	Farming, research
Sanjay Nirupam	Maharashtra	1	5	Real estate, education
Sanjeev Naik	Maharashtra	4	10	Technology, yachts
Shatrughan Sinha	Bihar	1	6	Food, entertainment
Shruti Choudhry	Haryana	7	15	Real estate, resorts
Smriti Irani	Uttar Pradesh	6	11	Entertainment, infrastructure

(Continued)

Table 3.A1 **Continued**

Politician Name	State	Number of different companies where the politician has equity stakes plus directorships	Number of companies where family members have equity stakes plus directorships	Sector
Sonia Gandhi	Uttar Pradesh	1	21	Hospitality, real estate, trading
Subodh Kant Sahay	Jharkhand	0	9	Trading, minerals
Supriya Sule	Maharashtra	12	22	Finance, travel
Sushil Kumar Shinde	Maharashtra	0	63	Entertainment
T. R. Baalu	Tamil Nadu	2	29	Real estate, entertainment, agriculture
Takam Sanjoy	Arunachal Pradesh	3	4	Entertainment, mining, minerals
Tathagata Satpathy	Odisha	3	4	Media, infrastructure
Veerappa Molly	Karnataka	2	7	Oil, finance
Vijay Inder Singla	Punjab	3	3	Energy
Vinod Khanna	Punjab	4	13	Infrastructure, hotels
Y. S. Vijayalakshmi Reddy	Andhra Pradesh	0	21	Real estate, energy, cement, infrastructure

Source: Data were collected from LiveMint database, initially collated by Aman Malik, a journalist. Aman Malik used the Ministry of Company Affairs to collate information about the political actors' business dealings. He used the same original source for all politicians. I transferred his data, analyzed it and further collated it to generate this table.

PART II

BUSINESS POWER ACROSS ISSUE AREAS

The Politics of India's Reformed Labor Model

RINA AGARWALA

We need a new theoretical framework to understand Indian labor in the twenty-first century. First, labor must be reunderstood to include formally protected and regulated workers (i.e., those usually equated in India to the "organized," industrial working class in India) *and* informal or precarious workers who operate outside the protections of traditional labor regulations (i.e., those who have long been omitted from standard definitions of the "working class" in India).[1] Second, labor must be re-envisioned to include manufacturing, as well as the growing sectors of construction and services. Finally, a twenty-first-century framework on labor must account not just for the market economy, but also for the *state, politics,* and *ideology.* Only then can we move past contemporary debates on labor, which are often stuck on superficial cries of "jobless growth." By intertwining the arguments of Antonio Gramsci and Karl Polanyi, this chapter offers a new labor framework that exposes exactly how the Indian state is using informal labor to organize consent for a powerful political project that undermines labor's twentieth-century gains, empowers large business, and simultaneously retains state legitimacy with a mass electorate in the contemporary era. In addition to exposing new hegemonic forces (of the Gramscian variety) from above, the reformulated labor framework enables us to expose budding countermovements (of the Polanyian variety) emerging from below. Each set of forces (i.e., hegemony and countermovements) must be evaluated in the context of the other.

For decades, academics, business associations, and policymakers trying to re-form India's economy have pointed to India's intricate web of labor laws as a chief hurdle to industrial productivity and competitiveness in exports (CII 2002; GOI 2006; Planning Commission 2001; World Bank 1995). Although Indian labor laws protect a range of workers' rights, costs, and securities, reformers have focused on one accusation—that is, labor laws create inflexible labor markets, which hinder capital's ability to hire and fire workers in accordance with market fluctuations. As a result, it is argued, capital incurs high direct transaction costs and inefficient production. The costs of job security were tolerated so long as employers could pass the costs on to consumers in the closed economy. But in the competitive environment of India's increasingly deregulated and globalized markets, increased costs undermine capital's ability to survive, let alone excel. Given this, both foreign capital and domestic capital lack the necessary incentives to invest in non-agricultural sectors and employ labor in large-scale, modern, registered enterprises, otherwise known as the "organized" sector. To facilitate economic growth through industrialization, therefore, pro-reform policymakers have repeatedly called for legislative changes in India's labor regulation framework. Underlying this is a call to remove state control in capital-labor relations, thereby increasing capital's power over production and accumulation. In return, reformers promise, Indian workers will enjoy increased employment in the ever-expanding, modern, non-agrarian sectors of industry and commerce.

To be sure, India's labor laws are not the lone culprits in hindering economic growth. Since the 1980s, labor reforms have stood in a long queue of other industrial, trade, and investment reforms that were deemed equally essential. Like labor reforms, these other reforms called for the removal of state interference in capital accumulation and a corresponding increase in business power and autonomy. Unlike labor reforms, however, many of the other reforms have been made. By 2002, most of the central government's controls over private investment had been dismantled, and the government's system of industrial licensing had been nearly abolished.[2] The list of industries reserved solely for the public sector had been drastically reduced. By 2014, the list of items reserved for production in the small-scale sector was finally deleted with the removal of the last remaining item—pickles. India's restrictive trade policy, which was said to protect inefficient domestic production, has also been progressively dismantled. As early as 1993, import licensing for capital goods and intermediates was abolished, a flexible exchange rate regime was launched, foreign institutional investors were allowed to purchase shares of listed Indian companies in the stock market, and procedures for foreign direct investment were greatly simplified. By 2001, import restrictions on consumer goods and agricultural products were removed, and since 1999, the privatization of public sector entities has progressed.[3] While these other reforms were controversial and sometimes stalled by opposition (particularly the removal of import restrictions on consumer goods), they were ultimately passed with support from business (especially big business) as a means to increased productivity.

In contrast, and despite heated debates on Indian labor laws, drastic labor reforms have *not* been made. The few reforms that have been made have been minor. Major reforms have been consistently blocked by Indian labor unions.

On September 2, 2015, all central trade unions organized a nationwide strike on and successfully stalled the government's proposed Labour Code on Industrial Relations, which offered several antiunion amendments to present legislation (Bhowmik 2015). In 2017, public sector bank employees launched a nationwide strike at the height of the tumultuous moment of demonetization to oppose labor reforms and outsourcing.

That Indian labor unions have attempted to stall labor reforms is not surprising. Since the early 1900s, Indian workers have organized into politically strong unions and fought hard to be formally recognized and to curtail capital's power through protective labor legislations. Although Indian labor suffered many losses at the hands of capital at independence (Chibber 2003), the labor laws and the state infrastructure behind them formed an important foundation through which labor managed to retain some power over capital. From the start, Indian labor exerted its power through two important avenues enshrined in India's labor laws. First, unlike many countries (including other social democracies), Indian labor laws give the state an enormous role in managing capital-labor relations. Underlying this is an assumption that the democratic pressures binding the state will also force the state to hold capital responsible for labor. Second, Indian labor laws apply only to large employers. Underlying this is an attempt to limit the power of big business and concentrated wealth, while acknowledging that the costs of labor rights may be too high to incur for the small-scale employers that are endemic to poor countries (and that are expected to diminish with growth). Therefore, from labor's perspective, reforming Indian labor laws not only threatens to undermine labor power, it also threatens the very ideals of democracy and equality on which the constitution was built.

While labor's resistance to reform is unsurprising, its success in stalling reforms in India is surprising. Deregulation, alongside increased privatization, was expected not only to accelerate productivity growth, but also to "weaken union power" (Zagha 1998). Labor unions, in India as elsewhere, are diminishing in terms of action and rhetorical power. Since the 1980s, there has been a sharp decline in strikes, while lockouts (initiated by the employer) have increased. Nevertheless, unions' ability to prevent any legal changes in Indian labor laws stands as a testament to the continuing *political power* they have long held in India's democracy. Since the early 1900s, new political parties in India have always been born with a new affiliated trade union attached; the new unions, in turn, have proved essential for drawing labor's vital votes from existing parties toward a new party. India is among the few (perhaps only?) countries in the world where every political party (across the political spectrum) has an affiliated labor union. In spite of the demise of labor power in India and elsewhere, Indian labor unions remain a strong political actor in India's political economy.[4]

To further economic growth in a liberalized and globalized environment, therefore, the postreform Indian state has had to take an *alternative* route with regard to labor. On the surface, it seems the state has "succeeded." For the first time in India's history, the nonagriculture sectors in 2011 were larger, at 56 percent, than the agricultural sector in terms of the share of labor. Even more striking is that since 1999, employment in formally regulated enterprises (otherwise known in India as the "organised sector") has grown more than in unregulated enterprises (otherwise known as the "unorganised sector"). (NSS 2012).[5] Analysts have highlighted these trends indicating that India is at long last undergoing the structural transition needed for capital accumulation (Ghose 2016; Shaw 2013; Thomas 2012).

How has the Indian state managed to make these shifts *without* reforming Indian labor laws? One common, and even official, answer is that the Indian state has had to turn to "jobless," "labor unfriendly," or "noninclusive" growth. Using manufacturing as the gold standard for mass labor absorption, scholars decry the turn to non-labor-absorbing channels of contemporary accumulation such as speculation, especially in commodities and real estate; "financialization"; and high-skilled services, such as information technology (Harvey 2005; Kannan and Raveendran 2009). These accounts of accumulation without mass labor (in India and elsewhere) have become ubiquitous in the Indian literature; they are important and indeed undeniable. But they are also insufficient. First, jobless growth arguments aggregate important differences across time, gender, and agricultural versus nonagricultural employment. Second, they gloss over the politics of this strategy and wrongly brush all labor aside. If the state is unable to resist unions in reforming labor laws, how can the state simply sidestep labor with a growth strategy that does not involve workers? In short, resorting to jobless growth arguments eclipses the powerful strategies and processes that the Indian state has used to interact with and gain favor from its labor constituents, while still facilitating capital accumulation in the postreform era. In addition, hiding state strategies with labor diverts our attention away from the new forms of labor organization that are emerging in response.

Toward a New Labor Framework

To understand the Indian state's recent strategies on labor, I draw from Michael Burrawoy's (2003) undercited but insightful arguments on the "complementary convergence" of Gramsci and Polanyi. Gramsci underscores the contradictory relationship that society (which he refers to as "civil" society) forges with the state under capitalism. As Burrawoy notes, "On the one hand, civil society collaborates with the state to contain class struggle, and on the other hand, its autonomy from the state can promote class struggle" (2003, 198). The contemporary Indian state's strategies toward labor reflect a deep (even if unarticulated) understanding of this contradiction.

Drawing from an analysis of Indian employment data, as well as my research with workers and employers across six Indian industries (construction, automobiles, garments, domestic work, garbage collection, and *bidi* [hand rolled cigarette]) since 2003, I argue that rather than reforming Indian labor laws, the Indian state has neutered these laws by shifting the locus of the capital-labor battle outside the twentieth-century legislative framework. To manage this, the state has employed a powerful two-pronged strategy that capitalized on two vulnerabilities in Indian labor legislation. In the process, the state has subtly undermined two central ideals of the Indian constitution—democracy and equality—thereby pushing forth a new hegemonic ideal that simultaneously organizes consent and constricts class struggle.[6]

First, the state has used its powerful role in labor relations to channel the public debates on labor reform toward a single issue—the need for labor flexibility. By never attacking labor's wages or other benefits, the state has sustained its democratic legitimacy. At the same time, the state has quietly undermined the power of all existing labor laws (protecting job security, wages, and nonwage benefits) by enabling state-level exceptions and reducing the resources of labor ministries designed to enforce them. These moves have been justified for correcting the bureaucratic excesses enabled by the state's earlier "inspector raj" system.

Second, the Indian state has capitalized on the Indian labor movement's lack of reach to create and promote a new political actor—that is, informal labor—that can provide business with a legitimate alternative to formal labor. In their attempt to control big business, Indian labor legislations excluded a majority of informal laborers, who were assumed to be working only in the small-scale sector, which in turn was seen as unable to afford labor regulations. Today, these very workers are meeting unregistered *and* registered business demands for flexible *and* low-cost labor. While informal work has long existed in India, the postreform state has openly promoted informal labor, even in public and private, registered enterprises (where labor laws are supposed to apply). The Indian state has used resources, institutions, and frameworks to officially define, sanction, count, and even offer some protection to informal workers. Throughout, the state has sustained informal workers' anger toward formal workers for years of exclusion, and helped shape informal workers' identity as separate from formal workers.

This two-pronged strategy has enabled the Indian state to shift the balance of power away from a protected labor class toward an empowered capitalist class (i.e., constricted class struggle), while still retaining its own democratic legitimacy through the promotion of informal workers (i.e., organized consent). In recent years, countless scholars have pointed to the rise of informal workers under neoliberalism. In reality, however, the share of the informal labor force has been relatively constant over time, hovering just above 90 percent. More important than a rising share of the informal labor force, I argue, is the composition and structural position of the informal labor force in India since the 1980s. First, low-cost informal work has grown in large, registered enterprises, thereby making unprotected labor the new norm, *even* among skilled workers. This move, which directly helps big business, may help explain India's rising inequality and concentration of wealth. Second, it has funneled more workers into the unprotected construction sector in the name of a structural transition out of agriculture. These workers are not enjoying higher-quality work, even with marginally higher wages. Third, it has resulted in a worrying drop in female labor force participation, especially in poor households. As a result of these trends, the informal labor force has become increasingly male, urban, and operating in the formally regulated enterprises of the so-called "organised sector". These trends suggest that the most important effects of India's probusiness, liberalization turn has been to alter the *politics* of informal labor.

The state's postreform strategy toward labor has also had an important fourth consequence: it has opened the door for informal workers to offer an alternative labor protection model in India—thereby showcasing the contradictory relationship of society to state. Herein enter Polanyi's countermovements. As Burawoy writes, "If Gramsci starts out from the way civil society, through its connection to the state, organizes consent and constricts class struggle, Polanyi starts out from the way active society counteracts the dehumanizing effects of the market economy" (2003, 199). To Polanyi, society is understood in its contradictory relationship to the *market*. "On the one hand, the market tends to destroy society, but on the other hand, society (re)acts to defend itself and to subordinate the market" (Burawoy 2003, 198).

Contrary to common perception, informal workers have not stood by as silent victims to be used as pawns by capital and the state. Rather, they have been organizing their own movements since the late 1970s. The state's new attention to their needs has given them new political opportunities that deserve our attention. After decades of being excluded from the formal labor movement, informal workers are now asserting a politics of recognition that aims to redefine *who* is "a worker" and increase the *number* of beneficiaries of labor protections, and a politics of welfare that aims to highlight the reproductive costs of all workers. In the process, they are reasserting the state's democratic responsibility to labor *citizens*.

That these developments occurred in the absence of labor reforms underscores the postreform state's ability to gradually and subtly chip away the very ideals of Indian democracy and equality. But these developments also serve as a harsh reminder that India's postindependence ideals were never translated into a reality that included the vast majority. In this context, informal workers' movements lend important insights into the ways (a redefined) labor is trying to assert a new twenty-first-century social contract. Karl Polanyi (2001) famously asserted that the pendulum of deregulation and decommodification swings back and forth as labor reasserts its rights against capital's onslaught. Karl Marx (1976) astutely highlighted how capitalism's contradictory social relations always yield working-class struggles. So if we use history as our guide, we should expect labor to reinvent itself. To understand the future of Indian labor, however, we must examine the strengths and limitations of this reinvention in the context of what Antonio Gramsci (1971) highlighted as the powerful hegemonic forces of the state.

Indian Labor and Legislation in the Prereform Era

Indian labor has been an active and organized political actor since the early 1900s. In 1919, Indian labor fought to make India a founding member of the International Labour Organization (ILO), and in 1920, Indian labor launched its first trade union federation, the All India Trade Unions Congress (AITUC), affiliated to the Communist Party of India (CPI). Indian labor was unique in the British colonies for having its own trade union. AITUC fought for Indian independence and led the effort to ensure protective legislation for workers under British colonialism and ultimately within India's constitution. Since AITUC, a plethora of new union federations have emerged in India. Historically, new union federations have arisen alongside new political parties designed to undermine existing political parties. On May 3, 1947, at the dawn of India's independence, the Indian National Congress Party (INC) famously formed the INC-affiliated Indian National Trade Union Congress (INTUC), to split the labor movement and undermine the growing power of AITUC and CPI. This practice continued over time, so that today every political party, at the national and state levels and across the political spectrum, has an affiliated union federation. Particularly striking in India is that even right-wing parties support active party-affiliated union federations. Today, the largest union federation in India, with twelve million members, is the Bharatiya Mazdoor Sangh (BMS), affiliated to the Bharatiya Janata Party (BJP). In recent years, there has also been a significant growth in independent unions and union federations. Despite the diversity of membership, party affiliations, and structures of Indian unions, they manage to come together for nationwide strikes and national-level debates.

At the heart of the Indian labor movement from the start has been a deep understanding of the unequal power relations that exist between employers and workers in any capitalist system. To help decommodify labor within this system, Indian labor focused primarily on establishing a legislative framework that the state could use to restrain capital. Today, a dizzying number of statutes, laws, and rules pepper India's national and state-level legislative frameworks on labor. In the contemporary debates around labor reform, even labor activists and scholars have called for a simplification of the existing labor laws (Nathan, Jeyaranjan, and Dayal 2014; Papola and Pais 2007). Some contemporary laws have their roots in the colonial era.[7] To ensure continued production in the face of labor demands, the British government passed a series of labor laws at the turn of the last century. After independence, several new laws were added.[8] At that time, the basic framework for labor legislation shifted from one of ensuring continued accumulation to one of ensuring social justice and a welfare state (Thakur 2007).

In other words, at independence, the Indian constitution enshrined a new social contract to ensure that in return for citizens' labor, the state would provide for labor's social regeneration and economic betterment. The constitution stipulated that the state would be responsible for securing public assistance for its citizens in the case of "unemployment, old age, sickness, disablement and other cases of undeserved want" (Papola and Pais 2007). Indian labor laws aimed to assist the state in fulfilling its promise by holding capital responsible for labor's needs. In return, organized labor promised industrial peace. This protective framework continued to grow through the early 1980s. For example, the 1947 Industrial Disputes Act, arguably the most contested labor law today, which protects workers against layoffs, retrenchment, and enterprise closures, was amended in 1972, 1976, and 1982—with each amendment giving ever more protections to workers (Papola and Pais 2007). Throughout, policymakers aimed (at least in their rhetoric) to eventually protect all Indian laborers under these laws (NCL 1969).

In addition to protecting labor against capital, Indian labor legislations in the prereform era featured two important features. On the one hand, these two features reflect progressive ideals that are slowly and subtly being chipped away. On the other hand, these features led to vulnerabilities that have been ironically instrumental in undermining labor in the postreform era.

Feature 1: Using a Democratic State

First, each of India's labor laws underline a massive state role in holding capital responsible for labor. It is this feature that has been highlighted in the postreform era as problematic for business, because it is said to invite government bribes, harassment, and other rent-seeking behaviors. Indeed India's strong state role differs from other labor-friendly welfare states, such as those in Scandinavia, where the state plays a minor (and unwelcome) role in capital-labor relations.

At the same time, this feature reflects a faith in the system of democracy that was expected to channel state attention to the needs of the majority.

In India, labor enforcement officers operate from the national to the district levels under the Labor Ministry and state-level labor departments to run routine "checks" on factory floors. State- and national-level tribunals and labor courts are responsible for resolving capital-labor disputes. Indian labor laws do not grant workers the freedom to choose the forum (civil courts or labor tribunals) where they may protect their contractual rights; rather, the state decides. The government provides permission for the firing of workers, and it administers employment exchanges, to which firms must notify vacancies and solicit applicants. As in many welfare states, the government is also the provider of mandated benefits. For example, its national network of hospitals and dispensaries provide the health benefits covered by ESI, and the state administers most pension funds.

The pronounced state role in India's industrial relations fit well with India's unique brand of a Fabian-socialist economy *and* its equally unique experiment with a democratic political system after independence. Unlike socialist countries, India maintained a mixed economy. Although the private sector owned most of India's productive assets and produced over 70 percent of the country's national product, the private sector was bound by state influence in how the assets were used (Zagha 1998). To exert this control, the state not only held extensive controls on international and domestic trade, prices, and private investment, they also controlled capital's use of labor. But the pronounced state role also fit well with India's experiment with democracy. Underlying the labor laws is an assumption that the democratic pressures that bind the state will force it to hold capital responsible for labor's rights, needs, and reproduction.

This assumption, however, opens the door to vulnerabilities that we know well, such as the state's ability to manipulate public interests or undermine legislation with weak enforcement. In the case of labor, however, this vulnerability could only be exploited when combined with a second vulnerability in Indian labor law.

Feature 2: Limiting the Power of Big Business

Another defining feature of Indian labor laws (which is less highlighted than the first) is their attempt to control big business and concentrated wealth. Indian labor has always assumed that the ability to retain profitability *and* absorb the costs associated with workers' rights is easier for large enterprises. Therefore, small-scale enterprises, which were understood as a temporary function of poverty, are exempt from most Indian labor legislations.[9] A handful of laws, such as the 1948 Minimum Wages Act and the Payment of Wages Act, aim to ensure that *all* workers subsist above the poverty line and thus apply even to small enterprises.[10] But they are rarely enforced. Under the Minimum Wages Act, an autonomous wage board is supposed to set and regularly revise minimum wages for all occupations by industry. But these boards are inactive, and revised wages are rarely indexed for inflation, so they often decline in real terms (Zagha 1998). Workers in large firms are unaffected, because their wages are determined by collective bargaining agreements and exceed the minimum wages. For workers in small firms, we know, the law does little to protect their incomes (NCEUS 2006).

Since business was assumed to grow with development, Indian labor laws focused on limiting big-business power by holding only them responsible for the decommodification of labor (which was also expected to grow). This was a progressive attempt to limit the concentration of wealth through its redistribution under capitalism, and it reflected an important ideal of equality.

At the same time, however, this attempt heralded a significant vulnerability that, combined with the first vulnerability around relying on a democratic state, has facilitated the recent downfall of India's twentieth-century labor protection model. The official and unofficial exemption that labor laws provided to small enterprises created an obvious disincentive to grow enterprises.[11] As a result, Indian business has long been notorious for managing multiple small-scale operations in unregulated conditions.[12] From 1984 to 1994, employment in firms with more than one hundred employees was stagnant, whereas it increased by 3.6 percent per year in firms with fewer than one hundred employees (Zagha 1998). The exemption also enabled a parallel labor force of unregulated, unprotected workers to remain extant in India, despite its progressive labor laws. This labor force, otherwise known as "informal workers," has always comprised the vast majority of Indian labor.

An unfortunate consequence of the exemption of unregistered enterprises (and their workers) from labor laws was that it justified the Indian labor movement's systematic exclusion of informal workers, which over time led to the limited reach of the formal labor movement. By definition, informal workers (who were assumed to be working only in small enterprises) did not have legal rights. Only once informal workers shifted into a standard employment relationship in the registered sector would they be entitled to join the labor movement and enjoy labor benefits. In the meantime, central trade unions and the state sanctioned the invisibility of informal workers by not counting them in labor force surveys, not expanding labor legislation to include them, and not considering their interests when making new labor policies. For some decades, informal workers and central trade unions fought to expand the formal workforce. However, capital had few incentives to give up the benefits of employing unprotected labor (albeit through small-sector enterprises). Therefore, the protected class of workers remained an entrenched minority and did not grow beyond

10 percent of the labor force, *even in the prereform era.* Over time, significant resentment arose toward formal workers among the vast majority of excluded, informal workers.

It was this resentment toward the formal labor movement, combined with the state's power in industrial relations, that the postreform Indian state capitalized on to undermine the formal Indian labor movement for the sake of capital accumulation in the 1990s. Let us now examine how the state used these vulnerabilities to advance business interests.

The Indian State's Political Project to Disarm Labor: A Two-Pronged Strategy

Since the 1990s, the Indian state has employed a powerful, yet subtle, two-pronged strategy to undermine formal labor without reforming protective labor legislations. The first part of the strategy employs the power vested to the state (in labor legislations) to shape the public debate in a way that retains the state's democratic legitimacy (even among workers) while highlighting business needs. The second part employs the resentment that has formed among the majority excluded from the labor movement (as a result of the labor movement's focus on big business) to create a competitive alternative to protected labor. Together, this two-pronged strategy exemplifies Gramsci's depiction of a state hegemony that constricts class struggle and organizes consent.

Part 1: Shaping the Debate and Weakening Enforcement

Since the 1990s, the Indian state has led an attack on Indian labor legislations. Throughout the discussions, the state has adeptly turned the social justice ideals undergirding labor laws on their head, while still claiming attention for key voter groups. For example, Indian labor legislations are vilified for hurting labor by hindering capital accumulation and thus employment opportunities (Geetha and Dutta 2012). Repeated depictions of India's "jobless growth" help power these claims. Additionally, labor unions are blamed for robbing marginal populations, such as scheduled caste and tribe members, Muslims, and women, of potential opportunities for poverty alleviation and equality (Planning Commission 2008).

But the state's attacks on Indian labor legislations are not universal. Democratically elected politicians cannot risk proposing to reduce employers' costs by lowering wages and nonwage benefits (such as social security and work conditions). Instead, every debate on labor reform since the 1990s has focused on the issue of *labor flexibility*. As Montek Ahluwalia notes, "Inflexibility in the labor market is [the] major factor reducing India's competitiveness in exports and also reducing industrial productivity generally" (Ahluwalia 2002, 76). Interestingly, the first laws on job security in the mid-1800s were passed to protect employers against workers leaving the job (ILO 1996). But in the postliberalization era, labor flexibility has been framed as a necessity for employers operating within global commodity chains where production is based on orders. Therefore, the state has focused the discussions on just two acts that govern job security. The first is the 1970 Contract Labour Act, which aims to abolish contract labor in "core" activities and regulate it in areas where it is deemed necessary; the purpose of this law is to limit employers' ability to avoid job security provisions.[13] The second is the 1947 Industrial Disputes Act, which protects job security by restricting employers' use of layoffs, retrenchment, and closures.[14]

India is not unique in protecting job security or even in legislating steps on how to dismiss and compensate workers. India's legal provisions (one month's notice in writing, and fifteen days' compensation for each year of service) are not even onerous by international standards (World Bank 1995). What is unique to India, however, is that government permission is needed before dismissal. By incorporating government permission into job security protections, Indian labor ensured that the state bore the social and political costs associated with mass retrenchment. It is this *political* incentive that has formed the bedrock of Indian job security since Indian independence. Therefore, it is not surprising that the state rarely granted this permission in the prereform era.

To empower capital's control over labor in the postreform era, reformers have tried to free capital from the democratic pressures that bind the state (at least in the areas where it is democratically acceptable to do so). For example, reformers have proposed to exempt more enterprises from these laws. At present, the job security restrictions of the IDA apply to enterprises with more than one hundred workers; reformers have tried to increase this number to one thousand (Ahluwalia 2002).

Although the state has failed to reform labor laws to cover fewer establishments at the central level, the state has managed to weaken these labor laws, while still retaining its own democratic legitimacy. By focusing attention only on flexibility (and not on wages and other benefits), the state has shifted the debate to a "need for jobs," rather than a commitment to "fair jobs." Even unions are beginning to voice agreement with the need for labor flexibility to ensure employment, and union strategies have shifted to ensuring monetary compensation for retrenchment, rather than government prevention of retrenchment (AITUC 1997; Ozaki 1999). In addition, the central government has allowed state-level governments to make their own amendments to national labor legislations. For example, the government of Gujarat has relaxed the use of contract labor, and the government of Rajasthan amended the IDA to exempt more firms (with fewer than three hundred workers). Third, the state has initiated new measures to reduce the formal workforce without going through the dismissal procedure of IDA, such as voluntary retirement schemes (VRS).[15] Finally, the state has significantly softened the enforcement of existing laws by slashing the resources of the Labor Ministry and labor departments and reducing the number of inspection officers, and corresponding inspections (Nagaraj 2004; Reddy 2007).

Part 2: Building an Alternative among Informal Workers

But as students of transformation know, it is not enough to simply weaken what *is*; we must also offer a palatable alternative. To this end, the state has capitalized on labor laws' exclusive focus on big business (and thus formal labor) to create a new political actor class of "informal" or "precarious" workers that can oppose formal workers and meet businesses needs for flexibility.

Portes, Castells, and Benton (1989) defined informal workers as those engaged in producing and providing legal goods and services who nevertheless operate outside labor, health, and financial regulation. Drawing on my findings of informal workers' organizing efforts in India, I qualify this definition to specify that informal workers are those not regulated or protected under labor laws based on a standard employer-employee relationship (Agarwala 2013). In other words, informal workers are very likely covered by state protections and certainly state regulations outside traditional labor laws.

Informal workers in India comprise contract workers and self-employed workers. Both groups operate outside labor legislation, with no employment contract, no nonwage benefits, and no legal rights to job security. Both groups operate in a diverse range of locations, including their own homes, employers' homes, unregistered work-sheds, the street, and even the factory floor. Contract workers are hired through subcontractors to avoid visibility and regulation, but are directly involved in capitalist production. Their principal employers can be registered or unregistered companies. The self-employed are owners of small, unregistered businesses. Self-employed owners and their workers provide cheap inputs for capital production (such as auto parts, transport, or products manufactured on order) and goods and services to middle- and upper-class capital owners (such as cleaning, elderly care, gardening, and waste collection) as well as to low-wage workers (such as food, clothing, and haircuts). In contexts where contract workers are protected under law, employers avoid regulation by claiming they "buy" their finished products from a self-employed worker, rather than a hired contract worker, though the product is ordered and designed by the employer. In these cases, self-employed workers resemble mislabeled or "bogus" contract workers.

After ignoring informal workers in labor force surveys and labor policy discussions for decades, the Indian state since the 1990s has financed multiple efforts to conceptually define informal work, improve statistics on informal labor, and disseminate empirical data on informal workers' productivity. These efforts have been instrumental in constructing "informal workers" as well-defined political actors that offer a legitimate and available alternative to formal workers. Doing so has helped the Indian state promote and facilitate the expanded and more open use of contract and self-employed workers, mainstreaming them as not only an acknowledged norm of the present day, but as an ideal for the future.

In 1997, the Expert Group on Informal Sector Statistics, commonly known as the "Delhi Group," was set up as a group within the UN Statistical Commission to address methodological challenges in counting informal workers. In 1998, the Indian Department of Statistics incorporated the Fifteenth International Conference of Labor Statisticians (ICLS) definition of the informal economy into Indian labor surveys. In 1999, the National Sample Survey Office (NSSO) conducted a household survey to count home-based and multiple-location workers.[16] The survey had detailed questions on employment status, location of work, enterprise characteristics, and workers' social and political conditions.[17] A follow-up survey was conducted on the enterprises identified as informal to better capture the details of output generated (NSSO 2001). Since then, the NSS has regularly included questions to capture India's mass of informal workers, as well as information on informal workers' employment, political, and social conditions (in and out of registered enterprises).[18] In 2004, the Indian government appointed the high-level National Commission for Enterprises in the Unorganized Sector (NCEUS) to promote increased productivity in the informal economy. In 2012, the National Statistical Commission wrote, "The development of the unorganized [i.e., informal] sector has a potent role in the 'inclusive growth' in the current paradigm of planning, and such a framework of statistics for formulation of policies and decision support is the need of the hour" (NSC 2012, 5).

These efforts from above created an enormous window of opportunity from below for civil society groups, which had been trying to draw attention to the needs of informal workers since the 1970s. Since the 1990s, organized groups of informal workers, activists, and researchers have worked hard to shape the state's attempts to increase informal workers' visibility through the use of facts and figures about their size and contribution to the economy (Agarwala 2012). Definitional issues were particularly at stake. For example, informal workers fought for a broad definition that could increase their numbers (and thus their political weight).

Rather than defining informal work as entrepreneurs and employees of small, unregistered enterprises, they fought to include all workers not covered under labor laws working in registered enterprises, unregistered enterprises, or households. This definition is also in line with the Seventeenth ICLS definition formed in 2003. To increase their bargaining position with the Indian state, local Indian informal workers' organizations formed partnerships with branded international knowledge brokers, such as Harvard University and the Global Labour Institute in Geneva. Rather than ignoring or sidestepping informal workers' demands, the Indian government has involved them as key advisers and even incorporated the broad definition of informal work into the NSS and policy discussions. By doing so, the state lent further legitimacy to its own stance on informal work.

In the process of exchange, new relations have formed between the Indian state and informal labor, sometimes replacing earlier relations between the Indian state and Indian formal labor, and further legitimizing informal labor. Government officials (at the national and state levels) today justify (at least in rhetoric) protective policies for informal workers. At the symbolic level, they often support informal workers' organization efforts. For example in 2007, then-prime minister Manmohan Singh inaugurated the formal launch of HomeNet South Asia, a transnational network of homebased workers' organizations. On economic grounds, government officials constantly repeat the contribution to gross domestic product (GDP) emerging from the informal economy. On political grounds, government officials (who ten years ago would rarely admit to the existence of informal workers in India) are now unanimous in their constantly repeated quotation that informal workers represent "93 percent of the Indian labor force." In return, informal workers' organizations have rarely demanded job security. They *have* made other demands (which I detail below). But they have generally agreed to remain flexible. Moreover, both parties invest considerable energy in distinguishing formal workers from informal workers.

As a result of these efforts, "informal workers" have become recognized, idealized political actors that enjoy legitimacy in the eyes of the Indian state. That this segment operates outside state regulations does not appear contradictory. More important is that informal workers have become a *distinct* actor class from the "formal workers." While some have read this as an attempt to divide the working class, others have read it as a chance to overthrow a long-entrenched labor bourgeoisie of formal workers who excluded informal workers. Both readings are correct. Let us now turn to the (often worrying) implications the state's efforts have had for Indian workers, as well as the (potentially hopeful) responses informal workers have launched. It is this ever-shifting dynamic that will bring us closer to understanding reality.

The Implications of and Responses to the Reformed Labor Project

The Indian state's open promotion of informal labor, *as a political project*, has had several important, often deleterious, implications for Indian labor and India's postreform economy. More than altering the size of informal labor, India's reformed labor model has altered the nature of informal labor to be more urban, male, and mainstream (i.e., operating in registered enterprises).

The contradictions inherent in these trends, however, have fueled important responses by informal workers, thereby reminding us of society's contradictory relationship with the state with consent on the one hand and resistance on the other. Currently, informal workers' movements are at an early, almost infant-level stage. Nevertheless, I argue that they are at a crucial stage. This is the stage that Peter Waterman captured when he first conceptualized the term "social movement unionism" (SMU)— the stage of *mobilizing and identifying people* under a common frame, the stage that precedes the attainment of legal rights, the stage that was equally important to formal workers' movements in formulating the twentieth-century social contract (Waterman 1993). Therefore, they should not be compared to formal workers' movements at their height, but rather at their early start. Informal workers' current responses indicate efforts to (1) unite formal and informal workers (as in automobiles); (2) hold big business accountable for labor's welfare (as in construction); and (3) assert the power of labor legislations once again (as in domestic work). The results of these efforts have been mixed. But they lend important insights into the future of Indian labor and its constantly shifting relations with the state and capital, thereby exemplifying avenues of what Polanyi described as countermovements that can potentially subordinate the market and the state.

Let us now examine this dynamic of implication and response in three areas.

The New Normal: Increasing Inequality with Informal Workers in Formal Enterprises

One of the most striking characteristics of the postreform era has been the state's active sanctioning of informal workers *in and by large firms*. These include two subcategories: a new category called "informal-regular" workers (which is in itself an oxymoron) and another called "casual workers." Although the former receive a finite contract guaranteeing the number of workdays, they receive neither nonwage benefits nor other labor rights. "Casual" workers earn less than "informal-regular," who earn less than "formal-regular" workers. Openly employing informal workers goes against the very grain of Indian labor laws that empowered the state to control and limit big business.

Since the late 1990s (when government data on informal work were first made available), there has been a sharp and steady increase in informal labor in registered (and thus large) companies in the public and private sectors. According to one estimate, the share of contract labor in registered factories increased from 12 percent in 1985 to 23 percent in 2002 (Pages and Roy, 2006). By 2011, this share rose to 51 percent (with 33 percent as informal-regular, and 12 percent as casual) (NSS 2012). In fact, the growth in informal work accounts for almost all the growth in employment in the registered sector since 1999. Between 1999 and 2011, the share of informal workers in registered enterprises grew three times as fast as formal employment in registered enterprises. Informal workers are even operating now in the public sector. In 2012, two million contract workers were estimated to work for the government and public sector enterprises (Sundar 2015). According to the NSS, between 1999 and 2011, the share of regular-informal workers increased from 13 percent to 18 percent in the public sector, and from 39 percent to 50 percent in the private sector.[19]

In other words, although the share of informal employment in India has remained fairly stagnant in India since the 1980s (hovering around 90 percent), the context of that informal employment has shifted from the so-called "traditional", unorganized sector to the "modern," organized sector. Informal, unregulated work has become the openly acknowledged new normal for India's modern economy. In my own research, I have seen this form of unequal, side-by-side employment in automobiles and export-oriented garment manufacturing.

These shifts have facilitated the growing inequality that has characterized India's postreform era. On the bottom end, the wages of informal workers in registered enterprises have remained stagnant since 1999. The only draw for workers has been more days of work offered. Although some have celebrated the resulting decrease in the share of small-scale, unregistered enterprises, others have noted the resulting decline in the quality of work in large enterprises, as measured by a work quality index (Ghose 2016). On the other end, these shifts have facilitated the growth and power of large business and concentrated wealth—a growth that labor legislation during the prereform era succeeded in helping to limit. This trend has been corroborated by others, who have shown that liberalization efforts since the 1980s have enabled the richest 0.1 percent to substantially increase their share of total income, thereby increasing the nation's income inequality (Banerjee and Piketty 2005).

At the same time, these shifts have also spurred important worker responses that may rechannel patterns in the years to come. Most importantly and for the first time in recent Indian history, they have inadvertently pushed formal and informal workers to join hands in organizing. This response threatens the very basis of the state's political project of defining informal workers as an alternative to formal workers. On February 20–21, 2013, for example, Indian workers held the largest and longest mass strike to take place since independence. Across the country, workers—including the unionized and nonunionized, the formal and informal—stopped work for two days. This strike, which saw active participation from all politically affiliated and most independent trade unions, was historic in that it highlighted the needs of India's diminishing formal workforce *and* its swelling informal workforce. Workers called for greater enforcement of labor laws, improved wages and benefits for contract workers, increased minimum wages, the compulsory registration of trade unions within forty-five days, and the ratification of International Labor Organization (ILO) Conventions 87 and 98.[20]

Another, even more famous, example is the autoworkers strike in the Manesar plant of Maruti Suzuki India Limited (MSIL) in Harayana in 2012, where workers, 65 percent of whom were nonpermanent contract workers, had been demanding improved provision of labor rights from management, particularly their right to form a union. After two months of protest, where managers refused to bargain with a newly formed union, violence broke out at the plant on July 18, and a manager was killed. MSIL declared a lockout and dismissed over two thousand workers, most of them contract workers. Over one hundred workers were arrested by the police without charges and denied bail and continue to remain in custody. The joint labor commissioner argued that the government had no obligation to promote collective bargaining and that management had the right to refuse to negotiate with a partner it did not like.[21] In contrast, the International Commission for Labor Rights (ICLR), which investigated the workers' allegations, found that the employer, supported by the criminal justice system, scuttled the workers' rights to collective bargaining, and the labor department (of the state of Harayana) had improperly favored management's interests and failed in its duty to act as an impartial adjudicatory body to settle industrial disputes.[22]

Although workers' protests were severely repressed in the Maruti case, workers' revolts altered business's future strategy with regard to informal labor. Very few manufacturing plants now employ informal and formal workers on the same shop floor.[23] In 2014, the Planning Commission and the CII "decided to launch a consultative process of working for a consensus between employers and trade unions on the desirable changes in labor force practices . . . without any change in the relevant laws," by conducting a study on "good practices" in manufacturing with regard to flexible labor (Nathan, Jeyaranjan, and Dayal 2014). The reports details three notable practices:

1. In new factories, contractors and contract workers earlier employed for non-core tasks have been replaced by outsourcing the jobs to outside *companies* that can take care of services such as logistics, food services, housekeeping, furnace operation and maintenance, and so forth.

2. Many large companies no longer employ any contract labor in production tasks. "Managers are very aware of the dangers arising from differential treatment of similar workers" (Nathan, Jeyaranjan, and Dayal 2014, 4). As a result, companies have begun to hire contract workers as "regular" workers in that they receive a contract for a fixed number of days. However, these workers are still not given nonwage benefits to which formal workers are entitled.

3. Companies have begun to retain skilled workers at a lower cost by offering fixed-term contracts (without nonwage benefits) after a long apprentice period.

These "good practices" indicate a shift toward lowering labor costs without reforming labor laws, even among skilled workers in large companies. In effect, formal labor is being undone.

A Flawed Structural Transition: Unprotected Construction as the Growth Sector

In recent years, several analysts have celebrated the fact that India may at long last be undergoing the structural transition out of agriculture that developmentalists have long been dreaming of. As noted above, in 2011 employment in the nonagricultural sector exceeded 50 percent (at 56.3 percent) for the first time in India's history. However, contrary to the experiences of other late-industrializing countries, India's employment has *not* shifted to manufacturing. Employment in manufacturing remains low, and growth since 1999 has been negligible (from 11 to 13 percent). Rather, agricultural workers are now turning to services and construction. Services, where labor law enforcement is notoriously weak, comprised 30.5 percent of the labor force in 2011, indicating steady growth since 1999, when it was 25.7 percent (NSS 2012).

Perhaps most striking, however, has been the massive growth in construction employment, from 5 percent in 1999 to 11 percent in 2011 (NSS 2012). This growth in construction accounted for a significant share of the structural transition out of agriculture. Agriculture and construction are deeply linked in India, as many construction workers are seasonal, rural migrants. Today, construction constitutes 11.3 percent of India's total economic output (NCAER 2014, viii). In 2014, the construction market totaled US$157 billion, an increase of US$4 billion since 2013 (PWC 2014).[24] According to Deloitte, India is poised to be world's third-largest construction market by 2025–30 (2014, 22). But employment in construction is almost entirely informal and unregulated (NCAER 2014, 20). Most workers operate through chains of subcontractors and rarely interact directly with the principal employer. Although average wages in construction are higher than in agriculture, the recent employment report noted that the average quality of employment in construction (organized and unorganized), measured by a work quality index, was worse than that in unorganized (read: informal) agriculture in 1999 and 2011 (Ghose 2016).

The unabashed promotion of informal work in India has ensured that even the structural transition, which has long been viewed as the foundation for development, is not leading to higher-quality jobs or livelihoods for Indian workers. How are workers responding?

Construction Workers' Legislations and Welfare Boards: Lessons to Learn

As I have detailed at length elsewhere, construction workers began organizing at a national level in the 1980s, and in 1996 they attained a comprehensive law designed to regulate construction work and an act requiring all state governments to enact a welfare board for construction workers (Agarwala 2013).

Informal workers' welfare boards are among the most innovative institutions that informal workers have launched in India and globally to ensure their welfare in the postreform era. Welfare boards are designed to be tripartite institutions, implemented by the state or central government, where government officials, employers, and workers have representation and contribute funds. Employers' contributions come from a tax on production, while workers' contributions come from board membership dues. To become a welfare board member, workers must prove their informal work status; unions normally educate workers about welfare boards and provide confirmation of workers' informal status. Construction workers' welfare boards are among the longest running and most successful. Today, they serve as a role model for informal workers in other industries, where welfare boards are also emerging. Some are trade based and include self-employed workers, such as garment workers and domestic workers. Others are general, aiming to provide welfare for all informal workers, under the 2008 Social Security Act for Unorganized Workers. These newer boards are even more problematic than the earlier boards in that some are no longer tripartite, and many lack a defined funding source. Nevertheless, informal workers' organizations across sectors remain committed to demanding and implementing welfare boards to help consolidate informal workers' identity, provide a forum for their concerns, and provide an institutional mechanism for the delivery of worker identity cards and benefits.

Although construction workers remain extremely unprotected and unregulated, my research with informal workers' organizations in construction, as well as site visits, indicates important benefits from the central legislation, especially when compared to other industries. For example, several unions mentioned the safety provisions in the act enabled them to hold employers accountable and take them to the labor court when they did not provide workers and their families with proper compensation for work-related accidents and deaths. Many interviewees noted the important role that left-leaning judges have played in assisting construction unions. These cases, although few in number, have served a major role in mobilizing members to the union and instilling a modicum of accountability in employers. Unlike in other informal worker-dominated industries, construction union leaders repeatedly pointed to employers as being responsible for their workers' safety. In addition, in my site visits, several workers reported having Sundays off and taking leave (albeit unpaid) for holidays in their home villages. Several unions have been particularly proud of their involvement in ensuring that employers and subcontractors provide timely payment to their workers and decrease the accusations of theft.

Even more than implementing the comprehensive legislation on regulation of construction work, however, I have found that enacting and implementing the Construction Workers' Welfare Board comprises the bulk of construction workers' activities. During the 2000s, construction welfare boards have proliferated across states, and their promised provisions have expanded. Most striking is how much money these boards have accrued across states. According to a recent Supreme Court ruling, each state's construction welfare board has hundreds of thousands of rupees. Unlike more recent boards (such as for domestic workers), construction welfare boards stipulated a tripartite source of income (from the 1–2 percent tax on large employers, government grants, and worker fees). To this end, they have reinserted labor's original call to hold big business accountable.

The welfare boards serve many functions. First, they provide (or at least aim to provide) welfare benefits to cover workers' reproductive costs. These include education scholarships, healthcare clinics, compensation for death and accident, pensions, and even housing. Second, the promise of these benefits have provided unions with the single most powerful draw to attract new members, thereby enabling unions to build group-level solidarity. Welfare boards are thus an effective mobilizational tool in an era when labor organization is bordering on extinction. Related to this, many unions claimed that the boards ease their access to building sites (so they can reach workers), because unions can claim they are not antibuilder and will not make the builder directly pay for workers' welfare. Rather, the union just needs the builder to help register workers, so the *board* can pay. Finally, the welfare boards and the identity cards that come with them have helped informal workers articulate their own identity as workers, thereby undoing decades of their exclusion from the recognized "workforce."

At present, welfare boards are also mired with challenges. They remain prone to the traps of neoliberal populism. The flush funds of construction welfare boards have already served as attractive pockets for politicians to utilize on an ad hoc basis. For example, in Rajasthan the welfare board was found to be distributing five hundred thousand rupees to fund the dowries of construction workers. In Karnataka, the government tried to use the welfare board money to build marriage halls and schools for construction workers. In other states, benefits were offered and then quickly retracted when there was a change of government. Similar trends were found among the domestic workers' welfare board in Maharashtra. Not surprisingly, the boards' implementation has been uneven. I have written elsewhere about the varying state-level conditions under which boards succeed and fail (Agarwala 2013). In some states, such as Tamil Nadu and Kerala, boards have been reasonably well implemented. In other states, the number of registered workers, let alone benefit recipients, remains low. Burdensome paperwork blocks registration, renewal, identity confirmation, and benefits. Recently, there has been increasing duplicity in schemes that workers can draw from, further slowing the process and fueling mistrust between workers and the state.[25] In some areas, boards have catalyzed a host of new, false, rent-seeking unions to emerge merely to register workers in boards, while taking a cut for themselves. And, of course, boards do *not* address workers' productive costs and cannot be seen as a replacement for earlier labor movements.

Despite these challenges, I argue that welfare boards remain the only attempt (*by* workers) that I have seen (across countries and in India) to address informal workers' reproductive costs. Ignoring them (or sidelining them as mere subsidies to capital) leaves them even more vulnerable to the pressures they are currently facing.

The Missing Women

The third impact of the India's state's reformed labor strategy is the striking disappearance of women from the labor force, especially at the lowest ends of the social structure. The female labor force participation rate (F-LFPR) has always been notoriously low in India. Many have noted that it explains India's low overall labor force participation rates (LFPR) (at 55.6 percent in 2011), relative to Brazil (at 69.9 percent) and China (at 74.1 percent) (Ghose 2016). Many have also noted that the informal nature of women's work means they are undercounted in India's labor force surveys (Hiraway 2010). But since the 1980s, despite the attempts to improve data on informal work, there has been a further *drop* in the women's LFPR. This is true for the nonstudent population and especially pronounced among poor households. Only the most educated women in the highest income bracket experienced a slight increase in employment rates in 2011 (NSS 2012).

This trend, which has been widely noted and termed the "defeminization" of Indian labor, has been credited for the drop in the overall labor force participation growth rate in India, which dropped to 1.4 percent a year (1999–2011) from 1.8 percent a year (1983–99) (Ghose 2016). Much of the drop in women's LFPR in the 1990s and 2000s can be attributed to the drop in contract work for unregistered enterprises, which fell by 10.4 million women workers between 1999 and 2011 (NSS 2012). Much of this work had been done by women. But these women seem not to have been reincorporated into the growing informal work in registered enterprises, where work conditions are said to be marginally better than in unregistered enterprises. Additionally, unemployment levels have also not increased.[26] Informal labor has thus become increasingly male.

But where then are the women? The recent employment report suggests that they have dropped out of the labor force due to the improved household incomes earned by their husbands (measured by the growing consumption rates across income brackets since 1999) (Ghose 2016). Given the continuing poverty levels choking a vast majority of the Indian population, this hypothesis seems unlikely. Clearly, much more in-depth research is needed to answer this question. At a very preliminary level, my own research with informal workers in domestic work, garbage collection, bidi manufacturing, garment manufacturing, and construction suggests that women are increasingly entering occupations that are even more invisible than in the past. This has led not only to a new set of challenges for labor, but also a new set of demands among labor organizers.

Unlike in many other countries, India's construction industry has long been known to incorporate the labor of women and children (Shivakumar, Sheng, and Weber 1991). In large part, this is a reflection of the manual nature of many of the jobs, even today. Women (and child) workers are hired to perform the tasks at the lowest rung of the labor hierarchy—such as carrying materials, fetching water, and manually cleaning and mixing cement. In some cases, they are also hired to do molding and roof work. In the rarest cases, women become masons. Estimates have placed the proportion of women working in construction between 30 (WIEGO) and 50 percent (Devi and Kiran 2013) of the total workforce. As India's construction industry has become increasingly mechanized (especially in large infrastructure projects, such as the Bangalore Metro), however, women are said to be losing jobs in construction (Madhok 2005). Women workers are rarely found on the large infrastructure projects (or "megaprojects") today. In our interviews, we were often told that many of these women are turning to paid domestic work instead.

Paid domestic work is not recognized as "work" in India, and is therefore not accurately counted in the NSS and not covered by any labor legislation, even the Minimum Wages Act. Although there has been substantial debate on the size of the domestic workforce (ranging from 10 million, according to the 2009 Labour Bureau statistics, to 3.9 million, according to the 2011 NSSO statistics), a less contested trend has been its increasing feminization in recent decades. Although a 1981 survey conducted by the Labour Bureau found that neither sex was dominant among full-time domestic workers, today, over 70 percent of domestic workers are female, according to estimates, making it one of the most prominent sources of female employment in urban areas (Neetha 2009, 492; Bhattacharya and Sinha 2010). In addition, there has been a notable expansion in the range of castes and religious communities willing to work in this sector, which indicates a break with earlier occupational enclaves and the desperate need for employment among poor women. With the rising costs of urban real estate, there has been a decline in live-in domestic work, and a subsequent rise in live-out domestic work conducted by first-generation female migrants (Neetha 2009; Jagori 2010; Rao 2011). Although a minority are employed through place-ment agencies, most domestic workers are "self-employed," finding employers through their personal networks.

Domestic workers' organizations today are fighting to (1) attain a compre-hensive law to regulate and protect the employment and working conditions of domestic workers (by fixing wages, holidays, medical leave, work safety, etc.) and (2) incorporate domestic work as a category covered by India's fourteen labor laws.[27] At first glance, these demands appear utopian in the current con-text of *declining* protective legislations for workers. But upon closer analysis, it becomes clear that domestic workers' fight for protective legislation is as much *a demand for recognition* (which is *not* a utopian impossibility). Although in-formal workers remain outside of these legislations in other sectors, the case of domestic workers highlights the beneficiary impact of simply *having* such legislations in place, *even* when they are not implemented or do not cover the in-formal workforce. First and foremost, they serve as an official recognition of who is a worker (being exploited in a wage relationship) and what is work. At pre-sent, domestic workers are not recognized as workers in India, their employers are not recognized as employers, their relationship is not recognized as exploita-tive, and the home is excluded as a potential place of work. Therefore, domestic workers' fight for protection (in terms of employment conditions *or* welfare) is impossible.

Second, the fight for protective legislation is a demand for the *threat of power*. Although informal workers are regularly excluded from labor laws in practice, having them in place enables unions and workers to exert some power over employers by using the threat of judicial action. Construction leaders regularly spoke about filing court cases and calling the police when employers refused to provide proper compensation to workers' families after work-related accidents. These cases were not numerous, but they served as an important tool through which unions could empower their members and mobilize new members. Domestic workers often spoke about the need to file such cases, so employers would have some "fear."

Although domestic workers' attempts to pass comprehensive legislation to recognize domestic work (which began in the 1950s) have all failed, their cumulative failures have galvanized a range of domestic workers' organizations to join hands at the national level.[28] In 2013, after the ILO Convention on the Rights of Domestic Workers, these organizations launched the National Domestic Workers Platform. They held a mass rally in 2014 in New Delhi to urge the government to adopt a central law on domestic workers guaranteeing their rights.

At present, the Indian government has agreed to form a "policy" for domestic workers, which will merely present a vision and advise state governments on potential regulatory options. It will not hold any judicial weight. Although domestic workers' organizations refuse to accept this as a replacement for the act, many whom I interviewed expressed that it was a first step that they would be willing to accept. The Draft Policy on Domestic Workers (which is currently pending approval in parliament) sets out a labor rights framework for domestic workers, and obliges the central and state governments to bring domestic workers into the ambit of existing labor laws and schemes and to set up legislative mechanisms to address issues that existing legislations do not address. It also obliges state government to set up an institutional mechanism that provides for social security, grievance redressal, and dispute resolution. It further urges governments to register workers, employers, and placement agencies and to promote skill development. Under these recommendations, governments will be urged to forbid sexual harassment and bonded labor and regulate working conditions by stipulating minimum wages, compulsory paid leave of fifteen days a year, maternity leave, one day per week off, and a safe working environment (see Planning Commission 2011).

Although the Indian government has refused to recognize domestic work under comprehensive legislation, it has now included domestic workers as an occupational category in a series of existing legislations (a contradiction that is not uncommon in Indian law). Domestic workers are now included as an occupational category under the 2008 Unorganized Workers' Social Security Act, the 2013 Sexual Harassment of Women at Workplace (Prevention, Prohibition and Redressal) Act, and the 2006 Child Labour Act (2006). There have been some additional legislative victories at the state levels.[29]

Domestic Workers' Welfare Boards

Welfare boards for domestic workers now exist in three states: Kerala's was established in 1977, Maharasthra's in 2008, and Jharkhand's in 2013. Further research is needed to examine the impact of Kerala's more established board. In Maharasthra and Jharkhand, I found the boards to be woefully weak. In Maharashtra, they are not connected to a secure funding source. In Jarkhand, they merely fold in existing schemes, which do not leave domestic workers better off. Implementation is a constant and unsurprising problem.

Nevertheless, these efforts among domestic workers indicate efforts from below to expand our notion of "work," recognize more occupations as "work," and increase the *number* of beneficiaries in labor protections. I found similar trends among bidi workers and domestic garment workers. Both groups work in the invisible confines of their homes, operating through subcontractors, who in turn buy and sell orders for large, registered enterprises. Bidi and garment workers have implemented welfare boards (at the national and state levels). Among export-oriented garment manufacturers, women are employed on the shop floor as informal workers. However, many union leaders noted that night shifts and safety concerns prevent women from retaining the jobs (AITUC interview).

Conclusion

The Indian state's increasingly close relations with Indian business has made the need for a new theoretical framework on Indian labor all the more pressing. Labor in the twenty-first century must be re-understood to include formal *and* informal workers. Contemporary labor must be re-envisioned to include manufacturing jobs, as well as those in the growing sectors of construction and services. The relationship of labor exploitation must account not just for the market, but also for state politics and ideology. Only then can we expose how the Indian state is using informal labor to organize mass consent for undermining labor's twentieth-century gains and empowering large business while still retaining its democratic legitimacy. Only then can we also examine the potential and limitations of countermovements emerging from below. Each set of forces (i.e., hegemony and countermovements) must be evaluated in the context of the other.

Contemporary debates on labor are often stunted by a stubborn attachment to twentieth-century labor frameworks that have long been misplaced in the Indian context. One of the most common complaints made about India's post-1991 economic growth is that it has been "jobless"—that is, that the growth of employment has not kept up with the growth of output. Indeed, this is true given

India's very high rates of economic growth in recent years. But is it surprising or interesting? No. First, a "jobless growth" argument is only relevant to labor demand for formal workers. But when we account for informal workers (as we must in India), we see that economic growth in India has never been constrained by labor shortages, because it is a labor-surplus economy. As a result, high economic growth always looks "jobless," while low economic growth looks "jobfull." Second, labor demand (which jobless growth suggests is too low) is an irrelevant proxy for employment in India, since the lack of universal welfare requires that people find *some* work to survive—hence, India's miniscule unemployment rates and massive rate of informal employment. Indeed, employment (i.e., formal and informal) between 1993 and 2011 in absolute terms (i.e., not relative to economic growth) *grew* in India (Thomas 2012).

Third, "jobless growth" arguments mask important details in India's employment situation. The slower growth in employment since 2004 that has been the subject of much debate is largely due to a decline in agricultural employment; nonagricultural employment (which covers less of the workforce) grew during this period. Unlike China and other East Asian economies that drew on their literate workforce to fuel a large manufacturing sector, India's economic and employment growth has come primarily from services and construction, where the jobs have been low quality and precarious (Ghose 2016). Moreover, the decline in employment growth has reflected a drop in female workforce participation (in addition to a drop in child labor and increase in student population). Some have heightened the danger of "jobless growth" by pointing to a so-called youth bulge or rising share of the working-age population in demographic terms. Again, these cries are misplaced, as the share of youth in the working-age population declined between 1999 and 2011. More importantly, the share of youth in the labor force (i.e., those seeking jobs) has been declining, from 52.3 percent in 1983 to 32.4 percent in 2011 (Ghose 2016). This has been attributed to the rising share of students and declining participation of young females in the labor force.

Finally, the focus on "jobless" growth veils the economic and political *strategy* that the Indian government is using with regard to labor and the important impact this strategy has on people's lives. Indian growth has not been fueled by avoiding or sidestepping labor (with technology, for example). Rather it has been fueled by a blatant consensus to step *on* labor. Investments in public education and healthcare are no longer seen as instrumental for growth, let alone morally required. Flexibility and precarity are becoming accepted norms across skill levels in small and large businesses. By building, showcasing, and using informal labor as a political actor, the Indian state has undermined the twentieth-century social contract and imposed a new hegemonic ideal of decommodified labor to serve capital's interests. More striking is that the Indian state has managed to retain its democratic legitimacy while bolstering accumulation on the backs of its own mass electorate. At the same time, history has shown us that labor rarely stands idle when being abused. Labor resists. Budding and extant efforts to resist new hegemonic ideals deserve our greater attention in India.

Acknowledgments

I am grateful to Ajit Ghosh for his time and patience in sharing with me his data and insights. I am also grateful to the excellent comments and feedback I received from the participants in the Princeton workshop held in May 2016, Sanjay Ruparelia (who offered excellent discussant comments), and to Atul Kohli, Christophe Jaffrelot, and Kanta Murali for their generous feedback-all of which greatly improved this chapter.

References

Agarwala, Rina. 2012. "The State and Labor in Transnational Activism: The Case of India." *Journal of Industrial Relations* 54 (4): 443–58.

———. 2013. *Informal Labor, Formal Politics and Dignified Discontent in India.* New York: Cambridge University Press.

Ahluwalia, Montek S. 2002. "Economic Reforms in India since 1991: Has Gradualism Worked?" *Journal of Economic Perspectives* 16 (3): 67–88.

AITUC (All India Trade Unions Congress). 1997. "Amendments to the ID Act: Proposals by AITUC." In *Trade Union Record,* 5–6. New Delhi: AITUC.

Banerjee, Abhijit, and Thomas Piketty. 2005. "Top Indian Incomes, 1922–2000." *World Bank Economic Review* 19 (1): 1–20.

Bhowmik, Sharit K. 2015. "Protecting Employers against Workers and Trade Unions: New Bill on Industrial Relations." *Economic and Political Weekly* 1 (29): 15–18.

Burawoy, Michael. 2003. "For a Sociological Marxism: The Complementary Convergence of Antonio Gramsci and Karl Polanyi." *Politics and Society* 31 (2): 193–261.

Chibber, Vivek. 2003. *Locked in Place: State-Building and Late Industrialization in India.* Princeton, NJ: Princeton University Press.

CII (Confederation of Indian Industry). 2002. "Competitiveness of Indian Manufacturing: Results from a Firm Level Survey." New Delhi: CII.

Devi, Kalpana and U. V. Kiran. 2013. "Status of Female Workers in Construction Industry in India: A Review." *IOSR Journal of Humanities and Social Science* 14 (4): 27–30.

Geetha, V., and Madhumita Dutta. 2012. "Roadblocks to Rights in 'Detroit of the South.'" *The Hindu,* July 29, 2012.

Ghose, Ajit K. 2016. "India Employment Report 2016: Challenges and Imperative of Manufacturing-Led Growth." New Delhi: Institute of Human Development and Oxford University Press.

GOI (Government of India). 2006. "Economic Survey 2005–06." Ed. Ministry of Finance. New Delhi: GOI.

Gramsci, Antonio. 1971. *Selections from the Prison Notebooks.* New York: International Publishers.

Harvey, David. 2005. *A Brief History of Neoliberalism.* Oxford: Oxford University Press.

Hirway, Indira. 2010. "Labour Market Adjustment and Female Workers: Global Production and Expiry of Quotas in India's Textile and Garments Industry." In *Labour in Global Production Networks in India,* ed. Anne Posthuma and Dev Nathan, 166–89. New Delhi: Oxford University Press.

ILO (International Labor Organization). 1996. "India, Economic Reforms and Labor Policies." New Delhi: ILO.

Kannan, K. P., and G. Raveendran. 2009. "Growth Sans Employment: A Quarter Century of Jobless Growth in India's Organised Manufacturing." *Economic and Political Weekly* 44 (10): 80–91.

Marx, Karl. 1976. *Capital.* Vol. 1. London: Pelican.

Nagaraj, R. 2004. "Fall in the Organised Manufacturing Employment: A Brief Note." *Economic and Political Weekly* 39 (30): 3387–339.

Nathan, Dev, J. Jeyaranjan, and Harishwar Dayal. 2014. "Good Practices: Contract Labour." New Delhi: Institute of Human Development.

NCEUS (National Commission for Enterprises in the Unorganised Sector). 2006. "Report on Conditions of Work and Promotion of Livelihoods in the Unorganised Sector." New Delhi: Government of India.

NCL (National Commission on Labour). 1969. "Report of the National Commission on Labour (NCL) Employment and Rehabilitation." Delhi: Ministry of Labour, Government of India.

Neetha, N. 2009. "Contours of Domestic Service: Characteristics, Work Relations and Regulation." *The Indian Journal of Labour Economics* 52 (3): 489–506.

NSC (National Statistical Commission). 2012. "Report of the Committee on Unorganised Sector Statistics." New Delhi: Government of India.

NSS (National Sample Survey). 2012. "National Sample Survey on Employment and Unemployment, 68th Round, 2011–2012." Ed. Ministry of Statistics. New Delhi: National Sample Survey Organisation, Government of India.

NSSO (National Sample Survey Organisation). 2001. "Informal Sector in India: Salient Features (1999–2000)." Calcutta: NSSO, Government of India.

Ozaki, Muneto 1999. "Negotiating Flexibility: The Role of the Social Partners and the State." New Delhi: International Labor Organization.

Papola, T. S., and Jesim Pais. 2007. "Debate on Labour Market Reforms in India: A Case of Misplaced Focus." *Indian Journal of Labour Economics* 50 (2): 183–200.

Planning Commission. 2001. "Report of the Task Force on Employment Opportunities."

———. 2008. "Eleventh Five Year Plan, 2007–12, Volume 1, Inclusive Growth." New Delhi: Government of India.

Polanyi, Karl. 2001. *The Great Transformation.* Boston: Beacon Press.

Portes, Alejandro Manuel Castells, and Lauren A. Benton. 1989. *The Informal Economy: Studies in Advanced and Less Developed Countries.* Baltimore: Johns Hopkins University Press.

Pratap, Surendra. 2011. "Trade Union Repression in India." Asia Monitor Research Center Research Paper. http://www.amrc.org.hk/system/files/Research%20Paper-Trade%20Union%20Repression%20in%20India.pdf.

Rudolph, Lloyd I., and Susanne Hoeber Rudolph. 1987. *In Pursuit of Lakshmi: The Political Economy of the Indian State.* Chicago: University of Chicago Press.

Shaw, Abhishek. 2013. "Employment Trends in India: An Overview of NSSO's 68th Round." *Economic and Political Weekly* 48 (42): 23–25.

Shivakumar, M. S., Y. K. Sheng, and K. Weber. 1991. "Recruitment and Employment Practices the Construction Industry: A Case Study of Bangalore." *Economic and Political Weekly* 26 (8): M27–M40.

Sundar, Shyam. 2015. "Contract Labour Law Debate: Do We Need More Flexibility?" *Deccan Herald*, November 26.

Teitelbaum, Emmanuel. 2011. *Mobilizing Restraint: Democracy and Industrial Conflict in Post-reform South Asia.* Ithaca, NY: Cornell University Press.

Thakur, C. P. 2007. "Labour Policy and Legal Framework in India: A Review." New Delhi: Institute for Studies in Industrial Development.

Thomas, Jayan Jose 2012 "India's Labour Market during the 2000s: Surveying the Changes." *Economic and Political Weekly* 47 (51): 39–51.

Waterman, Peter. 1993. "Social-Movement Unionism: A New Union Model for a New World Order?" *Review* 16 (Summer): 245–78.

World Bank. 1995. *World Development Report 1995: Workers in an Integrating World.* Delhi: Oxford University Press.

Zagha, Roberto. 1998. "Labor and India's Economic Reforms." *Journal of Policy Reform* 2 (4): 403–26.

Business Interests, the State, and the Politics of Land Policy

ROB JENKINS

Introduction

The legal and practical constraints on private investors' ability to obtain large tracts of land for industrial and commercial projects are matters of increasing interest to development practitioners. The ease of "accessing industrial land" is now measured at the country level as part of the World Bank / IMF data set on indicators of foreign direct investment regulations (World Bank 2010). In the case of India, the obstacles firms face when seeking to purchase or lease land for industrial purposes are a perennial complaint among investors domestic and foreign. States within India have competed for inward investment by promising expedited access to land—for production facilities, energy and transportation infrastructure, housing developments and other amenities required by future workers and managers.

Many multinational corporations that seek access to land in India are more accustomed to operating in countries where government expropriation of land—or changes to its use—is less circumscribed by legal and political constraints. This contributes to making India's regulatory framework, and the political environment that affects its structure and implementation, a subject of intense scrutiny in the investment community. Ernst and Young's "India Attractiveness Survey" for both 2014 and 2015 highlighted land availability as a major drag on private investment. Over the same period, the international consulting firm KPMG, in partnership with the Confederation of Indian Industry (CII), identified land issues as having a negative impact on the regulatory climate within which industrial projects were planned and financed.

This chapter examines the relationship between business interests and the Indian state through the lens of land-related policy issues. It focuses on the legal framework that governs the exercise of the state's power of "eminent domain"—that is, its authority forcibly to acquire private land for "public purposes" such as highways, power plants, and industrial estates, including those developed or operated by private sector firms. The chapter argues that India's recent history of land acquisition policy reform reveals a deep ambiguity in the nature of state-business relations.

On the one hand, in 2013 India's elected representatives and senior civil servants worked with social movement leaders, academic experts, and other non-governmental actors to enact a sweeping reform of India's land acquisition legislation. The Right to Fair Compensation and Transparency in Land Acquisition, Rehabilitation and Resettlement Act 2013 (LARRA) was designed to provide protections to landholders and the communities in which they lived. The bill that would become LARRA was almost universally denounced by India's business associations after it was introduced in parliament in 2011. Corporate opposition was not hard to understand: LARRA imposed significant new constraints on the state's ability to acquire land for industrial or infrastructure projects involving the private sector. Businesses would face increased costs, longer delays, and greater uncertainty. Given the considerable influence of organized business interests on Indian policymaking, their inability to prevent LARRA's passage in late 2013 is striking. The political leverage of India's private sector has been portrayed as having crossed a categorical threshold—toward a state-business ruling alliance (Kohli 2012). Yet on a policy matter of crucial importance to India's leading business associations, the Congress Party–led government of Prime Minister Manmohan Singh not only did not liberalize land acquisition laws in ways favored by the business community; it introduced significant new regulatory requirements. Even when the famously probusiness Narendra Modi became prime minister in 2014, private sector actors were unable to attain the policy change they openly coveted: the outright repeal, or at least substantial legislative amendment, of LARRA. In a major political embarrassment, Modi's government ultimately could not muster the parliamentary support necessary to amend LARRA, despite multiple attempts.

There is a second thread to India's land acquisition policy story, however—one that demonstrates the capacity of private sector interests to adapt to changing political circumstances. Despite the Modi government's failure to pass its LARRA amendment bill in parliament, business interests (acting through formal and informal channels) continued to influence policy change by supporting a range of *state-level* reform efforts. India's constitution allows states, under certain circumstances, to amend central legislation on subjects over which state and federal governments hold "concurrent" authority. During the early years of the Modi government, several states—notably Tamil Nadu, Rajasthan, and Gujarat—passed LARRA amendment laws through their legislatures, while others began the process of doing so. Business associations and individual firms have attempted to support and shape these state-level LARRA amendment laws, each of which accomplishes (in a single state) the same probusiness objectives— lower costs, faster acquisition, fewer uncertainties—that Modi's stalled LARRA amendment bill had sought to achieve nationwide. These policy victories have been the result of sustained, systematic engagement by national business groups in state-level politics. As we will see, the private sector's policy influence with state officials on land issues has increased due to its pursuit of a reform agenda that is both *wider* (including adjacent policy domains such as investment-incentive programs and urban-planning norms) and *deeper* (including issues beyond acquisition, such as land use and conversion, land pooling, title certification, and leasing arrangements).

The chapter is organized as follows. The next section provides essential background on India's land acquisition legislation, including major changes introduced in recent years. It is followed by a discussion of the factors that constrained the ability of private sector actors to see their preferred policy options adopted under two successive governments. The development of state-level land acquisition regimes is then assessed. The role of a widening and deepening of the policy agenda is examined in the subsequent section. The chapter concludes with a brief overview of some of the factors that may constrain continued business influence over policy reform.

Key Features of LARRA

The passage of LARRA in 2013 was of enormous practical and symbolic importance to Indian business. Introduced as the LARR Bill in 2011, the act came into force on January 1, 2014. LARRA was primarily an effort to enhance protections for landowners facing forcible acquisition by the state. The act aimed to accomplish its objectives by, inter alia, providing opportunities for collective action among landowners and involving local democratic institutions.

LARRA covers the rules, procedures, and oversight structures to be used when the state seeks to exercise its power of "eminent domain," as well as the responsibilities of state and private entities to individuals and groups adversely affected by the exercise of this power. This includes justifying the public purpose served by the acquisition (LARRA imposed higher standards), protecting certain categories of land (such as irrigated farmland), and assessing the likely social and economic impacts that forced acquisition will produce. The cross-party support for LARRA reflected the widespread belief that the Land Acquisition Act 1894 (LAA), introduced by the British colonial government (though amended periodically after independence in 1947), was inconsistent with the requirements of modern democratic governance. This was reflected in the seeming ubiquity of land-related controversy. One study, which uncovered a total of 252 substantial land disputes in 2013, found that a quarter of India's districts experienced a significant level of land-for-industry conflict, and that a majority of the most contentious cases involved the compulsory acquisition of land by state agencies (Society for Promotion of Wasteland Development and Rights and Resources Initiative 2014).

LARRA is a complex piece of legislation, but three features are worth noting at the outset. First, the act acknowledges that state-induced development can deeply disrupt the basis of social, economic, and political life for entire communities. LARRA therefore accords both voice and compensation not just to landholders, but to stakeholders in the local economy more broadly. Second, LARRA acknowledges that a project's "public purpose" must be justified with clear reasoning and documentary evidence, rather than vague principles and unduly optimistic forecasts. Under LARRA, officials must attest that the "land proposed to be acquired is the absolute bare-minimum extent needed." Third, LARRA specifies a set of participatory mechanisms through which ordinary people can hold officials accountable for the fulfillment of particular social and economic rights. This set of hybrid legal entitlements, which integrates civil and political rights with economic and social rights, amounts to what James Manor and I have termed "governance rights" (Jenkins and Manor 2017). For instance, the "views of the affected families" must be included in a social impact assessment (SIA) report, which nongovernmental actors are centrally involved in preparing. LARRA requires the "consent" of 80 percent of local residents when land is to be acquired for private companies, or 70 percent for public-private partnerships. Crucially, people also participate in "social audits" of the implementation of rehabilitation and resettlement programs, under which both firms and the state have specific responsibilities (Jenkins 2013).

The United Progressive Alliance (UPA) government's commitment to steering the LARR Bill through a parliamentary minefield during its final years in office—after a similar effort during the UPA's first term fell short—was closely connected to the effects generated by a law passed in its very first year in office: the Special Economic Zones Act (SEZA) of 2005. The politically inflammatory process of implementing SEZA, which involved large-scale land acquisition to create low-tax, low-regulation, export-oriented enclaves, had a major impact on the perceived need to develop a new legal framework for addressing the long-standing problem of development-induced displacement. SEZA, and the way in which state and central governments used it, created political and institutional conditions in which an integrated policy—addressing both the compulsory acquisition of land for industrial or urbanization purposes and the needs of affected people—became seen as a pressing demand (Jenkins et al. 2014).

Committees and study groups had considered these questions over the previous two decades, providing the Manmohan Singh government with a wealth of data and legal analysis on which to base its reforms (Ramanathan 2008). It is a testament to the unpopularity of compulsory land acquisition that there was no organized opposition to the final version of the LARR Bill, though changes had been made along the way. Many MPs were from parties that were sitting in opposition in state legislatures, where they had been vocal critics of high-profile land acquisitions by state governments.

The adoption of LARRA was more than just a "routine" policy reform. The difference between ordinary and extraordinary reforms is more than just the legal difference between a duly enacted statute and a policy directive issued by the executive branch. Replacing the 1894 LAA with LARRA, according to one commentator, signaled the arrival of a "progressive vision" of governance.[1] The scope, complexity, and likely political impacts of India's LARRA qualify it as what Grindle (2000) calls an "audacious reform." Perhaps the most notable feature of the law's passage was that it was enacted over the vociferous objections of virtually every section of India's business community, including some of its most well-networked industry associations and politically connected conglomerates. It would be an understatement to say that this outcome—and its durability, despite adverse political circumstances—was not predicted by prevailing theories of state-business relations in India. In fact, most researchers have found business interests becoming ever more enmeshed within the operations of the policymaking machinery, as well as increasingly able to exert influence over political elites operating outside the formal administrative hierarchy.

Patterns of Influence:
Implementation and Policymaking

Kanchan Chandra has argued that regulating access to land is among the key means by which the Indian state continues to function, at least in parts, as a "patronage democracy" (Chandra 2015). After three decades of economic reform, patronage has not been banished, but rather "relocated"—away from controlling production and access to capital, and toward natural-resource rents and rationed opportunities to participate in sectors formerly "reserved" for state-owned (or small-scale) enterprises. This is consistent with former Reserve Bank of India governor Raghuram Rajan's claim that India has transitioned from the "license-permit raj" to a natural-resource-based form of rent-seeking.[2] The processes of acquiring and developing land presents businesses with a succession of veto players. They must trace title documents—sometimes through several prior transactions—and obtain environmental clearances and "no-objection certificates" from agricultural offices (if rural land) or planning-related offices (if urban land).

Chandra (2015) points to ambiguities in LARRA that could allow discretionary decision-making to persist, though perhaps with higher transaction costs. While under LARRA senior political and administrative officials retain considerable latitude in deciding whether to initiate land acquisition on behalf of a private business, LARRA imposed requirements that, in theory, constrain the capacity of bureaucrats to forcibly acquire land. Moreover, rigging consent processes, stacking oversight committees, drafting alternative justifications, and so forth are all costly forms of evasive action—both for the officials that must orchestrate them and for the businesses that must bankroll the process and bear the risk of uncertainty, including potential adverse reputational consequences if corporate abuses are disclosed. Chandra also notes that, in general, and with respect to land acquisition in particular, the state has become in some respects more "plural" than it once was: there are more points of contact with which corporate entities must engage in order to acquire and, just as importantly, to "convert" land from agricultural to industrial use. The additional points of contact include the wider array of departments and agencies that must be consulted as well as the multiple levels of government involved.

That the increasing plurality of the state creates greater scope for engagement by business actors is borne out in the case of land-related policy in a variety of ways. For instance, LARRA implies, though it does not specifically demand, an increased role for India's judiciary (Wahi 2017). The ambiguities in the statute, including its relationship to preexisting laws, creates scope for a greater variety of lawsuits—both individual petitions and class actions—on a much wider array of legal grounds. Even prior to LARRA's enactment, judicial action impinged considerably on land acquisition. But LARRA provides enough interpretive latitude to invite even more lawsuits, and thus more judicial pronouncements on how the statute should be implemented.[3] A particularly contentious point of litigation following LARRA's passage concerned whether an award of land acquired under an earlier statute (the LAA or a similar state-level act) could be nullified due to provisions (notably, regarding time limits for taking possession of land and paying compensation) contained within LARRA.[4]

Industry groups were seriously concerned about the LARR Bill before it became law, though as late as early 2013, just six months prior to its passage, two India-based executives from multinational firms with operations in the country remained convinced that probusiness forces in the Congress Party were powerful enough to at least stall the bill's progress until parliament was dissolved in advance of the general election due the following year.[5] This would have caused the bill to lapse, the same tactic used to kill off similar legislation at the conclusion of the UPA's first term in 2009. For two solid years, from late 2011 through late 2013, India's three premier business federations—Assocham, CII, and FICCI—submitted memoranda to parliamentary committees and made presentations to informal groups of MPs and party leaders. Lobbyists outlined the allegedly prohibitive costs that would be incurred, and the potentially huge delays to greenfield projects that would result, if the LARR bill were enacted (see FICCI n.d.; Associated Chambers of Commerce and Industry n.d.; "Land Acquisition Bill" 2011).

Still, it would be wrong to see LARRA's passage as purely a case of business defeat. One indication of this was the extent to which the LARR Bill evoked criticism from the progressive Left. This included leading figures from the country's most visible social movement network, the National Alliance of People's Movements (NAPM), which regarded the LARR Bill's safeguards—for individuals and communities—as far too weak.[6] The NAPM was in any case sharply critical of encoding into statute (as opposed to its incorporation into case law) the principle that forcibly acquiring land for corporate entities was a legitimate means of achieving state-defined objectives. This was all in addition to a steady stream of proposed policy revisions from across the political spectrum (Ghatak and Ghosh 2011). Even groups that were sympathetic to the government's intention to improve the capacities of local communities to act collectively to prevent or mitigate the effects of development-induced displacement were nevertheless unhappy with the direction in which the bill was headed after industry groups had successfully pressed for modifications. Critics pointed to the fairly wide spectrum of exemptions from procedural and other requirements introduced into the version of the LARR Bill that received cabinet approval in December 2012 (Rajalakshmi 2012). Even the UPA's rural development minister, the bill's greatest champion, admitted that the government had been forced to concede on a number of provisions due to the realities facing countries that seek private-sector-led industrialization (see "We Have to Strike a Balance" 2012).

LARRA was among the last major laws enacted by the Congress-led UPA government of Prime Minister Manmohan Singh, which governed from 2004 to 2014. It was passed just eight months prior to India's 2014 general election, in which the Bharatiya Janata Party (BJP) won enough seats to form a parliamentary majority under Prime Minister Modi. During the election campaign, the effectiveness of the UPA government's rights-based approach to addressing poverty was loudly called into question, and just as loudly defended.[7] Radically overhauling, if not outright repealing, LARRA was a major priority for business groups that had closely aligned themselves with the BJP. The legislation's procedural requirements were held up by business leaders and procorporate policy analysts as emblematic of the kinds of bureaucratic barriers faced by private sector investors. That LARRA was a key target for much of India's business community, as well as political leaders from within and beyond the BJP, was evident from the routinely harsh condemnation of the act's structure, concept, and provisions.

After taking power in May 2014, the BJP-led government immediately began making good on its promise to defang what one commentator had called "The Law from Hell" (Nayyar 2014). It was striking that Modi was willing to radically overhaul legislation that every member of parliament (MP) from his party voted for just months earlier. This reversal reflected, in part, the extent to which MPs who backed LARRA did so primarily to avoid being seen as opposed to a bill touted as "profarmer." After assuming office in 2014, BJP finance minister Arun Jaitley argued that overhauling LARRA was essential to the Modi government's much-publicized plan to create "smart cities" across India ("Government Examining Land Act" 2014). Whatever the motivation, four main reform options were available to the Modi government: outright repeal of LARRA, national legislative amendments to specific provisions, the framing of new regulations to counter the act's effects, and encouraging state governments to initiate countervailing reforms, whether through regulation, legislation, or a combination of the two. Despite Modi's lack of a majority in parliament's upper chamber, the Rajya Sabha, the business constituency that helped to get the BJP elected as well as the network of like-minded intellectuals that had gravitated toward the party in the years preceding Modi's election pressed for decisive action on land policy at the center, rather than leaving the matter up to state governments. This meant amending (or even repealing) LARRA in parliament.

With an eye toward convincing parties not affiliated with the National Democratic Alliance (NDA) to support LARRA reform in the Rajya Sabha, the Modi government attempted to tap into rumblings of discontent among state governments run by these parties. Policy suggestions from state governments were sought as part of a consultation process organized by the central government's Ministry of Rural Development. Officials from every state governed by a regional party submitted complaints about particular aspects of LARRA, while claiming not to be against the act "in principle." West Bengal complained about urban-rural compensation norms. Uttar Pradesh chief minister Akhilesh Yadav called for greater latitude for acquisitions to take place in "urgent" cases. Even Congress-ruled state governments refused to embrace LARRA wholeheartedly ("Most Congress States" 2015).

The key feature of the Modi government's LARRA Amendment Bill in 2015 was a series of exemptions from LARRA's two main procedural requirements: (1) that projects involving the acquisition of land be subjected to an SIA (and a defined process for conducting, disseminating, and acting on the SIA); and (2) that public authorities seeking to acquire land must obtain local "consent," undertaken through public meetings convened by local elected institutions, or panchayats. The Modi government's proposed exemptions were framed so broadly—applying to projects that sought, among other things, to promote "rural infrastructure"—that critics feared any project could thereby evade LARRA's land-owner and community protections.

Opposition to the Modi government's LARRA Amendment Bill began even before it was introduced in parliament. It was one of the few issues that brought opposition parties together. The opposition was also emboldened by concerns about the Modi government's reform effort that were expressed by BJP-affiliated organizations—notably, those linked to the Rashtriya Swayamsevak Sangh (RSS).[8] This all occurred against a backdrop of growing civil society activism that cast the Modi government's attempted rollback of land-owner and community protections under LARRA as emblematic of what movement leaders called the BJP's procorporate, antipoor bias.

As the difficulties facing the Modi government's reform effort began multiplying—including complaints from business leaders from India and abroad that the government lacked the perseverance necessary to execute politically fraught reforms—Congress and regional party MPs sensed an unparalleled opportunity to embarrass the new prime minister. Modi had publicly promised to overhaul LARRA in high-profile public speeches in early 2015 ("Modi Govt Hasn't Delivered" 2015; "BJP, Led by PM Narendra Modi" 2015). The Modi government resorted to issuing an executive "ordinance" to bring the LARRA Amendment Bill's provisions temporarily into effect. Such ordinances lapse if they are not followed by parliamentary action within a stipulated time frame. In August 2015, when the last of its successive ordinances was due to expire, the Modi government announced that its efforts to pass the LARRA Amendment Bill, to which it had made revisions in a failed effort to win over fence sitters in parliament, had come to at least a temporary end ("Land Ordinance Gets a Burial" 2015). Political resistance had grown too debilitating, and in any case support in the Rajya Sabha was not forthcoming. If the NDA was going to increase its presence in the upper chamber, it would need decisive victories in state assembly elections, including the Bihar polls of late 2015. That did not happen. Nevertheless, in mid-2016, the Joint Committee of Parliament examining the government's LARRA Amendment Bill continued to deliberate ("Parliamentary Panel" 2016).

Political Adaptation and State-Level Engagement

The impasse reached by the Modi government's reform effort underscored the extent to which the private sector's capacity to continue influencing land policy increasingly depends on its ability to engage with state governments, which possess primary rule-making authority on land-related matters. India's constitution tasks the president (acting on the advice of the prime minister) with determining whether, for subjects assigned jointly to the central and state governments, a state law that contradicts elements of a federal law can still stand (Verma 2014). Article 254(2) permits state governments to pass statutes on matters contained in the "Concurrent List" of competencies. Because item 42 on the concurrent list includes land issues, a state-by-state approach to amending LARRA is possible. However, there is uneven capacity among state governments when it comes to managing, within their respective jurisdictions, the politically salient distributional conflicts that inevitably accompany policy changes of this magnitude.

Responding to this situation, private firms have organized themselves in a variety of ways—by sector, on the basis of size, zonally, and so on—to influence land-related laws and regulations at the state level. Doing so required ongoing relationships with politicians and civil servants in each of the states where change was sought. A crucial advantage for industrialists and business associations has been that the officials with which they have interacted in the past (sometimes extensively) to ensure that land-related policies were *implemented* in their favor provide important entry points through which they are increasingly able to influence how policy is *formulated*. While navigating (and, often, subverting the intention of) existing rules, businesses engage with state-level actors through a variety of mechanisms—some of a contingent, transactional sort; others involving a longer-term, broader-spectrum relationship. Some involve political figures, while others primarily engage with administrative officers.

Assisting passage of a state-level LARRA amendment bill requires business interests to work—directly and through intermediaries—with the handful of senior officials who shape state government reform agendas. In addition, a much broader array of contacts, and a more subtle appreciation of the political sensitivities involved in each state's political terrain, has also proven invaluable. Arguably, state governments are better positioned than authorities in Delhi to gauge the likelihood and severity of potential backlash against reform in their respective jurisdictions. India's national leaders have recognized this since the founding of the republic. In the 1950s, state governments were handed the responsibility of executing land reforms, which meant anticipating and dealing with the political fallout. Similar tactics have been used by market-oriented reformers since economic liberalization took off in the early 1990s (Jenkins 1999, chapter 5).

Despite the cross-party support LARRA received when it passed in late 2013, it was never popular with politicians at the state level, for whom operating relatively free of regulatory restrictions when acquiring land is an important resource for maintaining a political machine. The complaints state governments voiced in the federal consultative process ended up informing subsequent state-level policy adjustments, whether through legislation that amended LARRA or through administrative means. The latter included ambiguous provisions within state-level operational rules for implementing LARRA.[9]

As of early 2017, three states—Rajasthan, Gujarat, and Tamil Nadu—had passed legislation that substantially diluted LARRA's landowner and community protections within their respective jurisdictions. In all three cases, business groups were closely involved not only in proposing reforms, but also the iterative process of revising policy proposals to address political considerations raised by elected officials. Participating in such an intensive process relies on the expanded reach of business actors, whose knowledge of local power equations has improved as they have built networks that include agents, brokers, public relations experts, valuation consultants, and other actors. In Maharashtra, for instance, Reliance Industries Limited has reportedly constructed networks of junior officials in the rural land bureaucracy, all coordinated by outreach officers, who handle relations with landholders and community leaders as well (Majumdar and Menezes 2014). Shaping and channeling information provided through these networks is among the many mechanisms through which business actors influence policymaking.

Rajasthan was the first state to develop state-level legislation to amend LARRA. The Rajasthan Land Acquisition Bill, introduced in September 2014, sought changes beyond what the NDA government would eventually include in its central amendment bill (Government of Rajasthan 2014). While the central LARRA amendment bill identified certain exemptions from the SIA process, Rajasthan's initial draft bill removed the SIA provisions entirely and lifted the rehabilitation obligations on private sector firms that were stipulated under LARRA.

This aggressively probusiness agenda was consistent with the Rajasthan government's other economic reform measures, such as making more than twenty state-level amendments to four federal labor laws, all designed to reduce restraints on management decision-making. This approach has had imitators in other states, including Madhya Pradesh ("After Rajasthan" 2014). The architects of these state-led reform efforts were primarily motivated by a desire to maximize potential illegal profits for the coterie of political and bureaucratic officials who exercise formal and informal veto power over elements of land transactions. It would be a stretch to classify Rajasthan's reform efforts as any sort of "developmentalism" worthy of the name. Far more consequential was the BJP chief minister's desire to be seen carrying out a key element of Modi's agenda.

Rajasthan's draft bill was prepared by an interdepartmental committee whose ministerial leadership collectively represented a cross-section of the Rajasthan BJP. The text of the Rajasthan bill emerged after consultations with state and business leaders and central government entities. One set of politically savvy business leaders advised the Rajasthan government to offer the appearance of improving on existing district-level compensation rates, by indicating that the state government would pay between five and nine times this rate, without acknowledging that this would still place compensation far below a genuine market valuation, which is what LARRA calls for. State government officials also consulted industrialists on a maximum size for compulsory acquisitions. A ceiling of 1,000 hectares (roughly 2,500 acres) in rural areas, and 200 hectares (or roughly 500 acres) in urban areas, was considered unlikely to adversely affect any foreseeable project proposals. Even this ceiling could be exceeded by pursuing multiple, smaller projects, which could then be amalgamated as needed. (An amalgamation strategy had been adopted, out of necessity, by the developers of the Mahindra World City SEZ near Jaipur.) Rajasthan's draft bill was cleared within a week by the chief minister's office—an unusually rapid turnaround. The bill was posted online—in English, with no Hindi translation—before being introduced in the state legislature. Because the BJP held more than three-quarters of the seats, officials expected few substantial changes to what had been proposed in the draft bill ("Scrapping Key UPA Measures:" 2014).

Rajasthan's drafting team reverted, wherever plausible, to provisions of the LAA 1894. For instance, Chapter 9 of the draft bill lifted much of its language from Chapter 7 of the 1894 act, including clause 40(b). Section 46 of the LAA 1894 was also reproduced in Rajasthan's draft bill, which specified monetary penalties and jail time for "obstructing acquisition of land," whether through protest actions or other means. When asked about the reintroduction of such provisions—almost word for word in some cases—a state government official replied: "Yes, it's a copy-paste job. And, we are proud of it . . . we were in a hurry, as we want to speed up investments in the state" ("Rajasthan Assembly" 2014).

The drafters also introduced far-reaching exemptions from LARRA provisions they could not completely disable. LARRA Section 2's local consent provisions would not apply to roads and highways, power and telecommunication lines, schools and hospitals, sports and tourism projects, and variously designated investment regions. Rajasthan's bill also sought to empower the state government to exempt other project categories that might be specified in the future. In addition, the state could avoid paying full compensation for land acquired for irrigation works or forest-preservation initiatives.

Just days after the Rajasthan bill was introduced, a coalition of activist groups submitted a memorandum to Chief Minister Vasundhara Raje that outlined their reasons for opposing its passage. The memorandum questioned the motivations driving the bill and the haste with which it was introduced, and called on the government to focus instead on drafting state-level operational rules that would allow LARRA to be effectively implemented (All India Kisan Sabha et al. 2014).

Once the central government announced it would be introducing the LARRA (Amendment) Bill, the Rajasthan government said it would postpone further action until the parliamentary process was completed.

Rajasthan, like many other states, would become the site of organized opposition to the Modi government's LARRA (Amendment) Ordinance. Farmers organizations, including but not limited to the RSS-affiliated Bharatiya Kisan Sangh (BKS), undertook protest actions, including in the state capital of Jaipur. Opposition from among Adivasi rights organizations, including the Dungarpur-based Rajasthan Adivasi Sangh Gundikuva and the Sirohi-based Jana Chetana Sansthan, added weight to what the government sought to portray as the "gripes" of a "small section of relatively well-off farmers." The movement even managed to elicit the support of at least one BJP legislator, an Adivasi leader who argued that "tribal land should not be acquired in the first place" ("Dissent Grows" 2015). Business associations sought to counter such claims, as well as complaints that the Modi government was aiding corporate India at the expense of farmers. As an official of a regional business association stated, "It's wrong to say that the ordinance is pro-industrialist. It is pro-growth" ("Dissent Grows" 2015).

In late 2014 and early 2015, a select committee of the Rajasthan assembly considered the state's LARRA amendment bill. Cabinet members consulted privately with a number of business leaders, including companies involved in developing industrial installations in the state. This was in addition to submissions from business associations, which were reported to have been coordinated across sectors, with reform priorities ranked from most to least important, which in this case placed SIA and community consent at the top, and compensation rates near the bottom.[10] One of Rajasthan's largest business groups promoted the idea of leaving most of the onerous procedural provisions in place while creating two avenues for discretionary implementation: exempted project categories and broader "urgency" provisions.[11] Ultimately, the committee recommended higher compensation levels and greater funding for resettlement and rehabilitation for people affected by land acquisition ("Rajasthan Land Acquisition Bill" 2015). For land acquired on behalf of private firms, project-affected people would receive either 30 percent of the compensation level paid to landowners (a tripling of the 10 percent specified in the original bill) or an annuity to be paid over twenty years. The committee also deleted language that stated that "no court shall take cognizance of any offence under this Act which is alleged to have been committed except on a complaint in writing made by the Collector."

These were important changes to the bill, but due to "full on" lobbying by "the most well-connected businessmen in Rajasthan and from outside," other provisions that reversed the progressive intent of LARRA were left unchanged.[12] Rajasthan's legislation would provide broad exemptions from "consent" requirements for "infrastructure" projects. The SIA procedure was also eviscerated. It is notable that "outside" business interests—firms based in other states, with little direct operational presence in Rajasthan—felt the need to engage local lobbyists and consultants to shape the bill. Organizations such as the CII and FICCI had originally focused on influencing the Modi government's national-level legislation, calculating that BJP-ruled states would do what the party's national leaders instructed. In practice, however, business groups had to lobby in each state where legislation was being formulated—a costly endeavor. In 2016, after several procedural delays, Rajasthan's bill became law. Many large-scale land acquisitions will now be able to proceed in Rajasthan without all the protections that apply in states that did not pass similar legislation.

Tamil Nadu's LARRA amendment legislation was passed in early 2015 with relatively little fanfare. This may have been due to Tamil Nadu's history of attempting to amend central legislation on land issues, such as the Land Acquisition (Tamil Nadu Amendment) Act 1948. The state-level legislation passed in 2015 stipulated that land acquired by the state under the Tamil Nadu Highways Act 2001, the Tamil Nadu Acquisition of Land for Industrial Purposes Act 1997, and the Tamil Nadu Acquisition of Land for Harijan Welfare Schemes Act 1978 would not fall within the purview of LARRA's consent and SIA requirements. Because more than three-quarters of land acquisition in Tamil Nadu takes place under these three statutes, LARRA's effects would be severely mitigated (Mukherjee and Shekhar 2015).

The Tamil Nadu government's approach was shaped in consultation with industry associations, most of which maintain good relations with both of the state's two main (regional) political parties. Tamil Nadu–based firms' fairly positive experience with land acquisition was part of the reason why private sector associations refrained from publicly demanding a more radical overhaul by the state government. For a rapidly industrializing state, Tamil Nadu has been relatively successful in avoiding the politicization of land acquisition. As Vijayabaskar has argued, the state has since the late 1980s developed mechanisms for ensuring that landowners are offered decent terms. Agriculturalists have also had less reason to cling to their land thanks to economic opportunities in the state and their proven ability to diversify into them (Vijayabaskar 2010).

Another part of the explanation for the relatively muted political resistance to state-led land acquisition in Tamil Nadu was the willingness of business groups to work closely with agencies such as the State Industries Promotion Corporation of Tamil Nadu (SIPCOT) to reduce the political vulnerability of their projects. In 2011, just as Congress leader Rahul Gandhi was seeking to align himself (and his party) with high-profile land-related protest movements in north India, the president of the Tamil Nadu Association of Infrastructure Developers stated that Tamil Nadu businesses were willing to locate away from the state capital of Chennai. A business-backed strategy of industrial dispersal helped to avoid a familiar cycle found in other states—of protest action, leading to overreaction by state governments, followed by private sector disillusionment, and ultimately contamination of the political climate such that future acquisitions would face even greater uncertainty ("Tamil Nadu Shows the Way" 2011). Tamil Nadu's accompanying industrial policy specified that two-thirds of the industrial zones planned for the state would be at least two hundred kilometers from major cities, mainly in or near Tier 2 and Tier 3 towns ("Tamil Nadu Shows the Way" 2011). Such locations might seem to offer fertile soil for fierce resistance among farmers, who often have vocal and influential associations at the district level. But dispersing conflicts can also lead to their geographic containment, especially when acquisition takes place away from the media glare of the state capital, or in outlying land markets where lower levels of speculation make potential sellers more willing to engage in voluntary transactions rather than compulsory acquisition.

The third state to attempt a LARRA amendment act was Gujarat, where Modi served three terms as chief minister. Gujarat was a place of experimentation regarding methods for evading land acquisition norms as far back as the mid-2000s, when a Modi-led state government developed a system for "land pooling." This became a model for other state governments and the private sector actors with whom they would collaborate on the framing of regulations. In 2015, Gujarat accelerated progress on a long-discussed state-level land acquisition bill. But after the national LARRA amendment bill encountered legislative gridlock, the state government, over which the prime minister's political organization maintains control, built its legislation entirely around the dismantling of LARRA. Indeed, when introduced in January 2016, Gujarat's bill was named the Right to Fair Compensation and Transparency in Land Acquisition, Rehabilitation and Resettlement (Gujarat Amendment) Bill 2016.

Because Rajasthan drafted its amendment bill before Modi's government introduced legislation in New Delhi, Rajasthan's proposed legislation was not based on the centrally agreed "model." Rajasthan's draft bill had many homegrown features. By contrast, the LARRA amendment bill that Gujarat passed in 2016 hewed closely to the direction established by the central government. Gujarat's bill targeted the SIA process, but did so on the basis of broadly conceived exemptions—including "national security," a category that is poised to grow as India's IT and engineering companies expand their defense-related work. The Gujarat bill exempted (from LARRA procedures) any land acquired for "industrial corridors" and similar production or export zones. Opposition parties in the state claimed the bill was designed to please business interests, while social activists asserted that representatives of the Adani Group drafted key portions of the bill ("Gujarat Government" 2016; "Farmers Rally" 2016). The Adani Group's actions in Jharkhand had fueled opposition to proposed regulatory responses to LARRA in that state as well ("J'khand Oppn Demands Commission" 2016; Srivastava 2016; "Adani Group Got Land" 2014).

In addition to lobbying state-level governments *directly*, business groups have sought to influence state-level legislative and regulatory action *indirectly* as well. Influencing change at the state level, in fact, requires connections and leverage in New Delhi—because it is through central ministries and agencies that policy convergence across states is increasingly driven. The Ministries of Rural Development, Commerce, and Urban Development, as well as the Planning Commission and the National Advisory Council, were significant sites of policy diffusion regarding land-related matters during the UPA government. During the Modi government, the Rural Development Ministry, as we have seen, has played a similar role—at least insofar as it guided federal consultations on LARRA reform. Another site for policy diffusion under the Modi government is the Niti Aayog (or Policy Commission), a central government entity the Modi government created in 2014 to replace India's Planning Commission. Through the Niti Aayog and other channels, business actors have been able to shape policymaking at an earlier phase. And through partnership with government agencies, the CII, FICCI, and KPMG have collaborated to monitor reform activity across India's states (KPMG et al. 2015).

The viability of a state-by-state approach to overhauling LARRA was advocated by Niti Aayog vice chair Arvind Panagariya, though only after the national-level reform legislation became hopelessly stalled ("Centre's Bill on Hold" 2015). Panagariya pointed specifically to Tamil Nadu's legislation as a model that other states should consider emulating, though the differences between prior legislative frameworks in other states would require state-specific reform strategies. The Rajasthan government's (revised) approach to amending LARRA was also showcased as a potential model. At a July 2015 meeting of the Niti Aayog governing council, Rajasthan's chief minister outlined the ways in which a Rajasthan-style bill could help to fulfill the same purposes as the national LARRA amendment ordinance ("Land Bill to Expedite Development" 2015). FICCI and the CII offered "technical assistance" to help other state governments to take locally appropriate action.

Widening and Deepening Private Sector Engagement in Land Policy

Some legislative and regulatory changes that affect access to, ownership of, and use of land are effected through measures that are not primarily concerned with land, including—as we will see below—policy on industrial development and urban planning. Businesses are thus strongly incentivized to seek influence on policy issues beyond land acquisition. In doing so, they have had to adapt to local circumstances. But despite differences in how the process of amending LARRA was executed in Rajasthan, Tamil Nadu, and Gujarat, these three states had a lot in common. All three were known for the relatively low levels of political mobilization against land acquisition for industrial projects such as special economic zones. As noted above, several state-level economic and administrative factors that existed prior to the reform effort helped to explain why resistance to SEZ projects in Tamil Nadu was relatively weak, lacking in party-political support, and usually short-lived. In Rajasthan, according to Levien's analysis of SEZs in peri-urban Jaipur, the comparatively muted resistance to land acquisition stemmed from the entry of dominant social groups into land brokerage roles, which enlisted them into actions that dampened opposition from those further down local socioeconomic hierarchies.[13]

The reform agenda that the private sector must increasingly contend with at the state level has expanded along two dimensions: horizontally (making business engagement broader) and vertically (making it deeper). The horizontal axis refers to a widening of policy issues on which business and state officials collaborate, including both the land-related provisions in investment-incentive programs and regulations governing urban planning. For instance, Gujarat's 2009 special investment regions (SIRs) policy created expedited procedures for acquiring land, and SIRs are among the "economic infrastructure" projects whose obligations under LARRA are specifically waived under the provisions of the state's LARRA (amendment) act.

In Maharashtra, business groups, collaborating closely with officials with links to leading political figures, have pursued both types of agenda-broadening strategies to shape land-related regulations. A telling instance was a 2008 government order passed by the state's Urban Development Department (UDD). Citing the statutory authority provided by the Maharashtra Regional and Town Planning Act (MRTPA) 1966, the UDD announced that for all SEZs in Maharashtra, the state government would designate the SEZ's private sector developer/promoter as the "Special Planning Authority" (SPA) (Government of Maharashtra 2008). Section 40 of the MRTPA devolves to the SPA powers relating to building approvals, land use, taxes, and infrastructure. Businesses that were at the time planning industrial zones (under one of the many schemes and designations then in use) pressed for this provision to be included in the 2008 government order. Since the passage of LARRA in 2013, and the subsequent failure of the Modi government to substantially amend it, industrialists have prioritized the preservation and expansion of such regulations, which prevent local councils from blocking state-aided land acquisitions.

A major reason business directs its lobbying efforts into adjacent policy areas—which have a bearing on land availability but are not contained within land acquisition legislation itself—is to protect the clientelist practices built into existing regulations. Such arcane rules are always in danger of being undercut, or superseded, by new legislation or more recent regulatory decisions. An example is the Rajasthan Disposal of Land Rules 1979, which pertain to land obtained by the Rajasthan State Industrial Development and Investment Corporation (RIICO). The rules were devised pursuant to the statute that authorized RIICO's creation as well as subsequent decisions of its management. The Disposal of Land Rules not only do not bar resale of land allocated to private firms; notifications and circulars issued under these rules contain loopholes for those business-constraining provisions that do exist. One consultant noted that if "you pay RIICO officials a commission . . . they will call you in advance whenever a new industrial area is set up." Because no fully costed proposal is required to apply for a RIICO plot, the project's purpose "could be an *agarbatti* [incense] manufacturing project, which requires minimum investment." The lax rules allow firms to "hold the land as long as you want, until you want to sell it further." In fact, "Even if you do not start production, if you are influential enough you will not lose the land" (Sharma 2014). Rajasthan's business communities, both land speculators and otherwise legitimate firms seeking a form of hedging in case their projects are not successful, seek to preserve these lax regulations, which include flexible built-up-area limits and scope for changing the sector in which business is to be conducted.[14]

The second dimension of an expanded private sector policy-reform agenda on land involves a "deepening" of business engagement with processes directly related to land but transcending eminent domain. Deepening in this respect refers to four areas: (1) land conversion; (2) land pooling; (3) land certification; and (4) land leasing. In all four areas, policy reform is being undertaken by at least some states, with both direct and indirect input from business groups.

Several states have explored options for reforming the rules concerning conversion of land from one use to another. Some of this work began during the UPA government, particularly changes proposed within the framework of the JNNURM program (Government of India 2008). The Maharashtra government began studying methods for easing land conversion procedures soon after BJP chief minister Devendra Fadnavis was elected in 2014. Business leaders were consulted on ways of amending rules framed under the Maharashtra Land Revenue Code 1966. Officials reported that early action was sought to take advantage of the government's honeymoon period, indicating that they anticipated potential controversy in the state legislature.[15] In early 2015, the state government announced that its focus was on allowing farmland and government-owned land to be used for residential development—an initiative publicly justified by the state's "housing crisis," but also driven by the politically connected "builders' lobby" ("State Plans Easier Land Use" 2015). Other states, including Karnataka and Odisha, have pursued legislative and regulatory changes to ease the process of land conversion. Commercial property developers are typically based within the state where they do business, with close ties to government officials and political parties. The impulse to accommodate the policy preferences of such groups is strong, particularly when state-specific business groups see "outside" businesses engaged in large-scale land acquisition for industrial installations.

Land pooling has been an increasingly popular mechanism for ensuring land availability for industrial and infrastructural purposes. Land pooling does not involve the government forcibly obtaining privately owned property. Instead, landowners are encouraged to voluntarily cede their land in exchange for a stake in a site's future development. The Gujarat government, a leader in the field of land pooling, consulted closely with business groups in the state, including regional chapters of national chambers, when developing its approach from 2005 onward. Land pooling was used for scores of projects, and is seen to have undercut resistance from landowners, thus reducing the likelihood of drawn-out controversy. Land pooling in Gujarat has not been without its critics. The Dholera SIR, announced in 2007, revealed fault lines concerning the policy. Conceived as one of two dozen industrial hubs along the Delhi-Mumbai Industrial Corridor (DMIC), the Dholera project affected fifty thousand people, with land spread over twenty-two villages. The project revived when Modi became prime minister, but continued to attract complaints from local people ("Land Pooling Looks Fertile" 2016). One analysis found that planning, environmental, and other regulations had been repeatedly violated, despite assurances from elected officials that corrective action would be taken (Sampat 2016).

Andhra Pradesh chief minister Chandrababu Naidu was among the loudest voices denouncing LARRA's highly detailed procedures as too costly and time-consuming for investors seeking to respond to market signals. After taking office in 2014, Naidu's government, like several others, sought "workarounds" for LARRA strictures.[16] In developing a state-level policy, Naidu was criticized for diluting safeguards found in other states' land-pooling models so as to accommodate his corporate backers. The influence of business interests on Naidu's approach to land acquisition was a source of controversy from early in his tenure. A study team of Andhra Pradesh officials that visited another state was reported to have traveled in three aircraft supplied by companies interested in securing building contracts with the Andhra Pradesh government, and with the assistance of a member of parliament with an indirect stake in a number of business ventures ("Naidu Smitten" 2014). In Andhra Pradesh, much of the area to be occupied by the new state capital was obtained through a land-pooling system. By the end of 2015, the government had acquired thirty-three thousand acres of land. Building contractors and other business interests allegedly supplied legal experts to the government on an informal, pro bono basis to assist in devising a strategy for completing the assembly of the required land. The solution decided upon was to issue a government order that would exempt the project from the procedures contained within LARRA, and to do so during the period when the Modi government's LARRA Amendment Ordinance was in effect ("AP Issues GO" 2015). This would allow the state government to initiate forcible acquisition procedures against landowners that had elected not to take part in the (voluntary) land-pooling process. This approach was hailed as an effective public-private partnership, though the adverse impacts may well become a potent political issue for opposition parties in the years ahead, including with respect to a proposed new airport ("Land Acquisition: A New Capital City" 2015; "Land Pooling for Gannavaram Airport Expansion" 2016).

Reforming the process of securing transferrable land titles has been on state-level policy agendas since the 1990s. But legislative action with the aid of business interests has picked up in recent years (World Bank 2007). The first state to pass substantial legislation was Rajasthan. In April 2016, it passed the Rajasthan Urban Land (Certification of Titles) Act 2016. The law provides a means for landowners to obtain clear title to their property. It establishes an Urban Land Title Certification Authority, where title claims can be submitted and reviewed (Betala 2016). After issuing applicants with a provisional certification of title, two years must elapse before a fully authenticated title will be registered. The state government has committed to acting as a guarantor for title authenticated in this way, shielding landowners (and buyers) from future legal liability should claims arise from third parties. One of the laws' purposes was to increase incentives for willing-buyer/willing-seller transactions in Rajasthan's cities and towns. The legislation was among the reform proposals presented by a select group of Rajasthan's business leaders at a meeting held at the chief minister's residence in January 2014, very soon after the election that brought the BJP to power in the state. The meeting's purpose was to identify ways of streamlining state acquisition of land for industrial development. But through contacts in RIICO and the secretariat, two leading firms introduced proposals to ease constraints on private transactions, notably the lack of clear titles, the pursuit of which was a major reason why firms seek state help in acquiring land. Titles issued by governments are much harder, if not impossible, to challenge in court. This is another example of policy collaboration between state governments and private industry that is informed by an awareness of the political constraints facing reformers.

It is notable that even under Rajasthan's new Urban Land (Certification of Titles) Act, significant rent-seeking opportunities will exist. Officials who do the authenticating, and the political leaders who appoint these officials and to whom they answer, will be in a position of leverage over owners. There is scope for biased application of the rules on, for instance, what constitutes sufficient evidence for obtaining authentication certificates. Industrial firms seeking to purchase land will be incentivized to work with local brokers and agents to assist potential sellers to get their titles at least provisionally authenticated through the new regulatory authority. Private sector efforts to influence rule-*making*, in other words, are informed by an understanding of the need for ongoing business engagement in the process of rule *implementation*.

Land leasing is another area in which a deepening of business engagement with government officials on legal and regulatory matters has moved forward. Just as it did with state-level land acquisition legislation, the Government of India's Niti Aayog sought to disseminate workable approaches. It began this new direction just a week after the prime minister announced that the government would not be repromulgating its LARRA amendment ordinance.[17] Niti Aayog's vice chair became a major advocate for reforms to ease the regulatory constraints on leasing agricultural land, calling it a "win-win" opportunity for state governments (Panagariya 2015). At the end of March 2016, the Niti Aayog announced that a study panel appointed to develop a "model" land leasing statute had completed its work (Expert Committee on Land Leasing 2016). While the expert committee's report noted consultations with stakeholder categories, such as farmers' organizations and lawyers, it did not specifically indicate that industrialists were part of this exercise (Expert Committee on Land Leasing 2016, 55). Indeed, the focus of the model act is agriculture and allied activities. Still, there are reasonable grounds for suspecting that any such law would be part of a larger effort to increase land availability for industrial purposes. In fact, the Niti Aayog vice chair stated that due to "the difficulties in land acquisition under the 2013 land acquisition law, states wishing to facilitate industrialisation can further benefit from liberal land leasing if they simultaneously liberalise the use of agricultural land for non-agricultural purposes." States could overcome significant barriers through an "amendment of the law to permit non-agricultural use or by the introduction of time-bound clearances of applications for the conversion of agricultural land use in the implementing regulations."

Conclusion

This chapter has examined India's recent process of land acquisition reform. This case illustrates some of the limits on business influence over national policy reform as well as the political adaptability of the private sector, which has increased its engagement with state-level governments to achieve its policy objectives. The chapter argues that the influence of business lobbies over land policy *reform* depends in part on their ability to leverage prior relationships with state governments on issues of land policy *implementation*. It furthermore argues that business engagement with state-level officials on land policy increasingly involves a reform agenda that is both wider (including adjacent policy domains such as investment-incentive programs and urban-planning norms) and deeper (including issues beyond acquisition, to include land conversion, pooling, titling, and leasing).

By way of conclusion, let us consider factors that might influence the durability of these trends. Among the most significant is the fragmentation among various groups of private sector actors. This can harm the prospects for state-level land policy reform. Divergent interests, or even just differences in business culture, can seriously undercut the capacity for collective action among private sector actors, particularly when long-term engagement across a wider and deeper policy space is required, as this chapter has argued. Despite the considerable competition among business associations in the post-1980 era, a wide range of sectoral associations and federated chambers of commerce have shown considerable capacity for coordination, both before and after LARRA was enacted. One emergent fault line, however, is between a section of smaller, mainly locally based property development firms and a more recently arrived set of much larger companies from outside a given state. Some of these "outside" investors are backed by large sums of foreign capital earmarked specifically for property development ("Billionaire Piramal" 2015). Not surprisingly, a subnational protectionist impulse is evident, at least rhetorically, among regional business elites in some states. For instance, it was allegedly to assist medium-sized, state-level business interests that the Goa government passed the Land Acquisition (Goa Amendment) Act 2009 ("Legislature within Domain" 2016). The fear of displacement afflicts less nimble local business actors in many states. Advocating to preserve laws and regulations that, de facto, privilege local knowledge and connections, and thus benefit local firms, is a rational strategy under such circumstances—one that undermines, rather than supports, promarket reform.

Another potential challenge to even greater private sector policy influence at the state level is the acute vulnerability of land issues to politicization. As many parts of India have experienced firsthand, disputes over dispossession can very quickly transform a seemingly rational-legal process of land acquisition into a pitched battle between competing ideological or identity-based factions within local, district, and state politics. The implications for the policymaking and implementing machinery—and access by business thereto—can be enormous, as was the case in Odisha once opposition to the $12 billion POSCO iron-and-steel project began to be seen as affecting voting patterns among Adivasis.

Despite these and other headwinds, efforts by business groups to influence state-level land policy face certain advantageous conditions. The considerable exposure that Indian firms now have with official implementation machineries has endowed them with networks of contacts at the middle rungs of state administration who can be mobilized to persuade more senior officials to issue rule changes or rule "clarifications" in the interest of "administrative efficiency," presumably in exchange for a share of any illicit proceeds. In Rajasthan, these networks include managers in RIICO. For much of the period since it came into being at the end of the 1960s, just as the state-directed model of development was arguably in its most ascendant phase, RIICO focused on supplying credit to often politically affiliated borrowers, who for the same reason are difficult to re-coup debts from, and therefore a perennial budgetary liability. Since the 1990s, however, RIICO has become more intensively involved in acquiring land for in-dustry. It has been criticized for amassing far more land than is required for ex-isting or proposed projects. One analysis found that only one-third of the land RIICO acquired for industry was being used for industrial purposes (Sharma 2014). Similar discrepancies exist in other states, such as Karnataka and Madhya Pradesh (Government of India 2011). Maintaining ties to RIICO's managerial cadre, whether directly or through intermediary consultants, has been highly beneficial to business groups—not least because these officials serve as a con-duit to other parts of the civil service. The contacts developed through nodal agencies such as Rajasthan's erstwhile Bureau of Industrial Promotion become entry points for the private sector into policy discussions.

The influence of business interests on land policy issues appears set to con-tinue.[18] Having navigated the political currents that shape decision-making by elected leaders, private sector actors are arguably better positioned now than ever to assist state governments in addressing crucial constraints on land policy reform and implementation. Still, the substance of existing and proposed laws, and how they are being (or will be) implemented, has spurred mobilization and protest action by both movement groups and regional business interests who fear being sidelined by the arrival of better-resourced outsiders. Together, these sources of resistance, combined with increasingly effective legal challenges, may make it difficult in practice for business to exploit newly created regional loopholes in order to undertake (state facilitated) land acquisition for industrial and infrastructural purposes.

References

"Adani Group Got Land at Cheapest Rates in Modi's Gujarat." 2014. *Business Standard*, April 26. http://www.business-standard.com/article/companies/adani-group-got-land-at-cheapest-rates-in-modi-s-gujarat-114042501228_1.html.

"After Rajasthan, Madhya Pradesh to Tweak Labor Laws." 2014. *Centennial Asia Advisors*, September 11. http://www.centennialasia.com/after-rajasthan-madhya-pradesh-to-tweak-labour-laws-11-september-2014.

All India Kisan Sabha, National Alliance of People's Movements, Peoples Union for Civil Liberties (Rajasthan). 2014. "Memorandum to Chief Minister Vasundhara Raje on the Proposed Rajasthan Land Acquisition Bill 2014." September 19. Jaipur.

"AP Issues GO, Notification under Land Acquisition Act." 2015. *The Hindu*, May 15.

Associated Chambers of Commerce and Industry. N.d. "Land Acquisition, Resettlement and Rehabilitation Bill 2011: A Reaction. www.assocham.org/prels/shownews.php?id=3059.

Betala, Vinay. 2016. "Policy Brief: The Rajasthan Urban Land (Certification of Titles) Act 2016. Fitch/India Ratings and Research Group, April. http://www.indiainfoline.com/article/news-top-story/land-titling-law-to-ease-land-acquisition-india-ratings-116042000280_1.html.

Bhagwati, Jagdish N., and Arvind Panagariya. 2013. *Why Growth Matters: How Economic Growth in India Reduced Poverty and the Lessons for Other Developing Countries*. New York: PublicAffairs.

"Billionaire Piramal Seeks India Land with Warburg War Chest." 2015. *Bloomberg*, August 13. http://www.bloomberg.com/news/articles/2015-08-13/billionaire-piramal-seeking-india-land-with-warburg-war-chest.

"BJP, Led by PM Narendra Modi, to Clear the Air on Land Bill." 2015. *Economic Times*, April 5.

"Centre Opposes Reliance Plea against New Land Act Clause." 2016. *Indian Express*, February 19. http://indianexpress.com/article/india/india-news-india/centre-opposes-reliance-plea-against-new-land-act-clause/.

"Centre's Bill on Hold, States Move on Land acquisition." 2015. *Indian Express*, December 25. http://indianexpress.com/article/india/india-news-india/centres-bill-on-hold-states-move-on-land-acquisition/.

Chandra, Kanchan. 2015. "The New Indian State: The Relocation of Patronage in the Post-liberalisation Economy." *Economic and Political Weekly* 50 (41): 46–58.

"Dissent Grows against NDA'S Land Acquisition Ordinance." 2015. *Hindustan Times*, January 25. http://www.hindustantimes.com/india/dissent-grows-against-nda-s-land-acquisition-ordinance/story-OKXCCr0DReBt2RY4FgQ9OK.html.

Drèze, Jean, and Amartya Sen. 2013. *An Uncertain Glory: India and Its Contradictions*. Princeton, NJ: Princeton University Press.

Expert Committee on Land Leasing. 2016. "The Report of the Expert Committee on Land Leasing (NITI Aayog)." March 31. http://niti.gov.in/mgov_file/Final_Report_Expert_Group_on_Land_Leasing.pdf. Delhi: NITI Aayog.

"Farmers Rally on Apr 24 to Protest Dholera SIR." 2016. *Ahmedabad Mirror*, March 16. http://www.ahmedabadmirror.com/news/india/Farmers-rally-on-Apr-24-to-protest-Dholera-SIR/articleshow/51414735.cms.

FICCI (Federation of Indian Chambers of Commerce and Industry). N.d. "Memorandum: The Land Acquisition, Rehabilitation and Resettlement Bill 2011 (Submission to Lok Sabha Select Committee)."

Ghatak, Maitreesh, and Parikshit Ghosh. 2011. "The Land Acquisition Bill: A Critique and a Proposal." *Economic and Political Weekly* 46 (41): 65–72.

"Government Examining Land Act Provisions to Fix States' Concerns: Minister." 2014. *Zee News*, December 1. http://zeenews.india.com/news/india/govt-examining-land-act-provisions-to-fix-states-concerns-minister_1507783.html.

Government of India. 2008. "Legal and Procedural Framework For Conversion Of Agricultural Land To Non-Agricultural Purposes." Ministry of Urban Development. http://jnnurm.nic.in/wp-content/uploads/2011/01/Optional_Primer_primer.AGRICULTURAL.pdf.

———. 2011. "Performance Audit on Acquisition and Allotment of Land by Karnataka Industrial Area Development Board of Government of Karnataka." New Delhi: Comptroller and Auditor General of India. http://www.saiindia.gov.in/content/report-2011-performance-audit-acquisition-and-allotment-land-karnataka-industrial-area.

Government of Maharashtra. 2008. Government Order No. TPB 4308/465/CR-64/2008/UD-11, May 2. Mumbai: Urban Development Department.

Government of Rajasthan, Department of Law and Legal Affairs. 2014. Rajasthan Land Acquisition Bill 2014.

Grindle, Merilee Serrill. 2000. *Audacious Reforms: Institutional Invention and Democracy in Latin America*. Baltimore: Johns Hopkins University Press.

"Gujarat: After RIL, Essar, Cement Firm Challenge Land Act Clause." 2016. *Indian Express*, April 12.

"Gujarat Government Diluted UPA Land Act for Sake of Industrialists: Congress." 2016. *DNA*, March 31. www.dnaindia.com/india/report-gujarat-govt-diluted-upa-land-act-for-sake-of-industrialists-congress-2196674.

"HC Quashes Land Acquisition for Dewas-Shivpuri Road Widening." 2016. *Times of India*, March 18. timesofindia.com/city/indore/HC-quashes-land-acquisition-for-Dewas-Shivpuri-road-widening/articleshow/51451911.cms.

"India Inc Petitions Govt: From Land Laws to Levy, Ease It All." 2015. *Indian Express*, September 8. http://indianexpress.com/article/india/india-others/india-inc-petitions-govt-from-land-laws-to-levy-ease-it-all/.

"India Most Attractive Investment Destination: EY Survey." 2015. *Hindu Businessline*, October 14. www.investindia.gov.in/ey-attractiveness-survey/.

"J'khand Oppn Demands Commission on Land Acquisition Issues." 2016. *Outlook*, March 9. http://www.outlookindia.com/newswire/story/jkhand-oppn-demands-commission-on-land-acquisition-issues/932978.

Jenkins, Rob. 1999. *Democratic Politics and Economic Reform in India*. Cambridge: Cambridge University Press.

———. 2013. "Land, Rights, and Reform." *Pacific Affairs* 86 (3): 591–612.

Jenkins, Rob, Loraine Kennedy, and Partha Mukhopadhyay, eds. 2014. *Power, Policy and Protest: The Politics of India's Special Economic Zones*. Delhi: Oxford University Press.

Jenkins, Rob, and James Manor. 2017. *Politics and the Right to Work: India's National Rural Employment Guarantee Act*. New York: Oxford University Press.

KPMG, Confederation of Indian Industry, Federation of Indian Chambers of Commerce and Industry, and World Bank. 2015. "Assessment of State Implementation of Business Reforms." Delhi. https://www.kpmg.com/DK/en/.../kpmg-re-invest-survey-2015.pdf.

Kohli, Atul. 2012. *Poverty Amid Plenty in the New India*. Cambridge: Cambridge University Press.

"Land Acquisition: A New Capital City in Farmland." 2015. *Indian Express*, December 25. http://indianexpress.com/article/india/india-news-india/land-acquisition-a-new-capital-city-in-farmland/.

"Land Acquisition Bill Will Push Up Prices Five Times: CII Chief." 2011. *Hindu BusinessLine*, November 9.

"Land Bill to Expedite Development in Rajasthan: CM." 2015. *Times of India*, July 16. http://timesofindia.indiatimes.com/india/Land-Bill-to-expedite-development-in-Rajasthan-CM/articleshow/48091652.cms?from=mdr.

"Land Ordinance Gets a Burial." 2015. *The Hindu*, August 31.

"Land Pooling for Gannavaram Airport Expansion." 2016. *Times of India*, February 22. http://timesofindia.indiatimes.com/city/hyderabad/Land-Pooling-for-Gannavaram-Airport-Expansion/articleshow/51087854.cms?from=mdr.

"Land Pooling Looks Fertile but Dholera Farmers Not Reaping the Benefits." 2016. *Hindustan Times*, January 21. http://www.hindustantimes.com/india/land-pooling-looks-fertile-but-dholera-farmers-not-reaping-benefits/story-h0jvIaSWO5fklUADQYB9cN.html.

"Legislature within Domain to Bring Amendment Retrospectively: SC." 2016. *Times of India*, March 31. http://timesofindia.indiatimes.com/city/goa/Legislature-within-domain-to-bring-amendment-retrospectively-SC/articleshow/51629358.cms.

Levien, Michael. 2015. "From Primitive Accumulation to Regimes of Dispossession: Theses on India's Land Question." *Economic and Political Weekly* 50 (22): 146–57.

Majumdar, Rohit, and Benita Menezes. 2014. "Maharashtra: Institutional Politics and the Framing of Resistance." In *Power, Policy and Protest: The Politics of India's Special Economic Zones*, ed. R. Jenkins, L. Kennedy, and P. Mukhopadhyay, 239–71. Delhi: Oxford University Press.

"Modi Govt Hasn't Delivered on Promised Reforms." 2015. *CNBC: Money Control*, July 31. http://www.moneycontrol.com/news/economy/modi-govt-hasnt-deliveredpromised-reforms-moodys_2241381.html.

"Most Congress States Had Doubts on Original Land Acquisition Act." 2015. *Economic Times*, February 25. http://articles.economictimes.indiatimes.com/2015-02-25/news/59500123_1_land-acquisition-act-resettlement-act-land-amendment-bill.

Mukherjee, Ritika, and Sumit Shekhar. 2015. "Failure to Amend Land Law to Exacerbate Sense of 'Policy Drift.'" Mumbai: Ambit Capital, August 10. http://reports.ambitcapital.com/reports/Ambit_Economy_ExpertNote_Failuretoamendlandlaw_10Aug2015.pdf.

"Naidu Smitten by Naya Raipur Model, but Does the Opposite." 2014. *Times of India*, September 24. http://www.greatandhra.com/politics/political-news/naidu-smitten-by-naya-raipur-model-but-does-the-opposite-60026.html.

Nayyar, Dhiraj. 2014. "India's Law from Hell." *BloombergView*, November 7. www.bloombergview.com/articles/2014-11-07/indias-law-from-hell.

"Pachalam ROB: Landowners Seek Vigilance Probe." 2016. *Times of India*, February 19. http://timesofindia.indiatimes.com/city/kochi/Pachalam-ROB-Landowners-seek-vigilance-probe/articleshow/51051137.cms.

Panagariya, Arvind. 2015. "Land Leasing: A Big Win-Win Reform for the States," Delhi: Niti Aayog.

"Parliamentary Panel Gets Sixth Extension on Land Bill after Many States Failed to Furnish Vital Details." 2016. *Firstpost*, March 16. http://m.firstpost.com/india/parliamentary-panel-gets-sixth-extension-on-land-bill-after-many-states-failed-to-furnish-vital-details-2678398.html?utm_source=FP_CAT_LATEST_NEWS.

Rajalakshmi, T. K. 2012. "A Law and Its Losers." *Frontline*, December 29.

"Rajasthan Assembly to Push Land Bill Today." 2014. *Business Standard*, September 15. http://wap.business-standard.com/article/economy-policy/rajasthan-assembly-to-push-land-bill-today-114091400786_1.html.

"Rajasthan Land Acquisition Bill: Select Committee Insists on Higher Compensation." 2015. *Indian Express*, February 26. http://indianexpress.com/article/india/india-others/rajasthan-land-acquisition-bill-select-committee-insists-on-higher-compensation/.

Ramanathan, Usha. 2008. "Eminent Domain, Protest and the Discourse on Rehabilitation." In *Can Compensation Prevent Impoverishment? Reforming Resettlement through Investment and Benefit-Sharing*, ed. M. M. Cernea and H. M. Mathur. New Delhi: Oxford University Press.

"RBI Governor Raghuram Rajan Warns against 'Appellate Raj.'" 2015. *DNA*, February 21. http://www.dnaindia.com/money/report-rbi-governor-raghuram-rajan-warns-against-appellate-raj-2062771.

"Repeal the Land Acquisition Act!" 2011. "*New Red Indian*" blog, August 2. http://newredindian.wordpress.com/2011/08/02/repeal-the-land-acquisition-act/.

"RSS Affiliates Up in Arms against Modi Govt on Land Acquisition Bill." 2015. *Indian Express*, June 21. http://indianexpress.com/article/india/india-others/rss-affiliates-up-in-arms-against-modi-govt-on-land-acquisition-bill/.

Sampat, Preeti. 2016. "Dholera: The Emperor's New City." *Economic and Political Weekly* 51 (17): 59–67.

"Scrapping Key UPA Measures: Rajasthan Drafts Biz-Friendly Land Acquisition Act." 2014. *Economic Times*, August 11. http://articles.economictimes.indiatimes.com/2014-08-11/news/52687243_1_social-impact-assessment-study-land-acquisition-land-ownersEconomic Times, http://articles.economictimes.indiatimes.com/2014-08-11/news/52687243_1_social-impact-assessment-study-land-acquisition-land-owners.

Sharma, Supriya. 2014. "Rajasthan Rushes to Acquire More Land for Industry Even as Existing Industrial Land Lies Unused." *Scroll.in*, August 14. http://scroll.in/article/674079/rajasthan-rushes-to-acquire-more-land-for-industry-even-as-existing-industrial-land-lies-unused.

Society for Promotion of Wasteland Development and Rights and Resources Initiative. 2014. "Land Acquisition Related Disputes." http://www.rightsandresources.org/wp-content/uploads/Land-Conflicts-Map-updated-2013-14.pdf.

Srivastava, Arun. 2016. "Land Deals in Jharkhand." *Echo of India*, March 16. http://echoofindia.com/reflex-action/land-deals-jharkhand-105239.

"State Moots Radical Changes in Land Acquisition Act." 2014. *Times of India*, July 25. http://epaperbeta.timesofindia.com/Article.aspx?eid=31811&articlexml=State-moots-radical-changes-in-Land-Acquisition-Act-25072014002003.

"State Plans Easier Land Use Change, for a Price." 2015. *Indian Express*, March 24. http://indianexpress.com/article/cities/mumbai/state-plans-easier-land-use-change-for-a-price/.

"Tamil Nadu Shows the Way in Land Acquisition." 2011. *Business Standard*, June 8. http://www.business-standard.com/article/economy-policy/tamil-nadu-shows-the-way-in-land-acquisition-111060800029_1.html.

"Two Acquisitions That Lapsed Because Gujarat Delayed Taking Possession." 2016. *Indian Express,* January 12. http://indianexpress.com/article/india/india-news-india/two-acquisitions-that-lapsed-because-gujarat-delayed-taking-possession/.

Verma, Suyash. 2014. "Constitutional Law: Doctrine of Repugnancy and the Constitution of India (Centre-State Relations)." *Desi Kanoon,*May. http://www.desikanoon.co.in/2014/05/doctrine-of-repugnancy-and-constitution-of-india.html.

Vijayabaskar, M. 2010. "Saving Agricultural Labour from Agriculture: SEZs and Politics of Silence in Tamil Nadu." *Economic and Political Weekly* 45 (6): 36–43.

Wahi, Namita, ed. 2017. "Land Acquisition in India: A Review of Supreme Court Cases, 1950–2016." New Delhi: Centre for Policy Research.

"We Have to Strike a Balance: Interview with Jairam Ramesh." 2012. *Frontline,* December 29.

"Why All Eyes Are on Reliance's Land Acquisition Case." 2016. *Indian Express,* January 12. http://indianexpress.com/article/india/india-news-india/why-all-eyes-are-on-this-land-case/.

World Bank. 2007. "India: Land Policies for Growth and Poverty Reduction." Report No. 38298-IN. Delhi: World Bank.

———. 2010. "Investing across Borders: Indicators of Foreign Direct Investment Regulation in 87 Countries." Washington, DC: World Bank, Investment Climate Advisory Services.

6

Cabal City

Urban Regimes and Accumulation without Development

PATRICK HELLER, PARTHA MUKHOPADHYAY, AND MICHAEL WALTON

Introduction

It is difficult to imagine any setting in which the challenges of inclusive development are more sharply defined than the Indian city. India's megacities have played
a pivotal role in India's accelerated growth over the last two decades (World Bank
2013). High urban growth rates, however, have not translated into development.
Urban-based growth has instead been associated with widespread problems of
inadequate provisioning of urban services, infrastructure bottlenecks, and high
levels of pollution. If anything, patterns of urban growth have exacerbated social exclusion. More broadly, failures of urban governance—most notably in
providing basic infrastructure and creating a business-friendly environment—
threaten the sustainability of growth. These are common challenges of rapid
urban development. They are exacerbated by the fact that India is in a long phase
of large-scale urbanization.

Broad recognition of the "urban problem" has focused attention on the question of governance. We argue in this chapter that the malaise of Indian cities is
indeed largely now a reflection of issues of "governance." As much-cited reports
(GOI 2011; McKinsey 2010) have emphasized, resources matter too, and the
rate of investment in urban India has been woefully inadequate by comparative
standards.[1] But our point is that this shortfall is a *result* of a failure of governance
in India's current phase of development. But governance needs to be unpacked.
All too often the term is deployed as shorthand for "getting the policies right,"
as if there were self-evident, politically feasible policies that would resolve
urban problems. In this chapter, we explore the issues of urban governance by
drawing on the concept of "urban regimes." As developed in the literature, the
urban regime concept views governance as essentially a problem of coordinating

interests, with the degree of effective coordination fundamentally shaped by institutional settings and political processes.[2]

We develop the argument in several steps. First, we identify a modal "Indian urban regime" that is consistent with certain political processes. We argue that this regime has adverse consequences for both economic development and social inclusion. This is most directly manifest in systemic coordination failures, that is, the failure to effectively align public investments and policy interventions with social and economic objectives. This has proximate and ultimate causes. The proximate causes are a range of political accommodations that are stable and self-reproducing and hence represent a regime, but that nonetheless fracture the exercise of local state power. The ultimate source of the problem lies in the misalignment of political incentives and institutional power that results in the weak form of sovereignty that characterizes the Indian city.

The modal Indian urban regime is contrasted with the typology of the "growth machine" long held to be the archetypical US city. In the growth machine, a coalition of developers and politicians coalesce around the provision of infrastructure and other business-supporting investments to maximize land rents (Logan and Molotch 1988). At first blush, this would seem an apt characterization for the Indian city, which, in recent decades, has been often popularly referred to as the "land-grab raj." But the parallel obscures a key difference. While Logan and Molotch argue that the growth machine is fundamentally about maximizing the returns to land, the resulting processes of land development are subject to coherent governance and an overall economic logic. Insofar as land development is planned, regulated, and aligned with public investments, the resulting growth is sustainable and broadly inclusive, if not equitable. Compared to European cities, US cities do suffer more commonly from pockets of exclusion, most notably the hypersegregation of the ghetto (Wacquant 2008), but most urban citizens have access to basic amenities, public institutions, and affordable housing.

In contrast, we argue that in India, while relations between political and landed interests are at the core of the modal urban regime, this is at best a "growth cabal" and more often a "rent extracting cabal," in which the particularistic, and often informal, pursuit of land (and other) rents is only weakly aligned with either the coherent economic growth of the city or the construction of an urban living environment that could cater effectively to the basic needs of established and migrating populations. The result is not only that growth is hurt by failures in infrastructure provisioning, but that Indian cities are becoming increasingly unequal,[3] marked in particular by large swaths of spatial exclusion and basic services deprivation that adversely impacts even the middle class.

We argue that the dominant urban institutional formations of "growth or rent-extracting cabal" is shaped by three factors. First is the fragmented structure of state, and political interests, that is mirrored in particularistic business behavior. Second is the weak disciplining power of the state in constraining the pursuit of collusive rent-extracting deals. And third is the weak societal accountability of city-level political and administrative structures, owing to the very limited devolution of political authority to the city. These are interlinked: indeed the weak disciplining power of the state and the failure to devolve more political authority to the city (in spite of constitutional reforms) are themselves reflective of the underlying political structure.

Both the overall analytical construct of the modal Indian regime and the variations within it are illustrated by comparisons of three megacities: Bangalore, Delhi, and Mumbai. These three cities have contrasting stories: Bangalore as a modernizing center of the iconic, globalizing, IT industry; Mumbai as both the historic economic capital of India and the city with the largest concentration of slum-dwellers; and Delhi, the national capital, and also the only Indian megacity in which the jurisdiction of the state government is mostly aligned with the city of Delhi.

A Typology of Urban Regimes

The urban regime concept is a tool to identify the political pacts that govern cities. It has produced a wide range of types that range from the bookend of the "growth machine" to the "social city." If a market logic prevails in the former and a social logic in the latter, it is important to underscore that both involve effective coordination across social groups and political and economic processes.

Coordination in the growth machine is predicated on a broad-based link between city economic development and land rents. This is secured by an alliance between city political and business elites that forge an alignment between industrial service growth and increases in land value but still require for legitimation purposes reasonable provisioning of housing and public services. So even as growth machines in the United States are based on the "tendency to use land and government activity to make money" (Logan and Molotch 1988, 55), US cities have also been the sites of powerful democratic urban machines that organized immigrant and working-class voters and secured a modicum of inclusion in the city.[4] Rising land rents drive private behavior and lead to public revenues that support public interventions and investments geared to stimulating growth.

Coordination in the social city is based on balancing the use value with the market value of land. This can include cultural preservation, the maintenance and sustainability of urban life or redistribution. The social city can be built on a wide range of social bases, but these invariably have a majoritarian character that more or less keeps economic elites in check. Because the social city is a "pacted" city that brings together a highly diverse coalition of actors, it necessarily requires a high degree of coordination and an alignment of political and institutional power that can only be created and preserved through vibrant democratic politics. Examples of the social city would include cities that empha- size cultural heritage and actively resist growth (many older European cities), maintenance and sustainability cities in which the middle class generally plays a key role in controlling growth (Boulder and Santa Barbara), and cities where the local state plays an active role in promoting social inclusion by socializing land (e.g., large-scale public housing) and developing high-quality public serv- ices. This is the classic social democratic city of Europe, but can also be extended to some Brazilian cities (Heller 2017).

Turning to India, given the pervasive forms of social exclusion that mark all Indian cities, there is nothing that approximates the social city.[5] Furthermore, our analysis of Bangalore, Mumbai, and Delhi reveals that these cities have some of the formal trappings of a growth machine in terms of city plans, but actual functioning falls far short of this coordinated ideal. Close analysis of these cases instead reveals that India's megacities range between what we call the "growth cabal" and the "rent-extracting cabal."

In arguing that Indian cities fit neither the growth machine nor social city typologies, we highlight the absence of a coherent, city-based political coalition, backed by an ideology or narrative that shapes policy and investment, either for growth or for inclusion. Indian cities lack a dominant development coalition be- tween urban political and economic elites that could drive the infrastructure, regulatory, planning and business climate elements of a concerted growth dy- namic. Nor is there a political coalition that could represent an effective class compromise, on historical European lines (and to some degree of US industrial cities), with a mix of business support and broad-based provisioning of social services for the working classes.

Table 6.1 provides some basic indicators of the three megacities, with respect to population growth, share of slums, and access to basic services. All, and most dramatically Bangalore, experienced substantial population growth in the 2000s. While slum populations are immense in Mumbai and large in Delhi, they have declined in absolute number between 2001 and 2011. In all three cities, large proportions of slum-dwellers are deprived of basic water or sanitations services, and significant swaths of non-slum-dwellers lack access. When one considers that access to water includes nonpotable water of uncertain supply and that "flush toilets" are often little more than pit latrines that are unconnected to the sewerage system, the picture on the ground is much worse. For all their recent ec- onomic success, these cities are still marked by high degrees of social exclusion.

The robust growth rates reported in table 6.2 cut across a range of sectors (though much less pronounced for manufacturing) and paint a picture of ec- onomic dynamism. Much of this growth has, however, been dominated by

Table 6.1 **Basic Profile of Bangalore, Delhi and Mumbai**

City Parameters	Bangalore (BBMP)		Delhi (NCT)		Mumbai (MCGM)	
	Nonslum	Slum	Nonslum	Slum	Nonslum	Slum
Area km² (2011)	741		1,483		603	
Pop. density per km² (2011)	11,560		9,340		20,634	
Share of slum pop. (2001)	10.0%		14.7%		54.1%	
Share of slum pop. (2011)	8.3%		10.6%		41.8%	
No. households (2011)	1,949,435	165,341	3,068,106	367,893	1,644,429	1,135,514
Population (2001)	4,301,326	430,501	11,820,752	2,029,755	5,503,010	6,475,440
Population (2011)	7,882,692	712,801	15,002,551	1,785,390	7,235,900	5,206,473
Pop. growth (2001–11)	104%[a]	66%[a]	27%	−12%	31%	−20%
Assets in 2011: percentage of households with						
Two-wheeler	49%	21%	42%	18%	21%	9%
Television	88%	79%	90%	74%	89%	80%
Bank account	72%	35%	81%	55%	91%	81%
Tap drinking water (on premises)	71%	56%	73%	48%	87%	66%
Electricity	98%	97%	99%	97%	98%	96%
Flush toilet	80%	69%	63%	43%	63%	23%
Car	20%	3%	23%	5%	19%	4%

Note: Data for slum area and density not available. All figures for BBMP include outgrowths (OGs), which are defined as surrounding rural areas with urban infrastructure and amenities; MCGM stands for Municipal Corporation of Greater Mumbai and NCT for National Capital Territory.

[a] Bruhat Bangalore Mahanagara Palike (BBMP) was established in 2007 by expanding the erstwhile Bangalore Mahanagara Palike, increasing the area from 226 km² to 740.6 km². Hence, much of the population growth is attributable to area expansion. For comparison, the population of Bangalore Urban district grew from 6.53 million to 9.62 million over 2001–11. The share of BBMP in the district population grew from 72 percent to 90 percent.

Source: Primary Census Abstract and Town Directory, Census of India 2001 and 2011; House listing and housing data, census of India, 2011.

Table 6.2 **Economic Structure and Growth**

| Sector | Share 2012–13 | | Share 2006–7 | Annual growth | | |
| | | | | 1999–2000 to 2012–13 | | 1999–2000 to 2006–7 |
	Bangalore	Delhi	Mumbai	Bangalore	Delhi	Mumbai
Primary	1%	1%	1%	−0.9%	2.8%	−0.8%
Manufacturing	22%	5%	22%	7.0%	2.2%	3.3%
Public utilities	7%	1%	4%	17.5%	9.0%	3.8%
Construction	1%	4%	4%	−3.2%	5.5%	6.7%
Traditional services	26%	24%	26%	11.3%	6.0%	5.2%
Banking and insurance	11%	26%	16%	11.1%	10.0%	5.8%
Real estate, ownership of dwellings, and business services	26%	24%	17%	14.2%	14.7%	14.5%
Public administration	1%	4%	4%	−2.7%	5.8%	2.7%
Other services	5%	10%	6%	7.1%	8.1%	4.5%
Total	100%	100%	100%	9.5%	8.2%	5.8%

Source: Authors, drawing on a variety of official statistics, with state- and city-level data varying across the three cities.

rent-thick sectors. Our analysis moreover reveals two analytic types that we label the "growth cabal" and the "rent-extracting cabal." As with the growth machine, the "growth cabal" is organized around political-business deals that hitch infrastructure and public revenue to growth. But this type is closer to a political settlement—that is, a loose set of mutual accommodations—than an institutionalized regime. In contrast to the ruling coalition of a growth machine, the cabal is more particularistic, operating around rather than through institutions and is organized around niches or segments of city economic activity. Within these niches, some growth due to value-adding investments occurs. While in the growth machine coordination is institutionally organized, stable, and encompassing, the growth cabal lacks coordination and the ability to support sustained, and especially balanced and inclusive, growth. In India, Bangalore is the prototypical case. Though a dynamic and highly influential IT sector organized itself to shape governance and to enhance the competitive position of the city, extralocal political interests have prevented the consolidation of a full growth machine-type settlement and have carved out significant rental havens.

In the "rent-extracting cabal," the driver of the political-business settlement is organized primarily around rent extraction and rent-sharing, cemented by a mixture of private gains and political finance. Land rents are so central to the political pact that the link with underlying city growth dynamics is tenuous and can actually work against broader economic growth. Specific deals are mostly informal and particularistic, but nevertheless tightly woven into both political and business networks. Growth may occur, but mostly as a result of increasing land values driven by scarcity factors. This type captures the governance and developmental logic in Delhi and Mumbai, where landed interests have virtually monopolized the core of the city and where public investments and policy interventions service returns to land over broader development. It is also associated with the displacement of economic activity to the peripheries of the cities.

Our contention is that the urban regimes in India's megacities vary across the growth and rent-extracting cabal. These are both "cabals" in the sense that the dominant coalition consists of a fairly small group of actors who collude across the boundaries of state and market to maximize returns to scarce resources, most prominently land. State-market interactions are variable, networked, and often informal. Systematic and continued rent-sharing holds the system together and can make it resilient to change. The cabal stands in sharp contrast with the institutional rules and formal arrangements invoked by social pacts or by various forms of corporatism or organized participation emphasized in the urban regime literature. Of course, as stressed in the original formulation of urban regimes (Stone 1989), informal arrangements play an important role in all regimes but nonetheless tend to support institutional alignments that undergird effective governance. In our usage cabals are, much like all regimes, politically constructed, but on particularistic and opportunistic terms. Cabals prey on institutional weakness and are in fact organized around exploiting institutional gaps in governance.

The difference between a rent-extracting cabal and a growth cabal is one of degree and has to do with the extent to which the returns to rents are reinvested in the very social and political arrangements that generate rents or find their way into growth-inducing investments. As we show below, this distinction helps us differentiate New Delhi and Mumbai from Bangalore. In the democratic context of India, both forms of the cabal also need to generate political support from middle-class and poorer groups, but these are more likely to be based on clientelistic and populist linkages than coordinated forms of inclusion.

To understand exactly how and why "cabals" have become such a dominant feature of Indian cities, it is important to lay out the specific institutional, political, and socioeconomic conditions and dynamics that have given shape to the modal Indian urban regime.

Institutions of City Governance

By the *design* of India's political and bureaucratic structures, cities enjoy very little sovereignty, in contrast to the history of Western cities, and cities in many middle-income countries (e.g., Brazil, South Africa, and China). India is formally a federal system, with a constitutionally defined division of activities between the central (union) government and the (subnational) states, and a further division between the states and the third level of government—municipalities in urban areas and panchayats in rural areas. However, India's cities are effectively part of the political and bureaucratic processes of the subnational state. This is in spite of the Seventy-Fourth Constitutional Amendment that formalized the third level of government at the level of urban municipalities. Cities exist more as administrative than governing units, with the bulk of executive power over city designs residing at the level of the provincial state. This problem of sovereignty is compounded by a core problem of accountability. Thus citizens vote for city-level ward councilors/corporators (WCs), as well as state-level members of legislative assemblies (MLAs) and national members of parliament. But the real power lies in the executive of the state, and with most MLAs coming from rural areas the electoral logic dictates that political deals, rent extraction, and overall political alignments that impact the city are forged in networks and spaces outside the city. Because it is a city-state, this logic should not hold for Delhi, where all the MLAs are in fact urban. But in Delhi the center exerts so much power over urban governance that MLAs' and WCs' power is largely limited to petty patronage (such as getting water tankers into a slum), and the larger pattern of misaligned political authorization (in term of both autonomy and accountability) and institutional power holds firm.

The structure of city governance is presented, in stylized terms, in figure 6.1. The bulk of city planning, regulatory, investment, and service delivery responsibilities falls under the state (with some exceptions for Delhi). However, in the recent era of expanding central government revenues, the center has increasingly sought to influence activities at the state level through so-called centrally sponsored schemes, involving tied financial resources, conditional on states following specified investment guidelines and satisfying policy requisites.

There can be multiple executive agencies in a city, some in parastatals (usually at the level of the state), and there will typically be formal planning agencies. However, the most concentrated executive power resides in a city's commissioner, a position that is taken by an officer from the elite, national, career Indian Administrative Service (IAS), and is effectively in the hands of the chief minister. IAS officers also head the bureaucracies of each of the state's ministries, with substantial influence over a city's functioning and service delivery. In principle, planning agencies could integrate these various functions, but power and authority in practice lies in line departments that actively resist horizontal integration.

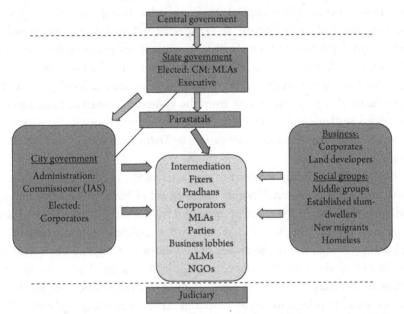

Organizational structures: a stylized account

Figure 6.1 A Schematic Presentation of Formal and Informal Governance for India's Megacities.

MLAs and WCs have legislative power but limited agency. Most legislative and legal action is developed by the state executive, in the nexus of the state's political leadership and the bureaucracy. Given their lack of power over policy, politicians have little choice but to resort to patronage to build support. This takes both fully legal forms, as in the disbursement of development funds that are allocated to MLAs, or in their role in distributing ration cards or pension awards, but also through an array of informal interventions such as targeted delivery of services, influencing contract allocation, and brokering land deals. The fact that the political power that matters for making policy is constituted at higher levels undercuts the incentives and potential for formation of coherent urban coalitions. As the city as a site of value creation is decoupled from the site of political and institutional power (including the power to tax), the coalitions that are able to mobilize political power are more geared to extraction (which requires minimal coordination) than investment (which requires coordination). In line with arguments made in this volume, for all the structural power business may enjoy in India, at the level of the city it is very difficult for business interests to assert their collective interest.

India's major cities undertake formal, if inadequate, planning and regulatory functions. The "urban-license raj" is alive and well and is especially evident in regulations over land use for large- and small-scale business, for infrastructure, and, not least, for housing and associated urban services. But much of this is dysfunctional for effective economic growth and urban living, and rather supports the generation of particularistic rents, specific political deals, and front-line rent-sharing systems between street-level workers, patronage politicians, and citizens—whether in the form of dispensing favors in local services or pensions by politicians, or the symbiotic relation between police and hawkers. It is also reproduces a range of exclusions, from the systematic denial of basic services to "illegal settlements" to prohibitions on informal economic activity such as small-scale manufacturing relocation in Delhi and actions against street vending.[6]

One might be simply tempted to characterize the entire legal and bureaucratic structures as captured by elite interests, as in Chatterjee's (2004) influential thesis that defines the space of rights and law (civil society) as the exclusive reserve of the middle class and relegates mass politics (political society) to political patronage and the tolerance of illegalities. But aligning the formal/informal binary along an elite/popular divide obscures the fluid and contested nature of formality. On the one hand, elites aggressively exploit the fluidity of the formal and the legal to extract rents and carve out privileges.[7] On the other, when exposed (e.g., recurring scandals over "land grabs") these practices come into sharp conflict with the normative resonance of democratic accountability and can invite institutional responses. As in many domains, India's urban regime is a hybrid between a "rules" and "deals"-based system. This is evident in an activist judiciary, especially in some (but by no means all) of the rulings of the Supreme Court, in periodic investigations of the Comptroller and Auditor General (CAG), and countless subnational examples—such as the reporting of Karnataka's Lokayukta (a state-level ombudsman) on corruption. This is sometimes in de facto alliance with a range of civil society-based initiatives.

The Socioeconomic Context

Key features of the socioeconomic profile of Indian cities are summarized in tables 6.2 and 6.3. Two features are particularly relevant. First, the relatively weak industrial employment growth, and associated absence of organized labor, has made collective mobilization of subordinate groups more difficult and typically limited to local neighborhoods, both in slums and outside. Second, the large increases in land prices in the postliberalization period has provided a rich seam of rents to be extracted and shared, especially between business, politicians, and developers.

There have been various degrees of industrial-service capital accumulation in our three cities. Mumbai has come closest to being an industrial city with its once-large textile sector, but has most recently become increasingly dominated

Table 6.3 **Share of Workers Engaged in Different Sectors over Time (%)**

City	Bangalore			Delhi			Mumbai		
Year	1999–00	2004–05	2009–10	1999–00	2004–05	2009–10	1999–00	2004–05	2009–10
Agriculture and mining and quarrying	1.1	0.9	0.0	1.2	0.1	0.1	1.2	0.5	0.7
Manufacturing	32.3	21.0	29.3	24.4	24.0	26.5	25.3	28.0	25.5
Electricity and water supply	0.4	0.7	2.5	0.4	0	0	0.3	0.3	0.6
Construction	11.4	11.6	5.9	3.7	5.2	3.5	6.1	5.6	4.2
Trade, hotel and restaurant	20.3	28.6	23.9	29.7	29.1	32.2	25.3	24.2	19.6
Transport	7.3	9.0	11.3	6.4	8.2	8,5	11.7	10.9	12.4
Services: all except above	26.5	22.7	25.2	30.2	30.3	25.7	24.6	23.7	30.7
Services: private household staff	0.7	5.4	1.9	3.6	3.2	3.4	5.4	6.6	6.3
Total	100.0	100.0	100.0	100.0	100.0	100.0	100.0	100.0	100.0

Source: NSS report Nos. 411, 462, 553, 564.

by the finance sector. Bangalore was long a city of government services, but has emerged as the iconic IT city. In Delhi, much of its industry has been moved to peripheral city developments, often outside its boundaries in neighboring states. But Delhi has leveraged its status as the nation's capital for economic gain in terms of both securing federal funds and developing a range of brokerage functions.

Delhi and Mumbai metro regions account for 11 percent of national manufacturing but 21 percent of "modern business services." In both cities, manufacturing employment growth was flat in the first decade of the twenty-first century, while modern business services grew in double digits. Both cities are classic "global cities" in Sassen's (1991) sense of the term, concentrating a high degree of high-end command-and-control functions. Mumbai and Delhi alone accounted for 42 percent of IT "headquarters" (as registered on the NASSCOM website).[8] In contrast, Bangalore dominated the export sector for IT-BPO, with 36 percent of the national total, compared to 15 percent for Mumbai (including Pune) and the Delhi region (including Gurgaon and Noida), but has also maintained a sizable garment sector.[9] Manufacturing also remains in Mumbai and Delhi, accounting for only 25.5 percent and 26.5 percent of workers respectively, but is surpassed by Bangalore (29.3 percent).

With respect to land, the key development concerns how liberalization and growth in the past twenty-five years has created new rents and made land salient as a commodity. Chakravorty (2013) calculates that by 2011 the price of land in Mumbai was almost as high as in New York, while in terms of the ratio of land prices to earning power it was ten times greater.[10] But growing land rents were not tightly linked to broad-based city infrastructure dynamics. Political constraints have limited investments in inclusive infrastructure. This operates most notably through the power of the land cabal to resist or circumvent taxation or effective development offsets/requirements such as providing basic services for new housing projects. Where resources were nonetheless abundant, such as in Delhi, this was due to political decisions to invest in large symbolic projects (stadia for the Commonwealth Games, conventions halls) or substantially middle-class megaprojects such as metros, flyovers, airports, and malls. At the national level, a major center-driven urban investment program (JNNURM) has been widely criticized for a project-driven logic more attuned to patronage than planning and has woefully underinvested in pro-poor initiatives (Sivaramakrishnan 2011).

In sum, in India's period of urban takeoff, land became central to rent creation but with weak links to city infrastructure development. Thus even as land rents rose rapidly, growth declined. This notably shows up in spatial patterns of population growth marked by declining centers but rapidly growing peripheries, where the costs of greenfield development are much lower. In Mumbai population growth in the decade 2001–11 in the core of the city was 0.4 percent and in Delhi 2.1 percent.[11] What growth did take place was in the periphery of the cities, 3.6 percent and 7.4 percent respectively. In Bangalore, where IT continues to occupy a central (but not exclusive) position in the city's political settlement, core growth was much more robust at 4.7 percent and much less dependent on greenfield development, with peripheral growth at only 1.6 percent. These core-periphery dynamics are also reflected in data on land prices. Chakravorty (2013), drawing on data from RSIDEX National Housing Bank, shows that land price polarization is dramatically higher in Mumbai and Delhi than in Bangalore. For Mumbai he calculated that the ratio of land price per acre from the lowest zone to the highest zone is a stunning 24, with Delhi at a more moderate 4 and Bangalore just under 2.

Politics

The possibility of a coherent political coalition that would underwrite either a growth machine or a social city is rendered unusually difficult by the weak political sovereignty of the city and the fragmented nature of sociopolitical interests, including a very limited industrial working class. This has resulted in a low-level equilibrium from the perspective of city politics. Political action in cities is either subservient to state-level political goals, or concerned with very local issues. Political actors strategically exploit institutional weaknesses to secure particularistic gains, which are then in turn reinvested in the existing institutional field and political alignments. This dynamic drives both elite and popular action.

At the elite level, a range of major private interests are primarily concerned with creating and sharing of rents—especially around land—in which private gains are misaligned with city economic growth, and yet are tightly linked to, indeed formative of, political and bureaucratic processes, at both the state and city levels of government. This can take many forms. Two major channels involve "front-running" (buying land ahead of planned land reclassification using "insider information") and protection. In addition, revenues can be generated from direct provision of basic services such as water supply—the ubiquitous "tanker mafia" in many cities, including Mumbai, as well as information rents from undocumented knowledge about de facto networks vis-à-vis de jure networks (Björkman 2015). Politicians and state agencies, in particular the "development authorities" that are responsible for land planning and zoning, secure and bundle public land for private gain, or valorize existing land through targeted value-enhancing investments. Land and land valorization as a major domain for rent creation and rent-sharing has underpinned and congealed alliances between political and economic elites—both for private gains and for the political finance that is crucial for re-election.

This is consistent with electoral politics because state-level elections are still primarily determined by the rural vote and because of the general absence of city-based political movements. This reflects the fragmentation of socioeconomic structures described above and means city-level political action is primarily at the local, as opposed to citywide, level and is characterized by patronage, intermediation, contracts, and local problem-solving.[12]

Within this equilibrium, nonelite groups have little choice but to adopt particularistic strategies that reproduce the low-level equilibrium. Middle- and lower-class groups have substantial political influence through voting, local mobilizations, and use of the judiciary. This includes the urban poor: most slum-dwellers have voting cards, vote in high proportions and engage with local politicians in ways that are very much political in nature (Das and Walton 2015). Political influence can be through vote-bank politics, clientelistic relations, or the informal pressures both middle- and lower-class groups put on local politicians (at both the level of city ward councilors/corporators and MLAs) to get issues of daily living solved. The demand for highly particularistic gains, or in some cases the club goods that accrue to a specific neighborhood or sector, in effect trump the possibility of demanding more encompassing goods. This is reflected in the finding that the level of services provided to any single settlement largely reflects local political settlements, that is, the specific ties that communities develop to local bureaucracies and politicians (see *Cities of Delhi* Centre for Policy Research).

Civil Society

Civil society in urban India is active, but relatively ineffective in terms of citywide policy. There are two problems here. The high level of social and economic differentiation has in general precluded horizontal linkages, and most civil society activism is group-, location- or sector-specific. This fragmentation is compounded by the legal-spatial segregation of the city, with different neighborhoods having very different levels of tenure security and consequent rights to services. The so-called middle class falls into two quite distinct categories. Those middle-class fractions living in planned or regularized areas of the city have often formed resident welfare associations that can effectively address local issues and even secure favorable treatment by the state.[13] They have also been proactive in using their associational power and political connections in pursuing projects of city improvement and beautification. These tend to have exclusionary effects by relocating street vendors or informal settlements.[14] In Delhi, the lower middle class tends to reside in unauthorized colonies that have yet to be regularized. Though they generally enjoy de facto security of tenure, their access to services is entirely negotiated (*Cities of Delhi* Centre for Policy Research). Much associational activity revolves around collective self-provisioning alongside activism around efforts to regularize their status. Slum-dwellers face far greater obstacles to collective action. Because of their basic insecurity of tenure, they are often beholden to patronage politicians or slumlords and enjoy limited associational autonomy. While unauthorized colonies in many cities are often "regularized," this is rarely true for slums. On the other hand, aided by rights-based NGOs and a judiciary that, while fickle, has at times extended legal protection to slum-dwellers, there is significant capacity to resist evictions.

This problem of differentiated and segmented class fractions is further compounded by the absence of institutionalized points of contact with the state. The provisions of the Seventy-Fourth Amendment and central directives to strengthen local-level ward committees notwithstanding, citizens enjoy few direct and responsive channels of engagement with the state. This limited institutional surface area, as noted earlier, puts a premium on intermediaries and brokers. The politics of patronage supplant the rights of citizens. A lack of collective cohesion, organizational capacity, and institutional access has largely limited civil society to defensive and often particularistic actions.[15] Citizens have insufficient structured influence to underpin an effective distributional deal, or even make much headway in pressing government agencies for effective service delivery. Overall, and in contrast to the strong civic pressures that have long been evident in Europe and more recently in Latin America (Le Gales 2002; Avritzer 2002), urban civil society in India has not had the strength or coherence to act as a countervailing force to market logic by ensuring that growth be more inclusionary (e.g., expansion of affordable housing, public services) and negative externalities—most glaringly pollution—more regulated.

A partial new exception is the rise of the Aam Aadmi Party (AAP), which has succeeded in linking middle-class grievances over corruption and bad governance to the service delivery concerns of the urban poor. That the AAP emerged out of a social movement and frames its platform as rights-based, makes it the quintessential civil society-based political formation, albeit with ambiguous characteristics.

If civil society has not struck any deep or broad roots, some NGOs that are focused on specific issues have developed important points of leverage. A range of NGOs focused on accountability have brought issues of corruption into public debate via reports from the CAG and Lokayuktas. Rights-based NGOs have used the judiciary to secure protection for hawker activities, based on the constitutional right to life, or assisted slum-dwellers in resisting eviction. But as a countervailing force to moneyed power and the land-grab raj, civil society remains largely impotent.

Contrasting Urban Regimes: Bangalore, Mumbai, and Delhi

We now turn to our three cases. While all share characteristics of the cabal regime, there are also contrasts, reflecting both their differing underlying socioeconomic processes and city-level political and institutional process. A sketch is provided in table 6.4.

Bangalore

No city has more explosively emerged as a center of the global information economy than Bangalore. Within a short span of time, a backwater administrative town with a large educational sector morphed into a leading center of production and innovation in IT, second only to Silicon Valley in the global hierarchy. The growth of this sector in turn generated extraordinary growth in

Table 6.4 **Variation across Three Megacities**

	Growth	Dominant coalition	Inclusiveness	Narrative
Delhi	Rent-extracting cabal based on external sources (Central funds) that drive land values and infrastructure rents	Developer and upper middle class (planned colonies)	Upper middle-class city, with organized exclusion	Aesthetic city (at expense of industrial city) but reinvestment partially in services/ information economy
Mumbai	Rent-extracting cabal focused on core land values	Coalition of developers and "world-class city" interests such as finance	Lots of small-scale entrepreneurs live in slums. Slums have more leverage than in Delhi.	World-class city, finance and culture (Mumbai is home to Bollywood, the base of Hindi cinema).
Bangalore	Growth cabal: Elements of a half-baked growth machine, in a sectorally based IT niche, alongside rent-extraction processes	IT, but garments excluded— unstable, and usurped by extracity mining interests	Slums are relatively small, with growth in the peripheral areas.	World class, high tech, service sector city with a comparatively large manufacturing sector that has survived

city income, territory and population, attracting skilled migrants from all over India and making Bangalore India's most cosmopolitan city. In terms of our typology of urban regimes, Bangalore has vacillated between a half-baked growth machine, marked by a relatively open interaction of business groups with governance mechanisms, and a growth cabal.

In colonial times Bangalore was mostly an administrative city, but in the 1960s–1980s it benefited from a concentration of high-tech government investments, such as Hindustan Aeronautics Limited, Indian Telephone Industries, Bharat Earth Movers Limited, Bharat Heavy Electricals Limited, Hindustan Machine Tools, and Defence Research and Development Organisation, and new higher-education public institutions. This set the stage for the takeoff of the IT sector.

For the 1990s and much of the 2000s Bangalore looked, at least from a distance, to be more growth machine than growth cabal: a dynamic urban center with a prosperous middle class that could compete globally. But this IT-driven growth machine ultimately had limited reach and didn't extend to other industries. City politics, as in other Indian cities, have always been embedded in broader state-wide issues. These have worked through a series of lobbies—from liquor to mining and land development. The politician-business nexus has become tighter over time, and increasingly embodied in the same people, as businessmen enter politics, and politicians enter business. There has been a failure of planning and infrastructure provision to keep pace with the demands of business and living, manifest in traffic congestion and service delivery bottlenecks. Divisions between identity-based groups have been recently politicized. From talk of the Bangalore and Karnataka "model" (Kadekodi, Kanbur, and Rao 2007), the main theme of recent years has been of corruption in the state. In many respects Bangalore has become a "normal" India megacity.

How can this trajectory be explained? The IT sector indeed had the potential to underwrite a growth machine based on innovation as well as expansion.

First, the sector itself was the most competitive in India, developing through competitive exports (rather than domestic rents), carried by a new business elite that prided itself on its independence from state tutelage and saw itself as a driving force of modernization. In Bangalore the sector was also well organized.

Second, the IT sector's dependence on a high-skilled, English-educated workforce that closely identifies with cosmopolitan attributes of city life (consumerism, associational freedom, cultural diversity) gave the sector a direct stake in developing a livable city, at least for the upper middle class.

Indeed, IT businesses did coalesce into a powerful force in city politics, securing extensive support in tax breaks and land allocations. The organized and modernistic spaces of the IT campuses that dot the Bangalore built environment are a testament to the sector's power. Beyond immediate sectoral interests, IT business leaders actively promoted "good governance." The formation, at the behest of the Congress Party chief minister, of the Bangalore Agenda Task Force (BATF) in 1999 has been widely recognized as a singular moment in Indian urban politics in which a business lobby assumed a direct role in city development. Indeed, with the quasi-governmental powers of the BATF, including a proactive role in shaping Bangalore's strategic planning, the IT sector exerted far more influence than in a typical growth machine. Discursively, the nascent growth machine projected an image of hypermodernity and progress, specifically invoking the cleanliness and efficiency of Singapore and providing public funds for "acquiring land to promote large corporate residential and work environments and related infrastructure such as multi-lane highways and dedicated power and electrical systems" (Benjamin 2000, 38).

Critics picked up on the underside of the analogy, pointing to the high-modernist and extrademocratic nature of privatized governance. But even here it is notable that criticisms of lack of inclusiveness and biases against established local socioeconomic areas (Benjamin 2000) point precisely to the advent of a modernizing growth machine.

But the growth machine was half-baked. What might have been a virtuous cycle of coordinated governance fostering agglomeration economies was ultimately ruptured by the reassertion of rent-seeking politics. The synergies that IT benefited from were not extended to other industries such as textiles (a larger source of employment than IT, though declining). Public investments were in fact highly skewed, favoring roads over public transportation, megaprojects over public services. And governance reforms promoted by BATF never really got off the ground. Committees were formed, plans were made, and a new vision was articulated, but in the end politics and institutional fragmentation won the day.

On the other hand, the returns to land development have skyrocketed. This increased the returns to the state's brokerage functions that in turn have further entrenched the politician-developer nexus. Goldman reports that in the 2008 statewide elections, twenty-three of thirty Bangalore MLAs had significant interests in real estate (2011, 567).[16] He summarizes his argument on "speculative urbanism" by concluding that "land speculation and active dispossession inside and surrounding the city of Bangalore [are] the main business of its government today" (2011, 557). The IT sector itself became a key player in real estate, investing significant resources in what were called "land banks" (Goldman 2011).[17]

There has in the past decade been a marked deterioration in the city's basic infrastructure relative to growing needs. Congestion has become notoriously bad. The city is experiencing increasing water problems, and its garbage system quite literally collapsed under the weight of poor management. A recent World Bank study finds that Bangalore's "economic success is creating its own infrastructure problems, including poor water quality, traffic congestion, and housing shortages" (World Bank 2013, 37). Even the city's iconic modernist project, the new international airport, has, because of political machinations, been poorly integrated into the metropolitan transport infrastructure.

But the most certain measure of the slide from a nascent growth machine into a growth cabal is the city's pattern of land development. In the 1960–1980s the periphery of the city developed in the form of massive colonies complete with infrastructure to house the workers of large public sector firms. But today, as Ranganathan neatly summarizes, "Bangalore's peripheries are perhaps best known for concentration of large-scale land speculation and illegalities" (2014, 593). Rent-seeking land interests have combined with the brokerage functions of government parastatals (Goldman 2011) to drive a relentless pattern of sprawl, with large private-estate megaprojects dominating the landscape. These are essentially self-provisioning gated communities, with most services provided on a private basis. Filling out the greenfield expansion have been unauthorized lower middle class developments. In contrast to the classic American pattern of sprawl, this growth has not been planned or accompanied by infrastructure development. Of our three cities, Bangalore's middle class has the lowest level of water provisioning (see table 6.1). Because new lower-class developments are not serviced, Ranganathan has dubbed this segment the "peripheralized middle class" (2014).

In explaining the failure of an otherwise favorable socioeconomic configuration to produce a governable city, one can only turn to the larger political and institutional equation in which Bangalore is embedded. Efforts to improve governance and planning in Bangalore (including BATF) were ultimately defeated by the reassertion of extralocal institutional power. BATF itself became a political football. Initially sponsored by a Congress chief minister, it was replaced by a task force packed with political appointees when the BJP came to power in 2008. A range of other parastatals asserted their power to run basic functions of the city (Benjamin 2000). All of this reflected underlying political alignments. For all its sectoral power, the rise of IT never diminished the significance of more traditional and politically entrenched rent-extracting and rent-sharing lobbies, such as liquor, higher education, and real estate.

The nascent growth machine was dealt a decisive blow by the rise of a new sectoral lobby, the Bellary mining group. This powerful lobby, which made its fortune by capturing the local state in the Bellary region of northern Karnataka and organizing a vast industry of illegal mining, not only bankrolled the rise of an opposition party formation—the BJP, which came to power in 2008—but also ended up controlling a number of ministerial positions and putting much of the state legislature on its payroll. As a report by the Karnataka Lokayukta (the state-level ombudsman) subsequently revealed, politicians were bought with land paid for by mining rents and appropriated by the state, in its brokerage role. This mining cabal—arguably the most coherent of its kind in India—eventually imploded when the Lokayukta exposed its capture of the political process, but not before the city had been rocked by a wave of land- and license-related corruption scandals in which the then-chief minister was directly implicated.

Wracked by corruption scandals, the BJP was ousted from power at the state level in 2013, a reminder that there are democratic limits to predatory behavior. But these democratic limits are far too reactive to generate a viable alternative to the growth cabal. A city that benefits from a cosmopolitan middle class has spawned a vibrant civil society, including a number of active NGOs in the governance sector. Some accountability reforms have met with success, notably the report card on urban services and targeted efforts at improving local-level planning and exposing corruption, including the activity of the ex-Lokayukta. The latter, in particular, illustrates how state agencies can be responsive to citizen pressure, and have had some effect. But in the absence of broader-based support, it is difficult to see how these initiatives can scale up politically. The urban poor and other workers remain largely unorganized. The middle class, while the most sizable in India relative to the size of the city, is highly fragmented, with a highly privileged, globally connected upper segment residing in self-provisioned gated enclaves, and a sprawling lower middle class consisting most of ancillary services to the export sector and government employment, scattered across communities of varying legality and service provisioning.

The IT sector remains economically dominant and continues to support a powerful discourse of making Bangalore into a world-class city. But lacking a significant political base in the city, and having ultimately to answer to external political demands, it has had little choice but to retrench into a growth cabal, a highly profitable, globally articulated sector with deep ties into the city's land rents that it shares, uncomfortably, with the state's assorted private-public rent-seeking cabals. As a recent government report on the encroachment of land remarked, having once been known as India's "Garden City" or IT city," Bangalore, "at this rate, . . . will become infamously the Land Grabbing Capital of India."[18]

Yet there are two respects in which Bangalore is still more a growth cabal than a rent-seeking cabal. Land has emerged as a critical source of rents, but these rents have been tied to the growth of IT and ancillary activities. Land development has been much more concentrated in the periphery, supporting the expansion of a middle class with relatively high incomes. This is reflected in the fact that core-periphery housing prices differentials are not as pronounced as in Mumbai and Delhi (where rent-seeking is concentrated in the core). Accumulation in this sense is still tied (somewhat) to development rather than just rent preservation. And even if overall governance and coordination remains poor, the pattern of growth has not been as socially exclusionary as in Delhi and Mumbai, with a relatively moderate share of people in slums (table 6.1). As Solomon notes (2000), the "local economy" of small, informal enterprises continues to thrive in the core of the city, and in this "producer-IT city," manufacturing continues to provide a significant amount of employment (table 6.3).

Mumbai

Mumbai represents a second type of missed opportunity, namely a failed Fordist compromise that has degenerated into a rent-seeking cabal.[19] Mumbai is India's historic economic capital, home to many of the country's entrepreneurial social groups, but also the city with the highest concentration of slums (table 6.1). Because it has such a long history as the dominant center of economic activity (emerging originally as a center of colonial commerce), Mumbai is, not surprisingly, the Indian city that has enjoyed the most distinctive form of urban politics. Once home to the country's largest communist-organized working class, it now hosts India's only urban political machine (the Shiv Sena).

Despite its status as an economic center, Mumbai's fortunes have been every bit shaped by the shifting Maharashtra political settlement. In the postindependence decades of Congress hegemony, rural sugar-based rents provided the financial resources underpinning the dominance of local Congress politicians. This resulted in relatively low levels of rent extraction from Mumbai itself and allowed the private sector to develop quite dynamically (Roy 2013). This in particular was aligned with reasonably rapid industrialization within India's license-based version of import-substituting industrialization. But as migrants kept pouring into the booming city, its highly restricted landmass (a water-bounded peninsula) inevitably produced a high proportion of informal housing in slums. The city did recognize the need to provide housing to the working class, and the Bombay Development Department (BDD) constructed hundreds of chawls (low-income apartment buildings) near the textile mills. But as Weinstein notes, the efforts were haphazard at best, as industrialists and developers profited from the limited supply of housing and the city's elites resisted efforts to increase levies to pay for a public housing program (2014, 36). In the absence of a development coalition, various efforts at comprehensive planning never took off, and Old Bombay, the densely packed core of the city, saw little investment in housing or infrastructure. This problem was compounded by the divide between the city of Bombay and the state of Maharashtra. The corporation, which was responsible for Old Bombay, had limited resources. In contrast, the Maharashtra Economic Development Council began planning New Bombay in the 1970s, favoring "the idea of building a new city as opposed to patching up the old" (Shaw 2004, 74, cited in Weinstein 2014, 45).

At the height of the city's reign as an industrial powerhouse, and with state politicians securing their core rents from the sugar lobby, a militant and highly organized working class could conceivably have formed the economic base for a Fordist class compromise. The dramatic defeat of the industrial working class in the textile mills strike of 1982–83, however, marked the beginning of deindustrialization and informalization of the labor market. This in turn gave rise to a classic rent-seeking cabal. As both capital and labor fragmented, accumulation was recentered around a land-mafia-politician nexus. The urban poor, politically empowered historically by unions and leftist politics and later represented, at least for native Maharashtrians, by the Shiv Sena, could successfully resist displacement and even make some claims on the city for services. This competitive, clientelistic, and increasingly identity-based politics of claim-making has left little room for programmatic reforms and more or less locked the city in a low-level equilibrium. The dominance of the land mafia, coupled with the capacity of the urban poor to assert minimal, defensive rights, has created a form of stalemate in which governance has been reduced to side payments. The net result is massive congestion, huge delays in infrastructure and slum redevelopment, absurd land regulations, and high-profile corruption. Unsurprisingly, a business-led effort to design a growth machine in the image of a world city unraveled quickly.

For all these governance problems, there were proto-Fordist elements to (then) Bombay in its industrial heyday. Most notably, the city was marked by a degree of inclusivity, at least compared to other Indian cities of the time. The housing stock was poor and the city was overcrowded, but a wide range of groups were able to take advantage of the city's economic dynamism. Bombay developed into India's most cosmopolitan city, attracting skilled professionals from all over India and unskilled labor from all across western and northern India. A wide range of large-scale businesses, most notably textiles, and small, more informal businesses flourished, most famously in the slum of Dharavi with its large, globally connected, informal sector.[20] This was *proto*-Fordism because class compromise was piecemeal and informal, with little of the coordination of class interests and comprehensive city planning that was the hallmark of Fordism in earlier phases of city development in now-industrialized countries. Thus, for all its resources and dynamism, Bombay was still caught in the clutches of the Indian model of urban governance. Planning remained extremely weak, and regulation high-handed and burdensome. Subordinate groups had sufficient power and organization to hold their ground and even claim some services in what Benjamin (2008) has evocatively labeled "occupancy urbanism." Most notably, evictions were often effectively resisted, but repeated reforms to upgrade slums, rather than leading to regularization, only created new points of negotiation. This was insufficient to effect substantive transformations of the urban service environment for the poor.

The core method for resettling the slum-dwellers is a scheme under the Slum Rehabilitation Authority, which entails the in situ redevelopment of a slum settlement (see Nijman 2008 for a description).[21] The eligible slum residents are resettled in high-rise apartments (25 square meters each) on site, and the remaining land is used for building apartments for commercial sale. The extent of commercial sale apartments depends on the number of rehabilitation tenements built. If the entire space available for commercial sale cannot be utilized on the site, the developer is allowed to transfer these development rights to another location, north of the development site. These development rights are tradable (TDRs) and can be sold to another developer. As Isaar notes, "In a city with high density of land use, extremely high land prices, and restrictive building height policies, TDR is akin to land. The political economy of floor space is the political economy of land in such a city" (Isaar 2013, chapter 4, p. 10). The transactional complexities of valorizing land not only have spawned an army of brokers and enforcers, but have created spaces for both large and small developers to engage in rent-seeking. This also means that densifying development occurs without the associated investment in network infrastructure, creating further opportunities for rent-seeking (Björkman 2015). Because elected ward corporators have always had a strong role to play in Mumbai, there is also broader involvement of politicians, which has in particular buttressed the strength of the Shiv Sena, which operates as a classic machine party in organizing and distributing retail rents.

The class stalemate has gone hand in hand with an active regulatory state. On the one hand, economic elites have effectively resisted the comprehensive planning and public investment required to transform the city and to integrate the lower classes. On the other hand, lower classes, and notably the majority of Bombayites/Mumbaikars who live in slums, have had sufficient power to press claims on the city and to carve out entrepreneurial niches. Rather than a political settlement that could have supported the integrative functions of the Fordist city, the stalemate instead led to the expansion of regulatory powers that created a vast swath of opportunities for front-line rent-sharing over land, housing, negotiated services, and informal economic activities. In Mumbai, the regulatory state has grown as a means to manage the sharing of spoils between the dominant classes, much like the Indian state described in Bardhan (1983). This endogeneity of regulation as a means of rent-sharing is expressed in many ways, most strikingly in the exemptions to the Floor Space Index (FSI) regulations governing buildings in Mumbai. This creates a hybrid regime in terms of legality and formality.

The proto-Fordist period began to unravel in the 1970s for three reasons. First, as rural interests outside the sugar zone emerged, the hegemony of the Congress system declined, opening opportunities for new political challenges, notably of the Shiv Sena. Second, the political defeat of the textile unions and the subsequent decline of industry eviscerated the organized power of the working class. Third, economic liberalization led to a massive increase in potential land rents, and shifts in the epicenter of both legal rent-extraction and criminal activity, from smuggling to land deals. These developments in turn produced new alignments that further corroded the governability of the city. The leaders of finance, the new dominant industry in the city, had little interest in tackling questions of governance and infrastructure. Its dominance was moreover completely compatible with rising land rents: finance is high return and requires little land. Industrial capital virtually fled the city core, migrating to the peripheries of Mumbai Suburban District, and Thane, where Navi Mumbai, a new city development built by the city and the Industrial Development Corporation of Maharashtra (CIDCO) is located.

If the Bombay of proto-Fordism sustained some growth, the Mumbai of today has become a clear case of a rent-seeking cabal. In the city core, investment has been entirely arrested and there is even evidence of declining economic activity (Sivaramakrishnan 2015). Bombay was well positioned to be a central node for the IT sector, but high rents have proved to be a challenge. Finance is a growing sector, but one that has little stake in seeing the city develop. As is true of all Indian megacities, real estate prices have soared. The contrast with Bangalore and Delhi is that the rent-seeking cabal is broad, diverse, and more embedded in city politics. In Delhi and Bangalore, much of the real estate growth is based on greenfield development and large infrastructure projects such as the Delhi Metro or the Bangalore ring road corridors in which the brokerage functions of parastatals like the Delhi Metro Rail Corporation, the Delhi Development Authority, and the Bangalore Development Authority (BDA) play a significant role. In Mumbai, much of the rent-seeking is organized around squeezing higher rents from an ever more densified core area, while the peripheries are managed by different local bodies, like Vasai Virar and Navi Mumbai, which are economically linked to Mumbai but not necessarily under its political control.

The legacies of the aborted proto-Fordist era are critical to sustaining the rent-seeking cabal. A vivid example is the dynamics of negotiations around the development of the old mill areas. These legacies of Mumbai's textile industry constituted a highly valuable resource of land. After extensive negotiations with various groups the city designed an arrangement in which a third of the area would be for low-income housing, a third for public spaces, and a third for commercial development. This was, however, trumped by the state, which confined this arrangement to the 10 percent of land not built up—constituting a massive distributional shift to the developers—supported on technical jurisdictional grounds by the Supreme Court.

However, despite pervasive informality and failures of governance, in particular over infrastructure and housing delivery, Mumbai is marked by a remarkably stable equilibrium held in place by acutely spatialized inequalities but also what Weinstein calls the "contentious politics of stability" (2014, ix). Slums have significant rights and also enjoy significant organized protection from politicians, both on routine matters of engagement with the local state and on policy process. Thus Mumbai's myriad "slum clearance" schemes driven by state-level interests remain robustly contested.

Delhi

Delhi has two clear advantages over other Indian megacities. As the capital, it secures a disproportionate share of national resources. As a city whose political boundaries are conterminous with the state, it does not suffer the problem of

being ruled by parties with largely rural constituencies. Yet despite these formidable advantages, from the perspective of both dynamic growth and social
inclusion, Delhi represents the most clear-cut case of failure.

While Delhi has grown dramatically over the past two decades, its growth
has been particularly rent-driven and highly dependent on public resources.
Unlike Mumbai and Bangalore, Delhi has never built a comparative advantage
in any particular economic sector and, indeed, has been so hostile to economic
activity that all the dynamism in the region has been located in adjoining satellite cities (Gurgaon and Noida) that are outside its jurisdiction. On the social
front, Delhi's planning and land development has systematically produced zones
of exclusion that have rationed the core of the city for its upper middle class.
Both these outcomes can be traced to the dominance of a rent-seeking cabal that
is particularly shaped by the outsized role and power of the center-controlled
Delhi Development Authority (DDA) and strategically placed politicians and
developers.

As the colonial capital Delhi inherited a highly segregated spatial form with a
clear demarcation between white-collar elites and the laboring classes, the latter
packed into the large, vibrant settlement of Old Delhi, which is formally a Slum-
Declared Area. Postindependence, Delhi was dominated, as an administrative city,
by the prototype of what Bardhan (1983), in his famous analysis of India's dominant classes, dubbed the professional-bureaucratic proprietary class. Partition
brought waves of refugees who were accommodated in settlements that had poor
service provision and slow regularization. The city has since been actively rationed,
with the DDA consistently underdeveloping land and underprovisioning low-
income housing relative to rates of population growth. This, as Bhan (2013)
shows, has produced concentric circles of exclusion in the form of unauthorized colonies and slums around a core of planned colonies. Eviction policies,
first in the Emergency between 1975 and 1977 and recently in the run-up to the
Commonwealth Games, have sharpened these spatial exclusions by removing
centrally located slums to peripheral "planned resettlements" that are in practice
nothing more than "planned illegalities" (Bhan 2013). In all, the city has managed to create eight differentiated settlement types defined by varying degrees of
tenure and planning and constituting what is in effect a grid of differentiated citizenship. As carefully documented in the *Cities of Delhi* project (Centre for Policy
Research), each settlement type enjoys a different bundle of basic services.

Such differentiation, of course, exists in Mumbai and Bangalore as well, but
is much more sharply defined in Delhi. There are basically three reasons for
this. First, the driving logic of the rent-seeking cabal is the preservation and the
rationing of the core of the city. The value of literally being close to power (and
the assorted brokerage functions that power invites) and the returns to massive
public investments have generated significant land rents.

Second, Delhi enjoys unusual regulatory and disciplinary power. Until the 1980s when it became a state, it was under the direct control of the center, with no territorial mechanisms of democratic accountability. The DDA was the model for development authorities, and the most powerful of them, enjoying a near monopoly over land development. More so than in any other city, it has been able to plan and enforce spatial differentiation and the rationing of the core. This power has extended to enforcement policies to keep most industry out of the city, including concerted efforts to control informal economic activity by, for example, prohibiting mixed zoning of residential and commercial activities, which has since been changed. The DDA is able to do this with impunity, in part because it reports not to the government that is elected only by the local electorate, that is, the Government of the National Capital Territory of Delhi, but to the union (federal) government, elected by the national electorate. As such, it is not responsible to the local population, such as the needs of the voters in informal settlements. Instead, it is supported by a powerful discourse of an "aesthetic" capital city that unites nationalist politicians, modernizing bureaucrats, big-project developers (notably in malls), and cosmopolitan upper classes against what this class perceives as a disorderly, undisciplined, encroaching mass (Ghertner 2015).

Third, administrative enforcement of differentiated citizenship has preempted horizontal alliances among the excluded. By the government's own estimates, only 24 percent of the city's population resides in "planned settlements," with the balance living in settlements that must negotiate their relationship to the state and to public services through patronage bargains. With the city fractured into more than two thousand colony-based political settlements, it is hardly surprising that Delhi has no history of organized mobilization, either from slum-dwellers as in Mumbai or the "occupancy urbanism" that is widespread in Bangalore (Benjamin 2008).

The dominance of a rent-seeking cabal is apparent both in the city's socioeconomic profile and in its political-institutional processes. Delhi's elites have always owed their privileged position to state power, and the city's commercial or industrial class that once comprised large textile firms like Shriram's is now largely petty traders, who organized to contest the implementation of zoning laws. The dominant economic activity was for a long time administrative and public services, but in the globalization era Delhi has morphed into an important command-and-control center for the national economy. The broader Delhi economic region has become home to corporate headquarters and processing centers, but most of this new activity has in fact been located outside of Delhi's city boundaries in the satellite cities of Gurgaon and Noida. The broader Delhi region is second only to Maharashtra (including Mumbai) in attracting FDI, accounting for 20 percent of all flows from 2000 to 2015.[22]

Delhi has seen its modern business services (MBS) sector grow rapidly, but much of this growth has had less to do with new business ventures than with coordinating activities such as banking, insurance, legal services, and more generally brokerage with the state. The manufacturing sector, which was never large to begin with, has been shrinking. From 1999–2000 to 2009–10, MBS grew by 12 percent while the share of formal manufacturing in the core actually shrank, as did services (while the share of informal manufacturing remained steady).[23]

This new economic profile reflects the politics of the "aesthetic city." With planning focused on "improving the environment in the core city" (Kundu 2003, 3530) the city has never been friendly to industry. In the 1980s the DDA actively pushed emerging IT enterprises to satellite cities. There have also been repeated efforts to control and shrink existing informal manufacturing activity. Coupled with slum removals and planning policies that have kept illegal settlements at bay (no unauthorized colony has been regularized in the past twenty years), the net effect has been to insulate and ration a modern, relatively well-planned, and regulated core consisting of the New Delhi Municipal Council area and its immediate ring of planned colonies from a rapidly expanding periphery.

That the cabal is organized around rent-seeking more than growth is evident from a pattern of public investment that has been single-mindedly geared to elevating the enclaved core to world-class city status. Investments in malls, a new international airport, an expansive metro system, sports facilities, and parks have all but crowded out investments in public transport, water provisioning, sanitation, and local economic development. The rent-seeking cabal is organized both around capturing the returns to centrally funded infrastructure projects and working with the DDA to develop new land for commercial ventures (e.g., malls) or educational and health institutions.

However, two factors tilt the locus of rent-seeking to infrastructure projects rather than land. First, the availability of the national budget makes it possible to fund really large infrastructure projects, principally, the Delhi Metro (350 km in phases 1 to 3—a phase 4 is also planned, which will expand the network by another 30 percent) and the Commonwealth Games, with a combined budget of around US$22 billion at current exchange rates (JNNURM projects are also part of this, but they were accessible to other cities also; in Delhi their importance is relatively smaller, while being absolutely large, at US$1.6 billion). Second, the planning norms of the DDA, which restricts high-rise development, make it harder to monetize land in Delhi than in Mumbai, for example.

In the past two decades, the DDA, which was originally conceived in the Nehruvian vision as an agent of socialist planning, has become an aggressive broker and bundler of land, amassing billions of dollars in cash reserves. The returns to the cabal have been high, as witnessed by rising land prices in the core and the massive cost overruns of megaprojects. Politically, the project has been made feasible by the incorporation of the educated middle class through DDA-subsidized housing and a range of implicit and explicit subsidies, as well as participatory schemes for planned colonies with resident welfare associations.

This social compact in turn has been sealed by the rotation in power of two parties—the BJP and the Congress, until the rise of the AAP—that had a direct stake in the rent-seeking cabal, all the more so because the massive rents from the capital helped support national party structures. Tellingly, both parties have refused to devolve significant power to the local Delhi municipal corporation.

The failings and unsustainability of the rent-seeking cabal are increasingly apparent. As the core has become rarified, the periphery has exploded in size and activity, but also in its disorganization. Over the past decade, growth in the core has stagnated, while the periphery has grown steadily in terms of both population and economic activity. Yet investments still skew in favor of the core, and this has left a clear mark. There is now ample evidence that spatial inequality in service delivery is acute (Sidhwani 2015; Singh 2014). Little progress has been made in slum upgrading despite major schemes. Remarkably, as noted earlier, Delhi has been able to allot only 4 percent of the housing for the poor. Similarly, efforts to regularize unauthorized colonies have made little headway. The Delhi Metro—the largest urban infrastructure project in Indian history—has been a success, but has come with opportunity costs of underinvestment elsewhere, not least in the bus system, which services lower-income segments, and is falling dramatically behind. Traffic has worsened, and the flyovers that have claimed the largest portion of JNNURM funding have had the net effect of truncating the city.[24] Nowhere are the failures of governance more visible than in Delhi's new status as the most polluted city in the world, and this in a city with little industry.

The problem of how political authority shapes governance is posed in quite stark terms in the case of Delhi. While the authority of the State of Delhi is largely coterminous with the city boundaries (with the notable exception of the core of the city), this has not led to a more coordinated political economy, as in the growth machine paradigm. The State of Delhi is in fact dominated by central government interests, most institutionally manifest in the role of the DDA, and these interests are generally more preoccupied with rationing the "aesthetic" city than with investing in the city, be it for dynamic economic growth or inclusion. Delhi as such emerges as a vivid example of a "rent-extracting cabal," reflecting the collision of the greater rent-extracting opportunities of the capital city, the relative dominance of landed business interests in urban space as opposed to industry, and the fragmentation of urban politics.

We end this section by highlighting that precisely because regimes are politically and institutionally constructed, they can also be subject to political transformation. The rent-seeking cabal in Delhi has imposed a low-level equilibrium on the city, one in which a nonproductive privileged core exploits democratic deficits to monopolize public investments and rents. But the regime has been recently politically challenged. The rise of the Aam Aadmi Party represents a revolt of the periphery. Riding the wave of the national anticorruption movement that shook Delhi in 2011–12, AAP first made inroads in state elections in 2013 by capturing most of the city's outer wards (Ramani 2013). It subsequently (2014) won the most commanding majority (sixty-seven of seventy seats) in Indian state election history, and this in the immediate aftermath of the BJP's national electoral victory under Narendra Modi. The social base of AAP consists of slums and unauthorized colonies and progressive elements of the upper middle class, but most telling is that AAP, as a new party, captured the voters' imagination by promising to strengthen Delhi's sovereignty, promote people's participation, and deliver public services. AAP to date has had at best mixed results, in no small part because of its own internal problems. Most revealing, however, have been the constant and increasingly bitter conflicts between the AAP-led state government and the center-government lieutenant governor, who, under the unique status of the state of Delhi (officially the Government of the National Capital Territory of Delhi), has final authority over the government and has effectively blocked a range of reforms. The AAP's sudden rise to power is symptomatic of the acute problems of urban governance in Delhi but also exposes the fundamental institutional blockages to political change.

Conclusion

Focusing on India's urban regimes brings into sharp relief Kohli's (2012) succinct diagnostic of India's developmental travails: a vibrant democracy that is badly governed. We began this chapter by making the claim that one should be skeptical of overly structural explanations that point, for example, to neoliberal globalization and focus instead on the political and institutional conditions that underwrite any given urban regime. Nowhere is this point illustrated more dramatically than in India's cities. Globally, the success of both industrial capitalism and the new post-Fordist services-driven economy has been driven in large part by agglomeration effects and the concentration of local public goods and state-supported innovation environments that are the hallmarks of competitive cities. Indian cities have certainly benefited from agglomeration effects, including some clear cases of state-driven investments, most notably in the case of Bangalore. Moreover, the most dynamic sectors of the Indian economy—high-tech manufacturing and ICT—are highly concentrated in megacities (World Bank 2013, 30). Yet more recently these cities have experienced a significant deacceleration of growth. Exhortations aside, there is little evidence that Delhi is becoming London, Mumbai Shanghai, or Bangalore Singapore. Instead, high levels of growth have been sustained by rent-thick activities that have not supported a commensurate expansion of public services and infrastructure. As a result, even policymakers now widely acknowledge that Indian cities face significant challenges in sustaining growth.

We have argued that this problem stems primarily from the failure of Indian cities to congeal into functional urban regimes, by which we mean pacts of elite economic actors and public officials working in a more or less coordinated fashion to provide the investments and services cities need to leverage their agglomeration advantages. Business interests are of course powerful, and some, as the cases of BATF in Bangalore and Bombay First illustrate, are certainly foresighted enough to want to address these challenges. But the institutional and political environment of the city undermines effective collective action.

As we have shown, the lack of local level sovereignty that defines center-local relations in India and gives the provincial state, to which cities are politically subservient, an outsized development role has all but ensured that Indian cities cannot govern themselves. Absent institutional resources and political opportunities to build the urban regimes that could manage the formidable coordination challenges of urban governance, India's cities have been dominated by cabals of selective business interests and politicians that are partially countervailed by the need to maintain electoral support from middle- and lower-class groups. Though the precise configuration of business-political alliances that underwrite the loose, informal, but nonetheless systemic forms of rent-seeking that feed the cabal varies across cities, the developmental effects are clear. In the absence of planned and coordinated policies of investment and infrastructural development, it has become increasingly difficult to sustain value-adding economic activity in India's megacities. What is good for a highly fragmented set of business interests, which are increasingly dominated by rent-seeking fractions, has not been good for a dynamic, productive form of capitalism. This pattern of accumulation without development has generated perverse and increasingly entrenched forms of social exclusion that are spatially demarcated and legally encoded. The result is that citizenship in Indian cities is becoming increasingly differentiated, making the formation of broad-based reformist popular coalitions less likely. In sum, institutional forms and socioeconomic developments have made programmatic citywide political mobilization unusually hard, while providing incentives for both particularist rent-extraction and rent-sharing, and a focus of the poor and middle-class urban citizens on local, and often defensive, political action.

References

Avritzer, Leonardo. 2002. *Democracy and the Public Space in Latin America*. Princeton, NJ: Princeton University Press.

Bardhan, Pranab. 1983. *The Political Economy of Development in India*. Oxford: Oxford University Press.

Benjamin, Solomon. 2000. "Governance, Economic Settings and Poverty in Bangalore." *Environment and Urbanization* 12 (1): 35–56.

———. 2008. "Occupancy Urbanism: Radicalizing Politics and Economy beyond Policy and Programs." *International Journal of Urban and Regional Studies* 32 (3): 719–29.

Bertorelli, Ebony, Patrick Heller, Siddarth Swaminathan, and Ashutosh Varshney. 2014. "Citizenship in Urban India: The Evidence from Bangalore." A Report by the Janaagraha-Brown Initiative Citizenship Index Bangalore.

Bhan, Gautam. 2013. "Planned Illegalities: Housing and the 'Failure' of Planning in Delhi: 1947–2010." *Economic and Political Weekly* 48 (24): 58–70.

Björkman, Lisa. 2015. *Pipe Politics, Contested Waters: Embedded Infrastructures of Millennial Mumbai*. Durham, NC: Duke University Press.

Chakravorty, Sanjoy. 2013. *The Price of Land: Acquisition, Conflict, Consequence*. New York: Oxford University Press.

Chattaraj, Shahana, and Michael Walton. 2016. "Functional-Dysfunction: Mumbai's Political Economy of Rent Sharing." Working paper, Sheffield University and Harvard Kennedy School.

Chatterjee, Partha. 2004. *The Politics of the Governed: Reflections on Popular Politics in Most of the World*. New York: Columbia University Press.

Centre for Policy Research. *Cities of Delhi*. Various reports available at http://citiesofdelhi. cprindia.org/.

Das, Veena and Michael Walton. 2015. "Political Leadership and the Urban Poor: Local Histories." *Current Anthropology* 56 (S11): 44–54.

Dobbs, Richard., and Shirish Sankhe. 2010. "Comparing urbanization in China and India." *McKinsey Quarterly* 7: 1–3.

Ghertner, D. Asher. 2015. *Rule by Aesthetics: World-Class City Making in Delhi*. New York: Oxford University Press.

Goldman, Michael. 2011. "Speculative Urbanism and the Making of the Next World City." *International Journal of Urban and Regional Studies* 35 (3): 555–81.

GOI (Government of India). High Powered Expert Committee. 2011. *Report on Indian Urban Infrastructure and Services*. New Delhi.

Government of Delhi. Delhi Economic Survey. 2008–2009.

Government of Delhi, Delhi Development Authority. 2007. *Delhi Master Plan*.

———. Various years. *Annual Plan*.

Hashim, S. R. 2009. "Economic Development and Urban Poverty." In *India: Urban Poverty Report 2009*, ed. Ministry of Housing and Urban Poverty Alleviation, 3–27. New Delhi: Oxford University Press.

Heller, Patrick. 2017. "Development in the City: Growth and Inclusion in India, Brazil and South Africa." In *States in the Developing World*, ed. M. Centeno, A. Kohli, and D. Yashar, 309–38. Cambridge: Cambridge University Press.

Issar, Sukriti. 2013. "The Slum in Urban Governance: Policy, Politics and Institutional Transformation in Mumbai, 1880–2010." PhD dissertation, Brown University.

Kadekodi, G., R. Kanbur, and V. Rao. 2007. "Governance and the 'Karnataka Model of Development.'" *Economic and Political Weekly* 42 (8): 649–52.

Kohli, Atul. 2012. *Poverty amid Plenty in the New India*. New York: Cambridge University Press.

Kundu, Amitabh. 2003. "Politics and Economics of Land Policies: Delhi's New Master Plan." *Economic and Political Weekly* August 23: 3530–32.

Le Galès, Patrick. 2002. *European Cities: Social Conflicts and Governance*. New York: Oxford University Press.

Logan, John R., and Harvey L. Molotch. 1988. *Urban Fortunes: The Political Economy of Place.* Berkeley: University of California Press.

McKinsey Global Institute. 2010. *India's Urban Awakening: Building Inclusive Cities, Sustaining Economic Growth.*

Molotch, Harvey. 1976. "The City as a Growth Machine: Toward a Political Economy of Place." *American Journal of Sociology* 82: 209–30.

Mossberger, Karen, and Gary. Stoker. 2001. "The Evolution of Urban Regime Theory: The Challenge of Conceptualization." *Urban Affairs Review* 36 (6): 810–35.

Nijman, J. 2008. "Against the Odds: Slum Rehabilitation in Neoliberal Mumbai." *Cities* 25 (2): 73–85.

Ramani, Srinivasan. 2013. "The Aam Admi Party's Win in Delhi: Dissecting It through Geographical Information Systems." *Economic and Political Weekly* 48 (52). https://www.epw.in/journal/2013/52/web-exclusives/aam-aadmi-partys-win-delhi-dissecting-it-through-geographical

Ranganathan, Malini. 2014. "Paying for Pipes, Claiming Citizenship: Political Agency and Water Reforms at the Urban Periphery." *International Journal of Urban and Regional Research* 38 (2): 590–608.

Roy, Pallavi. 2013 "India's Vulnerable Maturity: Experiences of Maharashtra and West Bengal." In *In the Shadow of Violence: Politics, Economics, and the Problems of Development*, ed. D. C. North, J. J. Wallis, S. B. Webb, and B. R. Weingast,198–232. New York: Cambridge University Press.

Sassen, Saskia. 1991. *The Global City.* Princeton, NJ: Princeton University Press.

Sengupta, Ranjana. 2007. *Delhi Metropolitan: The Making of an Unlikely City.* New Delhi: Penguin.

Sidhwani, Pranav. 2015. "Spatial Inequality in Big Indian Cities." *Economic and Political Weekly* 20: 55–62.

Singh, Gayatri. 2014. "Freedom to Move, Barriers to Stay: An Examination of Rural Migrants' Urban Transition in Contemporary India." PhD dissertation, Department of Sociology, Brown University.

Stoker, Gary., and Karen. Mossberger. 1995. "Urban Regime Theory in Comparative Perspective." *Environment and Planning C: Government and Policy* 12: 195–212.

Stone, C. 1989. *Regime Politics: Governing Atlanta, 1946–1988.* Lawrence: University Press of Kansas.

Sivaramakrishnan, K. C. 2011. *Re-visioning Indian Cities: The Urban Renewal Mission.* New Delhi: Sage Publications.

———. 2015. *Governance of Megacities: Fractured Thinking, Fragmented Setup.* New York: Oxford University Press.

Stone, Clarence N. 2006. "Power, Reform, and Urban Regime Analysis." *City and Community* 5 (1): 23–38.

Vithayathil, Trina, and Gayatri Singh. 2012. "Spaces of Discrimination." *Economic and Political Weekly* 47 (37): 60–66.

Wacquant, Löic. 2008. *Urban Outcasts: Towards a Comparative Sociology of Advanced Marginality.* Cambridge: Polity Press.

Weinstein, Liza. 2014. *The Durable Slum: Dharavi and the Right to Stay Put in Globalizing Mumbai.* Minneapolis: University of Minnesota Press.

World Bank. 2013. *Urbanizing beyond Municipal Boundaries.* Washington, DC: World Bank.

Media in Contemporary India

Journalism Transformed into a Commodity

C. RAMMANOHAR REDDY

As in many democracies, the media in India is independent, noisy, and questioning of the powerful, whoever they may be.[1] At the same time, also as in many democracies, it can show a tendency to defer to the state, to be selective in its questioning, and to be prone to sensationalism.

Where the media in India is now different from that in many countries is that since the early 1990s, print as well as broadcast have been expanding very rapidly. There has been an accompanying explosion in advertising revenue, again in both print and TV. The structure of ownership in the media, too, has been changing. Traditional family ownership has been joined by the entry of new owners (both family and corporate), business empires have extended their reach to the media, and there has been vertical integration as well. During this period, the media's relationship with advertisers has been modified, and editorial practices have changed.

This chapter asks if and how all these changes are connected, how the continuing transformation is affecting the practice of journalism, and how this transformation influences the reading and viewing public. It looks at the past quarter-century, broadly coterminous with the sweeping changes in India's economy, society, and politics.

The focus here is on the print and broadcast (described here also as TV) news media. Social media, which is increasingly important, is not discussed here. Radio, which is changing, too, even if very slowly, and remains largely under state control, is also not discussed here.

Growth of the Indian Media

It is by now well known that India is one of the few countries where print and TV are growing. In print, instead of circulation falling, profitability declining, and newspapers/magazines closing down, as is happening in the advanced markets, exactly the opposite is happening in India. In TV as well, new channels are launched every year, and viewership is simultaneously growing.

There are different sources of information on the media in India, and not all of them are consistent. But all point toward a healthy media sector.

In print, according to the government agency Registrar of Newspapers of India, both the number of publications and their circulation has been rising.[2] Circulation of newspapers has been growing since the late 1980s.[3] More recently, the daily circulation of newspapers published in all languages rose continuously almost four-fold from 98.8 million to 371.46 million between the Indian financial years (April–March) of 2006–7 and 2015–16. The growth of circulation of all print publications was only slightly slower: from 192 million to 610 million between the same two years. The most rapid growth has been in the Indian languages, especially Hindi. English too has grown, but it has begun to see a slowdown in the pace of increase.

This story of continuous growth for two decades and more was broken in 2016–17, when there was a 25 percent drop across the board in circulation, to 488 million. This decline was attributed to the disruptive event of demonetization in November 2016, when 86 percent of the currency in circulation in a highly cash-dependent economy was delegalized. This affected economic activity across sectors, with newspapers and periodicals being one of the more severely affected sectors.[4] But in 2017–18 circulation recovered, though it was acknowledged that it would take a couple of years before the earlier growth momentum would return.[5]

There has been a rapid increase of coverage in TV as well.[6] In 2017, 61 percent of the households in India had a TV, up from 47 percent in 2011. These numbered an estimated 181 million households (Media Research Users Council 2018). According to an earlier report of a management consultancy (KPMG-India 2015, 9), India had by 2015 become the second largest TV-viewing country in the world.

It was in 2000 that the first satellite TV channel was licensed to uplink and downlink programs from India. By 2005 there were 154 such channels; by 2010 there were 603, and by December 2017 there were as many as 877 licensees, of which 389 were news channels and the rest general entertainment channels (Ministry of Information and Broadcasting, *Annual Report 2014–15* and "Status at a Glance" 2018).

Whichever data one looks at, TV viewership is now higher than readership of dailies. For example, in 2017, 75 percent of individuals above the age of twelve had watched TV at least once the previous month, while the corresponding figure for newspaper readership was nearly half that, 39 percent (Media Research Users Council 2018).

The new story is the growth in internet usage. At the end of 2017, India had 363 million users of internet broadband, which was about 27 percent of the population (Telecom Regulatory Authority 2018). The numbers have grown rapidly in recent years as Indians turn to mobile phones to access the internet.

The Facebook-using population was estimated to be as large as 240 million in mid-2017, making India the country with the largest number of users of this social media platform (*LiveMint* 2017). The Twitter population in India was 15.8 million in 2014.

While one can take note of the tremendous growth in readership of newspapers and the size of the TV audience, we need to also note the large numbers still not covered. With only 75 percent literacy, that still leaves a quarter of the population, or more than 300 million people, unable to read a newspaper in any language. Those who are not literate or are barely so may try to obtain news from TV, but 39 percent of all households (more than 115 million households, with more than 575 million people) remain without access to TV in their homes. The Facebook and Twitter populations are much smaller even in relative terms, even if they are noticeably large in particular population segments. The Facebook-using population was only 18 percent (2017) of the national population and the Twitter population just 1.2 percent (2014).

Given the pace of growth in the past ten to fifteen years, one can visualize newspaper readership and TV viewership reaching near universal levels over the next decade.

The Many Faces of the Indian Media

The numbers on readership of newspapers, viewership of TV, and the growth in the number of dailies and TV channels may all look impressive, but the practice of journalism itself faces challenges on many fronts in India.

Here are a few examples from 2016 and 2017.

In September 2017, Gauri Lankesh, an editor of the weekly *Gauri Laknkesh Patrika*, who was known for her vociferous criticism of the forces of the Hindu Right, was shot dead outside her home in Bengaluru. The killing evoked a great deal of public protest. As of early 2018, the killers had not been brought to justice, but it is widely believed that Gauri Lankesh was killed for the views she and her journal expressed.

Gauri Lankesh was the best-known example of violence against journalists, but there have been many instances of unexplained killings, assaults, and state harassment. A compilation of violence against journalists found that in 2017, eleven journalists were killed (in three cases there was a direct link to their work as newspersons), there were twenty-seen cases of police arrests, detentions, and filing of cases, and forty-six instances of attacks by the public (TheHoot.org 2018a).[7]

In 2017, the government's Central Bureau of Investigation raided the offices of the news channel NDTV and the residences of the main promoters and editors following a private complaint of many years standing (*Hindustan Times* 2017). The year before, in October 2016, the government of India had ordered NDTV, which has a bouquet of TV channels, to go off the air for a day because one of its news channels, the Hindi NDTV India, had transmitted live details of a terror attack (*Indian Express* 2016b). Protests by journalists, professional associations like the Editors' Guild, and opposition political parties saw the government placing the order in abeyance.

Other forms of state control, however, did not attract the same degree of protest and attention. In 2016, a newspaper in Kashmir, *Reader Kashmir*, was shut down by the state government presumably because it was asking difficult questions of the Indian state during months of sustained protests against the state and central governments (Scroll.in 2016). In 2017, a photo journalist was arrested in Kashmir because he was allegedly involved with terrorism. In the same case, in court filings in early 2018, the investigating agency outlined the duties and responsibilities of a reporter and explained how the arrested journalist had not performed these roles (Scroll.in 2018).

In 2016, sections of the media took to self-censorship and compromise on the idea of freedom of expression, when they decided that "national security" came first. In September and October 2016, in the midst of heightened tension between India and Pakistan, many decided that they would not be "antinational" in their reporting, and some TV channels in particular took to commentary that could only be described as warmongering (Bhatia 2016).

TV news channels at times abandoned their neutrality and took up openly prejudiced stands especially against Muslims and Kashmiris, so much so that a government negotiator had to call on the central government to ask TV channels to stop fostering hate (*Hindu* 2018).

At times, the media continued to surprise, with journalism of the highest order of public purpose. In February 2018, The Wire.in, a web magazine, published a detailed documentation of a series of extrajudicial killings in Uttar Pradesh (Dixit 2018). This was a topic mainstream newspapers had referred to but never followed up on. Earlier, the same publication had published an investigation into the finances of the son of the chief of the ruling Bharatiya Janata Party (Singh 2017), which other publications did not follow up on, but for which The Wire.in was served a gag order and defamation notice.

In general, the smaller publications appear to take their investigative duties more seriously, while the mainstream newspapers and TV channels turn away. Thus in late 2017, *Caravan* magazine published an explosive two-part report on allegations of an attempt to bribe a judge and then the sudden death of the same judge, who was trying one of the most powerful political personalities in the land (Takle 2017). Yet, until the case reached the courts, most publications other than a couple of online outlets ignored what in any other circumstance would have been a major story.

These are just a few examples—from the English press—of how the media functions and the conditions under which it operates. What they indicate is that the Indian media can show different faces. It can be fearless and take on authority but can also defer to the state. The media can strike an independent path but can also internalize the thinking of the state and actively encourage the most pernicious of attitudes. It can be united in defending the freedom of expression but can also be selective in doing so.

Underlying the Growth of the Media

The Indian media growth story over a longer period of the quarter-century from the early 1990s is the outcome of a number of factors at play, some unique to print, some unique to broadcast; and some unique to the Indian-language media.

In print, the single most important factor underlying the rapid growth in the number of publications and total circulation is the spurt in literacy. In 1971, the literacy rate in India (population aged five and above) was only 35 percent. Over the next forty years it rose fairly quickly (but not fast enough), more than doubling to 73 percent in 2011. The consequent expansion in the size of the literate population (the total population itself more than doubled over the four decades 1971–2011) certainly expanded the market for newspapers. The distance to be traveled to universal literacy also suggests how much more of a potential there remains in the newspaper market.[8]

The second explanation is that alongside the increase in literacy, the growth in per capita income by more than 3 percent a year since the early 1980s and the corresponding reduction in poverty—however slow the progress may have been—have together increased readership of newspapers.

The third reason, relevant to Indian-language media, is the combination of two unique factors, as identified by Robin Jeffrey in landmark studies since the mid-1990s. One, technological change in newspaper printing, in the 1980s transformed the speed of production of Indian-language papers and helped make possible an expansion in circulation. Two, an aggressive attempt by publishers of Indian-language newspapers to be part of the national "market" and the simultaneous recognition by national advertisers that there was a local and nonmetro demand for consumer goods, worked with the change in technology to help drive advertising income and circulation.[9]

However, Jeffrey's explanation does not give sufficient agency to the readers themselves. In the Hindi language, it is an acknowledged fact that the aggressive mobilization of what was called Hindu "sentiment" in north India, which was voiced in Hindi newspapers in the late 1980s and early 1990s, contributed significantly to the rising circulation of newspapers. Another factor was the mobilization of the lower castes—especially the Other Backward Classes (OBCs)—which also found expression in the Indian-language press. The OBC mobilization acquired momentum with the acceptance in 1990 of the Mandal Commission report giving reservations in government jobs, around the same time that newspaper circulation started rising.

In the Hindi-language press, perhaps the most comprehensive explanation is given by Ninan (2007), who locates the expansion of the number of newspapers and readership in the "localization of news" that created a new public sphere in the 1990s at a time when the economic, social, and political landscape of the Hindi heartland was being transformed.

In broadcast a different set of factors has been driving the terrestrial and satellite TV explosion since the 1990s. TV in India hardly grew until the early 1980s, essentially because government policy frowned on the medium as a source of communication and entertainment. In the 1980s, there was first a loosening of regulations on the importation or manufacture of color TV sets, and then there was the establishment of transmitters across the country for terrestrial TV broadcast by the public broadcaster. This was followed by the arrival of cable and satellite TV in the early and mid-1990s and then by the removal of restrictions on transmission by private channels, both of which helped broadcast to expand dramatically.

What all these explanations for the growth of the media in India miss is that the explosion has been facilitated by the larger transformation of the Indian economy over the past quarter-century. The sweeping changes that came by way of what has been called "liberalization" transformed many parts of the Indian economy. An integral part of this structural change was the emergence of a consumer economy in both rural and urban India. This played an important role in expanding the media and in attracting old and new forms of private capital to the sector.

The Advertising Surge in a Rapidly Expanding Economy

One of the ways in which the Indian economy changed in the early 1990s was in the expansion of choice for a variety of consumer goods. This was followed by an expansion in private services in healthcare, insurance, and then education. In the late 1990s, the expansion of bank credit to households also saw the growth in loans for housing, giving a fillip to middle and high-income housing.

An economy that after the early 1990s could create new demand for goods and services and offer a wider choice than before was one where it became important for producers to make large advertising outlays to attract consumers. It was not only consumer advertising for new products (personal computers) and new brands (from Kellogg's to Ford) that fueled the growth of advertising. Services of many kinds—finance (banking and insurance products) and education (training schools and private colleges) were two—saw substantial amounts of advertising. Then, later, when finance for housing became widely available, advertising by housing companies became important in print.

This surge in advertising was a significant factor in driving the growth of the media. Between 1991 and 2012, advertising outlay in print, grew almost fifteen-fold, from Rs. 10.69 billion to Rs. 150 billion; on TV (the "new" medium) the growth on a tiny base was explosive, a thirty-fold jump from a paltry Rs. 3.9 billion to Rs. 124.8 billion over the same period (Kohli-Khandekar, 2013; table 0.2, p. xxxii).[10]

Advertising spending in both print and TV continued to rise in the 2010s. The annual KPMG-India report on the media, which has become the most frequently cited source of information, estimated that by 2016, advertising outlay in both print and TV had both grown even more, each to over Rs. 200 billion (KPMG-India 2017, 73 and 114).

Advertising has become so important for print and broadcast companies that the biggest and most profitable ones now state that they are in the advertising, and not media, business. A 2009 statement made by Vineet Jain, managing director of Bennett Coleman Company Ltd. (BCCL), the publishers of the Times group of publications, for an article in the media has gone into folklore as emblematic of the media in India today and the change wrought by the biggest media group in the country:

> "We don't go by the traditional way of doing business." His [Vineet Jain's] company's dominance can be explained simply, he added, though its methods are not taught in most Western journalism schools. "We are not in the newspaper business, we are in the advertising business," he said. With newspapers sold so cheaply and generating little

circulation revenue, newspapers depend more on ad revenue, he said, and, "if ninety per cent of your revenues come from advertising, you're in the advertising business." (Auletta 2012)

Even as advertising income was growing sharply, in relative terms circulation income (not circulation numbers) was declining.

Ever since the early 1990s, when large newspapers began an aggressive pricing war to grab market share in circulation, the prices of newspapers have been brought down to extremely low levels, and with that the share of circulation revenue has declined.[11] For the entire industry, revenues from circulation now contribute only a third of total income, while advertising contributes to two-thirds; that is, advertising revenue brings in twice as much as circulation revenue (KPMG-India 2017, 121).[12] The picture is much the same in broadcast media, with subscription revenue being only 32 percent of total revenue in 2016 (KPMG-India 2017, 80). Advertising, then, is king in the Indian media.

Talking about the media in the United States in the 1980s, Herman and Chomsky (1994) referred to income from advertising as an "advertising subsidy" that gave publications that received a large income from advertising an advantage over others, but which made the media as such vulnerable to external pressure.

In India this is now more of an "advertising dominance," especially in print. Newspapers depend on advertising—corporate advertising at that—and this must make them circumspect about how far they will go in questioning particular corporate interests. Advertising is important for TV, too, though new regulations in the 2010s requiring subscribers to channels to install set-top boxes that controlled and metered access, shifted the balance of power from local distributors to the TV companies, thereby potentially increasing the share of subscription income in total revenue.

Expansion of Corporate Ownership

The past quarter-century has seen many changes in the form of ownership, substantial new investment, as well as considerable vertical and horizontal integration. All this resulted in healthy profitability for both privately and publicly owned companies, though as in any other industry there was a range of outcomes.

The lucrative advertising business in traditional print and TV was not the only driving force behind the expansion of investment. The changes in technology— essentially digital—meant that new forms of dissemination of information (video, through the internet on desktops, tablets, and eventually the mobile phone) became possible and these could be monetized. Conglomerates also saw an expansion into entertainment as a route to a larger volume of business. The new business was called "infotainment"—a combination of information and entertainment. This in some cases came to have a negative impact on journalism as public purpose.

Expansion of Investment

The media in India has always largely been privately owned. The state has had a dominant presence only in radio, and until the early 1990s it had control over TV. In print, ownership has traditionally been in the hands of closely held family enterprises, many of which had direct or indirect links with political parties.

What has changed since the early 1990s is a modification of the old forms of ownership, the entry of new kinds of owners, and a new kind of connection to politics. There are also differences between print and the newer medium of TV, though as we shall see, there has been a criss-crossing of interests between the two.

Jeffrey (2015), analyzing the ownership profiles of the ten most widely read newspapers in 2012, concluded that "all were controlled by families; none was a fully public company controlled by its shareholders. Four had a limited number of publicly traded shares." In the boom of the past quarter-century, there has been some movement toward corporatization of family enterprises, with the original owners retaining control (see the discussion in Jeffrey 2015, 29–31 of such changes in the leading Hindi daily, *Dainik Jagran*). The new development has been the expansion of corporate entities already in print or TV to other media segments and, most significant, the diversification of business empires into the media through acquisitions and new ventures.[13]

In TV, where, unlike in print, there were no "legacy" entities, the emergence of new corporate entities was most marked.

The ownership pattern in TV is of four kinds. One, new companies have made their foray into media through TV (for example, Zee TV initially in Hindi, NDTV in English). Two, another set of new companies has entered into tie-ups with foreign partners (TV18, which is part of the Network 18 group, is an example). Three, the older print companies, like BCCL, HT Media, and the India Today group, have expanded into TV. The fourth kind is the most recent and potentially most consequential for media autonomy: the diversification of conglomerates into the media.

The presence of business groups diversifying into the media, too, is not new. The 1950s and 1960s did see industrial groups like the Tatas and Birlas acquire interest in English newspapers. But in scale and intention, the entry of the conglomerates into the media today outstrips that in the 1950s. India's largest business group, Reliance Industries, now has stakes in a number of media companies. In a complicated funding and investment exercise that began in 2012, Reliance took full control in 2014 of the Network 18 media group and acquired a substantial stake in the Eenadu media group of companies. Network 18 has news channels in TV in English and Indian languages, publishes magazines, and runs popular news and entertainment websites. Eenadu, which started as a new and radically different Telugu newspaper, has acquired a large footprint across the country in both English and a number of Indian languages (Hindi, Bengali, Odia, and Telugu, to name just a few) in news and entertainment TV channels. Reliance now has control of all non-Telugu businesses of Eenadu (Guha Thakurta 2013).[14]

The Aaditya Birla group, another of India's large conglomerates with interests in telecom, finance, power, cement, textiles, and more, took a 27.5 percent stake in Living Media, the holding company of the prominent India Today stable, which publishes a daily and a weekly newsmagazine, and also has news and general entertainment TV channels in both English and the Indian languages (India Today.in 2012).

The rationale for the two conglomerates' entry into media is to gain and control access to digital content to feed the subscribers in the groups' telecom networks. The Aditya Birla group has been in telecom since the 1990s, and in 2016 Reliance re-entered the telecom business with a major investment which quickly made it the second largest telecom company in the country. The telecom business is now driven not by voice but by data, which requires access to content. Whatever the rationale, the fact is that some of the biggest business groups in India now own large chunks of the media, especially TV.[15]

Horizontal and Vertical Integration

Alongside the entry of conglomerates into the media sector, companies have spread their wings horizontally and vertically. This has been driven by the need to straddle as many markets as possible.

In the first instance, the more successful print companies (in both English and the Indian languages) have embarked on horizontal integration across different forms of media. Whereas in the 1990s there were few cross-media operations, such operations are now the norm. Two halfhearted attempts at introducing legislation to regulate cross-media holdings were made, first in the late 1990s and then again in the 2000s. Both were abandoned, mainly due to resistance by the larger media companies.[16]

The BCCL/Times group is in newspapers, magazines, television, radio, internet—and in films too. It also has footprints in English, Hindi, and other Indian languages (Kannada). BCCL is not alone. HT Media has expanded far beyond its traditional base of print in English and Hindi. It now has TV channels in English and Hindi. The Living Media group is in print and TV (English and Hindi). Zee TV is in broadcast (Hindi and many Indian languages) and print.[17]

Second, there has been vertical consolidation in broadcast, with the major TV channels setting up distribution companies as well, thereby extending their hold from production to transmission and then to distribution. Companies fronting for political ruling parties have also entered distribution, since they see political gains to be had from controlling the distribution of TV signals to consumers. In Tamil Nadu, the battle over distribution ebbs and flows with every change in the state government. The political parties in power in Chhattisgarh and Punjab have both on occasion tried to control distribution by setting up front companies. Nationally, major TV channels like Zee TV have also set up separate distribution companies (Mehta 2015, 30–32).[18]

Ownership and Profitability

There have not been many insights into the financials of media companies, partly because many of them remain closely held private entities. However, analyses of the public limited companies among them as also investigations by enterprising journalists show a profitable industry, though it is vulnerable like any other to the vicissitudes of the marketplace.

One set of analyses carried out by TheHoot.org during 2016–18 showed that the big media companies were extremely profitable. The biggest among them, the BCCL/Times group, recorded earnings before interest and tax of 23 percent on sales in 2015–16. This was in the middle range, higher than that of HT Media and the ABP group but lower than that of Zee TV. Analyses of other media houses such as Jagran Prakashan (publishers of the most widely circulated daily in India, *Dainik Jagran*), TV Today, Sun TV, HT Media, and the Indian Express Group show a similar picture of very healthy profitability.[19]

The same analysis that noted the healthy profits of BCCL also revealed the extent to which it was dependent on advertising. In 2015–16, advertising contributed to 65 percent of the media and nonmedia operations of the entire group.[20] In keeping with BCCL's aggressive pricing strategy to garner market share, circulation income from all media businesses (print, TV, radio and the internet) brought in only 7 percent of group income for the year.[21]

These are, of course, numbers of the bigger media groups. How many of the medium-sized and small media enterprises are making profits and, if they are not, why they are in operation are questions for which one can only offer tentative answers.

In 2011, T. N. Ninan, editorial director and part owner of the *Business Standard*, offered summary data to argue that (1) print and not TV was the healthier sector, with profit after tax returns ranging between 8 percent and 20 percent of sales (similar to the numbers presented above), (2) in TV it was the entertainment channels and regional news channels enjoying dominance that were in the pink, and (3) English news channels, with just 1 percent of the total viewership, were in bad shape, with the listed firms at the time losing 80–90 percent of their market valuations (Ninan 2011).

It is unlikely the picture has changed much in the years since. One could add that the Hindi press has continued to thrive and so too print in the other Indian languages.

Media Owners and Political Parties

If the consensus is that while print is thriving and the situation is not quite the same in broadcast, why are there so many satellite TV channels being launched every year? Who is doing so, especially in Indian-language broadcast, where the numbers are growing the fastest? And why does India have so many news channels?[22]

It is not just the presence of corporates like Reliance and the Birlas in the media that we need to explore. There is also the individual politician or political party's desire to own or have a stake in a TV channel and, somewhat less so, in a newspaper. The media's link with politics is not something new in India. One of the platforms for India's independence movement was newspapers and magazines. M. K. Gandhi himself had a weekly magazine, *Young India*, in 1919 and then in 1932 the *Harijan*. Later the Congress Party, which led the national movement, established *National Herald* in the 1930s to act as a mouthpiece for the party and the anticolonial struggle. Across the country, similar newspapers and periodicals were launched in the decades ahead of independence in 1947, in both English and Indian languages. After independence, a number of other political parties had their own publications—the Communist Party of India did, and then after a split in 1964 the Communist Party of India (Marxist) started its own publications, as did regional parties like the DMK.

What is different now is that the new media ventures with direct or indirect political links are not part of a larger movement of any kind, nor are they meant to spread a larger political idea. They are for the most part ventures to project a particular individual or family in politics (see Ninan 2013 and also Parthasarathy 2013; Bhushan 2015).

Guha Thakurta (2015) has a useful listing of thirty-eight well-known cases of important political personalities who now control or are linked to media outlets—mainly TV channels. The personalities are from across the political spectrum, both those in power and those in opposition, and the ownership is of Hindi and other Indian-language channels. Leading members of parliament, too, are owners of media outlets.

With the considerable financial resources that political parties and individuals have at their command, the launch of private TV channels and newspapers poses no great challenge, even to regional parties. The costs involved are not large if you are a well-endowed political organization. The licensing fee for both news and entertainment channels whose programs are uplinked from India is a very low Rs. 200,000 per annum, and licenses are given for a decade. To initially obtain a license for a news channel, one needs to have a net worth of Rs. 200 million and Rs. 50 million for every additional news channel (Ministry of Information and Broadcasting, *Annual Report 2015–16*, 88–89).

In his interesting but not fully documented study of TV in India, Mehta (2015, 34–35) places the cost of starting up and operation at a low level. In Hindi and other north Indian-language channels, small news channels are, Mehta argues, set up for as little as Rs. 5–6 million of capital expenditure, with annual running costs of Rs. 15–25 million. In the south, where production values are higher, his numbers are of Rs. 100–500 million for capital expenditure and Rs. 200 million for annual running expenditure.[23]

For individuals or organizations with large (sometimes illegal) funds and fronting for political groups, these numbers are very affordable, especially when owning a TV channel can buy you prestige and influence. Based on interviews in the TV industry, Mehta (2015, 25–28) suggests that the owners and operators of India's satellite TV channels are (1) politicians, (2) businesses with interest in real estate and personal finance schemes, and (3) corporates. This is somewhat the same conclusion that one study of Odia media came to (Pattnaik 2014). "Politicians" here refers both to political parties that have started TV channels via front organizations and to individuals setting up TV channels, also with front organizations.

One can argue with the limited and somewhat impressionistic information we have that (1) owning and operating a TV channel is a source of prestige and doable if you have illegal funds that can be recycled, (2) political groups and individuals seek to use TV more than print to push across their ideas because they see viewers as more impressionable than readers, (3) for political groups with funds, the costs of a license and capital investment for a satellite TV are reasonable and are therefore an attractive option ahead of elections,[24] and (4) there are nonpolitical entities such as media companies in other sectors that wish to expand their footprint by expanding into TV.

Private investment in the Indian media, then, takes different forms and has different motivations. At one end there are large corporate entities belonging to old and new media businesses (BCCL, HT Today, Living Media, NDTV, and Zee TV) and new entrants that are conglomerates (Reliance Industries). At the other end, especially in Indian-language broadcast, there are innumerable small- and big-time political operators running satellite TV channels, starting with news and current affairs and then building a bouquet of entertainment channels.

Transformation of the Media in a Rapidly Growing Economy

Advertising may have been growing continuously, but for individual media companies the task is to promise advertisers a larger and growing readership or viewership. So to attract advertising, media companies turned their newspapers and TV channels into consumer products like any other in order to expand the audience.

In newspapers, while price competition was one thing driving circulation strategies, a transformation in the nature of the medium and its content was another. Beginning in the mid-1990s, almost all general newspapers in all languages began to give more space to recreational content to a greater or less degree. This inevitably moved in the direction of sensationalizing news, playing up scandals and more generally heading in the direction of a tabloidization. A similar process took place in TV from the late 1990s, when licenses for private broadcast started to be handed out in large numbers—sensationalism in both news and entertainment began to grow in the search for eyeballs.

In the process, the media lost its traditional character of being first and foremost a provider of news. It increasingly became a commodity like any other that had to be sold in the largest numbers in order to acquire the maximum amount of advertising. This is not to deny that the media had always been a commercial enterprise, with owners having to keep an eye on income and expenditure. What has been different in recent decades is that journalism has been defined not so much by the authenticity, reliability, and depth of its coverage but by how well it sold itself (including in packaging) as a commodity. This is true of the publications of all media companies—the older family-owned companies, the new entrants to the media, and the business empires that entered the media, both print and broadcast. While there were, of course, notable exceptions among newspapers and magazines, less so in TV, the overall complexion of the media changed—away from serious reporting and toward, to put it strongly, trivialization. (The complexity of the media—or what I call the two-headed nature of the media—is discussed in detail in the concluding part of this chapter.)

The packaging of the media as a commodity is not unique to India. The trivialization-cum-tabloidization process took place in the Western democracies as well, perhaps earlier, from the 1980s onwards. What was unique to India is that the process took place at the same time that the economy, too, was transformed in a rapid manner. Growth rates moved to a higher level, credit to bankable households fueled spending, consumer spending in such households shifted toward high-end goods, and the introduction of newer products and services kept consumer spending of a certain kind going.

The transformation of both content and packaging had a two-way connection with the transformation of the Indian economy. The changes in the economy influenced the media, including its finances. The media too developed an interest in an economy that was on a high-growth path and in the maintenance of a framework that pushed the economy in that direction.

The process of commodification of the media, then, had two effects on journalism in both print and broadcast. First, commodification invested publishers and owners with an interest in an organization of the society and economy that facilitated market expansion. This was reflected in a perspective and coverage that focused on factors and processes promoting (or inhibiting) growth and a corresponding neglect of livelihood and social concerns. The neglect in the media of important social issues like health fits into the same perspective and has been highlighted by many commentators (see Dreze and Sen 2013 for just one example).

The second important aspect of what can be called the "commodification" of the Indian media was that in the race for eyeballs and in the trivialization that was taking place in an overall scenario of rapid growth, professional journalism practices were gradually abandoned. A part of this process was deference to the demands of advertisers, who came to wield enormous influence.

The impact of commodification can be seen in newspaper practices in which advertising takes precedence over the priorities of journalism. Since the early 1990s, the following practices relating to advertising, which were earlier the exception (if not prohibited altogether by editorial/news departments), have now become conventions:

1. Entire front pages are sold to single-page advertisers; on occasion even the masthead is sold to advertisers.
2. Right-hand pages are routinely handed over in full to advertisers.
3. Block ads are placed in the middle of news articles.
4. There are often explicit reference to "sponsors" in entertainment, business, and sports news stories and features.
5. Most scandalous is the phenomenon of "paid news"—which, as its name suggests, sees advertisers paying for news space where adverts masquerade as

news. This happens during elections, when candidates buy news stories. The practice is to be found in both the English and Indian-language press and is not as uncommon as one might hope (Raman 2009 and Sainath 2010).

6. We also have practices pioneered by the BCCL/Times group (since adopted by others) to publish "advertorials"—advertising supplements that look like news supplements (with notices discernible only on close examination). They also sign "private ad treaties" with select advertisers, under which a newspaper enters into a contract to provide advertisement space in exchange for a stake in the advertising company's equity (Shukla 2008).

Similar practices can be observed on TV too. For example, on popular programs and channels a distracting proportion of the screen is taken over by running advertisements.

Journalism in the Transformed Media

The overbearing direct and indirect influence that advertising has on the media does not mean that newspapers and TV programs are now little more than consumer products. There is a vast difference between media outlets, with the smaller ones (in print) tending to be braver than the larger enterprises and having imbibed a sense of public purpose. They can on occasion speak truth to power. Journalism does not shy away from covering stories of corruption when they do break. They also invest considerable resources in covering "crisis" events. An illustration of the latter was the coverage that print, TV, and even radio gave to the disruption that the 2016 demonetization of 86 percent of currency in circulation caused to human lives (Reddy 2017, chapter 9).

The credibility and therefore the salability of print and broadcast are also based on their ability to provide news and opinion. They must therefore periodically establish their legitimacy as providers of news and opinion, and not as carriers of advertising.

However, as argued, the larger changes that have taken place in the Indian economy since the early 1990s have had an influence on journalism practices in print and TV.

Adapting Kohli's (2012, 49–51) explanation for a probusiness tilt of the readers of newspapers themselves, one can argue that in the current setting, journalists, too, see that the expansion in job opportunities and rise in compensation levels in the media have been coterminous with the years of rapid economic growth. They thus begin to develop a similar stake in the reproduction and expansion of the economy in the same form. All of this has less to do with greater corporate influence in the media than with commodification of the media.

Market expansion or economics is, however, not the only agenda driving media priorities. There are other new dimensions in which the media now show an open partiality to certain worldviews. From the time of the boom years of the economy (2003 to about 2009 or 2010), the media served as a mouthpiece for the idea that the time has come for India to take its place at the high table of world affairs—to become a "great power" in political and economic matters. This approach has been given new strength during the tenure of the Bharatiya Janata Party (BJP)–led government that took office in May 2014. Both print and broadcast speak with some uniformity on national security matters, and there is an aggressive and even chauvinistic posturing on India's security interests, especially with respect to Pakistan, China, and Bangladesh.

This follows from both an unquestioning acceptance of government policy and an uncritical acceptance of briefings on national security. Dissenting voices are given token space. By and large the media narrative is that India must aggressively work to secure its place at the high table when it comes to global affairs. From such a position it is a short step to suspending one's critical perspective, as the media has done over the "antinational" argument that assumed prominence in 2016 and was aggressively used by the government and the ruling BJP to control criticism (Bhatia 2016).

Ram (2011), making an overall assessment of the state of contemporary media in India, recognizes their weaknesses but takes an overall positive view. Where there are weaknesses, the pattern is one of "two worlds"—the old world (essentially print) upholding the values of an independent press, and the new world (essentially satellite TV) not carrying out the roles expected of it. This is a sanguine view of the media today.

I would instead characterize the media as "Janus-faced," with the two faces present in both print and broadcast. One face is independent, questioning and articulating people's concerns. The other face shows an unhealthy willingness to curry favor with the (central and state) government and corporate India; it only selectively questions the government and takes up issues of public importance episodically and only fleetingly. At the same time, it is prone to a herd mentality when it does carry out investigations. It frequently conducts a trial by media, shows little respect for privacy, and sensationalizes news. There are, of course, differences between publications and across platforms, but the overall trend is in one direction and this is a noticeable shift over the past quarter-century. In the absence of in-house training and mentoring and with the breakdown of the larger guiding principles and norms surrounding journalism, standard journalistic practices have tended to lose their rigor and autonomy.

From the foregoing discussion one can argue that the overall outlook of the media has changed in the decades since the early 1990s, a consequence of the sweeping changes in India over the decades since then. The media has embraced the market and is also now more aware of the financial bottom line. In the process it has lost the larger capacity for independent thinking and the ability to stand outside, both of which are required of the free press. It has instead internalized the values of the dominant paradigm in a rapidly changing economy. The result is that the media and the journalists who people them by and large develop a certain outlook and speak a language that is similar to that of the dominant classes.[25]

This change has less to do with corporate ownership of the media than with imbibing an outlook consonant with that of the corporates. The greater influence on the practice of journalism is less that which comes with corporate ownership of the media than that which comes from internalizing the dominant tendencies of the larger society in which the media function.

This is not to say that the new forms of corporate ownership and the corporatization of the old pattern of family-held ownership have no influence on the practice of journalism. They certainly do. Journalists have been asked to leave media organizations when ownership changes hands.[26] Media owners who have other business interests are also known to use their newspapers and TV channels to either directly or indirectly push the agenda of their nonmedia business.[27]

More significantly, the commodification of the media is becoming complete with owners and publishers altogether abandoning the idea of journalism as public purpose, and developing individual "brands" to meet the needs of individual "markets." Rajeev Chandrasekhar, a member of parliament and an investor in more than one major media publication and TV channel, said in one interview in 2017:

> I think the mandate in the newsrooms of the media brands I have invested in is very simple. . . . You have got to have a large share of the market. You have to do what you have to do to get a large share of the market. That's my only brief. If that happens to be a slight leftist slant in a market that requires a leftist slant, they do that, if it requires a certain slant in another market, they do that.

In this perspective, credibility is also defined in terms of the size of the market:

> For us, it's about looking at building brands that are credible. . . . Credible is important from the size of the audience, and that the audience believes in it. That is the only measure of it. (Venkataramkrishnan 2017)

This is not an isolated view. In early 2017, BCCL launched a second English news channel, Mirror Now, which adopted a more moderate in reporting than the leading English news channel from the same stable, Times Now, which is known for its hectoring tone of political opposition and at the same time an unwillingness to question the government. When it was launched, its owners called Mirror Now "a differentiated product" (*Economic Times* 2017).

Media and Political Choices:
Case of Narendra Modi, 2014

The change in the media's reporting and its loss of autonomy can be illustrated with the political preferences that the media expressed in the run-up to the May 2014 parliamentary elections.

The media does not finally determine the specific political choices of the voter; a whole host of other factors also play a role. But to my mind the more pernicious and, to use a strong word, insidious influence is in the molding of the larger worldview. This is now the broad consensus among political scientists,[28] though debate on the media's effects on the political values of individuals continues (literature cited in Stromback 2008, 232).

During the 2014 elections the BJP—or rather the Narendra Modi campaign—skillfully managed all media platforms (print, commercial radio, TV, social media, and outdoor advertising) to trounce the ruling United Progressive Alliance (UPA) on the hustings. Indeed, writing in the midst of the campaign, the political scientist Suhas Palshikar argued that the 2014 contest was turning out to be a "mediatised" election.[29]

After the dramatic outcome of the 2014 elections, many commentators observed that the media had showed a high degree of partisanship toward Narendra Modi and simultaneously ran down the record of the Congress Party–led UPA. The Congress Party, decimated at the polls, was itself quick to blame TV channels for selling out to the public relations agencies managing the Modi campaign.[30]

Should we say, then, that 2014 was a watershed, with the Indian media in all forms and in most languages organizing an electoral victory for one particular candidate? While the BJP campaign did work to consolidate the Hindu vote, the stronger message was that Narendra Modi, the architect of the "Gujarat miracle," would oversee a similar transformation at the national level. This, with the equally effective denigration of the UPA and Congress Party record, helped push into the background Modi's responsibility for the 2002 post-Godhra communal carnage in Gujarat.

A somewhat similar argument has been made as part of the National Election Study 2014:

> Modi managed to connect to voters with higher media exposure with
> his promise of reducing the role of the state in the economy and his
> image as a pro-business reformer. We hypothesise that voters with

higher media exposure were more likely to support economic reform, and this was the reason why media exposure had such a large effect on the choice of the BJP in 2014. (Verma and Sardesai 2014, 87)

Indeed, the influence of the media in Narendra Modi's march to power in 2014 can be explained in these terms rather than as the result of an overt endorsement of the BJP's prime ministerial candidate.[31]

The media in India, then, has a political influence that is exercised in a broad manner. As argued earlier, the growth in the number of outlets and their readership and viewership, the new dominance of advertising, and corporate ownership have worked together to make the media very much a commodity. The media's interest in continued expansion of this commodity has made it embrace a worldview that puts a premium on rapid economic growth and a simultaneous expansion of the consumer market.

This perspective is increasingly one that sees India as becoming a major economic (and military) power that will take its place in the world. In this worldview there is also a need for firm action by the state. The media therefore favors—through providing disproportionate reporting, comment, and space and time—political parties and individuals who express such a worldview and promise to act on it. So it is not so much a case of corporate owners dictating to their outlets whom or what to favor and endorse. It is instead the orientation of the transformed media of the post-1990s looking for and favoring political platforms that espouse a certain worldview, which, of course, is in consonance with that of the corporate owners.

Political preferences, then, are not expressed in favor of particular individuals as dictated to by the corporate owners. They are expressed instead in terms of parties and candidates who express and promise to act on what is now the dominant perspective in the media. Simultaneously, the political parties and individuals who disagree with such a perspective are given less space and more critical comment.

There is, of course, no single and homogenous worldview. There are differences within the media. But within the differences and in the midst of the media acting as an independent institution, there is a dominant perspective that influences political perspectives.

Conclusions: Media's Faustian Bargain with Commodification

With the kind of fault lines we have discussed, the Indian media today appears to fit Herman and Chomsky's "propaganda model" of the US media in the 1980s.

The five filters Herman and Chomsky saw in this propaganda model seem applicable to the Indian context:

(1) the size, concentrated ownership, owner wealth and profit orientation of the dominant mass media firms; (2) advertising as the primary income source of the mass media, (3) the reliance of the media on information provided by government, business, and "experts" funded and approved by these primary sources and agents of power, (4) "flak" as means of disciplining the media and (5) "anticommunism" as a national religion and control mechanism. (Herman and Chomsky 1994, 2)

All that one has to do is replace "anticommunism" with "national security" and "antinationalism," and the filters perfectly fit the Indian media today. However, Herman and Chomsky themselves admitted that their propaganda model "leaves many nuances and secondary effects unanalyzed. There are other factors that should be recognized" (304). Indeed, while important fault lines weaken the Indian media, one must recognize that here as well one needs to offer a nuanced and multilayered understanding.

In spite of all their weaknesses, print and TV in India are far from consistently frivolous or deferential to the state and the powerful in business and society. The exposés on corruption and the investigations into state abuse of human rights (occasional as they may be) and the wariness of governments and political personalities toward the media also suggest that they remain free and lively. Sections of the media are also willing to take up new forms of investigation—as they did in 2011 with the Wikileaks papers (*The Hindu* 2011) and then more recently in the investigation into the Panama Papers (*Indian Express* 2016a).

One should also explicitly acknowledge cases of bravery where journalists have taken on the state and the powerful and, especially in district capitals and small towns, have paid the price with criminal defamation cases slapped on them, arrests (Seshu 2016), and even death, as most shockingly in the murder of Gauri Lankesh in September 2017.

It is the Janus-faced nature of the media in India today that gives rise frequently to the use of Dickensian phrases to capture its complexity.[32] One can perhaps understand this double nature by positing that publishers and owners of media outlets realize that their legitimacy in the eyes of their audience is derived from the idea of "media autonomy." Newspapers and private TV channels may wish to turn their "product" into a commodity that can be sold to the largest number of "consumers" and provide advertisers with the largest reach possible, but they can do so only by continuing to assert that they are the fourth estate. The media is quick to assert its autonomy when needed and makes frequent calls to guard its independence. And publications and TV channels can convince their audiences that they are independent only if they do carry out credible informational, adversarial and watchdog roles, as outlined by Ram (2011), even if only occasionally and within limits, all the while pushing the boundaries toward greater and greater commodification.

When I use the term "commodification," I do not suggest that the media could perform, if it wished to, a role as watchdog without regard to meeting costs or without a concern for profitability. Nor must the media be independently funded so that no publisher need look at the bottom line.[33]

I argue instead that with Herman and Chomsky's "advertising subsidy" in the United States turning into "advertising dominance" in India alongside a simultaneous search for a rapid growth in readership and viewership based on price competition driving cover prices lower and lower, the media must perforce become a commodity. This advertising dominance is the outcome of entrepreneurs discovering that the media has a potential for immense profitability. This potential can be realized if the hunger for news and entertainment can be met, suitably packaged into a commodity that is sold to both advertisers and consumers. If the product sells more if the contents are trivialized, the entrepreneur-publishers will do so. Yet the product must retain an aura of public service performed by a watchdog.

However, the entrepreneur-publishers enter into a Faustian bargain as they aggressively seek to enhance their market share while claiming to be watchdogs. As Ninan put it perceptively:

> The true power of the media comes from the perception that it is a public good. The Constitutional scheme under which freedom of the press is a part of the freedom of expression relies essentially on the social sanction given to the media, to be a public voice for the common good. . . . The fatal temptation to which publishers succumbed was therefore not political but economic, to look at the media increasingly as a business, and less and less as a part of the public space in a democracy. (Ninan 2011, 10–11)

As part of this drive to expand the market and obtain a greater share of the growing pie, the norms of journalism and publishing are first weakened and then abandoned. The media in India, while strongly resisting state intervention, has paid only lip service to self-regulation.[34]

In presenting the media in contemporary India as dual-faced, it would be erroneous to simultaneously argue that there was an earlier idyllic phase when the media exercised its autonomy and fulfilled the roles traditionally expected of a watchdog. One can argue instead that after the Indian press fulfilled its mission during the anticolonial movement, it transformed itself into an ally of the state in independent India. This changed with the opportunities thrown up by economic liberalization and the subsequent expansion of the market. In the absence of any serious self-regulation, the media fell victim to the dictates of the market.

While there has been a dramatic change from the pre-1990s era to the post-1990s decades, there is a continuity as well. Then as now, the press was largely privately owned; then as now, a handful of newspapers had a large circulation; then as now, the media did not fully exercise its power as an autonomous institution. As argued in this chapter, within this continuity, however, major changes have taken place. These changes broadly reflect the changes in India's society and politics.[35]

References

Auletta, Ken. 2012. "Citizens Jain: Why India's Newspaper Industry Is Thriving." *New Yorker*, October 8. http://www.newyorker.com/magazine/2012/10/08/citizens-jain.

Bhatia, Siddharth. 2016. "When Journalists Become Jingoistic Cheerleaders." September 24. http://thewire.in/68389/journalists-become-jingoistic-cheerleaders/.

Bhushan, S. 2015. "'Regulation' and 'Non-media' Money in the Media." *Economic and Political Weekly* 50 (7): 21–23.

Dixit, Neha. 2018. "Chronicle of the Crime Fiction That Is Adityanath's Encounter Raj." The Wire.in, February 24. https://thewire.in/226426/chronicle-crime-fiction-adityanaths-encounter-raj/.

Dreze, Jean, and Amartya Sen. 2013. *An Uncertain Glory: India and Its Contradictions*. New Delhi: Allen Lane.

Economic and Political Weekly. 2014a. "Anger, Aspiration and Apprehension." Editorial, May 24. Volume 49 (21).

———. 2014b. "The Fourth Estate That Vanished." Editorial, May 24. Volume 49 (21).

Economic Times. 2017. "Times Network Launches a Second English News channel Mirror Now." March 23. https://economictimes.indiatimes.com/industry/media/entertainment/media/times-network-launches-second-english-news-channel-mirror-now/articleshow/57782109.cms.

Guha Thakurta, P. 2013. "Curbing Media Monopolies." *Economic and Political Weekly* 48 (16): 10–14.

———. 2015. "Media Ownership Trends in India." Paper presented at a workshop at the Indian Institute of Advanced Studies, Shimla, November.

Herman, E. S., and Noam Chomsky. 1994. *Manufacturing Consent*. 2nd ed. London: Vintage.

Hindu. 2011. "The India Cables." http://www.thehindu.com/news/the-india-cables/.

———. 2016. "Editors Guild Condemns One-Day ban on NDTC India." November 4. http://www.thehindu.com/news/national/Editors-Guild-condemns-one-day-ban-on-NDTV-India/article16436556.ece.

———. 2018. "Vicious Propaganda against Kashmiris by Some TV Channels Affecting the Peace Process Says Special Representative." January 10. http://www.thehindu.com/news/national/other-states/dineshwar-sharma-flags-propaganda-on-tv/article22413701.ece.

Hindustan Times. 2017. "CBI Raids NDTV's Prannoy Roy, Wife over 'Bank Fraud.'" June 17. https://www.hindustantimes.com/india-news/cbi-raids-homes-of-ndtv-s-prannoy-roy-his-wife-in-2008-bank-fraud-case/story-HJOdY5DmNpbZNmZhcIuMBK.html.

India Today.in. 2012. "Aditya Birla Group Acquires 27.5% Stake in India Today's Holding Group Living Media India." May 19. http://indiatoday.intoday.in/story/aditya-birla-group-india-today-group-living-media-india/1/189418.html.

Indian Express. 2016a. "Indians in Panama Papers" April 5. http://indianexpress.com/article/india/india-news-india/panama-papers-list-amitabh-bachchan-kp-singh-aishwarya-rai-iqbal-mirchi-adani-brother/.

———. 2016b. "Take NDTV India Off Air on November 9 for Pathankot: I&B Panel." November 4. http://indianexpress.com/article/india/india-news-india/1-day-ban-on-ndtv-india-proposed-for-its-pathankot-coverage/.

Jeffrey, Robin. 2010a."Monitoring Indian Newspapers: Understanding the Indian State." in *Media and Modernity*, ed. Robin Jeffrey, 147–65. New Delhi: Permanent Black.

———. 2010b. "Advertising and Indian-Language Newspapers: How Capitalism Supports (Certain) Cultures and (Some) States, 1947–1996." In *Media and Modernity*, ed. Robin Jeffrey, 166–99. New Delhi: Permanent Black.

———. 2015. "Newspapers in India: Diversity, Ownership and Future." In *Media at Work in China and India: Discovering and Dissecting*, ed. Robin Jeffrey and Rononjoy Sen, 25–42. New Delhi: Sage.

Kaushik, K. 2015. "The Tempest: Have Radhika and Prannoy Roy Undermined NDTV?" *Caravan*, December. http://www.caravanmagazine.in/reportage/the-tempest-prannoy-radhika-roy-ndtv.

Kohli, Atul. 2012. *Poverty amid Plenty in the New India*. Cambridge: Cambridge University Press.

Kohli-Khandekar, V. 2013. *The Indian Media Business*. 4th ed. New Delhi: Sage Response.

KPMG-India. 2015. *Indian Media and Entertainment Industry Report 2015*. https://assets.kpmg.com/content/dam/kpmg/pdf/2015/03/FICCI-KPMG_2015.pdf.

———. 2017. *Indian Media and Entertainment Industry Report*. https://home.kpmg.com/in/en/home/insights/2017/03/kpmgmediaoutlook.html.

Kumar, Sashi. 2011. "Hegemony in Contemporary Culture and Media: Need for a Counter Initiative." *Economic and Political Weekly* 46 (51): 38–43.

LiveMint. 2017. "India Now Has the Highest Number of Facebook Users, Beat the US: US Report." July 14. http://www.livemint.com/Consumer/CyEKdaltF64YycZsU72oEK/Indians-largest-audience-country-for-FacebookReport.html?utm_source=scroll&utm_medium=referral&utm_campaign=scroll.

Media Research Users Council. 2018. "Topline Findings: Indian Readership Survey 2017." http://www.mruc.net.

Mehta, Nalin. 2015. *Behind a Million Screens: What Television Tells Us about Modern India*. New Delhi: HarperCollins.

Ministry of Information and Broadcasting. 2015. *Annual Report of Ministry of Information and Broadcasting (2014–15)*. New Delhi: Publications Division.

———. 2016. *Annual Report of Ministry of Information and Broadcasting (2015–16)*. New Delhi: Publications Division.

———. 2018. "Status at a Glance of Private Satellite Channels (as of Dec 31, 2017)." http://mib.gov.in/sites/default/files/Status%20at%20a%20Glance%20of%20Permitted%20Private%20Satellite%20TV%20Channels%20as%20on%2031.12.2017%20.pdf.

———. 2018. *Press in India (2016–17): 60th Annual Report of the Registrar of Newspapers of India*. http://rni.nic.in/pin201617.htm.

Muralidharan, Sukumar. 2007. "Broadcast Regulation: Narrow Consultations, Indifferent Results." *Economic and Political Weekly* 42 (37): 3690–92.

———. 2010. "Media: Stenographer to Power." *Economic and Political Weekly* 45 (49): 10–14.

———. 2014. "TRAI Report on Media Ownership: The Press's Curious Response." *Economic and Political Weekly* 49 (36): 10–13.

News Laundry. 2014. "Who Owns Your Media?" February 5. https://www.newslaundry.com/2014/02/05/who-owns-your-media-4.

Ninan, Sevanti. 2007. *Headlines from the Hindi Heartland: Reinventing the Public Sphere*. Sage: New Delhi.

———. 2013. "A Surrogate Media Ownership." November 14. http://www.livemint.com/Opinion/FbTn976LbPqSWvs9RukmUN/A-surrogate-media-ownership.html.

Ninan, T. N. 2011. "Indian Media's Dickensian Age." CASI Working Papers 11-3.

Palshikar, S. 2014. "Modi, Media and the Middle Class." *Seminar*, April. No. 656. www.india-seminar.com/2014/656/656_suhas_palshikar.htm.

Parthasarathy, Suhrith. 2013. "The Broken Estate." *Caravan*, December. http://www.caravanmagazine.in/perspectives/broken-estate.

Pattnaik, Sudhir. 2014. "Who Does the Odia Media Serve." *Economic and Political Weekly* 49 (14): 74–81.

Ram, N. 2011. "The Changing Role of the News Media in Contemporary India." Patiala, Punjab. The Indian History Congress, December 10–11.

Raman, Anuradha 2009. "News You can Abuse." *Outlook*, December 21. http://www.outlookindia.com/magazine/story/news-you-can-abuse/263242.

Reddy, Rammanohar. 2017. *Demonetisation and Black* Money. Hyderabad: Orient Blackswan.

Sainath, P. 2010. "Paid News Undermining Democracy: Press Council Report." *The Hindu*, April 21. http://www.thehindu.com/opinion/columns/sainath/Paid-news-undermining-democracy-Press-Council-report/article16371596.ece.

Scroll.in. 2016. "Daily Newspaper *Kashmir Reader* Says It Has Been Banned by the Kashmir Government." October 2. http://scroll.in/latest/818092/daily-newspaper-kashmir-reader-says-it-has-been-banned-by-j-k-government.

———. 2018. "J and K Journalist Arrest: Real Journalist Should Cover Government's Development Activities, Says NIA." February 16. https://scroll.in/latest/868900/j-k-journalist-arrest-real-reporter-should-cover-governments-development-activities-says-nia.

Seshu, Geeta. 2016. "Bastar Journalists and Jail: A Year On." July 14. http://www.thehoot.org/free-speech/media-freedom/bastar-journalists-and-jail-a-year-on-9489.

Sharma, Supriya, and Mridual Chari. 2017. "He Said He Was Stressed: Tracking CBI Judge Brijgopal Loya's Last Journey from Nagpur to Latur." Scroll.in, December 2. https://scroll.in/article/859981/he-said-he-was-stressed-tracking-cbi-judge-brijgopal-loyas-last-journey-from-nagpur-to-latur.

Shukla, Archna. 2008. "Should Private Treaties Be Made Public to Newspaper Readers." January 15. http://www.livemint.com/Companies/kVh5CLOMwo02BWqLODiL9M/Should-private-treaties-be-made-public-to-newspaper-readers.html.

———. 2014. "3 Dozen in 5 months: News Channels Crowd News Space." *Indian Express*, May 5. http://indianexpress.com/article/india/india-others/3-dozen-in-5-months-new-channels-crowd-news-space/.

Singh, Rohini. 2017. "The Golden Touch of Jay Amit Shah." The Wire.in, October 8. https://thewire.in/185512/amit-shah-narendra-modi-jay-shah-bjp/.

Stromback, J. 2008. "Four Phases of Mediatization: An Analysis of Mediatization of Politics." *International Journal of Press/Politics* 13 (3): 228–46.

Takle, Niranjan. 2017. "A Family Breaks Its Silence." *Caravan*, December. http://www.caravanmagazine.in/vantage/shocking-details-emerge-in-death-of-judge-presiding-over-sohrabuddin-trial-family-breaks-silence.

Telecom Regulatory Authority of India. 2018. "Press Release on Telecom Subscription Data as of December 31 2017." February 16. http://www.trai.gov.in/sites/default/files/PR_No.23_TSD_Eng_16022018.pdf.

The Hoot's Analyst at Large. 2017. "The BCCL Empire: Towering over the Competition." TheHoot. Org. http://www.thehoot.org/media-watch/media-business/the-bccl-empiretowering-over-the-competition-10255.

TheHoot.org. 2018a. "The India Freedom Report: Media Freedom and Freedom of Expression in 2017." http://www.thehoot.org/public/uploads/filemanager/media/THE-INDIA-FREEDOM-REPORT-.pdf.

TheHoot.org. 2018b. "Section: Media Business." http://www.thehoot.org/media-watch/media-business.

Venkataramkrishnan, Rohan. 2017. "It's All about Market Share." Scroll.in, August 11. https://scroll.in/article/846434/its-all-about-market-share-arnab-goswamis-funder-rajeev-chandrasekhar-on-republic-tv-and-more.

Verma, R., and S. Sardesai. 2014. "Does Media Exposure Affect Voting Behaviour and Political Preferences in India?" *Economic and Political Weekly* 49 (39): 82–88.

PART III

REGIONAL EXPERIENCES

Business-Friendly Gujarat Under Narendra Modi

The Implications of a New Political Economy

CHRISTOPHE JAFFRELOT

In Gujarat, close relations between a robust business community and the state politicians as well as the bureaucracy crystallized at an early date.[1] In fact, this is one of the states where the—exceptionally developed—sense of entrepreneurship of the locals resisted most effectively the Nehruvian system, with the help of politicians and bureaucrats. Aseema Sinha has shown how after independence the business community circumvented some dimensions of the state-owned economy regime (Sinha 2005). Under the license raj, the state of Gujarat, for instance, promptly allocated the quota permits decided by the Planning Commission to the private sector. The state government also played a pioneering role in the 1970s, when it created an "investment promotion cell" that fostered a hybrid form of state capitalism. This development resulted as much from the resilience of its capitalists as from the mindset of the politicians and bureaucrats who were immersed in a business-oriented milieu.

The state was so business-friendly that Sinha described its economic model as that of "bureaucratic-liberalism." Congress chief ministers trained under Indira Gandhi like Madhavsinh Solanki had no inhibition in following this "ism" even before the much-vaunted 1991 liberalization. In the mid-1980s Solanki claimed that he would turn his state into a "mini-Japan." At that time, Gujarat had become the second most industrialized state in India, "as its government, in cooperation with the private sector, launched many projects in power development, electronics, fertilizers and many other industries" (Wood 1995, 158).

Then, in the 1990s, Gujarat liberalized its economy more quickly than most other states in India.[2] That was partly an unintended consequence of a deep fiscal crisis (the fiscal deficit represented 7.37 percent of the state's net domestic product in 1990–91 (Sinha 2010, 134)). Similarly, in the mid-1990s, Gujarat evolved a ports policy in the framework of which the government decided to give "complete control of two ports to the private sector" (Sinha 2010, 142). The chief minister who presided over this policy was a Congress man, Chimanbhai Patel. Keshubhai Patel continued with the same policy after he became CM in 1995.

Years before Narendra Modi—on whose terms I'll focus in this chapter—took over, the Gujarati economy was "pushed forward very much by deliberate state interventions that resemble the interventions of the developmental state of East Asia," which means that "Gujarat's rapid economic growth [wa]s propelled by a close working alliance between the region's political and economic elite" (Kohli 2012, 192, 179). Gujarat indeed continued to exemplify a business-friendly pattern,[3] more than a "market-friendly" economy,[4] even after the Indian economy got liberalized in the 1990s. While market-friendly economies minimize interventions from the state, in a business-friendly economies, politicians (and "their" bureaucracies) intervene in favor of the companies they seek to favor, their cronies—hence the notion of crony capitalism.

Modi's economic policy in the years 2000s gave a new dimension to this business-friendliness. What has been publicized by the longest-serving chief minister (2001–14) as the "Gujarat model" benefited first the large corporate houses. As argued below, the special relationship that developed between the government (and more precisely the chief minister) and big companies had implications not only for the economy (as evident from the problems that small and medium enterprises started to face—as well as the exchequer), but also for the society (big firms need fewer workers than SMEs) and the polity (grand corruption was a corollary of this pattern).

The first section of this chapter examines the facets of the special equation that the Modi government developed with big corporate houses in terms of policies and more or less illicit arrangements. The second section analyzes the implications mentioned above in economic, social, and political terms. The third focuses on the specific case of the relations between Narendra Modi and Gautam Adani as a multifaceted case study.

Big Is Beautiful
The Making of New Public Policies

The state of Gujarat has traditionally made a point to follow well-articulated public policies that reflect the political agenda of the chief ministers. Before the BJP took over, the liberal leanings of the chief ministers mentioned above were systematically balanced by more social policies, including reservations-based positive discrimination in the 1980s. In 1990, the new employment policy was aimed at guaranteeing employment in backward talukas (subunits of a district) and laid down that "80% posts in new industries should go to local people and 50% posts of managerial and supervisory posts should go to local people" (Hirway et al. 2014, 146). The 1995 and 2000 industrial policies were in the same vein. Archana Dholakia and Ravindra Dholakia point out that the 1990, 1995, and 2000 policies spelled out by the government "focused largely on interest subsidies and incentives for small and tiny manufacturing sectors. Industries that were employment-intensive, export-oriented, using modern technology, ready to locate in backward regions, and set up by social groups like Scheduled Castes and Tribes and other backward castes were given incentives" (Dholakia and Dholakia 2015, 251).

Things changed in 2003, when the new industrial policy "was designed and implemented under the leadership of the Chief Minister, Narendra Modi" (Dholakia and Dholakia 2015, 252). First, the new policy "called for labor reforms to the extent permissible at the state level. Inspections carried out under the labor department substantially reduced in numbers and so also the harassment to the industries." Second, "A large number of industries were exempted from obtaining No-Objection Certificate (NOC) from Pollution Control Board." And third, "Relatively easy and quick possession of land through the 'urgency' clause, simplification of administrative processes to release agricultural land for industrial use, liberal land pricing strategy for unused government land and efficient land acquisition policy were all fallout of the 2003 policy, attracting large number of entrepreneurs to the state" (Dholakia and Dholakia 2015, 252).

In 2004, the Gujarat Special Economic Zones Act was voted by the state assembly (it was to be amended in 2007) (see below) in order to make access to land still easier and labor laws still less strict. Five years later, a new industrial policy was decided by the state government in order to think big (or bigger). Indeed, in January 2009 the Gujarat Special Investment Region Act was passed in order "to come up with a legal frame work to enable development of mega investment regions and industrial areas in the State." (Government of Gujarat 2009a, 20). Its aim was more precisely to create "global hubs of economic activity supported by world class infrastructure, premium civic amenities, centers of excellence and proactive policy framework." The SIRs were supposed to develop around the Delhi-Mumbai Industrial Corridor initiated by the center in 2007. The 2009 act established a Regional Development Authority—appointed by the state government—whose mission was to control all economic initiative, including the making of new buildings in "its" area.

The 2009 industrial policy was explicitly designed for "making Gujarat the most attractive investment destination not only in India but also in the world" (Government of Gujarat 2009b, 3). It targeted not only the "prestigious units"

(Rs. 3 billion and more since 1991), but even more the "megaprojects" that implied Rs. 10 billion and more investment in projects and direct employment of two thousand persons—hence a ratio of Rs. 500,000 per job (Hirway et al. 2014, 147). The priority to big-business operations was reiterated several times in the document, where it was written, for instance, that "to ensure that the state transforms into a global investment destination, development by way of establishment of several mega projects is considered necessary" (Government of Gujarat 2009b, 13). To attract big companies, access to land was considered as a key element: "Since the availability of land with right kind of infrastructure is the key to competitive operations, adequate provisioning would also have to be made so as to provide the land in an appropriate manner. The policy adequately dwells upon this important aspect "(Government of Gujarat 2009b, 13). The Gujarat Industrial Development Corporation (GIDC) started to give land to industrial units on ninety-nine-year lease and created more SEZs (see below). In 1990–2001 it had acquired 4,620 hectares, but this figure rose to 21,308 hectares between 2001 and 2010–11 (Hirway et al. 2014, 161–63).

To sum up: till the 1990s, "New industrial units were entitled to incentives/ subsidies when they were small or/and located in backward *talukas*. Gradually [in the 2000s] the larger units have also been included. . . . The conditionality of employment has also been watered down substantially. In the early years of the 1990s it was mandatory for the beneficiary units to employ 100 permanent workers each, and to employ local workers who would constitute 80% or more of the total workers each, and to employ local workers who would constitute 50% or more of the managerial and supervisory staff. The condition of employing 100 permanent workers turned into 100 regular workers and then *just* 100 workers" in the 2000s (Hirway et al. 2014, 149).

To attract big investors, the Gujarat government has also made significant concessions in terms of tax deduction and other fiscal subsidies. The amount of such subsidies per year (in terms of sales tax incentives and sales tax deferment), "which was on an average Rs. 1,253.56 crore between 1990–1 and 1999–2000, jumped by almost five times to Rs. 5,966.72 crore per year during the period from 2000–1 to 2006–07. Also, there was a big jump in the total sales tax subsidy per unit in the second period. It rose from Rs. 3.37 crore in 2000–01 to Rs. 83 crore per unit in 2004–05 and to Rs. 101.4 in 2006–07. This jump is likely to be due to the rising number of 'prestigious' units in the total units. . . . This means that the state government let go of 40% of its revenue from its main source of income" (Hirway et al. 2014, 156).

Incentives to attract investors also included the multiplication of special economic zones. Bibek Debroy emphasizes that "the attractiveness of SEZs in Gujarat had quite a bit to do with the SEZ Act's provisions on the labour market. For example, there is easier exit, more flexible provisions on hiring and terminating labour and the concept of fixed term employment" (Debroy, 2012, 71). Besides relaxing labor laws, SEZs are also areas in which industrialists are invited to set up production units (generally export-oriented) in exchange for various tax concessions and subsidies. Debroy and Bhandari define SEZs as follows: "Tax breaks are given, regulations are also fewer and less intrusive in SEZs. SEZs offer a free-market atmosphere to traders, implying a higher level of economic freedom" (Debroy and Bhandari n.d., 11). By June 2010, the government of India had given "approval to 60 SEZs in Gujarat covering an area of 31,967 hectares" (Dholakia and Dholakia 2015, 255). By that time, the government had "allotted more than 20,000 acres of land to the roughly 27 SEZs that had already been notified" (Asher 2014, 140).

Engaging the Big Businessmen

Indian investors appreciated not only the public policies described above, but also Modi's modus operandi, including the speed of procedures and decision-making as well as the concessions made to them, as evidenced by the case of the Nano factory. In August 2008 Ratan Tata abandoned the idea of building this low-cost car in Singur, in West Bengal, when the peasants' protest was backed by Mamta Banerjee. It seems that Modi then sent a one-word SMS to Ratan Tata: "Suswagatam" (welcome). Ratan Tata said later in an interview that his company had been contacted by seven state governments, but that Modi had delivered land more quickly: "The speed and the fact that Gujarat could transfer possession of the land without any hassles to Tata Motors was perhaps the singular reason that made us decide on Gujarat" ("15 Minutes" 2012, 6). Ratan Tata adds that "Narendra Modi is an extremely easy person to deal with—very informal, compatible and pleasant, and capable as well. It is very difficult not to feel comfortable with him. The fact remains that he has taken a personal interest in the project to ensure that everything moves smoothly."

The Nano deal was wrapped up in fifteen days, Tata Motors opting for the site at Sanand that Modi had preselected (among others) for the new factory. To woo Ratan Tata, the chief minister moved very fast but also offered many concessions. Some of them were made public by the government of Gujarat in January 2009, including a soft loan of Rs. 9,570 crore at 0.1 percent interest rate and repayable in twenty years and the fact that the existing policy regarding 85 percent recruitment of locals would not apply ("Gujarat Government Reveals Offers" 2009). Other concessions leaked later. First, "For 1,100 acres of land allegedly sold at Rs. 900 per sq m, while its market rate was around Rs. 10,000 per sq m, the Tatas were given facility of payment through installments" (Mishra 2011). Second, the company got exemption of stamp duty of "20 crore rupees levied on the sale of land, deferred payment of Value Added Tax (VAT) on the sale of twenty years" (Nag 2013, 119). Third, the loans amounting to Rs. 9,570 crore represented 330 percent of the investment—Rs. 2,900 crore.[5]

While this deal is the most high-profile one, others were made in similar conditions. Larsen and Toubro was, for instance, "allotted 8,00,000 sq m of prime land in the industrial zone of Hazira, Surat, without auction, at the rate of Re 1 per sq m ... thereby costing the state exchequer a few hundreds crores rupees" (Mishra 2011). In the same vein, the Essar group was "allotted 2.08 lakh sq m of disputed land for a steel plant on the CRZ [Coastal Regulation Zone] and forest land that can't be allotted as per Supreme Court guidelines. . . . The occupier is unauthorised but no action has been taken by the state machinery" (Mehta 2012). Similarly, a comprehensive study showed in 2012 that in one case Reliance Industries had paid for land between Rs. 21 and Rs. 390 per hectare—that is, less than the market price ("Forest Land" 2012; Behavioural Science Centre 2012, 47).

The Comptroller and Auditor General (CAG) discovered these "irregularities" several years later (Comptroller and Auditor General of India 2013). In a very detailed report, it accused the Gujarat government of causing an important loss to the exchequer by bestowing "undue" favors to large companies, including Reliance Industries, Essar, the Adani Group, Larsen and Troubo, and Ford ("CAG Indicts Modi Govt." 2013, 10). Land allotment was the main issue, but not the only one: "During the last five years, the audit reports have highlighted cases of non/short levy, non/short realization, underassessment/loss of revenue, incorrect exemption, concealment of turnover, application of incorrect rate of income tax, incorrect computation, etc worth Rs. 5,287.48 crore" ("CAG Finds" 2013, 3; "State Lost" 2013, 1).

This indictment came after the CAG asked more than five thousand queries and made 15,100 audit observations.[6] None of these interventions made any difference, and the Gujarat-based companies mentioned above have continued to register good results. The market capitalization of the Adani Group (see below) has allegedly increased by 8,615 percent between 2002 and 2012, that of Essar, by 4,507 percent, and that of Reliance Industries by 1,357 percent (Centre for Education and Documentation 2013, 2).

The industrialists' appreciation of the Modi government was most obvious on the occasion of the "Vibrant Gujarat" meetings. The chief minister conceived this special event—which was to occur every alternate year—in 2003 in conjunction with chambers of commerce and industry in order to attract Indian investors, including those residing abroad, and to publicize his economic credentials. In contrast to the policy of previous governments, this program did not rely on competitive bids, but on calls for projects. Hundreds of companies were attracted to this get-together, and promises of investment totaled 66,000 crore rupees in 2003 ("Investors Back Out" 2008). In January 2005, 106,160 crore rupees of investment commitments were made in the form of MoUs, of which 60 percent—allegedly—materialized (Nag 2013, 113). Two years later, the promises of investments reached 465,309 crore rupees, by the end of the decade, in 2009, 1,239,562 crore rupees, and in 2011, 2,083,047 crore rupees (Nag 2013, 113, 116, 121). The realization of promised investments declined steadily over the years, but by the middle of the first decade of the century, investment in Gujarat had risen significantly and Modi had become one of the favorite chief ministers of Indian businessmen. They made a point of attending the Vibrant Gujarat meetings and of showering praise on him. Among them, the Gujaratis were usually the first to appear on the platform, the most prominent ones including Mukesh and Anil Ambani, Shashi Ruia (Essar group), and Gautam Adani, probably the closest of all to the chief minister, as we shall see in the last section of this chapter.

In 2007, Mukesh Ambani declared: "Narendrabhai is a leader with a grand vision . . . amazing clarity of purpose with determination . . . strong ethos with a modern outlook, dynamism and passion."[7] In 2013, Anil Ambani, who had already projected Modi as the next prime minister of India, seized the opportunity of the Vibrant Gujarat meeting to liken him to Mahatma Gandhi, Sardar Patel, Dhirubhai Ambani (his father) and Arjuna, the hero of the Mahabharata, before calling him "king of kings."[8]

While Modi has not attracted many foreign investors (only 4.5 percent of FDI went to the state from 2000 to 2012, as against 32.8 percent in Maharashtra, 19 percent in Delhi, 5.6 percent in Karnataka, 5.2 percent in Tamil Nadu, and 4 percent Andhra Pradesh),[9] he has been very popular among Indian businessmen.

Reliance, for instance, developed a huge petroleum refinery whose capacity jumped from 27 million metric tons per annum to 62 million tons per annum in 2008, after the building of a second factory on a three-thousand-hectare SEZ.[10] In the same year, also in Jamnagar, Essar inaugurated another refinery, of a 20 million tons per annum capacity.[11] The same group also set up between 2005 and 2008 a big steel plant in Hazira, close to Surat in south Gujarat, that represented a Rs. 300 billion investment.[12]

These investments boosted the growth rate of Gujarat. While in the 1990s Gujarat was already ahead of all the other states of India, it remained so in the years 2002–3 to 2011–12, and lagged behind Bihar by a single percentage point in the years from 2006–7 to 2012–13, when Gujarat became number three, neck and neck with Maharashtra.

This performance needs to be disaggregated sector-wise. Unsurprisingly, the most dynamic sector has been industry, in which most investments have been concentrated. With an average yearly growth rate of 10.64 percent from 2005–6 to 2011–12, Gujarat recorded the fourth best performance in India—the national average being 7.5 percent.[13] As a result, in the beginning of the present decade, it accounted for 20 percent of India's industrial output, including 24 percent of its textile production, 35 percent of its pharmaceutical products, 51 percent of its petrochemical production—and 22 percent of its exports (Dev 2012, 157).

The Social, Fiscal, and Environmental Implications of the "Gujarat Model"

What Jobs?

By focusing on "megaprojects," the "Gujarat model" has relied on big companies that have boosted the growth rate but have not created many good jobs, not only because the rules pertaining to job creation have been relaxed, as mentioned above, but also because big companies are very capital intensive. The petrochemical industry and the chemical industry are cases in point. They have been so dynamic that they represent respectively 34 percent and 15 percent of the industrial output,[14] but they are not labor intensive at all.[15] Manufacturing is more labor intensive, but automation is also gaining momentum in the large factories. For instance, the Nano plant never had more than 2,200 employees—for an investment worth Rs. 2,900 crore, hence a ratio of more than Rs. 1.3 crore per job created directly (indirect job creation needs to be taken into account but is more difficult to measure). Between 2009–10 and 2012–13, Gujarat was the state where investment in industry was the highest (above Maharashtra and Tamil Nadu), but that did not translate into job creation as much as in these states, where the enterprises tended to be smaller and more labor intensive (Ethiraj 2015). The comparison between Gujarat and Tamil Nadu—where big firms are not so prominent—is illuminating in that respect: in 2013, Gujarati industry represented 17.7 percent of the fixed capital of India but only 9.8 percent of the factory jobs, whereas the industry of Tamil Nadu represented 9.8 percent of the fixed capital but 16 percent of the factory jobs (ISED Small Enterprise Observatory 2013, 39).

In Gujarat, fixed capital multiplied by a factor of 3.6 in ten years, from Rs. 66,601 crore in 1999–2000 to 240,381 crore in 2009–10, but the annual growth rate of employment declined from 2.4 percent in the years between 1999–2000 and 2004–5 to 0.1 percent in the years between 2004–5 and 2009–10. Not only has the growth rate of urban employment hardly increased, from 4 percent to 4.9 percent, but wages have lagged behind too.[16]

The quasi-stagnation of job creation is partly due to the crisis of the SMEs, which are four time more labor intensive than the average for all firms. A study by the Institute of Small Enterprise and Development, which the Gujarat Industrial Development Corporation has sponsored, showed that in 2013, the non performing assets of the

SMEs of Gujarat had grown by 43.9 percent. Besides the economic slowdown (including in terms of exports), that growth was mainly attributed to the rise of the price of gas and electricity (sometimes decided to please big companies—see below) and poor financial support that the SMEs got because of the indifferent policy of the local banks (ISED Small Enterprise Observatory 2013, 99). Indeed, the share of the MSMEs' (micro, small, and medium enterprises) credit in as a percentage of the gross bank credit had declined from 12.98 percent in 1997–98 to 6.34 percent in 2006–7. It started to rise again afterwards to reach 10 percent in 2009–10, but it remained below the late 1990s figure (ISED Small Enterprise Observatory 2013, 80). These financial tensions were partly due to the crisis of the district cooperative banks, which are in a bad shape after financial irregularities almost sealed the fate of eight of them in the early 2000s: Madhavpura Mercantile Cooperative Bank, Charotar Cooperative Bank, Vishnagar Cooperative Bank, Laxmi Cooperative Bank, Diamond Jubilee Cooperative Bank, Suryapur Cooperative Bank, General Cooperative Bank, and Baroda People's Cooperative Bank ("Another Co-operative Bank" 2002). The failure of the Madhavpura Mercantile Cooperative Bank had the largest repercussions on the sector. Four of the eight banks had to be liquidated. The BJP government did not help cooperative banks, not only because, in its eyes, small is not beautiful but also because the cooperatives are traditionally strongholds of Congress in Gujarat.

This financial situation has precipitated the crisis of many MSMEs. According to the Union Ministry of MSMEs, the number of sick units jumped from 4,321 in 2010–11 to 20,615 in 2012–13 and 49,382 in 2014–15—a figure second only to Uttar Pradesh (Mishra 2015). Between 2004 and 2014, 60,000 MSMEs shut down in Gujarat (Singh 2015). Clearly, the MSMEs were not in a position to hire as many people as before.

Not only has the growth rate in jobs not increased in proportion to the growth rate of the state GDP—something the government of Gujarat admitted in 2009[17] and even more explicitly in 2016[18]—but the quality of the jobs has not improved, as evident from the informalization process at work on the job market.[19] Formal employment remained almost stagnant (+0.3 percent) between 1999/2000 and 2009/2010. In contrast, informal employment increased by 4 percent. According to the National Sample Survey, in 2009/2010, the informal sector represented 84.1 percent of the working force in Gujarat and only 74.9 percent in Maharashtra. The proportion of male workers in the urban informal sector increased in Gujarat from 74.1 percent in 2004–5 to 80.6 percent in 2009–10, while it decreased in Maharashtra (from 72.3 percent to 61.3 percent), in Tamil Nadu (from 76.7 percent to 74.7 percent), and in India at large (from 73.9 percent to 68.5 percent) (Mahadevia 2014, 347). In the Nano plant, out of 2,200 employees, 430 were "permanent workers" in 2016. They earned Rs. 12,500 in 2016, whereas the informal workers earned about Rs. 3,300 a month ("Workers Strike at Tata Motors" 2016; Johari 2015).

Indeed, the informalization goes on a par with stagnation of wages. One of the reasons why industrialists have invested in Gujarat is also, precisely, the low level of wages, which is largely due to the inflow of migrant workers, men from Orissa, Bihar, and UP whose presence is very much resented by local laborers. According to the report of the National Sample Survey of 2011, Gujarat has some of the lowest average daily wages for casual laborers in the urban area. These wages are not only much below the national average, but on a par with those in Uttar Pradesh (see table 8.1).

This situation resulted in tensions: in 2014, Gujarat was the state with the most strikes, twenty-six (against nineteen in Tamil Nadu) ("Workers' Strike: Guj Tops the List" 2015). One of the longest strikes took place in the Nano factory. In February 2016, 422 of the 430 permanent workers had gone on strike. They protested against the suspension of other workers for indiscipline, but besides demanding reinstatement of the 28 suspended workers, they had other demands, including union formation and wage increases ("Strike at Tata" 2016). A compromise was found after one month, when most of the suspended workers were reinstated, unions were recognized, and negotiations on wages started.

Loss for the Exchequer and Impact on Social Expenditures

Partly because of the business-friendly policy described above, the financial situation of Gujarat has not improved as much as its growth rate could have permitted.

First, to attract big companies in Gujarat, the Modi government has given them facilities with fiscal exemptions, as mentioned above. Second, many companies did not pay taxes. They owed Rs. 12,000 crore in taxes to the state in 2011 (Dave 2011). Essar, alone, owed Rs. 8,000 crore of sales taxes in 2012 (Khanna 2012). Third, according to a March 2012 report from the CAG, the Gujarat state company, Gujarat State Petroleum Corporation, took a loss of Rs. 5,000 crore to the exchequer by buying natural gas on the open market and selling it to the Adani Group for a price lower than the purchase price, giving Adani Energy an "undue benefit" of Rs. 70.54 crore (see below) (CAG 2012, 74, 101).

Focusing on stamp-duty exemptions and duty forgone on customs and imports, Asher points out that between 2006 and 2014, the treasury lost "tens of billions of rupees. To illustrate, Reliance Group's Jamnagar SEZ benefited from more than Rs 50 billion worth of exemptions; the Adani Group's Mundra SEZ Rs 18 billion; the Kandla SEZ Rs 8 billion; and the Dahej SEZ Rs 1.3 billion" (2014, 140).

Partly for these reasons, the fiscal liabilities of Gujarat have increased from Rs. 45,301 crore in 2001–2 to Rs. 96,452 crore in 2007–8 and Rs. 138,978 crore in 2011–12 (CAG n.d.-a). The internal debt of Gujarat, then, represented

Table 8.1 **Average Wages of Casual Workers in Urban Areas in Selected Indian states in 2011 (other than public work)**

States	Average wages of casual workers in urban areas (Rs.)
Kerala	30,990
Jammu & Kashmir	21,047
Tamil Nadu	20,834
Haryana	20,446
Punjab	18,795
Andhra Pradesh	17,834
Karnataka	17,405
Rajasthan	17,367
Uttarakhand	17,041
India	**17,010**
Himachal Pradesh	16,723
Bihar	15,733
Assam	15,538
Maharashtra	15,462
Gujarat	**14,452**
Uttar Pradesh	14,320
Chhattisgarh	10,616

Source: *Key Indicators of Employment and Unemployment in India,* National Sample Survey, 2011, 66, 102 and 103. http://www.indiaenvironmentportal.org.in/files/file/key%20indicators%20of%20 employment%20and%20unemployment%20India%202011-12.pdf.w

76 percent of these liabilities, making Gujarat the third most indebted state in India, behind Uttar Pradesh (Rs. 158,400 crore) and West Bengal (Rs. 192,100).[20]

The lack of resources affecting the state has been an additional factor explaining the low level of social expenditures.[21] From the mid-1980s, the state has stopped spending a lot of money in this domain, partly, in the 1990s because of the decline of its growth rate (for more detail, see Jaffrelot 2015). During the Modi years, the growth rate was one of the best in India, but some of the social spendings among the lowest. In 2010–11, Gujarat spent 15.9 percent of its budget on education, when Bihar, Chhattisgarh, Haryana, Kerala, Maharashtra, Orissa, Rajasthan, Uttar Pradesh, and West Bengal spent between 16 and 20.8 percent, the national average being 16.6 percent.[22] Over the years

2001–2 from to 2012–13, Gujarat spent 13.22 of its budget on education, when the national average was slightly above 15 percent.[23] From 2000–2001 to 2012–13, only four states out of twenty-one spent less than Gujarat on education. With 13.22 percent of expenditure devoted to educational provision in the period, Gujarat was almost 2 percent below the national average of 15.02 percent.[24] Partly for this reason, only 53.8 percent of the primary schools had toilets, against 56.77 percent as an average in India (Iyengar 2014).

The situation was slightly more favorable as far as public health was concerned. With 2.8 percent of its budget devoted to health-related expenditures, Gujarat ranked last out of seventeen large states in 2000–2001; with 4.2 percent in 2010–11, it ranked number seven.[25] But the "ratio of doctors in public sector health care to population was 1:19,000, as against 1:9,000 in Tamil Nadu."[26]

"Grand Corruption"

According to the weekly magazine *Business India*, already in 1994 Gujarat was renowned for corrupt practices:

> If Gujarat is flooded with investment it is partly due to a corrupt but well-organized regime. Industrialists know that in Gujarat everything has a price. Land, water and power concessions, not to mention environmental clearances are hassle free if one has the right political connections. Similarly files move fast and lengthy duplicate procedures are simply non-existent if one knows which palms to grease. (Quoted in Sinha 2005, 228)

Lately, according to Jennifer Bussell, Gujarat is particularly known for its "*grand* corruption"[27]—related to large economic transactions that the promotion of megaprojects implies. In 2005, Gujarat was second only to Delhi as far as this kind of corruption is concerned, whereas it did better than all other states (except Himachal Pradesh and Kerala) in terms of "petty corruption" (Bussell 2012, 43, 107, 188). For Bussell, this state of affairs can be explained by Gujarati politicians being eager not only to attract big investors, but also to outsource public services, in the name of reforms, to private firms. This "company model," as Bussell explains,

> provides three important potential benefits to politicians and bureaucrats. . . . First there may be only one or two companies signing contracts, limiting the number of occasions in which state officials might be caught receiving a bribe. Second, the scale of the partner and the contracts . . . implies that state actors may be able to acquire a much

larger single payment from the transaction. . . . Finally, because this model deals with high-profile contracts, it is also more likely to involve state leadership directly, thereby limiting the number of hands through which bribes will have to pass before reaching the highest political levels and maximizing the rents for top officials. (Bussell 2012, 184)

To sum up, the very fact that the Gujarat government has given increasing priority to big investors has impacted the state in many different ways. The cooperatives and SMEs, which used to epitomize the Gujarati entrepreneurial ethos, have not continued to benefit from the traditional attention of the state, and this evolution has affected the labor market—where jobs have been few and where wages have not increased. The state has also suffered financially, which partly explains its indebtedness and the low level of social expenditures. Last but not least, this pattern of economic growth laid itself to "grand corruption." Some of these facets of the Gujarat model are well illustrated by a specific case study.

The Rise of Gautam Adani

Today, Gautam Adani stands as India's largest private trader of coal, operates India's biggest private port, Mundra, and additionally owns two more ports, four ships, and India's largest private railway line. His companies also have a presence in compressed natural gas (CNG), real estate, and the edible oil and food storage industries. They currently trade in over thirty commodities and in twenty-eight countries. In one of the email interviews he gave, Gautam Adani made his ambition clear: to become "a globally admired leader in integrated infrastructure businesses with a deep commitment to nation building" (Adani 2014).

The combined market value of Adani Enterprises, Adani Power, Adani Ports, and special economic zones is now close to the value of Reliance Industries. In comparison, the Adani Group stood about five hundred times smaller than Reliance in 2001. Lately, the rise of the Adani Group accelerated: the market capitalization of its companies increased by 250 percent between September 2013—when Narendra Modi was declared the BJP's official candidate for the prime ministership—and September 2014.[28] According to a September 2014 issue of *Forbes*, Adani had "added $ 4.5 billion to his net worth since 2013," a record increasing his wealth to $7.1 billion (or Rs. 43,000 crore) ("Forbes India Rich List" 2014). Then Adani's wealth zoomed 48 percent more between May 2014 and May 2015 because of soaring shares of his companies that operated in trading, power, ports, and edible oil (Sasi 2015). The media explained this prosperity by his close relation with Narendra Modi—which became obvious when Modi used Adani's chartered plane on his campaign trail across India in the run-up to the 2014 elections. On May 22, 2014, the day he was sworn in as prime minister, he flew to New Delhi from Ahmedabad in the private aircraft of Adani, the Indian flag embossed on the aircraft to his right, and on his left, an embossed logo of the Adani Group. Subsequently, Adani accompanied the PM as his private guest in most of his travels abroad (Langa 2015).

But Gautam Adani had already shown his proximity to Modi when he was chief minister of Gujarat—at that time they visited China, Japan, Singapore and Russia together. Two months before Modi became PM, he declared: "We are in the infrastructure sector. Government policies, government facilitation, and support is very critical in implementation of large project like ours. Thus we have to work closely with the government" (Adani 2014).

The proximity of Gautam Adani to Narendra Modi is one of the reasons why the turnover of the group had already started to rise in the first decade of the 2000s when Modi was the chief minister of Gujarat—it rose more than twenty-fold, from Rs. 3,741 crore in 2001–2 to Rs. 75,659 crore in 2013–14 (Thakurtha 2015), the period on which I shall focus in this section.

A Rewarding Good Equation

Gautam Adani was born in 1962 in a Jain family, in Ratan Pol (a locality of the old city of Ahmedabad), from parents who had migrated from north Gujarat. At the age of eighteen, he dropped out of Gujarat University and moved to Bombay, made a stint as a diamond sorter at Mahindra Bros., and then became a diamond trader (*Gautam Adani Biography* n.d.). He moved to Ahmedabad in 1981 to help his brother, Mahasukh, who was starting a business manufacturing plastic film. This company was very much dependent on PVC. The sole producer of PVC in India at that time was IPCL, which used to supply the Adani brothers two tons of PVC per month. But the rapidly growing business needed over twenty tons per month. This is when Adani began importing plastic granules into the Kandla port, which was India's largest port till 2013, when Adani's Mundra Port adjacent to it unseated it. Then Gautam Adani diversified his activities. In 1988, he set up a commodities trading venture called Adani Exports. In the next four years, his import orders grew from 100 metric tons (MT) orders to entire 40,000 MT shiploads (Rajshekhar 2013).

In 1991–92, Adani and an agribusiness group, Cargill, were given three thousand acres of coastal land in Kutch, including Mundra, by the Chimanbhai Patel government for salt production. The project fell through after protests by George Fernandes and others, and Cargill pulled out. Adani held his land and began thinking of converting Mundra into a private port. In the framework of the nascent liberalization, the Gujarat Maritime Board decided to allot ports to private companies in a joint venture with the state—an initial list of ports was created, which included the Mundra port. This port was 14 meters deep (deeper than Kandla at 12 meters), and this allowed it to berth larger ships of 200,000 MT and above (Rajshekhar 2013). In 1993, the company was incorporated into a limited company with two promoters, Adani himself and Rajesh S. Adani, his younger brother. In 1997, Adani Exports Ltd. entered into a joint venture with the Gujarat government to build a megaport at Mundra. Around that time the Adani Group established a base in Dubai, where two of the five Adani brothers are still primarily in charge of the supplying chain of Adani Exports. In 1999, Adani ventured into coal trading for the first time, with a shipment landing at Mundra. In 2000 Adani let P&O Australia, one of the world's largest port operators, set up a container terminal in Mundra.

There is no evidence of relations between Gautam Adani and Narendra Modi before the latter became chief minister. Their rapprochement was precipitated by the 2002 pogrom. In the aftermath of this event, which disrupted the state economy for weeks, senior members of the Confederation of Indian Industry (CII)—including Rahul Bajaj, Jamshyd Godrej and Azim Premji—criticized Modi during a meeting that took place in Delhi in February 2003. In reaction, CII members from Gujarat formed the "Resurgent Group of Gujarat" in order to counter what they regarded as "a concerted attempt by a section to defame Gujarat" ("Gujarat Inc. Guns" 2003). Among them were Dr. Karsan Patel and Ambubhai Patel (Nirma group), Indravadan Modi (Cadila Pharmaceuticals), Pankaj Patel (Cadila Healthcares), Chintan Parikh (Ashima), Anil Bakeri (Bakeri group), and, last but not least, Gautam Adani, who was also a newcomer to the world of big companies and who took the lead.[29]

When the first Vibrant Gujarat meeting took place in September–October 2003, Adani went further than his colleagues and pledged Rs. 15,000 crore of investment (Guha Thakurtha 2015). This was a major turnaround for the Adani-Modi relationship.

The Adani Port and SEZ (APSEZ) at Mundra (Kutch District) was created in 2003 to provide cargo handling and other port services. It soon became India's first multiproduct port-based SEZ, after Adani was granted 3,585 hectares of land, including 2,008 hectares of forest and 990 hectares of *gauchar* (village grazing) land. Two converging investigations have alleged that the Adani Group bought this land, in one area, at a rate ranging from Rs. 1 to Rs. 32 a square meter, when the market rate was over Rs. 1,500 a square meter (Behavioural Science Centre 2012, 16), and, in another area, at the cost of Rs. 10 per square meter, when the market price there was between Rs. 700 and Rs. 800 per square meter (George 2011; see also "Gujarat State Government" 2012).

In Mundra, Adani acquired up to 7,350 hectares. *Forbes* argues, on the basis of the texts of the original agreements, that for most of this area "he got the

30-year, renewable leases for as little as one U.S. cent a square meter (the rate maxed out at 45 cents a square meter). He in turn has sublet this land to other companies, including state-owned Indian Oil Co., for as much as $11 a square meter. Between 2005 and 2007 at least 1,200 hectares of grazing land was taken away from villagers" (Bahree 2014).

During the 2009 Vibrant Gujarat summit, the Modi government signed MoUs allowing the Adani Group to invest for a "Rs. 15,000-crore expansion of its SEZ over the next 15 years. The Modi government topped off its largesse of land to the Adani group with five-years tax breaks of over Rs. 3,200 crore, almost four times what it had marked for redeveloping Kutch after the 2001 earthquake. Government data shows an investment of Rs. 1,31,702 crore in the Adani SEZ, port, and power plant, but only 38,875 jobs created. That comes to an astonishing figure of Rs. 3.38 crore for creating one job" (Yadav 2011). This is a clear indication of capital intensity.

In 2013, a CAG report pointed out that in the SEZ of the Adani Group in Mundra, "14 lease deeds for an area of 4,84,326 sq. mt. in MPSEZ were registered during the period from December 2008 to November 2011. However, the Collector had given permission to only one unit. . . . Accordingly, the transfer of land admeasuring 4,65,728 sq. mt. by way of lease in the remaining 13 cases were irregular" (CAG 2013). The CAG also indicted the Gujarat government for buying electricity from the Adani Group at an abnormally high price. It pointed out that this "non adherence to the terms of Power Purchase Agreement led to short recovery of penalty of Rs 160.26 crore and passing of undue benefit to a private firm" (CAG n.d.-b).

In 2012, the Modi-Adani connection was targeted by Arvind Kejriwal, the leader of the Aam Admi Party, who, the year before, had taken part in anticorruption campaigns along with Anna Hazare. He accused the Gujarat government of buying power from the Adani Group at Rs. 5.45 per unit when the Gujarat Mineral Development Corporation had made a better offer ("Kejriwal Targets Modi" 2012). I have already mentioned that gas was another source of income for the Adani Group, as it had also acquired a monopolistic position in the supply of CNG in Ahmedabad.

In its last report dealing with the Modi government in Gujarat, the CAG reiterated the critique it had made in 2012. Indicting explicitly the Adani and the Essar groups, it pointed out that "the purchase of power from the private sector increased to 37.22 per cent (2012–13) from 15.22 per cent (2008–09). Of this increase, the share of Private IPPs in power purchased from private sector, increased to 82.75 per cent (i.e. 22,562.17 Mus) in 2012–13 from 66.59 per cent (i.e. 5,653.24 Mus) indicating an increase of 300 per cent in purchase of power from them during 2008–09 to 2012–13" (Comptroller and Auditor General of India 2014).

Not only did the Adani Group benefit from special treatment in financial terms, it was also allowed to flout the environmental rules of the state in Mundra.

Breaching Environmental Norms

The adverse consequences of the politicians-businessmen nexus on the environment is a general problem, but it is especially obvious in the case of the Adani Group, which circumvented ecological rules and regulations, even drawing criticism from BJP leaders like Kanubhai Kalsariya, an MLA from Gujarat. Coastal Regulation Zone rules were violated, mangroves were illegally cleared, and inadequately treated wastewater contaminated fishing grounds.

The Gujarat Coastal Zone Management Authority (GCZMA), in May 2006, formed a subcommittee headed by Professor Nikhil Desai, director of the Gujarat Ecological Education and Research (GEER) Foundation, who reported that the company had built many bunds in the intertidal area and blocked many creeks feeding water to the mangrove patches. To no avail. Four years later, in December 2010 the Ministry of Environment and Forests (MoEF) sent an inspection team under one of the ministry officials because of the complaints of the local inhabitants. The report, presented after the visit, found many instances of noncompliance. It made the same observations regarding large-scale destruction of mangroves and obstruction of creek systems and natural flow of seawater because of reclamation. It made no difference.

On September 14, 2012, the minister of MoEF, Ms. Jayanthi Natarajan, constituted a committee under the chairmanship of Sunita Nair, the director general of the Centre for Science and Environment, for inspection of the Mundra port. It came to the same conclusions as its predecessors (*Report of the Committee* 2013, 19ff.).

All the inspectors and experts have also observed that the Mundra thermal plants of Adani and Tata released fly ash, in spite of the terms of the 2007 clearance. In 2011 the Gujarat Pollution Control Board inspection revealed that about 27,127 MT of fly ash was disposed of in low-lying areas of the MPSEZ. When Megha Bahree visited the place, she noticed that "fly ash and saline water from Adani Power and a nearby Tata Power Co. Ltd. plant are spoiling the crops and making the soil less fertile" (Bahree 2014).

The Sunita Nair committee recommended a Rs. 200 crore environmental restoration fund (ERF), but no penalty was imposed on the company by the government (Mukherjee 2016). In 2016, the Gujarat High Court appointed another committee to enquire about the degradation caused by the Mundra port. It came to the same conclusion as its predecessor, but, says environmentalist Mahesh Pandya, "If you ask the Gujarat Pollution Control Board or the state environment and forest department how many notices they have served to the company, you will find none" (cited in Mukherjee 2016).

Beyond the political connections of the Adani Group, the link between the Gujarat state and the group have become somewhat organic after a large number of former Indian Administrative Service officials in Gujarat have gone on to join Adani's companies. In 2002, Sanjay Gupta, a 1985 batch IAS officer who had played a pivotal role in the Gujarat State Petroleum Corporation after resigning from the IAS, briefly joined the Adani Group as the CEO of the Adani Infrastructure Project.[30] P. N. Roy Chowdhury, a former head of the Gujarat Maritime Board and principal secretary to the Government of Gujarat, Agriculture & Co-operation Department, became joint president of strategic planning at Adani Ports and Special Economic Zone Limited.[31] In October 2012, former home secretary G. K. Pillai joined the board of Adani Ports. In July 2013, the advocate-general of Gujarat, Kamal Trivedi, represented Rajesh Adani in a duty evasion case made by the Enforcement Directorate. When confronted with this apparent conflict of interest, his answer was, "I do not cease to be a lawyer just because I am the advocate general." According to lawyer Anand Yagnik, more than twenty lawyers who fought cases against the Adanis are now on the group's retainership (Rajshekhar 2013).

The meteoric rise of Gautam Adani is not very different from Dhirubhai Ambani's in the 1970–1980s.[32] But at that time, corrupt practices were conveniently attributed to the license raj. Liberalization was supposed to rid India of this kind of debilitating effect by making market rules supreme.

Conclusion

In the last page of a book whose title—*Gujarat: Governance for Growth and Development*—echoed Narendra Modi's program, Bibek Debroy summarized the state's economic policy as follows: "What is the Gujarat model then? It is one of freeing up space for private initiative and enterprise and the creation of an enabling environment by the state" (2012, 165). In fact, it is more about business-friendliness than market-friendliness, as evident from the nonmarket price some companies pay their land. Gujarat has a long tradition of business-friendliness, but in the past it allowed a dense network of SMEs to blossom in the state, besides bigger players like the Ambanis.

In the 2000s, the BJP government has prioritized "megaprojects" and tried hard to attract big companies. This shift may be explained in many different manners. First, after the 2002 pogrom, the party wanted to prove wrong the entrepreneurs who had argued that Gujarat would not attract investors any more, and Narendra Modi wanted to change his image to appear as the "development man" (the "Vikas Purush"). Second, he wanted Gujarat to be singled out because of its growth rate—a magic figure everybody was obsessed with at that time. Third, to attract big companies was the best way to finance his political activities by retaining a small number of donors while emancipating oneself from the BJP leaders (including Prime Minister A. B. Vajpayee) who had expressed their displeasure with the 2002 violence. Fourth, to give priority to megaprojects enabled Modi to boost the career of emerging figures who were prepared to help him, like Gautam Adani—a man who was not part of the establishment either.[33]

This strategy had many implications for the economy, the society, and the ecology of Gujarat. First, big firms developed at the expense of the SMEs, which had to pay more for the gas and the power produced by the big players, had to face new competition (in the market and with the banks, which lent them less money), and had to wait for their new masters to pay for their bills (these delays are one of the SMEs' complaints in Gujarat). Second, the decline of the SMEs, one of the finest assets of a state known for its entrepreneurs, affected the labor market in terms of the number of jobs available (SMEs are notoriously more labor intensive than the big firms) and, possibly, in terms of the quality of these jobs—with wages remaining very low, partly because of the large number of migrant workers. Third, the big companies that have been attracted to Gujarat have been offered so many incentives—the price of land, the interest rates of loans, and tax deductions—that the exchequer has suffered (as evident from the growing indebtedness of Gujarat). These fiscal constraints have further reduced the ability of the state to spend for social expenditures (education, health . . .)— something Gujarat was good at in the 1980s, but not anymore. Last but not least, the clout that big companies acquired at the highest level in the Gujarat government allowed them to resist pressures from the regulators in charge of environmental norms.

In a democracy, elections and the rule of law are supposed to offer corrective mechanisms when imbalances have become unbearable. In 2015 Patel youth demonstrated in order to have access to government jobs quotas. This massive protest showed that good jobs had become an acute need. Soon after, the BJP lost local elections in the rural parts of Gujarat, and in 2017 it also lost to Congress in rural constituencies, a clear indication of the crisis the peasants, the artisans, and the cottage industry were facing. One of the factors of this crisis is land: land is now a source of tensions between the agriculturalists and the industry, in part because the latter has sometimes polluted both the surface and the subsurface water tables. Whether the voters are in a position to change the center of gravity of the political economy remains to be seen. But the rule of law is also at work. For instance, the Directorate of Revenue Intelligence (DRI) has accused the Adani Group of "over-invoicing coal imported from Indonesia to the tune of Rs. 29,000 crore," of making "illicit gains through 'compensatory tariffs' awarded by electricity regulators," and of "over-invoicing of power plant equipment to the tune of Rs. 6,000" (Guha Thakurta 2015, 12–14). Josy Joseph, one of the journalists who covered these accusations, points out that, according to his "contacts in the SIT (Special Investigation Team) on black money . . . the Adani case is the biggest one they handle" (Joseph 2015a, 215). Whether these investigations will bear any fruit will provide an indication of the degree of crony capitalism in India.

References

"15 Minutes and Gujarat Had Won Over Tatas." 2012. *DNA*, November 3, 6.
Adani, Gautam. 2014. "We Have to Work Closely with the Government." *Outlook*, March 10. http://www.outlookindia.com/magazine/story/we-have-to-work-closely-with-the-government/289726.
"Another Co-operative Bank in Gujarat in Liquidity Crisis." 2002. *Economic Times*, September 4.
Asher, Manshi. 2014. "Gujarat and Punjab: The Entrepreneurs Paradise and the Land of the Farmer." In *Power, Policy, and Protest: The Politics of India's Special Economic Zones*, ed. R. Jenkins, L. Kennedy, and P. Mukhopadhyay, 137–69. Oxford: Oxford University Press.
Bahree, Megha. 2014. "Doing Big Business in Modi's Gujarat." *Forbes India*, March 24. http://www.forbes.com/sites/meghabahree/2014/03/12/doing-big-business-in-modis-gujarat/.
Behavioural Science Centre. 2012. "Development' versus People: Gujarat Model of Land Acquisition and People's Voices." Ahmedabad: Behavioural Science Centre.
Bondre, Shobha. 2013. *How Gujaratis Do Business*. New Delhi: Random House.
Bussell, Jennifer. 2012. *Corruption and Reform in India: Public Services in the Digital Age*. Cambridge: Cambridge University Press.
CAG (Comptroller and Auditor General). 2012. *Report of 2011—Performance Audit on Commercial of Government of Gujarat*, March. http://cag.gov.in/content/report-2011-performance-audit-commercial-government-gujarat.
———. 2013. "Audit Report (Revenue Receipts) for the Year Ended 31 March 2012—Report n°2 of 2013." http://saiindia.gov.in/english/home/Our_Products/Audit_Report/Government_Wise/state_audit/recent_reports/Gujarat/2012/Report_2/Chap_3.pdf.
———. N.d.-a. "Audit Report n°1 (State Finances), for the Year Ended 31 March 2012." http://saiindia.gov.in/english/home/Our_Products/Audit_Report/Government_Wise/state_audit/recent_reports/Gujarat/2012/SF/Chap_1.pdf. =
———. N.d.-b. "Chapter III, Transaction Audit Observations." http://saiindia.gov.in/english/home/Our_Products/Audit_Report/Government_Wise/state_audit/recent_reports/Gujarat/2012/Report_1/Chap_3.pdf.
"CAG Finds State's Public Land Policy Poor, Suggests Immediate Reforms." 2013. *Times of India*, April 4.
"CAG Indicts Modi Govt. for 'Undue' Favours to Firm." 2013. *The Hindu*, April 15, 10.
Centre for Education and Documentation. 2013. "Critical Concerns—Deciphering Gujarat's Development, Mumbai and Bangalore." http://www.doccentre.net/cc/gujarat-final7.pdf.
Comptroller and Auditor General of India. 2013. "Report No. 2 of 2013 Government of Gujrat—Report of the Comptroller and Auditor General of India on Revenue Receipts." http://saiindia.gov.in/english/home/Our_Products/Audit_Report/Government_Wise/state_audit/recent_reports/Gujarat/2012/Report_2/Overview.pdf.
———. 2014. "Report of the Comptroller and Auditor General of India on Public Sector Undertakings for the Year Ended 31 March 2013 (Report No. 3 of the year 2014)."
Das, Rathin. 2013. "Anil Ambani Says Modi King of Kings, India Inc Adds Praise." *The Pioneer*, January 12.
Dave, H. 2017. "More Than 80% Engineers Are without Jobs." *Ahmedabad Mirror*, March 28. http://ahmedabadmirror.indiatimes.com/ahmedabad/cover-story/more-than-80-engineers-are-without-jobs/articleshow/57880536.cms?prtpage=1.

Dave, Kapil. 2011. "Firms Owe Rs 12,000 Cr in Taxes to State Govt." *Indian Express*, February 2011.
————. 2012. "Over 5,000 CAG Queries Awaiting Modi Govt Reply!" *Times of India*, November 27.
Debroy, Bibek. 2012. "Gujarat: Governance for Growth and Development." New Delhi: Academic Foundation.
Debroy, Bibek, and Laveesh Bhandari. N.d. "Economic Freedom for States." New Delhi: International Management Institute.
Dev, Nirendra. 2012. *Modi to Moditva*. New Delhi: Manas.
Dholakia, Archana, and Ravindra Dholakia. 2015. "Policy Reform in Economic Sectors." In *The Making of Miracles in Indian States: Andhra Pradesh, Bihar and Gujarat*, ed. A. Panagariya and M. G. Rao, 246–64. New Delhi: Oxford University Press.
"Did Modi Offer Rs. 30,000 Crore in Sops to Tata Motors?" 2008. *The Hindu*, November 12.
Dupont, Veronique. 1995. *Decentralized Industrialisation and Urban Dynamics*. New Delhi: Sage.
Ethiraj, Govindraj. 2015. "Quietly, Maharashtra and Tamil Nadu Outrace Gujarat." *IndiaSpend*, January 16. http://www.indiaspend.com/cover-story/quietly-maharashtra-tamil-nadu-outrace-gujarat-25529.
"Fall of Sanjay Gupta: From IAS to Conman." 2015. *Economic Times*, May 20. http://articles.economictimes.indiatimes.com/2015-05-20/news/62413387_1_gujarat-state-petroleum-corporation-sanjay-gupta-neesa-group.
"Forbes India Rich List: Mukesh Ambani Tops, Adani Moves Up." 2014. *Forbes*. http://www.moneycontrol.com/news/business/forbes-india-rich-list-mukesh-ambani-tops-adani-moves-up_1188269.html.
"Forest Land Allotted to Corporates in Gujarat." 2012. *DNA*, March 7.
"Fortunes of Indian Promoters Rise Significantly; Gautam Adani Witnesses the Maximum Surge." 2014. *Economic Times*, May 17. http://economictimes.indiatimes.com/markets/stocks/fortunes-of-indian-promoters-rise-significantly-gautam-adani-witnesses-the-maximum-surge/articleshow/35226427.cms.
Gautam Adani Biography. N.d. Business Maps of India.
George, P. T. 2011. *Special Economic Zones and People's Struggles in Gujarat*. New Delhi: Intercultural Resources.
Government of Gujarat. 2009a. Gujarat Act no.2 of 2009. January. http://www.gidb.org/pdf/sirord.pdf.
————. 2009b. "Industrial Policy—2009." January. http://www.ic.gujarat.gov.in/pdf/industrial-policy-2009-at-a-glance.pdf.
Guha Thakurta, Paranjoy. 2015. "The Incredible Rise and Rise of Gautam Adani: Part One." *The Citizen*, April 26.
"Gujarat Government Reveals Offers That Drove Nano into State." 2009. *Indian Express*, January 20.
"Gujarat Inc. Guns for CII." 2003. *Times of India*, February 20.
"Gujarat State Government Gifts Adani Group Land in Kutch for Peanuts." 2012. *Ahmedabad Mirror*, February 29.
Hirway, Indira, Neha Shah, and Rajeev Sharma. 2014. "Political Economy of Subsidies and Incentives to Industries in Gujarat." In *Growth or Development: Which Way Is Gujarat Going?*, ed. I. Hirway, A. Shah, and G. Shah, 139–92. New Delhi: Oxford University Press.
"India Inc Hails Narendra Modi's 'Vision.'" 2013. *Indian Express*, January 11.
"Industrial Policy to Usher Investment in Gujarat." 2003. *The Pioneer*, November 8, 11.
"Investors Back Out, Vibrant Plans go Awry." 2008. *Times of India*, March 4.
ISED Small Enterprise Observatory. 2013. "Gujarat Micro, Small & Medium Enterprises Report 2013." Cochin: Institute of Small Enterprise and Development.
Iyengar, Sudarshan. 2014. "Education in Gujarat: A Review." In *Growth or Development: Which Way Is Gujarat Going?*, ed. I. Hirway, A. Shah, and G. Shah, 477–516. New Delhi: Oxford University Press.
Jaffrelot, Christophe. 2015. "What Gujarat Model? Growth without Development and with Socio-Political Polarisation." *South Asia: Journal of South Asian Studies* 38 (4): 820–38.
————. 2016. "Quota for Patels? The Neo-middleclass Syndrome and the (Partial) Return of Caste Politics in Gujarat." *Studies in Indian Politics* 4 (2): 1–15.
Johari, Arefa. 2015. "Casteism, Brides and a Failed Gujarat Model: What the Patel Demand for Reservations Is Really About." *Scroll.in*, September 14. http://scroll.in/article/753595/

casteism-brides-and-a-failed-gujarat-model-what-the-patel-demand-for-reservations-is-really-about.

John, Paul. 2012. "Gujarat's Hall of Shame." *Times of India*, February.

Joseph, Josy. 2015a. *A Feast of Vultures: The Hidden Business of Democracy in India*. New Delhi: HarperCollins.

Joseph, Tony. 2015b. "Adani's $ 10-Billion Gamble." *Business Today*, January 18.

"Kejriwal Targets Modi, Alleges Favouritism in Giving Away Gas Wells, Land Allotments." 2012. *Indian Express*, December 5.

Khanna, Sumit. 2012. "Has Essar's Proximity to Modi Become Too Taxing?" *DNA*, July 18.

Kohli, Atul. 2012. *Poverty amid Plenty in the New India*. Cambridge: Cambridge University Press.

Langa, Mahesh. 2015. "Gautam Adani, PM Modi's Constant Companion on Overseas Trips." *Hindustan Times*, April 16. http://www.hindustantimes.com/india/gautam-adani-pm-modi-s-constant-companion-on-overseas-trips/story-CMDqyMTSNxoewGpQVqEeDK.html.

Mahadevia, Darshini. "Dynamics of Urbanization in Gujarat." In *Growth or development: Which Way is Gujarat Going?*, ed. Indira Hirway, Amita Shah, and Ghanshyam Shah, 340–79. New York: Oxford.

McDonald, Hamish. 2010. *Ambani and Sons*. New Delhi: Roli Books.

Mehta, M. 2012. "Corporate Cronyism in Vibrant Gujarat." *Hardnews*. http://hardnews media.com/2012/07/5445?page-show.

Mishra, Piyush. 2015. "Only UP Has More Sick MSMEs Than Gujarat." *Times of India*, December 4.

Mishra, Pravin. 2011. "Whose Gujarat Is Vibrant." *Ahmedabad Mirror*, March 28.

Mukherjee, Arindam. 2016. "Mundra: The Port of No Call." *Outlook*, August 1. http://www.outlookindia.com/magazine/story/mundra-the-port-of-no-call/297572.

Mukherjee, Atri. 2011. "Regional Inequality in Foreign Direct Investment Flows to India: The Problem and the Prospects." Reserve Bank of India Occasional Papers 32, no.2.

Nag, Kingshuk. 2013. *The NAMO Story: A Political Life*. New Delhi: Roli Books.

Nair, Avinash. 2017. "Over 13.95 Lakh New Jobs in Gujarat since July 2011." *Indian Express*, April 11.

National University of Educational Planning and Administration. 2013. "*DISE 2011–12. Elementary* educationDISE 2011-12. Elementary Education." New Delhi: National University of Educational Planning and Administration. http://www.dise.in/Downloads/Publications/Publications 2011-12/Flash 2011-12.pdf.

Naudet, J., A. Allorant, and M. Ferry. 2018. "Heirs, Corporate Aristocrats and 'Meritocrats': The Social Space of Top CEOs and Chairmen in India." *Socio-economic Review* 16 (2): 307–39.

Naudet, J., and C.-L. Dubost. 2016. "The Indian Exception: The Densification of the Network of Corporate Interlocks and the Specificities of the Indian Business System (2000–2012)." *Socio-Economic Review*, January. https://academic.oup.com/ser/search-results?page=1&q=Naudet&fl_SiteID=5245&allJournals=1&SearchSourceType=1.

Pathak, P. G. 1982. "Industrial Structure in Gujarat: A Study in Spatial Dimension." In *Gujarat Economy: Problems and Prospects*, ed. D. T. Lakdawala, 441–75. Ahmedabad: Sardar Patel Institute of Economic and Social Research.

Parekh, Sunil R. 2014. "Some Facets of Industrialisation in Gujarat (1999–2009)." In *Growth or development: Which Way is Gujarat Going?*, ed. Indira Hirway, Amita Shah, and Ghanshyam Shah, 193–224. New York: Oxford.

Rajshekhar, M. 2013. "The Other Big." *Times of India*, September 5. http://epaper.timesofindia.com/Repository/ml.asp?Ref=RVRNLzIwMTMvMDkvMDUjQXIwMjIwMA==.

"Ratan Tata Takes Mistry to Modi." 2011. *Indian Express*, December 30.

Report of the Committee for Inspection of M/sadani Port & SEZ Ltd. Mundra, Gujarat. 2013. New Delhi: Ministry of Environment and Forests.

Rutten, M. 1995. *Farms and Factories: Social Profile of Large Farmers and Rural Industrialists in West India*. New Delhi: Oxford University Press.

Sasi, Anil. 2015. "Indian billionaires: Gautam Adani, Dilip Shanghvi see highest growth." *Indian Express*, May 31, 2015. http://indianexpress.com/article/business/business-others/indian-billionaires-gautam-adani-dilip-shangvhi-see-highest-growth.

Shah, Ghanshyam. 2013. "Politics of Governance: A Study of Gujarat." *Studies in Indian Politics* 1 (1): 65–77.

Shah, Rajiv. 2009. "State Debt Set to Cross Rs 1L Crore." *Times of India*, January 2.

Singh, Pragya. 2015. "How Much Growth Can Absorb All?" *Outlook*. http://www.outlookindia. com/printarticle.aspx?295246.

Sinha, Aseema. 2005. *The Regional Roots of Developmental Politics in India: A Divided Leviathan.* Bloomington: Indiana University Press.

———. 2010. "Reforming Public Services in a High Growth State." In *Public Service Delivery in India: Understanding the Reform Process*. New Delhi: Oxford University Press.

"State lost, Big Business Gained from Govt's Land Policy: CAG." 2013. *DNA*, April 3.

"Strike at Tata Motors Sanand Plant Ends." 2016. *F*.

Sud, Nikita. 2012. "Liberalization, Hindu Nationalism, and the State a Biography of Gujarat." New York: Oxford University Press. http://myaccess.library.utoronto.ca/login?url=http:// books.scholarsportal.info/viewdoc.html?id=/ebooks/ebooks2/oso/2012-09-10/1/ 9780198076933-Sud.

"Vibrant Gujarat." 2013. *The Economic Times*, January 12.

Wood, John. 1995. "On the Periphery but in the Thick of It: Some Recent Political Crisis Viewed from Gujarat." In *India Briefing: Staying the Course*, ed. P. Oldenburg, 23–46. Armonk, NY: M.E. Sharpe.

"Workers Strike at Tata Motors, Sanand, Gujarat, in India." 2016. *Libcom.org*. https://libcom.org/ news/workers-tata-motors-sanand-gujarat-14032016.

"Workers' Strike: Guj Tops the List in India." 2015. *DNA*, August 11.

Yadav, Anumeha. 2011. "Vibrant Gujarat? Your Coast Is Not Clear Mr. Adani." *Tehelka*. http:// archive.tehelka.com/story_main48.asp?filename=Ne260211DEVELOPMENT_ CONFLICTS.asp.

Business and Politics

The Tamil Nadu Puzzle

JOHN HARRISS AND ANDREW WYATT

We have made it a point not to interact with government very much.

In Tamil Nadu, there is a division of roles between politicians and business. Politicians concentrate on the social sectors, leaving entrepreneurs pretty much to themselves.

Government runs on liquor.[1]

Introduction

Tamil Nadu has seen a distinctive trajectory of development. According to recent data, it is second only to Maharashtra in terms of the size of the economy (given by GSDP); it has the third largest manufacturing sector, after Gujarat and Maharashtra; and a service sector that is second only to that of Karnataka ("Maharashtra is Biggest State Economy" 2015). An analysis by Kumar and Subramanian shows that, over the period from 1993 to 2009, the growth rate of NSDP per capita in Tamil Nadu, of 5.37 percent, was only a little lower than that of Gujarat (5.77 percent) and Kerala (5.8 percent), and about the same as that of Andhra Pradesh (5.38 percent)—these four states being ahead of all the other major states (Kumar and Subramanian 2012, table 1). At the same time, in regard to many indicators of social welfare Tamil Nadu is second—among the major states—only to Kerala,[2] though recent calculations of the human development index across these states by the Institute of Applied Manpower Research place Tamil Nadu also a little behind Punjab and Maharashtra. It has come to be recognized, therefore, that Tamil Nadu combines relatively successful economic growth with a positive performance in regard to social development, in a way that is distinctive, if not absolutely unique, among the more important Indian states. It certainly seems to be more of a "model" than Gujarat.[3]

Yet, as a writer for *The Mint* has put it, "Conventional wisdom dictates that rampant populism, autocratic administrations and widespread corruption—all endemic to [the politics of Tamil Nadu] since MGR's reign [referring to M. G. Ramachandran, popular chief minister of the state 1977–87], with little to choose between the All India Anna Dravida Munnetra Kazhagam (AIADMK) and the M. Karunanidhi-headed Dravida Munnetra Kazhagam (DMK) that have alternated terms since then—are antithetical to economic growth and human development" ("Why Tamil Nadu's Freebie Culture Works" 2016). But, as the writer goes on to say, "In Tamil Nadu they have always coexisted comfortably." How has this been possible? What is commonly described as "populism"—reflected in Tamil Nadu especially in government spending on the distribution of free consumer goods, or "freebies," intended to garner votes—is generally considered to be in conflict with sustained economic growth; and corruption is thought to undermine effective governance. Yet Tamil Nadu is clearly among the most successful of India's major states. This is the puzzle of the political economy of Tamil Nadu.

Our argument is that successive governments of Tamil Nadu have worked with big-business groups to secure economic growth, albeit having to qualify, and to an extent to disguise, this support because of the ways in which they have mobilized and maintained their electoral bases among middle and lower castes or classes. The competition between the Dravidian parties has also driven them to deliver in regard to social welfare, through a combination of clientelistic and programmatic policies.[4] Given the particular character of Tamil politics, and the Dravidian political culture, it is neither a developmental nor a social democratic state, while having some elements of both, but approximates rather to Bonapartism.

Atul Kohli argues that three political tendencies "compete for ascendancy in India's states: *neo-patrimonial, social democratic,* and *developmental*" (2012, 143). These are ideal-typical distinctions, and so it is unsurprising that Tamil Nadu corresponds neatly with none of the three. With respect to neopatrimonialism, Kohli (2012, 143) says, "Instead of using state authority and resources to pursue the broader public good, ruling elites use their power either for personal gain or to benefit a narrow political community that they define as their 'own.'" Ruling elites in Tamil Nadu have certainly used their power for personal gain, while also distributing patrimony to loyal followers—as evidence presented later in this chapter demonstrates. Yet there is also an important sense in which their power rests on the support of lower castes and classes, and this Kohli associates with the social democratic tendency. The outcomes of government action in Tamil Nadu, too, in regard to social democratic objectives, are much more clearly successful than are those of West Bengal under Left Front governments (which Kohli takes as his example, and of which he has a more positive view than many others).

Lastly, as Kohli puts it, "A few of India's states have started moving toward becoming developmental states of sorts, in which the government works closely with business groups to promote economic growth" (2012, 144). Gujarat is his example, though he refers to Maharashtra as well.

This chapter will present evidence that in Tamil Nadu, too, government works with business groups to secure growth. At the same time, our evidence from Tamil Nadu leads us to question Kohli's presumption that the enhanced role of business groups in politics (in India's "developmental states," and now, in the period of the Modi government, at the center) means that these groups are able to use their power to influence state behavior in a way that was not true before. With Christophe Jaffrelot and Kanta Murali, Kohli has proposed that "at the heart of India's new model of development [which is focused on "the goal of growth promotion via support for private enterprise"] is the enhanced role of business groups in politics. . . . With economic success, the power and influence of business groups has grown enormously. Business groups now use this power to mold state behaviour" (Kohli 2016). We will show that in Tamil Nadu the power and influence of business groups has *not* grown enormously, and that they do not mold state behavior.

The political economy of Tamil Nadu presents something of an enigma, therefore. As we will explain, we find some inspiration, in resolving the enigma, in the idea developed by the historian David Washbrook (1989), thirty years ago, that Tamil Nadu has characteristics of a Bonapartist state, in which the political elite rules to an extent, at least, on behalf of the capitalist class, which does not itself directly exercise political power. In practice, over the quarter-century since the inception of India's economic reforms, and even further back than this, governments of Tamil Nadu, whether led by the AIADMK or by the DMK, have done a great deal to encourage private investment. In 1996, for example, the National Council for Applied Economic Research ranked Tamil Nadu as the state with the most attractive package of investment incentives (NCAER report, referred to by Kennedy 2013). Since then, while successive governments have not always acted according to the priorities of corporate business—and businessmen complain quite vociferously of the "indifference" of government— the state has continued to be attractive to private investors, and the various incentives offered by the state have not been irrelevant to this. Tamil Nadu has, fairly consistently, sought to take advantage of economic liberalization, and to encourage the private sector, even while governments have not generally advertised the fact.

Loraine Kennedy shows, in her comparative study of how governments of Tamil Nadu and Andhra Pradesh handled the economic reform process in its earlier years, that the former were much more discreet about it than the latter, reforming "by stealth," without much fanfare. Governments of Andhra often did less than they announced, while those of Tamil Nadu did more than they claimed. Kennedy explains the difference as being the outcome of the greater political fragmentation and mobilization in Tamil Nadu, where the Dravidian parties compete for the political support of middle and lower castes and Dalits. These conditions made for strong incentives for governments "to avoid overt political identification with economic reforms" and to avoid the appearance of support for upper castes—who predominate in the ownership of big business, as we show in this chapter, and who were the most visible supporters of economic liberalization in the earlier years (Kennedy 2004, 52).

As Washbrook argued, in the context of his discussion of Bonapartism, the Dravidian political culture accommodates elite privilege. In spite of the promises of the Dravidian movement in its early years, the Dravidian parties in power, their left-of-center and egalitarian political idiom notwithstanding, have not pursued a radically redistributive agenda. It seems that both parties, in office, have realized the importance of growth, for instrumental reasons—the financing of expansive social welfare requires sufficient government revenues—as well as to generate jobs (growth has been relatively broad-based in the state, as compared to Gujarat, for example). Hence, their pragmatic approach to industrial development and their relatively probusiness attitude. Wealth has been made legitimate "by appearing to be held and used for the benefit of other members of the Tamil 'community'—providing employment and distributing largesse" (Washbrook 1989, 254). But at the same time, given their support bases among subaltern groups, neither the DMK nor the AIADMK must be seen to pander to upper-caste interests. This explains the ambivalence in the relationships of the Tamil political elite and big business that emerged very clearly in interviews with businessmen from the corporate sector, conducted for this chapter.[5]

There is of course another side of the relationship between business and politics: party funding. It was widely thought that part of the explanation for the dramatic success of the campaign led by Narendra Modi in the 2014 general election in India was that he raised huge sums of money from big business to finance campaign activities (Jaffrelot, in this volume). Subsequently, in office, Modi was constrained to try to counter the perception that he was in the pocket of the corporate sector (Sen 2015). Kohli, Jaffrelot, and Murali (2016) have suggested that politicians have become increasingly dependent "on resources controlled by the wealthy." In Tamil Nadu, however, politicians have secured their own sources of wealth, partly through corrupt means, as we show in the later part of this chapter, which is concerned particularly with the relationships of business and politics at local levels—where they are deeply imbricated within each other. There is a sense, indeed, in which politics and business merge into each other, when individuals act as entrepreneurs both in politics and in business.

The structure of the chapter is as follows. We begin by reviewing the history of economic development in Tamil Nadu and what are commonly considered to be its inherited advantages. We proceed to examine what successive governments of the state have done to encourage private business, to substantiate the case that they have worked with business, more or less effectively, to promote economic growth. We then go on to consider the relationships of business and politics from the perspectives of businessmen in the corporate sector, showing that, even if the state does support private capital, big business certainly does not "mold state behavior." Finally, we assess the connections of politicians with business, especially at local levels, where such activities as agro-industry, transport, real estate, and mining and quarrying are involved. We conclude by developing our explanation of "the Tamil Nadu puzzle."

The Character of the Tamil Nadu Economy: Inherited Advantage?

Tamil Nadu, in common with Maharashtra and Gujarat, inherited economic advantages that reflect what Krishna Bharadwaj (1982, 609) referred to as the "historical legacy of port-enclave development" in the colonial period. The initial advantages of Bombay (the states of Maharashtra and Gujarat) and of Madras (present-day Tamil Nadu and the coastal districts of Andhra Pradesh), in regard both to overall economic growth and industrial development, have generally been maintained, though those of Calcutta (West Bengal) have not, or at least not to the same extent. Rather than the gaps in terms of economic growth between the major states having been closed over time, as some economists expected, and as the quinquennially appointed finance commissions have sought to bring about, the disparities between them have grown larger. The RBI now classifies Goa, Gujarat, Haryana, Maharashtra, and Tamil Nadu as "higher income states," followed by Kerala, Punjab, Karnataka, Andhra and West Bengal ("middle income states"). The initial advantage in terms of economic development of the old presidency states—together with the states of the northwest (Punjab and Haryana) that benefited from investment especially in irrigation and agricultural infrastructure in the colonial period—has been maintained, therefore.

Tamil Nadu has generally lagged behind Maharashtra and Gujarat in terms of industrial investment, but now has many more factories than either of the two western Indian states—in fact more factories than any other state—and the highest level of factory employment in the country. Gujarat leads in terms of fixed capital investment, but lags behind both Tamil Nadu and Maharashtra in terms of the number of factories and the level of factory employment (RBI 2016, tables 76–83). Tamil Nadu had 3.1 million small and medium enterprises (SMEs) in 2006–7, compared with just 3 million in Maharashtra and only 2.1 million in Gujarat. Tamil Nadu then employed 8.1 million people in these SMEs, Gujarat only 4.7 million. The differences between Tamil Nadu and Gujarat, in particular, are very striking and surely are a reflection, in part, of the greater success of Gujarat in attracting large-scale private investment, as Aseema Sinha (2005) showed in her comparative study. The severe constraints acting on the agricultural economy of Tamil Nadu, on the other hand, together with the high level of urbanization of the state (it is the most urbanized of the major states) and its relatively good road network and public transport, have provided incentives ("push" and "pull") for smaller-scale investment outside agriculture, which has also suited the political interests of the Dravidian parties (Vijayabaskar 2010, 38). Historical path dependency may go a long way in explaining the varying economic success of different Indian states, therefore, but these dynamics are influenced by political action.

It is widely held that Tamil Nadu has several advantages in relation to other states, and that these have significantly influenced the state's economic performance. According to some businessmen, indeed, insofar as Tamil Nadu is successful in terms of economic growth it is a reflection of these inherited advantages. These include especially the numbers and quality of the state's educational institutions, and the availability of skills; a disciplined labor force;[6] a relatively competent bureaucracy; infrastructure that at least compares favorably with other states (even if one overlooks recent woes over power);[7] and the existence of a number of "enterprising" communities,[8] such as the Nadars, the Rajus (of Andhra origin) and the Gounders and Naidus (also of Andhra origin) of western Tamil Nadu, as well as the Brahmans and the Chettiars. There is also a recognition that the quality of social provisioning of the state is in the long-run interests of business, because it makes for social stability as well as for relatively high-quality human resources—even though the immediate costs may be a source of concern for some.

Basic education is generally regarded as being better in Tamil Nadu than in most other states, and as having been so for a long time. A major advantage of the state lies in the numbers of engineering colleges that it has, and even though the quality of many of them is deplorable, there are still a number of private engineering colleges—perhaps fifty, according to one of our informants—that do compare with the best public institutions and produce competent, employable engineers. The number of private colleges is seen as one of the "gifts" to the state of the charismatic chief minister, and former film star, MGR, in the 1980s. Though he may have encouraged the privatization of college education in order to satisfy some of his cronies, who saw profit-making opportunities, the state has derived a lot of public benefit from its colleges. The advantage that Tamil

Nadu has over most, perhaps all other, states in terms of an educated workforce is clear.

More debatable is the claim, commonly made, that the state benefits from a relatively competent bureaucracy. Joshi and McGrath report a perception that Tamil Nadu has a relatively disciplined cadre. The same authors also speak of a "higher degree of politically motivated transferring of officials in Gujarat" than in Tamil Nadu (Joshi and McGrath 2015, 476). They supply no evidence for this, however, and an analysis by Lakshmi Iyer and Anandi Mani of transfer rates of Indian Administrative Service (IAS) officers in the major states over the period 1980–2004 does not show that Tamil Nadu is marked out by a particularly low rate of transfers. Indeed, the transfer rate in the state was slightly higher than that of Gujarat (Iyer and Mani 2012, figure 1). It is argued that the high rate of often politically motivated transfers, especially of senior officials, is one of the most important causes of low levels of bureaucratic performance in India (Saxena 2016). One might have supposed, therefore, that if indeed Tamil Nadu is characterized by a notably competent bureaucracy, the state would have had a particularly low rate of transfers. But this not the case; and Iyer and Mani (2012, figure 2) also present data showing high rates of transfers associated with changes of government in the state.

The high transfer rate notwithstanding, the idea that a superior bureaucratic performance helps to account for Tamil Nadu's success gains some support from recent studies of government performance by Mundle, Chowdhury, and Sikdar (2016), who rank the state as second only to Gujarat both in 2001 and in 2011. One of our business informants said that in his experience, bureaucrats in Tamil Nadu interact with business much more than is the case in other states, and there is no doubt of the important role played by various IAS officers as industry secretaries, or in other positions, at various junctures. The role of the then-industry secretary, M. S. Srinivasan, in the later 1990s was, for instance, clearly important in the establishment of the TIDEL Park, which played a significant role in boosting the IT industry in the state. Srinivasan's story of what happened in that period draws attention to an aspect of Tamil politics that may, in some ways, be an advantage, while in others constituting a problem.[9] The story is that the then-chief minister, Karunanidhi, was determined that he himself (as a matter of personal prestige) and the state should lose out no longer to Chandrababu Naidu and Andhra Pradesh in the development of the IT industry, and he put all his authority behind Srinivasan over the TIDEL Park.

The aspect of Tamil politics in question is that government is very highly personalized. Whether under Karunanidhi, MGR, or Jayalalithaa, authority was highly centralized. Rule is autocratic, and—as was reported to us by many informants—nothing moves without the authority of "the Leader."[10] This can be the source of big problems, as we go on to explain. But it can also mean that things work very well indeed because of the backing given to officials by the chief minister or "Leader." This was the case in Srinivasan's experience of his work as industry secretary under Karunanidhi.[11] The high rate of transfers associated with changes of chief minister in Tamil Nadu is not necessarily indicative of a problem, therefore. It is a double-edged phenomenon. It may facilitate corruption (and we provide some evidence of this later in the chapter); but it may also facilitate effective performance in the delivery of vital services.

Tamil Nadu does have inherited advantages, but we should not underestimate the contribution made to the economic performance of the state by the actions of successive governments. That businessmen complain a lot about the "indifference" of government, particularly in the recent past—as we recount later—is indicative, somewhat ironically, of the significance of government action for capital.

Industrial Policy in Tamil Nadu

In 1994 Padmini Swaminathan (1994, M64) reported that "while maintaining its position as one of the three leading industrial states of the country [with Maharashtra and Gujarat], Tamil Nadu has nevertheless over the years lost considerable ground and many opportunities." Private investment in the state, she found, had been low by comparison with the two western Indian states. A key finding was "*the interaction between government and industry is at a very superficial level*," and implicitly she argued that Gujarat and Maharashtra functioned as developmental states (in the way that Kohli uses this term) and that Tamil Nadu did not (Swaminathan 1994, M74; emphasis added). If, indeed, the concept of "developmental state" is identified with what Peter Evans (1995) refers to as "embedded autonomy"—the idea that a positive relationship between state and business is one in which politicians and the state bureaucracy are not in the pockets of businessmen, and (having autonomy) are able to implement an industrial policy, yet are well networked with business people (they are still "embedded")—then Tamil Nadu, according to Swaminathan, clearly was not a developmental state. Swaminathan's characterization of the relations of business and government in Tamil Nadu is one that is recognized by businessmen themselves.

These arguments are in line with the findings of Aseema Sinha in her comparative research (from the late 1990s). She points out that Tamil Nadu (in common with West Bengal) relied heavily, in the early postindependence decades, on public sector investment, while Gujarat combined public and private investments. Then Tamil Nadu, though an industrially advanced state, saw "a marked decline in its industrial indicators from 1965 onward" (2005, 10). The public sector strategy paid off very well, Sinha says, "until the end of the 1960s, with regional party leaders effectively lobbying the central state" (2005, 17). After the DMK took power in the state from Congress in 1967, however, "the political logic of a regionalist movement . . . necessitated an anti-center strategy from the 1970s through to the mid-1980s" (Sinha 2005, 17). Then the declining political dividends from this strategy "led the regional leadership to pursue lobbying and cooperation with the central government"; until in the 1990s the influence of the Dravidian parties in India's new minority governments and co-alition politics at the center lent them significant power (Sinha 2005, 114). The AIADMK government supported the minority Congress government after 1991 and made use of that linkage "to launch a regional strategy of liberalisation"; and after 1996 (when the DMK was re-elected into office in Tamil Nadu), the DMK politician Murasoli Maran, as minister for industry in the central government exercised a very important role "in informing Tamil Nadu's officials" about po-tential investors.[12]

Sinha's analysis emphasizes the significance in the economic history of Tamil Nadu, of the taking over of power in the state by the Dravidian parties from 1967. In line with her argument, one businessman put it that "the DMK taking power in 1967 brought a tremendous churning, with people from the bottom of society taking over powerful positions." It represented, he thought, a big cul-tural change that was difficult for the established businesses in the state, run by forward castes—mainly Brahmans and Chettiars—to negotiate.[13] He recalled that when Kamaraj was chief minister of Tamil Nadu, and T. T. Krishnamachari was a member of the union cabinet, they would come to his father's house in the evenings to play cards. Such relationships between politicians and the long-established business houses of Tamil Nadu have not obtained, he thinks, since the takeover by the Dravidian parties.[14] There was a "cultural problem" that helped to make Tamil business generally risk averse. On the side of the Dravidian politicians there has been a tendency to be suspicious of the corpo-rate sector, and businessmen are somewhat looked down upon. Another of our interviewees saw the lack of trust (a "trust deficit") between businessmen and politicians as a problem.

Whatever the merits of the argument about a "cultural problem," it corresponds with Sinha's observation that both Dravidian parties have "excluded productive classes within their fold,"[15] though she goes on to say that "the DMK, over time, did benefit from support from the local business groups" (Sinha 2005, 202–3). This is borne out by the strong suggestions in our interviews that, on the whole, the DMK in office has been easier to work with, and more actively sup-portive of business interests, than the AIADMK.[16] Yet, just as Sinha observed earlier, there are still reports that state governments in Tamil Nadu, whether AIADMK or DMK, have been subject to the "whims and dictates of the chief minister without much predictability" (2005, 207). We have argued, above, that the centralization of authority in Tamil Nadu is a double-edged phenomenon, and not invariably negative. Sinha's final argument that there has been "active neglect of infrastructural and industrial development" overstates the case (Sinha 2005, 207).

The AIADMK government in 1991 was among the first state governments to try to bring in private investment. It streamlined procedures, established the Industrial Guidance and Export Promotion Bureau in 1992, provided tax holidays and capital subsidies, put in place measures to facilitate the acquisition of land, and continued to establish industrial estates. Investors were permitted to begin construction without waiting for local authority approval.

In 1995 the AIADMK government clinched a deal with Ford (in a joint venture with Mahindra and Mahindra) against competition from other states, thanks to a package of incentives devised by government officials. The interest taken in this by Chief Minister Jayalalithaa is believed to have been extremely important. Though the DMK accused the government of pandering to a multinational corporation, when it came back to power in 1996 it agreed to the terms of the MoU with Ford, and to a very similar deal with Hyundai and later with the glassmaker Saint-Gobain. The establishment of the Ford and the Hyundai plants stimulated further investments in the automotive industry that have made Chennai and its region into "the Detroit" of India (Kennedy 2004, 35–36). Both Renault-Nissan and Daimler have opened major facilities outside Chennai, and industrial parks outside the city host, as well, the "Nissan Suppliers Park," Apollo Tyres, Bosch Electrical India, Bridgestone, BMW, and Caparo. It seems reasonable to think that these investments might well not have come to the state had the government interventions of the 1990s not been made. In 2016 the state was very actively competing for a further major investment in the auto industry, on the part of the Korean company Kia.[17]

In a similar vein, in 2005 the AIADMK-controlled state government offered incentives to attract a Nokia plant outside Chennai. As well as compensating Nokia via generous sales tax rebates, the company was allowed exemptions from various employment regulations. The DMK also backed the investment, both at the center (where it was part of the UPA government) and after it returned to power in the state in May 2006. The package was later criticized for being excessively generous—though the employment gains were significant and Tamil Nadu won some cumulative advantages ("Death of a Dream" 2014; Dutta 2009).[18]

We have referred to the way in which the DMK government of 1996–2001 sought to encourage the development of the IT industry, explicitly in competition with Andhra Pradesh. And successive governments have actively encouraged industrial development, involving local, as well as national and international, business, through the Tamil Nadu Industrial Development Corporation (TIDCO), and the State Industries Promotion Corporation of Tamil Nadu (SIPCOT)—founded in 1972, and which was setting up industrial estates in the 1970s and 1980s.[19] These agencies have also been responsible for creating a land bank that proved very useful when the state, one of the first to do so, began promoting special economic zones (SEZs).

The Government of Tamil Nadu has a detailed industrial policy, proclaims its enthusiasm for promoting industry, and has plans for developing infrastructure (outlined in the Vision Tamil Nadu 2023, which was launched in 2012). However, it is not clear that the depth of commitment is equal to that shown in other business-friendly states (such as Gujarat). In some areas, the Government of Tamil Nadu does keep pace with Gujarat's priority for business. Similar tax breaks and subsidies are granted in Tamil Nadu. Yet to the disappointment of business, infrastructure development in Tamil Nadu has not kept pace with demand. The fiscal commitments of the government confirm only qualified support for business. Tamil Nadu spends nearly half of its revenue budget on social services, and it is constrained when it comes to capital spending. Revenue spending on economic services, which might be used to help business, was skewed toward agriculture in the 2013–14 financial year. Overall, economic services accounted for 17.9 percent of the revenue expenditure and 56.3 percent of the capital spent in Tamil Nadu. The comparable figures for economic services in Gujarat in 2013–14 were 20.9 percent of revenue and 67.1 percent of capital spending. Furthermore, Tamil Nadu, a state with a larger population, spent less on capital projects, in absolute terms, than Gujarat in 2013–14. The same outcome is shown in the budget estimates through to 2015–16. Tamil Nadu's fiscal record indicates a government that gives priority to the immediate needs of voters over the sectional interests of big business.[20]

Swaminathan's and Sinha's analyses suggest that relationships between politicians and officials, on one side, and business people, on the other, that would make for a consistent flow of information, both ways, from business to government and from government to business (as in Evans's idea of embedded autonomy) did not obtain in Tamil Nadu in the later twentieth century. But business interests are now better organized than they were, and bureaucrats and business may be more effectively networked together than before. There is an institutional mechanism, as well as a consultative committee of the State Planning Commission—the government selects a representative of "industry" as a member of the commission—though it is widely felt that "in general more happens in private meetings with bureaucrats than in public meetings." An industrialist in the automobile components industry said it was important to take advantage of casual meetings with ministers and senior officials at motor shows.

Much depends, it seems, on the capabilities and the accessibility of senior officials.

The significance for business of the actions of senior civil servants is very clearly shown up in the response of the government of Tamil Nadu to the controversial Land Acquisition, Rehabilitation and Resettlement Act passed by the UPA government in 2013 (and which the BJP government subsequently sought to modify, partly, at least, to satisfy business interests). Tamil Nadu was the first state to seek and to receive presidential assent for excluding three major categories of land acquisition (for highways, for industrial purposes, and for Harijan Welfare Schemes, together accounting for about four-fifths of land acquisitions in the state) from the purview of the act—relaxing, therefore, its requirements in regard to consent, and for the conduct of social impact assessments. One media source speaks of Tamil Nadu offering a "tutorial" to other states on how to deal with the land acquisition legislation. That it has been able to do so is down to the actions of senior civil servants ("Tutorial from Tamil Nadu" 2015; Vijayabaskar 2010).

Business associations do now have some influence. The Confederation of Indian Industry (CII) is described as having been a "National Partner" in the Global Investors Meet that took place in Chennai in September 2015; the Federation of Indian Chambers of Commerce and Industry (FICCI) is described as "Event Partner"; and both ASSOCHAM (Associated Chambers of Commerce of India) and the Madras Chamber of Commerce and Industry are listed among various "Partner Organisations." CII is very active in Tamil Nadu and articulates especially the views and interests of the larger corporates. Several of the big businessmen who were interviewed have served as directors of the Southern Region of CII. The Chennai chapter of FICCI has an active membership among somewhat smaller companies, as well as including the Hindustan Chamber of Commerce, the Tamil Chamber of Commerce, and the Madras Chamber of Commerce. ASSOCHAM has relatively little presence.

Both the CII and FICCI exercise some influence over government policy, as for example in the identification of the priority sectors that are listed in the Tamil Nadu Industrial Policy of 2014,[21] and in making the case for the development of industrial corridors (such as that between Madurai, Tirunelveli, and Thoothukudi, which is especially emphasized in the industrial policy statement). The industrial policy lays out an array of incentives for industry, including commitments over power and water supply, as well as a battery of fiscal incentives, including special packages that are intended to encourage investment in the southern districts of the state, and to diversify away from the current concentration of industrial activity in the vicinity of Chennai. Aerospace industry is listed among the priority sectors, and FICCI played some part in this, having submitted a "Proposal for Creation of an Aerospace Cluster in

Tamil Nadu" to the Department of Industries in 2012. It was active in making the case for the inclusion of pharmaceuticals as well. The Auto Components Manufacturers Association of India (ACMA) is another business association that has been somewhat successful in influencing policy, sometimes by using the strategy of playing off one state against another. The association has recently sought to persuade government in Tamil Nadu to define the auto components industry as a public utility, so making strikes illegal. Chandrababu Naidu in Andhra has now done this (very largely using words taken from an ACMA policy document), which is putting some pressure on the government of Tamil Nadu to follow suit.

The industrial policy framework in Tamil Nadu still leaves room for discretionary action by senior politicians, as is the case in Gujarat,[22] whereby a chief minister can intervene to speed up a project by, for example, making land available or providing additional incentives.[23] More broadly, there can be a lack of transparency or rigorous procedure in allocating contracts to supply services to the state. This is particularly true in the state-controlled market for alcohol (discussed below) but it also applies in other areas. In July 2015, a representative of the Adani Group, in the presence of the chief minister, signed an agreement to supply solar-generated electricity to the Tamil Nadu Generation and Distribution Corporation ("Adani Group" 2015). The agreement was reached though a preferential process. Opposition parties and critics objected to the price of Rs 7.01 per unit when it was revealed that in a nearly simultaneous auction in Madhya Pradesh the Adani Group offered to supply solar power at the lower price of Rs. 6.04 ("Tamil Nadu's Adani Deal" 2015).

There is abundant evidence, therefore, that even if governments led by the Dravidian parties in the 1970s and 1980s were not business friendly and failed to offer "systematic political or institutional support for industrial development" (Sinha 2005, 203), this has not been the case since the inception of India's economic reforms in 1991. Over the last twenty-five years successive state governments in Tamil Nadu have intervened very actively to encourage private capital investment and to support business. Still, an awkward relationship between business and the state is revealed in the political commitment to attracting investment and export promotion. A number of Indian chief ministers have taken a personal interest in "paradiplomacy" and traveled overseas with delegations of business leaders seeking investment, export opportunities, and external finance for infrastructure development. Both Narendra Modi and Chandrababu Naidu have used these overseas trips to support businesses based in their own states, and such activities are evidence of a convergence between regional political and business elites. The pursuit of investment has not been entirely neglected in Tamil Nadu, and we return to this theme in the next section, but the opportunities for paradiplomacy have not been exploited by the chief ministers of Tamil Nadu (Wyatt 2017). The relationship between capital based in Tamil Nadu and government remains an ambivalent one.

A Business-Friendly State?

Travelers passing through Terminal 5 at London's Heathrow airport in August 2015 were confronted by a whole flight of banners hanging from the ceiling, proclaiming the strengths of the south Indian state of Tamil Nadu and advertising a Global Investors' Meet (GIM) to be held in Chennai in September. The GIM took place in Chennai on September 9–10, 2015, amid much fanfare, and one big businessmen suggested that its importance was marked by the fact that the chief minister, J. Jayalalithaa, was in attendance on two occasions. That he thought this was remarkable is a reflection of the fact that in the perception of many businessmen the chief minister—at least in the period of the AIADMK government that assumed office in 2011—was "indifferent" to business interests (Kandavel 2015a). It is possible that, as one CEO suggested, Jayalalithaa had been stung into organizing the event because of the favorable publicity surrounding the meets organized by Narendra Modi while he was chief minister of Gujarat. Whether there is truth in this suggestion or not, there is no doubt of the importance of the Chennai event in the context of the competition for investment between Tamil Nadu and Gujarat, and other states such as Rajasthan (which held a similar meeting, the Rajasthan Partnership Summit, in November 2015) and West Bengal (which held a global summit in January 2016). It was said that it represented an important signal from Jayalalithaa to her bureaucrats.

Opinions inevitably varied between observers as to how successful the GIM was (Kandavel 2015b). Still, the view that the GIM was at least partly directed at countering negative perceptions of investment prospects in Tamil Nadu carries conviction. *The Hindu* reported that the state received only 3.5 percent of the total number of industrial investments coming into India between 2008 and 2012, and that "even Andhra Pradesh and Telengana have caught up . . . (and) . . . bagged investments that were initially supposed to come to the state," while firms such as Ford were said not to be keen on expansion in Tamil Nadu (Kandavel 2015a, 2015b). There were suggestions of an "investment flight" from the state,[24] with the recent history of power crisis held to be partly to blame for these trends. There was a suggestion too that problems relating to unrecognized unions were a factor. Even though the number of strikes in Tamil Nadu had dropped from 110 in 2003 to 28 in 2013, "the old scars still remain; even now firms globally look at TN as a state with labour unrest" (Kandavel 2015b). But probably of greater significance was the shutdown of the Nokia plant at Sriperumbudur in November 2014, which had been the Finnish company's largest factory. It was left out, however, from the deal concluded by Nokia for the purchase of its worldwide handset business by Microsoft, because of the tax issues faced by Nokia's Indian company. The European Union put the blame on "lack of support from the state." The EU ambassador was reported as saying, "I have not understood why there was no support from the state government [on the issue] which resulted in significant loss of employment" (*Times of India*, December 9, 2014). The charge was vigorously refuted by the state government, which argued that blame attached rather to the UPA government, because of its tax policies, but the ambassador's suggestion that the whole affair had cast a negative light on how European companies looked at Tamil Nadu as a destination for investment was probably justified.[25] The Nokia closure had knock-on effects, too, when the Taiwan-based company Foxconn also closed its facility in Sriperumbudur in February 2015, giving as the reason the loss of business following the shutdown of the Nokia plant—though a history of labor disputes in 2010 may have had a part in the decision. Salt was rubbed in the wound for Tamil Nadu when, in August 2015, Foxconn announced an investment in Maharashtra of $5 billion over five years.

The suggestion that Tamil Nadu is not very friendly to business was raised again not many days after the GIM when the results of an "Ease of Doing Business Survey," comparing Indian states, conducted by the World Bank with the government of India, were published. The *Economic Times* reported the findings that the easiest states in which to do business were Gujarat, closely followed by (residual) Andhra Pradesh. Tamil Nadu came in twelfth, behind such states as Jharkhand, Chhattisgarh, Madhya Pradesh, Rajasthan, and Uttar Pradesh.[26] The methodology of the survey may be criticized, but Tamil Nadu could clearly have done without such negative findings. Are they justified?

The Problem of Autocratic Leadership

The recent problems that big business in Tamil Nadu has experienced, and which may well have produced a negative image of the state, have to do with what we have described as the "double-edged" phenomenon of highly centralized political leadership. That so much depends on the "whims and dictates of the chief minister without much predictability," as Aseema Sinha (2005, 207) put it, is an indication of the limits of the structural power of the corporate sector. When chief ministers have put all their weight behind major business projects or social policies, they have often been highly successful (as was the case with the Ford plant, and as also happened with the state's well-known noon meals scheme, introduced and strongly supported by M. G. Ramachandran as Chief Minister). But if that support is withdrawn or is not available, as was the case in the period of the AIADMK government of 2011–16, at least until the setting up of the Global Investors' Meet—according to our informants, and confirmed in commentaries on Jayalalithaa's career, following her death in December 2016—then projects tend to founder (e.g., Muthukumar 2016).

Our informants, in late 2015, agreed that in the period of the 2011–16 government, Ms. Jayalalithaa was inaccessible even to the biggest and most influential business people—at least until the GIM. It was said by interviewees that "there have been no significant new investments in the state during the period of this government, and those that have come up were all negotiated during the period of the preceding DMK government—and even those have been obstructed." A notable case in point, commonly referred to, was that of the plant set up by the French tire company Michelin, negotiated by the DMK government in 2009, and intended to be the largest of the company's plants outside France, with ambitious objectives for exporting from India. It was supposed to have begun production in 2013, but the start was delayed by almost two years because of problems over clearances and access to power and to water. There were many stories about delays created by the chief minister, on one hand, and, on the other hand, about the successful resolution of problems through her intervention, once some means had been found of gaining direct access to her. A significant achievement between 2011–16 was to have addressed the long-running power problems of the state (Ramesh 2016).

Aseema Sinha's conclusion, that in Tamil Nadu, government and the fates of even big-business investments are subject to the whims of the chief minister, remains a fair assessment. Jayalalithaa behaved differently toward business in earlier periods in government, especially when her government concluded the important deals with Ford and Hyundai. The DMK also displays ambivalence toward big business, though it is said that DMK governments have allowed more interaction and opportunity for dialogue (in the words of one interviewee, "At least the DMK government gave access"). When the DMK is in office, one businessman said, "You can be sure how to fix your problem"—and this somewhat enigmatic statement seems to reflect the view that though the governments of the two Dravidian parties are equally corrupt, side-payments are more likely to be effective under the DMK.[27]

The DMK government that was in office in 2006–11, like that of 1996–2001, had the considerable advantage of being part of ruling coalitions at the center, and through the control of important ministries was able to bring significant investment to the state. We referred earlier to the role of Murasoli Maran, first in the United Front government and later in that of the NDA. Maran's son Dayanidhi and A. Raja followed suit as DMK ministers in the UPA government, until their fall from grace over corruption scandals, especially that over the allocation of the 2G spectrum (Thakurtha 2015). As DMK ministers in coalition governments at the center, the Marans' role in channeling industrial investments into Tamil Nadu provides an outstanding example of how regional parties have been able to leverage national industrial policy for their own states' benefit.

Still, "Tamil Nadu is in a terrible state," according to the CEO of the Indian subsidiary of an international company. The events of recent years such as the misadventures of the Michelin plant, problems encountered at the ITC Grand Chola Hotel, the closure of the Nokia plant, and the shutdown of the Foxconn facility, as well as problems of power supply (until the final years of Jayalalithaa's third government, 2011–16), the reputation of the Pollution Control Board for corruption, and the state's labor laws, have meant that less investment has come into the state than might have been the case. The general level of corruption was ramped up, it was widely claimed, under the AIADMK government of 2011–16. "Where lakhs were paid, now it is crores," one respondent said, though SMEs are those that are most adversely affected. One economic consultant wondered why businesses stick to Tamil Nadu and speculated that though there is inertia because of the inherited advantages of the state, a tipping point may not be far away. In some sectors, there is a tendency that could become more significant for companies to set up in Andhra, where the regulatory environment is more friendly, and whence it is possible still to take advantage of assets such as the availability of skills in Tamil Nadu.

Another factor that may influence decisions over establishing new plants in Tamil Nadu is that there is quite a history of popular protest against major investments. In western Tamil Nadu, protests over land acquisition for a gas pipeline that the Gas Authority of India sought to construct between Cochin and Bangalore and from which the state may well have benefited caused the project to be called off ("GAIL Calls Off Pipeline Work" 2014). Another case is that of opposition to the Sterlite copper smelter near Tuticorin. Protest orchestrated by political parties, over what turned out to be a false accusation that the company was responsible for dangerous gas leaks, caused the plant to be closed for several months ("Sterlite's Pollution Problem" 2013; "NGT Reverses Closure Order" 2013).

In sum, with the partial exception of the IT industry, there is little evidence that governments of Tamil Nadu, whichever of the two Dravidian parties has been in office, have pursued *consistent* industrial policies or have always been friendly to the corporate sector, or on the other hand that the corporate sector is able to "mold state behaviour." The structural power of big business is limited in the context of the particular politics of Tamil Nadu, and the personal power exercised by the leaders of the two Dravidian parties. It clearly makes sense, to most corporate leaders, not to get too close to the party in office, given that over the last twenty-five years (until 2016, when the AIADMK was returned to power), it has been likely that the same party will not be there after the next election.[28]

There is, therefore, usually an arm's-length relationship between the corporate sector and the state. But this is not the whole story of the relations of business and politics in Tamil Nadu. At another level business and politics are intrinsically intertwined.

Politicians and Business

In Tamil Nadu, as elsewhere in India, politics is sometimes seen as a kind of business in itself.[29] A great deal of investment is required to win office at different levels, and it is commonly considered that very many of those who enter politics do so in order to secure personal gain, by using their office to occupy gate-keeping roles and exploiting economically sensitive information. State regulation remains extensive, opening many possibilities "for entrepreneurial activity, expanding and limiting markets for different activities, creating or squeezing opportunities for profit." Office seeking is a costly affair : "One MP from Tamil Nadu in the 2009 Lok Sabha election spent several million rupees making payments of 200 rupees to voters, obliging him to sell properties and get into debt until he could begin to enjoy his returns from office." But it is not only offering rewards to electors that calls for financial resources. Money is needed, too, for legitimate campaign expenses, and—after electoral success—for financing constituency work, for maintaining a staff, for contributing to party funds, and, often, for financing bids for nomination. "At a minimum this [latter] might be a fee to purchase a nomination form or an application fee. The fees used by the DMK [1,000 rupees for the form and a deposit of 25,000 rupees to accompany a completed form in the 2016 state assembly elections] deters some frivolous candidates and boosts party funds." The fee charged by the DMK appears modest indeed by comparison with what is reported of other parties, when payments may have to be made several times over. "One AIADMK aspirant reported that he had paid five million rupees in the hope that he would be given the party nomination for a mayoral election" (Wyatt 2015a). Participation in politics is seen, therefore, as a form of entrepreneurship: it calls for investment in the expectation of turning a profit—though it should not be assumed that this accounts for the motivation of all politicians. There are local politicians whose political careers have been costly, and not always profitable, and in several cases their sacrifices seem to have been driven by motives other than financial gain (Wyatt 2015b). But there is no doubt about the financial demands that seeking political office involves.

It is evident that a lot of money is required to enter politics. Some candidates are recruited from among those who have already built up a business, but it is much more common for ambitious politicians in Tamil Nadu to combine a career in politics and business, accumulating and spending resources as they rise through the local ranks of their party. Several DMK district secretaries have done this, and an analysis of affidavits completed by candidates in 2011, and of other evidence, shows that about half of the DMK elite has business interests.[30] These are spread across different sectors, including transport, small-scale manufacturing, rice mills, retail, and real estate. And whereas people from modest backgrounds were once, in the earlier years of the Dravidian parties, able to gain economic and social status through their political careers, it is now doubtful whether the DMK still offers many opportunities for such accelerated social mobility. In the 2011 state assembly elections, only four of the DMK candidates declared assets of less than a million rupees (about $15,000). There is, on the other hand, a small group within the DMK elite, who are members of the regional capitalist class, often with interests in private education, and there are a few such, notably, as the Marans, whom we referred to earlier, and who have very successfully used the platform provided by a successful political career to join the national bourgeoisie. Both of the sons of Murasoli Maran, and grand-nephews of Karunanidhi, have prospered in the media sector. Dayanidhi Maran is active within the DMK, whereas Kalanidhi Maran, who is a dollar billionaire and one of the wealthiest men in India, keeps a certain distance from party activities (Wyatt 2015c).

Politicians have particular advantages in business activity where illegal practices are common. These include mineral extraction, real estate, and the liquor business, areas that are highly regulated and where the state has a particular interest in regulation owing to concerns for public safety or, ostensibly at least, the protection of the environment, and the taxation or revenue that flows from them. The enforcement of rules creates opportunities for profit and rent-seeking. Sales of alcohol, quarrying of granite, sand mining (both from riverbeds and from beaches where monazite can be obtained), and scams over the acquisition of land all contribute very substantial sums to ruling parties, and to the private fortunes of politicians. Tamil politicians are not at all dependent upon resources controlled by the wealthy.[31] They have their own sources of wealth. It may be, too, that rent extraction does not have to derive from the delivery of public goods to the extent that occurs in other states. Unlike the national parties the Dravidian parties do not centralize party funding; rather they encourage ambitious cadres to raise funds and pass them up the party hierarchy. The party leaders also have their own assets and enterprises that generate funds. Candidates are expected to fund their own election campaigns. These arrangements encourage lower-level leaders to go into business and give aspirants with business backgrounds an advantage. Owners of smaller enterprises in the mofussil have an advantage over business leaders in Chennai, as both parties strongly prefer candidates to fight elections from their home district (Manikandan 2016, 165–66).

The corporate sector may, generally, hold politicians at arm's length, as business leaders claim, and, in many ways, this is reciprocated by party leaders keen to maintain control of their own organizations. Activists are hostile to industrialists attempting to buy their way into party activities. Accordingly, in the DMK it is considered acceptable to combine a political and business career, as many DMK district secretaries do, but cadres bristled in 2014 when a few nominations for Lok Sabha seats were given to wealthy associates of M. K. Stalin with no track record of party work.

Below the corporate level, business and politics are quite fundamentally intertwined. Politicians run many SMEs. There is a wide range of ways, some entirely legal, and others not, in which politicians, at different levels, are involved in business activities, sometimes directly, and sometimes as rent-seeking agents. Politics *is* business in Tamil Nadu, but this does not mean that the power and influence of business groups is such as to enable them to mold state behavior in the way that Kohli has suggested. Politicians also need to manage the electorate and have to be ready in some circumstances to sacrifice business interests.

Conclusions: How Tamil Nadu Works

The two most reflective of the businessmen interviewed for this chapter both offered the same analysis of the state in Tamil Nadu—that which is expressed in the second of the three epigraphs with which this chapter begins : "In Tamil Nadu, there is a division of roles between politicians and business. Politicians concentrate on the social sectors, leaving entrepreneurs pretty much to themselves." The evidence presented in this chapter provides support for this idea, so far as the corporate sector is concerned. While politicians may leave entrepreneurs "pretty much to themselves," the problem of corruption is not absent. But corruption affects companies very differently. Larger businesses can avoid making side-payments by waiting out delays in providing infrastructure or regulatory decisions. We have come across no evidence that suggests that large businesses, outside of the liquor sector, are required to make regular payments to politicians or seek the protection of patrons. Corruption does cause some difficulty in Tamil Nadu, but business does not face a predatory state.

"Entrepreneurs" in SMEs, on the other hand, are likely to depend much more on the intermediation of politicians, in negotiating the still extensive state regulation of economic activity, and to be more actively involved in politics. Some, as we have seen, start out primarily as politicians. At their level, business and politics are intertwined, and business interests may influence government policy. Certainly, the liquor policy of the government of Tamil Nadu appears to have been written to accommodate those around successive chief ministers

(Srinivasan 2015). In addition, both education and land policy might also be biased to suit politicians with business interests.

The idea of the division of roles between politicians and the corporate sector, however, recalls David Washbrook's conclusions from his analysis of the Tamil state:

> Classically,[32] the bourgeoisie, or the elite of wealth, withdrew from a formal position of control over the state apparatus and the constitutional political process. Not only was their direct control no longer necessary for the purposes of capital accumulation but their attempt to exercise it, or rather the sight of their attempting to exercise it, provoked resistance and instability. Formal control was passed to a cadre of political managers who on the basis of a populist ideology, mollified resistance by turning what was left of the state into a welfare agency and by stirring up feelings of patriotism and atavism.[33] By these means the elites [the forward castes—Brahmans, Chettiars, Reddiars, Rajus, Kamma Naidus, and others] "disappeared" so that they could preserve their privileges and abilities to accumulate (in black money) at very little cost, while the illusion of democracy permitted the people to imagine that they ruled. (Washbrook 1989, 258)

This is a harsh judgement, perhaps, but it reflects pretty well what happened when the DMK took power in Tamil Nadu in 1967, causing what our elite Brahman businessman informant described as a "cultural problem." Those from his cultural background and social class have not occupied "formal positions of control over the state apparatus and the constitutional political process" since 1967. Yet they have continued to occupy the heights of the business world of the state.[34] The only business communities in the state that have been very directly involved in politics since 1967 are those of the Nadars and the Gounders.[35] Damodaran (2008) lists several Nadar businessmen who have gone into politics, but he makes no reference to leading businessmen from Brahman, Chettiar, or Naidu backgrounds having had such engagements. And no doubt, in the light of the success of the mobilizations of lower castes (though not the Dalits) by the DMK, the "sight of the Forward Castes attempting to exercise control" would have "provoked resistance and caused instability" by the later 1960s (Washbrook 1989, 258). Yet, as Washbrook suggests, "the final and most amazing of all the transformations the Dravidian ideology was to undergo was that which turned it from a vehicle of anti-elite protest into one which accommodated privilege in Tamil society" (Washbrook 1989, 254).[36]

This describes very well what happened after 1967. The elites from among the historically forward castes lost political prominence but were able to carry on building their businesses (including, over the last quarter-century, highly successful IT companies), while the Dravidian politicians managed the state (Fuller and Narasimhan 2013, chapter 3). As argued above, given the findings of earlier studies by Padmini Swaminathan and Aseema Sinha, and the observations of those interviewed for this chapter, neither the DMK nor the AIADMK has operated in government in such a way as unambiguously to favor big-business interests. Indeed, in the 1970s and 1980s, and even to an extent in the first years of the present century, and since 2011 under the AIADMK, the ways in which the parties have behaved in government have sometimes not been at all favorable to corporate interests. There are ways in which Tamil Nadu is not particularly "business friendly," and the claim that business in the state has succeeded in spite of, rather than because of, government carries some conviction. Yet the politicians have not invariably been obstructive or predatory; and senior bureaucrats have quite often been positively helpful. The problem has been, as we have argued, that so much depends upon the "whims and dictates of the chief ministers"—which is double-edged in its implications. It can make for speedy and effective decision-making, or it can represent a serious obstacle to investment. And there is also another level of business that is thoroughly intertwined with politics (and which is where—somewhat contra Washbrook—much of the "black money" probably lies). Politics is funded through the business that is carried on directly and indirectly, legally and illegally, by politicians, rather than by depending on resources controlled by the wealthy.

But then, how has Tamil Nadu succeeded in delivering so effectively, by comparison with most other states on most significant measures, social and human development? Competitive populism in Tamil Nadu has delivered for the mass of the Tamil people (Harriss 2003a), partly, at least, because public administration probably works better than in most of the country (Vivek 2014) and because—for all that the radicalism of the Dravidian movement was always shallow[37]—the Dravidian parties, in very successfully building a broad base of support, have espoused an ideology of "inclusion."[38] Former senior civil servants who worked closely with MGR attest very strongly to his commitment, in particular among the senior politicians whom they have served, to the poorer people of the state. The distribution of largesse to the people—not only the "freebies" scorned by the elite,[39] but also and much more importantly the noon meal at school, and cheap (now free) rice made available through the Public Distribution System—has, of course, been paid for, in part, by taxes paid especially by poorer people (through tax on the sales of liquor) (Guhan 1988; Lakshman 2011), but there is no doubt that the policies pursued by the two parties have become increasingly programmatic rather than clientelistic (Wyatt 2013).

In his study *The State and Poverty in India*, Atul Kohli argued that propoor redistribution is most likely to be achieved where there is "a tightly organized ideological party (that) can penetrate the rural society without being co-opted by the propertied groups," with coherent leadership, ideological or organizational commitment to exclude propertied interests from direct participation in the process of governance, and a pragmatic attitude toward facilitating a nonthreatening as well as a predictable political atmosphere for the propertied entrepreneurial classes (Kohli 1987, 8). This comes close to describing a social democratic regime, and in later work Kohli talks of the possibility of a "democratic developmental state," taking as an example the case of West Bengal (Kohli 2012). Can Tamil Nadu be described in these terms?

The democratic culture of the state is ambiguous even though electoral participation in Tamil Nadu is relatively high, the Tamil press is flourishing, and civil society is active. This is because so much depends on the devotion that is inspired by the great leaders, first Annadurai, then (and especially) MGR, and later Jayalalithaa—Karunanidhi, too, though he has never quite exercised the charisma of the other three. The other face of devotion is that "the leader" is able to behave in an autocratic manner, with the consequences that we have emphasized in this chapter.

The ideas of devotion to the Tamil language and to the Tamil nation, fostered by the genius of Annadurai, Karunanidhi, and others in producing and projecting a mytho-history of Tamilian greatness, have been extended, Ingrid Widlund argues, "to leaders who were projected, or perceived, as embodiments or at least protectors of the nation and its associated values," and legitimize "a conception of political relations as inherently unequal" (Widlund 2000, 377, 378). She suggests that "the DMK's version of Tamil identity and pride, despite the party's rhetorical emphasis on equality, served as an ideological device for legitimizing the relations of subservience between . . . the leaders and their followers," and that this feature was accentuated even further in the AIADMK (Widlund 2000, 380). Such ideas and relations stand, Widlund argues, "in contradiction to basic democratic values" (2000, 380).

These aspects of the Dravidian parties are reflected in the fact that Tamil politicians, whether from the AIADMK or from the DMK, have generally been resistant to decentralization. The state has been notably tardy in devolving responsibilities to local government. One of the parties, the DMK, certainly once had significant local organization, while the AIADMK has always been much more of a following of charismatic leaders. Internal party democracy in the DMK has been threatened by the dominance of the Karunanidhi family, and though the party ran organisational elections in 2015, there was little doubt that the patriarch would be succeeded as leader of the party by his son Stalin. Various governments of Tamil Nadu have behaved in a repressive manner, certainly as regards labor, as Narendra Subramanian (1999) records. He also concluded that "although the inclinations of paternalist populism toward social control were tempered by the prior strength of social pluralism, civil rights were abridged when MGR's government faced radical challenges and when Jayalalithaa's felt beleaguered" (1999, 299).

Tamil Nadu represents a very distinctive case indeed. It has some of the attributes of a developmental state, but the partnership between the political and business elites is marked by tensions and constrained by mistrust. It has some of the features, too, of what Kohli describes as a "democratic developmental state," and it has seen the realization of at least some of the outcomes that are expected of such a regime, yet without having either a politics or a culture of social democracy. Tamil Nadu has certainly seen the mobilization of a coherent political collectivity, but around identity, and depending upon populist appeals. The politics of the state, remarkably perhaps, have remained fundamentally centered on caste (Gorringe 2012). It has lacked class politics and even has a political culture that is in tension with basic democratic values. Group rights have been pursued with particular vigor, but the state has sometimes been repressive, certainly of workplace rights—even though competition between the two Dravidian parties has, led to the delivery of welfare benefits to unorganized workers, and to recognition of their status as "workers," to a much greater extent than has been the case elsewhere (with the possible exception of Kerala) (Agarwala 2013). The Dravidian parties are no longer embedded in a broad social movement, but the voice of civil society has ensured that the competition between the two Dravidian parties channeled into responsiveness to popular concerns. There has been a kind of a tacit, Bonapartist agreement between political leaders and the corporate sector that has ensured capitalist development, but nothing resembling a social democratic pact between capital, labor, and the state.

Acknowledgments

We are grateful to friends with *The Hindu* group of newspapers who made the interviews with businessmen referred to in this chapter possible: N. Ram, N. Ravi, Mukund Padmanabhan, and especially N. Murali. We are grateful, as well, for their advice and help over many years, to Professor M. Vijayabaskar at the Madras Institute of Development Studies and Dr. J. Jeyaranjan. We also thank the editors, Professor Kunal Sen of the University of Manchester, and Dr. Nate Roberts of the University of Göttingen for their comments on earlier drafts.

References

"Adani Group to Set Up Rs 4,536 Crore Solar Power Park in TN." 2015. *Hindustan Times,* July 5.

Agarwala, Rina. 2013. *Informal Labor, Formal Politics, and Dignified Discontent in India.* Cambridge: Cambridge University Press.

"Ashwin Muthiah Pulls Spic Back from the Brink." 2015. *Business Standard*, November 9.

Bharadwaj, Krishna. 1982. "Regional Differentiation in India: A Note." *Economic and Political Weekly* 17 (14–16): 605–14.

Damodaran, Harish. 2008. *India's New Capitalists: Caste, Business and Industry in a Modern Nation*. Basingstoke: Palgrave Macmillan.

"Death of a Dream." 2014. *Business Today*, August 17.

Dreze, Jean, and Reetika Khera. 2015. "Child Development: How are Indian States Faring?" Ideas for India, December 18. www.ideasforindia.in.

Dutta, Madhumita. 2009. "Nokia SEZ: Public Price of Success." *Economic and Political Weekly* 44 (40): 23–25.

———. 2016. "The Nokia SEZ Story." *Economic and Political Weekly* 51 (51): 43–51.

Evans, Peter. 1995. *Embedded Autonomy: States and Industrial Transformation*. Princeton, NJ: Princeton University Press.

Fuller, C. J., and Haripriya Narasimhan. 2013. *Tamil Brahmans: The Making of a Middle-Class Caste*. Chicago: University of Chicago Press.

"GAIL Calls Off Pipeline Work in Tamil Nadu." 2014. *The Hindu*, April 21.

Gorringe, Hugo. 2012. "Caste and Politics in Tamil Nadu." *Seminar* 633, May 2012. Accessed at www.india-seminar.com.

Guhan, S. 1988. "State Finances: Trends and Policy." In *Tamil Nadu Economy: Performance and Issues*. Chennai: Madras Institute of Development Studies.

Harriss, John. 2003a. "Do Political Regimes Matter? Poverty Reduction and Regime Differences across India." In *Changing Paths: International Development and the New Politics of Inclusion*, ed. P. Houtzager and M. Moore, 204–32. Ann Arbor: University of Michigan Press.

———. 2003b. "The Great Tradition Globalizes: Reflections on Two Studies of 'The Industrial Leaders' of Madras." *Modern Asian Studies* 37 (2): 327–62.

"Industrialist AC Muthiah Relieved after the Ouster of M Karunanidhi." 1991. *India Today*, March 31.

Iyer, Lakshmi, and Anandi Mani. 2012. "Traveling Agents: Political Change and Bureaucratic Turnover in India." *Review of Economics and Statistics* 94 (3): 723–39.

Jeyaranjan, J. 2011. "Women and Pro-poor Policies in Rural Tamil Nadu: An Examination of Practices and Responses." *Economic and Political Weekly* 46 (43): 73.

Joshi, D. K., and K. McGrath. 2015. "Political Ideology, Public Policy and Human Development in India: Exploring the Gap between Gujarat and Tamil Nadu." *Journal of Contemporary Asia* 45 (3): 465–89.

Kalaiyarasan, A. 2014. "A Comparison of Developmental Outcomes in Gujarat and Tamil Nadu." *Economic and Political Weekly* 49 (15): 55–63.

Kandavel, Sangeetha. 2015a. "Top Corporate Leaders to Attend Investors' Meet." *The Hindu*, September 3.

———. 2015b. "Will Pegasus Help TN Reach for the Skies?" *The Hindu*, September 6.

Kennedy, Loraine. 2004. "The Political Determinants of Reform Packaging: Contrasting Responses to Economic Liberalization in Andhra Pradesh and Tamil Nadu." In *Regional Reflections: Comparing Politics across India's States*, ed. R. Jenkins, 29–65. New Delhi: Oxford University Press.

———. 2014. *The Politics of Economic Restructuring in India: Economic Governance and State Spatial Rescaling*. Abingdon: Routledge.

Kohli, Atul. 1987. *The State and Poverty in India: The Politics of Reform*. Cambridge: Cambridge University Press.

———. 2012. *Poverty amid Plenty in the New India*. Cambridge: Cambridge University Press.

Kohli, Atul, Christophe Jaffrelot, and Kanta Murali. 2016. Background paper for the workshop "Business and Politics in India," Princeton University, May.

Kumar, U., and A. Subramanian. 2012. "Growth in India's States in the First Decade of the 21st Century." *Economic and Political Weekly* 47 (3): 48–57.

Lakshman, Narayan. 2011. *Patrons of the Poor: Caste Politics and Policymaking in India*. Delhi: Oxford University Press.

"Maharashtra is Biggest State Economy, Says Report." 2015. *The Hindu*, December 2.

Manikandan, C. 2016. "Caste in Political Recruitment: The Study of Two Major Dravidian Parties in Tamil Nadu." Pondicherry University, Pondicherry.

Manikandan, C., and Andrew Wyatt. 2014. "Elite Formation within a Political Party: The Case of the Dravida Munnetra Kazhagam." *Commonwealth & Comparative Politics* 52 (1): 34.

Mundle, Sudipto, Samik Chowdhury, and Satadru Sikdar. 2016. "Governance Performance of Indian States." *Economic and Political Weekly* 51 (36): 55–64.

Muthukumar, K. 2016. "More Development Bang for the Buck." *Business Line*, December 6.

"NGT Reverses Closure Order for Sterlite's Tuticorin Plant." 2013. *Down to Earth*. http://www.downtoearth.org.in/news/ngt-reverses-closure-order-for-sterlites-tuticorin-plant-41275.

Radhakrishnan, R. 2016. "Jayalalithaa and Governance." Chennai: Hindu Centre.

Rajasekharan, Ilangovan. 2015. "The Mother of All Loot." *Frontline*, 32 (14) July 24 http://www.frontline.in/cover-story/the-mother-of-all-loot/article7391496.ece)

Ramesh, M. 2016. "Where She Served, Where She Didn't." *Business Line*, December 6.

RBI (Reserve Bank of India). 2016. *Handbook of Statistics on Indian States*. Mumbai: RBI.

"Sand Mining System Entails Annual Loss of at Least Rs 3000 Crore." 2013. *The Hindu*, December 3.

Saxena, N. C. 2016. "Governance Reforms in India." In *Reinventing Social Democratic Development*, ed. O. Tornquist and J. Harriss, 131–67. Copenhagen: Nordic Institute of Asian Studies.

Sen, Ronojoy. 2015. "House Matters: The BJP, Modi and Parliament." *South Asia* 38 (4): 776–90.

Singh, Prerna. 2015. *How Solidarity Works for Welfare: Subnationalism and Social Development in India*. New York: Cambridge University Press.

Sinha, Aseema. 2005. *The Regional Roots of Developmental Politics in India: A Divided Leviathan*. Bloomington: Indiana University Press.

Srinivasan, R. 2015. "Of Revenues, Bribes and Regulation." *Frontline* 32 (8) May 1. https://www.frontline.in/cover-story/of-revenues-bribes-and-regulation/article7098243.ece

"Sterlite's Pollution Problem." 2013. *Business Standard*, April 14. http://www.business-standard.com/article/companies/sterlite-s-pollution-problem-113041801267_1.html.

Subramanian, Narendra 1999. *Ethnicity and Populist Mobilization: Political Parties, Citizens and Democracy in South India*. Delhi: Oxford University Press.

Swaminathan, Padmini. 1994. "Where Are the Entrepreneurs? What the Data Reveal for Tamil Nadu." *Economic and Political Weekly (Review of Management)* 29 (22): M64–M74.

"Tamil Nadu's 'Corrupt' Cash Cow TASMAC: How Politics and Liquor Came to Form a Potent Mix in the State." 2015. *Economic Times*, January 11. http://articles.economictimes.indiatimes.com/2015-01-11/news/57940995_1_tasmac-illicit-liquor-quality-liquor/2.

"Tamil Nadu's Adani Deal under Scanner." 2015. *Times of India*, July 18.

Thakurta, Paranjoy Guha. 2015. "The Business of Politics: Sun TV and the Maran Brothers." *Economic and Political Weekly* 50 (35): 30–35.

"Tutorial from Tamil Nadu for States to Get Around Land Acquisition." 2015. *Firstpost*, September 3. http://www.firstpost.com/business/tutorial-from-tamil-nadu-for-states-to-get-around-land-acquisition-2419440.html.

Vijayabaskar, M. 2010. "Saving Agricultural Labour from Agriculture: SEZs and Politics of Silence in Tamil Nadu." *Economic and Political Weekly* 45 (6): 36–43.

Vijayabaskar, M., and Andrew Wyatt. 2013. "Economic Change, Politics and Caste: The Case of the Kongu Nadu Munnetra Kazhagam." *Economic and Political Weekly* 48 (48): 105–6.

Vivek, S. 2014. *Delivering Public Services Effectively: Tamil Nadu and Beyond*. Delhi: Oxford University Press.

Washbrook, David. 1989. "Caste, Class and Dominance in Modern Tamil Nadu: Non-Brahminism, Dravidianism and Tamil Nationalism." In *Dominance and State Power in Modern India*, ed. F. Frankel and M. S. A. Rao, 204–64. Delhi: Oxford University Press.

Weiner, Myron. 1967. *Party Building in a New Nation: The Indian National Congress*. Chicago: University of Chicago Press.

"Why Tamil Nadu's Freebie Culture Works." 2016. *LiveMint*, May 12. http://www.livemint.com/.

Widlund, Ingrid. 2000. "Paths to Power and Patterns of Influence: The Dravidian Parties in South Indian Politics." Uppsala University, Uppsala.

Wyatt, Andrew. 2013. "Combining Clientelist and Programmatic Politics in Tamil Nadu, South India." *Commonwealth and Comparative Politics* 51 (1): 27–55.

———. 2015a. "The Comparative Advantages Enjoyed by Entrepreneurial Politicians."

———. 2015b. "Political Service and the Use of Money in a South Indian Town."

———. 2015c. "Politicians as Entrepreneurs: The Business Careers of DMK Politicians in Tamil Nadu."

———. 2017. "Paradiplomacy of India's Chief Ministers." *India Review* 16 (1): 106–24.

10

Business and State in Odisha's Extractive Economy

SUNILA S. KALE

Introduction

Among India's states, Odisha stands as a paradox. Unlike other states with episodes of marked hostility to business, Odisha has had an almost unbroken succession of probusiness governments from independence onward. A rich subsoil resource base—roughly three-fourths of India's bauxite, a third of iron ore reserves, almost all of the chromite, and a quarter of the country's coal—has long held out the promise of resource-intensive extractive industrialization for the state's political class. However, unlike developmental probusiness states that nurtured industry to produce jobs and higher rates of economic growth, economic policies in Odisha have failed to produce either sustained economic growth or a substantial economic transformation. Business-state relations in Odisha instead display "neo-patrimonial tendencies" (Kohli 2012, 15): the government extends support to entrepreneurs with no attendant discipline, and in order to succeed, economic actors must access personal connections rather than proceed via institutionalized channels. As in other neopatrimonial states like Uttar Pradesh and Bihar, governance in Odisha has tended to be "underinstitutionalized" and has served to advance narrow interests rather than a broader public welfare.

Despite attempts from the 1950s onward to catalyze industrialization, the state has remained a primarily rural and agrarian one, where more than 60 percent of the population continues to rely on agriculture as a base of livelihood.[1] For most of this period until the recent decade and a half or so, Odisha has experienced lower than average economic growth rates (table 10.1), and Odisha's population of 41.9 million (roughly 3.5 percent of India's total) continues to experience poorer conditions on almost all measures of socioeconomic well-being.

Table 10.1 **Annual Average Growth in GSDP in Various Sates and All India, 2013–14**

Odisha	6.7%
Tamil Nadu	9.0%
Gujarat	9.3%
All-India	7.6%

Source: IndiaStat. Data for 2014–15 not available; average for is for 2013–14

The state's poverty figures remain higher than in the faster-growing economies discussed in other chapters of this volume, Gujarat and Tamil Nadu (table 10.2). Moreover, the rate of poverty has declined at a slower pace in Odisha than in either of those states.

In this chapter I develop one part of an explanation to Odisha's puzzle, focused on the nature of state-capital relations. I do so by drawing from and responding to literature on developmental states, which is focused on explaining why some states have been able to facilitate industrialization. State-capital relations in Odisha have stood in contradistinction to the successful models of developmental states found both within India's subnational units (Sinha 2005 and Jaffrelot, this volume) and outside of India. The developmental state literature suggests that states embedded in, and yet sufficiently autonomous from, dominant social forces are able to catalyze industrial transformation that can lead to high overall economic growth (Evans 1995). A successful developmental state needs both to support capital—through credit, market linkages, coordination across sectors—and to discipline capital. The latter is essential to advance

Table 10.2 **Population below Poverty Line in the Various States and All-India (%)**

	2004–5			2011–12		
	Rural	*Urban*	*Combined*	*Rural*	*Urban*	*Combined[a]*
Odisha	60.80	37.60	57.20	35.69	17.29	32.59 (–43.0)
Tamil Nadu	37.50	19.70	28.90	15.83	6.54	11.28 (–60.9)
Gujarat	39.10	20.10	31.80	21.54	10.14	16.63 (–47.7)
All India	41.80	25.70	37.20	25.70	13.70	21.92 (–41.0)

[a] Figures in parentheses indicate percent change from 2004–05 to 2011–12, calculated by author.

Source: IndiaStat; poverty figures based on the Tendulkar methodology.

an economic agenda that benefits society as a whole, as opposed to one that rewards only individual firms or capital exclusively. Extending this argument, another set of scholars has argued that the state's autonomy from dominant capitalist actors can only be guaranteed through selective alliance with other social groups. Chibber (2003) ascribes India's failed developmentalism to the state's inability to collaborate with labor, the one social actor whose strength in numbers could have enabled the state to discipline capital. Davis (2004), who makes a related argument using contrasting empirical cases from East Asia and Latin America, suggests that the rural middle classes can also serve as a bulwark to give a developmental state the latitude to restrain and direct capital.

With respect to the first condition for developmentalism, Odisha's postindependence history provides ample evidence of state support to capital, in the form of enabling policies and preferential access to vital inputs like electricity, mineral resources, land, and credit. It is in the second condition—for discipline—that the state has fallen short. Moreover, as successive governments supported capital, the state forged durable alliances with neither labor nor its vast agrarian sector. Odisha has less of the kind of labor activism and mobilization associated with the politics of other states in India, like West Bengal (Alivelu, Samal, and Sen n.d.); neither does Odisha have a politicized rural middle class or middle peasantry of the type that allied with the Park regime in Davis's account of South Korea, or in Indian versions of developmental states like Maharashtra and Tamil Nadu. Compared to other states in India, the state's underinvestment in agriculture—seen in poor provision of irrigation, extension services, assistance with mechanization, inputs, credit, and market linkages—is long-standing and has only deepened in the last twenty-five years (Mallik and Padhi 1995; Sarap and Sahu 2016).

To understand why Odisha fails to exhibit the qualities of a developmental state requires examining the nature of the state itself, its relationship to the society it governs, and the individuals who compose it. The state elite in Odisha over seventy years has been drawn from a narrow band of upper-caste elites who straddle political, social, and economic milieu. Anthropologist F. G. Bailey (1963) describes these characteristics of Odisha as a facet of the state's sociopolitical structure, in which a small group of elites is bound together by "multiplex" ties that cross spheres of social, political, and economic life. In contrast to societies where relationships are more specialized, in Odisha "the same set of people interact with one another in politics, in ritual, in making a living" (220). As part of a comparative study of caste dominance in India's states, Mohanty (1989) characterizes Odisha as a case of upper-caste hegemony, where two jatis—Brahmans and Karans—have commanded much of public life since independence. So little changed in the subsequent twenty-five years that Mohanty echoed this characterization with little modification in a more recent analysis of

Odisha's politics (2014). This sense that the state elite is composed of a narrow band of individuals, networked through relations of caste and class, was reinforced by my own interviews in Odisha in 2016.[2]

In other parts of India over the last century, the social and political dominance of forward or upper castes has been challenged by movements from below. By contrast, Odisha, which has one of the highest proportions of Adivasi and Dalit populations outside of the northeast (22.8 and 17.1 percent of the total state population, respectively), has not witnessed the sustained caste-based or Adivasi mobilization that has disrupted electoral politics elsewhere, from the Dalit revolution of Uttar Pradesh and the rise of Other Backward Classes in Bihar to Adivasi claims to power in Jharkhand. Rather than forming independent parties, the politicians who contest elections in scheduled caste- and scheduled tribe-reserved constituencies are well enmeshed in mainstream national and regional parties (Baral 1987, 557).[3] Odisha has a vibrant sphere of social movements and peoples' movements that oppose the prevailing model of mineral-led development, but political parties have failed to make these issues essential to their electoral strategies, as happened around land acquisition in West Bengal at Nandigram and Singur. Over the last twenty years vocal movements in the state to oppose Utkal's aluminum refinery at Kashipur, Vedanta's bauxite mining in the Niyamgiri hills, Tata Steel's plant at Kalinganagar, and the Korean steel firm POSCO, among others, have received national and international attention, particularly around dramatic events like a police firing at Kalinganagar in 2006. In another part of India, any of these individually might have been used to bring down or at least weaken an incumbent government. But in Odisha, the Naveen Patnaik–led Biju Janata Dal has only strengthened its electoral position and now rules for a fourth consecutive term, the last two without coalition partners, a rare show of incumbency strength in India. These sociopolitical aspects of Odisha's political field—upper-caste dominance and the lack of independent political mobilization among subaltern groups—have remained more or less constant throughout the postindependence period.

Corresponding to the relative stability of the sociopolitical field, economic policy in the state has likewise remained more or less consistent from independence forward. In the 1950s and 1960s landed interests, former princes, and zamindars, alongside others from the state's western districts, organized themselves politically in the local Ganatantra Party, which later merged with the national Swatantra Party and seemed to entertain a different approach to economic development (Bailey 1959).[4] For the last thirty-five years however, the probusiness stance of economic policy has become more defined, despite alternations in power between the regional BJD (1991–95, 1999–present) and the Congress Party (1980–89, 1995–99). To succeed in Odisha, successful business actors operate through networks that link them with bureaucratic and political offices. Instead of producing virtuous cycles of industrial growth, business-state relations in Odisha instead display "neo-patrimonial tendencies" (Kohli 2012, 15): the government extends support to entrepreneurs with no attendant discipline, and in order to succeed, businesses must access personal connections rather than proceed via institutionalized channels. As in other neopatrimonial states like Uttar Pradesh and Bihar, governance in Odisha has tended to be "underinstitutionalized" and has served to advance narrow interests rather than a broader public welfare.

The chapter is organized as an account of state-business relations delineated in three phases from independence to the present. I rely on a variety of data and sources, media reports, government documents, and secondary literatures. For the middle and latter periods, I also use insights from a range of interviews with bureaucrats and officers in the state-owned lending agencies, entrepreneurs, politicians, journalists, and heads of regional business lobbies. In some cases, particularly when something controversial but still on the record was stated in the course of an interview, I note the institutional location of an interviewee but refrain from giving the name.

To briefly preview the chapter, in the first chronological phase, from the 1950s through the 1970s, the state used a variety of means to support large-scale extractive industries, including by allocating scarce resources and through efforts to encourage and benefit a nascent regional capitalist class. This connection between politicians and business groups generated tremendous political opposition, ultimately resulting in several judicial enquiries over allegations of corruption. And yet the patterns established in this period—of mutually beneficial, personalistic relations between political and economic elites that failed to spur the kind of widespread economic growth that emerged in other parts of the country—were repeated in modified forms in subsequent decades.

Beginning in the late 1970s and continuing through the 1980s, regional politicians shifted their focus to a dual track. On the one hand, state leaders renewed lobbying, with moderate success, for large-scale central public investments in mining and mineral-processing, essential since much of this sector continued to exclude private investment. The second focus of the governments in power during the 1980s was a renewed attempt to support small- and medium-scale entrepreneurs, but the state's generous incentives in the form of credit and land came without the kind of discipline that was the hallmark of successful developmental states. Instead, state support to entrepreneurs seems to have been part of an electoral agenda rather than a programmatic developmental effort. The result was a transfer of public wealth to private hands, as the main beneficiaries were a coterie of young, first-time entrepreneurs, a vast majority of whose ventures failed.

From the 1990s onward, by when many mining and metallurgy sectors had been deregulated, state-capital relations in Odisha entered a third phase: the engine of investment shifted to the private sector, though the state's focus remained on large-scale mining and metallurgical projects, a resource-based economic sector that now produces far fewer jobs than in the past. By contrast, Odisha's small- and medium-scale sector—the one with the most promise for generating employment—has remained small compared to other states in India. The current government's industrial policy (Government of Odisha 2015) includes a focus on downstream manufacturing, but so far this has had limited success. Among the successful firms set up by homegrown entrepreneurs, most have required access to networks that connect political and business worlds. Although on paper and in policy statements, Odisha has the requisite features of a probusiness environment, in practice the state falls short in implementation. Particularly so in the case of regional businesses and in the micro, small, and medium enterprise (MSME) sector, successful economic actors remain closely tied to the political and bureaucratic machinery; either they emerge from within that interlinked network, or to succeed, they must embed themselves in that milieu by building and cultivating relationships within the network.

The 1950s to the 1970s: State Capital and a Nascent Neopatrimonial Bourgeoisie

The most prominent state leaders from the 1950s through the early 1960s spoke of the goal of industrial transformation based on the state's mineral wealth. In presenting budgets to the legislative assembly in 1946 and 1947, the state's first chief minister, Mahatab (1946–50), emphasized the need for industrial development and for policies that would privilege the interests of local entrepreneurs in particular (Das 2007, 111–16). The reality is that much of the industrial development during this period was concentrated in large-scale plants, decisions over which the state elite had little effective control. Prior to independence there was some large-scale private investment in Odisha, notably the aluminum industry initially set up by Indal, the Indian subsidiary of the multinational aluminum company Alcan, which later became part of the Birla group's Hindalco (Padel and Das 2010, 79, 115). Odisha's first major public sector investment after independence was also India's first integrated steel plant, set up in Rourkela by the government of India in northern Odisha, just south of what is now the border of Jharkhand. As one of a handful of Nehruvian steel towns set up in the early 1950s with foreign technology and financial assistance, the area on which the steel plant sits was completely transformed by the arrival of the plant. A hitherto exclusively rural landscape and economy became one of India's new industrial townships. The Indian government has rightly been charged with failing to discharge its obligations to communities displaced for construction (Strumpel 2014), and yet Rourkela also provided new opportunities and avenues for social mobility like those created by the steel townships at Bhilai and Jamshedpur (Parry 2014; Sanchez 2012).

These large industries were supported by an outsize share of development resources, chief among which was an assured supply of electricity, so scarce in the context of a newly forming power sector but economically essential to the energy-hungry extractive sector. Odisha's modest electric capacity at independence grew substantially when the large hydroelectric dam at Hirakud and the smaller dam at Machkund came online. Most of this new capacity was set aside in advance for large industrial consumers, leaving little for either agricultural consumers, agro-industries, or even expanding household access to electricity (Kale 2014, 114–15). Even two decades later, amid the green revolution's emphasis on large-scale rural electrification programs throughout India, the subsidies for industrial electricity tariffs continued to exceed those for rural electrification. The government and the Orissa State Electricity Board (the government utility) were explicit about the goal of using electricity as a tool of development (OSEB 1975, cited in Kale 2014, 120–21).

In the shadow of these few but outsize industries, the state elite also attempted to encourage a regional industrial and mining class, a project that took several forms, including efforts to recruit entrepreneurs to the state (resulting in the establishment of regional companies like Indian Ferro Metals and Alloys); setting up state-owned public sector undertakings (PSUs), like the Orissa Mining Corporation; establishing industrial promotion and financial bureaucracies; and giving preferential treatment in public contracts to local firms. Looking northward to the example of West Bengal, where one of India's oldest business associations, the Bengal Chamber of Commerce, had been functioning since the 1850s, Biju Patnaik, whose first stint as chief minister was in the early 1960s, convinced a cohort of exporters and local manufacturers based in the old capital city of Cuttack to form an analogue for Odisha, the Utkal Chamber of Commerce and Industry, which has grown since its formation in 1964 into the state's largest business lobby by membership.[5] To provide skilled human capital for industrialization, the state also reorganized and expanded a premier engineering school in the coastal city of Cuttack and set up technical training institutes at various other locations during the 1950s and 1960s.

On paper, these state efforts looked to be essential ingredients for materializing a regional capitalist class. In practice, however, the state's political elites were too tightly engaged with economic actors to provide the kind of discipline necessary for successful developmentalism; in more cases than not, political actors were themselves economic agents, as was the case with Biju Patnaik, who was involved in a suite of mining and manufacturing ventures in the state before joining politics. In the latter half of the 1960s the opposition political parties began to call out the connections between industrial and political elites in the Congress Party as examples of deep-seated corruption. These allegations finally compelled the appointment of a judicial commission in the late 1960s. The Khanna Commission, named after the retired chief justice who served as its chair and sole member, was charged with investigating the improper use of public office by prominent Congress politicians. At the center of the controversy was Biju Patnaik, chief minister in the early 1960s and again from 1990 to 1995. The resulting report provides important evidence of how the state and businesses operated together during the 1960s. In all, fifteen politicians who held office from 1961 to 1967 were charged in seventy counts of alleged corruption, three of whom were found to be guilty of impropriety. In considerable detail, the nine-hundred-page volume recounts repeated instances of unseemly closeness between regional capitalists and the state machinery. In some instances, these involved the selective awarding of public contracts to closely allied private companies, as in the case of a construction firm registered in the name of the wife of the deputy chief minister, and in others the offloading of non- or underperforming private companies to public ownership, as in the case detailed below.

The Khanna Commission's first lengthy chapter focuses on the transfer of Kalinga Iron Works to state ownership. The text of the report includes copies of letters from the then-chief minister, H. K. Mahatab, to ministers in the central government requesting loans and guarantees for Kalinga Industries, as well as letters to and from Patnaik and various government officials regarding financing for his project, and later regarding ownership transfer of the company to the public sector. Just after independence in 1948, Patnaik, who returned to his home state a nationalist hero, founded Kalinga Refrigerators Corporation. The state government was both a lender to the firm and an owner; by 1955, the state had a 25 percent ownership stake. Over the next decade, Patnaik's industrial holdings diversified and expanded dramatically, in directions that took advantage of the new mineral wealth that came to the state following the merger of British-controlled Orissa with the native states of western Odisha, where much of the mineral wealth is located. In 1952, Patnaik acquired a mining lease from the state for 3,900 acres of land in Kendujhar (also spelled Keonjhar) District, near the town of Barbil and spanning large deposits of iron ore and manganese. The lease agreement was issued to Patnaik with the provision that once his corporation was given dedicated electricity supplies, the firm would be obligated to build and operate a ferroalloy manufacturing unit within three years. After securing the mining lease, Patnaik began negotiating with German firms to import the capital goods technology for a low-shaft furnace to produce pig iron, an industrial technology that was not yet in use in India.

Kalinga's difficulties revolved around financing for the new plant. Chief Minister Mahatab wrote successive letters to the union finance minister as well as the vice chairman of the planning commission, requesting permission to issue a state guarantee so that Kalinga could finance the project through private resources. Twice during the negotiations to secure financing, first a state-level bureaucrat and then a bureaucrat in the central industrial ministry denied Patnaik's requests for financing, stating that the high cost of the imported technology would make production prohibitively expensive relative to the older method of iron production. But both times, Kalinga Industries sidelined bureaucratic efforts to impose quality control on state lending by appealing directly to elected officials.

After the plant began producing pig iron in early 1960, the flaws in the business model became apparent almost immediately. In June 1960, Patnaik wrote directly to Prime Minister Nehru, requesting that either capacity be expanded to exploit economies of scale or the central government assume ownership and follow a similar plan but in the public sector. As Patnaik put it, he feared that "unless some rational approach is made to tackle this problem, this first successful Indian effort to make iron [using new technology] . . . would remain economically unsound and become a national waste" (Khanna 1969, 81). The central government responded by giving Patnaik permission to expand production, but in 1961, the Congress won a majority of seats during the state assembly elections, and Biju Patnaik became chief minister. At this point his wife became the chairman of Kalinga Industries. Rather than press for the pig iron plant to be absorbed by the central public sector, as Patnaik had earlier requested, the government of Odisha created a new vehicle for public ownership at the state level, the Industrial Development Corporation, which assumed ownership of the plant in 1963 at Patnaik's suggestion (Khanna 1969, 125).

Patnaik's political opponents argued that, from start to finish, the process demonstrated state favoritism toward a private firm. Particularly egregious was the fact that after state ownership of the failing manufacturing unit, Patnaik retained the mining lease as part of B. Patnaik Mines Private Limited (Khanna 1969, 152), thereby contravening the original conditions that linked the mineral rights to an iron production facility. These and other accusations of impropriety that involved Patnaik, his family members, and his political associates were taken up in parliamentary debate in New Delhi. The national media reported biased contracts at Rourkela Steel plant in the late 1950s, which favored a mining firm owned by Patnaik rather than the public sector Metals and Minerals Trading Corporation. Conservative parliamentarians from Swatantra joined with leftists from the Communist parties to criticize the Congress governments at the center and in the state for failing to live up to their socialist rhetoric (*Times of India* 1966). Despite the evidence, though, the Khanna Commission concluded that there was no requirement for a criminal investigation. A slap on the wrist and a public shaming, accomplished by the report itself, was considered sufficient.

Biju Patnaik and his allies dismissed the report as politically motivated and biased in its conclusions. Indeed, the appointment of the commission became one battle in a war of commissions that saw Patnaik's allies counterattacking by demanding judicial enquiries against his onetime ally, H. K. Mahatab, which compelled additional investigations and produced the Mudholkar Commission Report in 1967 and the Sarjoo Prasad Commission Report in 1972. Like the Khanna Commission, this latter report, too, found the main accused guilty of taking private benefit from public office and playing favorites with close associates (Swami 1968). Given the political rivalry in which the Khanna Commission Report forms one chapter, it seems clear that demands for the enquiry by Patnaik's electoral opponents was politically motivated. However, the chairman of the judicial commission, H. R. Khanna, and his findings should nevertheless be respected as the work of a fine jurist, remembered by many as the lone dissenting judge who tried to stem the tide against threats to civil liberties during India's constitutional "Emergency" from 1975 to 1977 (Guha 2007). Moreover, a 1964 Central Bureau of Investigation report on Patnaik and his colleagues had suggested a similar conclusion (Baral and Banerjee 1997, 446), which is what paved the way for the full commission that followed.

One real consequence of the episode was electoral. The repeated allegations of financial and political misdeeds made it difficult for Biju Patnaik and the Congress Party to maintain power. The Congress lost decisively in the 1967 state elections to a coalition of the Swatantra Party and a local Congress off-shoot that styled itself the Jana Congress. State-capital relations and the larger industrial policy framework within which they were embedded were somewhat incoherent for the remainder of the 1960s and 1970s; this larger political turmoil is attested by New Delhi's declaration of President's Rule four separate times during the 1970s.

A Flawed Developmental Effort in the 1980s: "1000 Industries in a 1000 Days"

Several trends coincided to give new shape to Odisha's probusiness stance toward the end of the 1970s. First, by the late 1970s, several influential politicians from the state had joined the Janata Party and began working from within the central government to direct public investments to the state in the mining and minerals sectors. And second, within the state a stable, probusiness Congress government was elected in 1980, helmed by J. B. Patnaik, who would go on to serve two consecutive terms as chief minister. From that point onward, there would be no successful political party in the state either to oppose or to voice criticism of business or to counter the model of development based on the state's resource wealth; neither would the state produce a political party to champion the still-numerically dominant agrarian sector as a viable strategy for economic growth. Rather, the state's political parties consistently since the 1980s have articulated a consensus that favors mineral-based development as the primary goal of economic policy.

One prong of the strategy to industrialize in the late 1970s and 1980s concentrated on directing central public sector investments to the state. After Rourkela, Odisha had to wait almost three more decades for another sizable public sector investment. Despite political efforts coordinated by organizations like the Ispat Karkhana Sangram Samiti and the Orissa Steel Plant Action Committee, efforts that crossed party lines (even uniting erstwhile opponents like Biju Patnaik and those who had accused him of corruption) and presented to New Delhi a united demand for industrial investments, the next several public sector steel plants bypassed Odisha's extensive iron ore and coal supplies (*Times of India* 1970; Dharmarajan 1970). In an analysis of the steel plant planned during the Fourth Plan period, Das (1997) argues that political calculations drove locational decisions of public investments. Although independent evaluations pointed to Odisha as the most efficient location for a large-scale steel project (close to port, coal supplies, iron ore deposits, rail linkages), the state was bypassed several times for locations in the southern states of Karnataka, Tamil Nadu, and Andhra Pradesh.

The pace of central public sector investments to Odisha picked up in the late 1970s. Following the post-Emergency return to parliamentary governance, the regional politician Biju Patnaik, who had by this point left Congress and joined the Janata coalition, used his position in the central government as minister of steel and mines from 1977 to 1979 to secure large-scale public sector investments to Odisha's extractive sector. Although Charan Singh's Janata government was shifting planned expenditures to agricultural development, Biju Patnaik's ministry was trying to develop the steel and mines sector by inviting foreign investments, which he pledged would not detract from the government's rural agenda (Thapar 1977; BM 1980). At the same time, under Patnaik, the steel ministry also put more emphasis on steel and iron exports, which in 1977 accounted for a quarter of the Steel Authority of India's total production (BM 1977).

Since he was unable to set up a second steel plant in Odisha despite his position in the union cabinet, the most prominent heavy industry for which Patnaik laid the groundwork was an integrated aluminum production facility that included bauxite mines, an alumina refinery, captive power plant, and an aluminum smelter, under the auspices of the newly formed National Aluminum Company, or NALCO. NALCO's operations in Odisha constituted India's largest mining and metallurgy operation at the time, and its effects on the state's finances were proportionately significant. In just five years from 1985–86 to 1989–90—by when the first stage of NALCO's mining, refining, and smelting operations had become fully operational—the percentage of revenue from mining royalties to the state's total nontax internal revenue stream grew from 7.5 percent to 26.0 percent (Government of Orissa 1991, 54). The bulk of this revenue came from the two large public sector metallurgy operations at Rourkela and NALCO, and a small number of large private sector firms near Hirakud dam.

A second strategy for industrialization was promised as part of J. B. Patnaik's successful electoral platform in 1980. Patnaik, who helmed the Congress Party as chief minister for the 1980s and again from 1995 to 1999, pledged to promote one thousand industrial units worth one thousand crores in one thousand days, about which he was keen to show progress right from the start (*Times of India* 1980). More dynamic, regionally oriented industrial, entrepreneurial, and agro-industrial business sectors had already begun to emerge in Gujarat, Maharashtra, and Andhra Pradesh, many of which had their origins in productive agrarian economies. In Andhra Pradesh, the wealthy landowners of coastal Andhra became the seedbeds of future entrepreneurs in the state. As Alivelu, Srinivasulu, and Reddy (2013) argue, in Andhra Pradesh it was an "aggressive rural rich" (199–200) who, along with an educated urban class, found in entrepreneurship new avenues for social mobility outside of agriculture. One key to entrepreneurship in Andhra Pradesh was that earlier investments in agriculture enabled farmers to generate surpluses that were then redirected to industrial and manufacturing pursuits. A similar pattern obtained in western India, where surpluses from agriculture in Maharashtra and Gujarat alongside state development support first engendered a base of agro-industries and then were put to other industrial uses by homegrown entrepreneurs. In Odisha, by contrast, entrepreneurship was not spurred by assets and capital accumulated through agricultural or mercantile surpluses. Instead, state leaders tried to make up for this lack of investible surplus and indigenous entrepreneurs by incentivizing entrepreneurship through public funding, dispensed through the Odisha State Finance Corporation (OSFC), for micro and small enterprises; and the Industrial Promotion and Investment Corporation of Odisha Ltd (IPICOL), for medium enterprises. Of the two, OSFC was meant to have a greater, because more widespread, effect.

Originally established in 1956 under the central State Financial Corporations Act, 1951, OSFC's lending during its first decade and a half of existence was modest; relatively few small-scale entrepreneurs applied for loans, and of these, the rates of sanction were likewise modest. Things changed dramatically after 1980, when JB Patnaik's promise to transform the state's entrepreneurial profile came to be reflected in the bank's lending policy and practice. As the annual report from the bank's silver jubilee in 1981–82 notes, to align itself with the government's industrial policy, OSFC "liberalized its procedure for disbursement thoroughly" (OSFC 1982, 21). In principle, the increasing numbers of entrepreneurs coming forward to apply for loans and the higher loan sanction rates might have had a positive effect on the state's industrial development, particularly in the job-creating MSME sector. The problem was that the bank's lending was increasingly precarious, with an ever greater share of lending to first-time entrepreneurs, those without experience, assets, or viable business plans. To meet the promise of a thousand industries, OSFC officers were instructed to sanction loans to all pending applications, relax their appraisal norms by lowering margin rates, and aggressively increase their sanction rates.[6] These changes were felt almost immediately after Patnaik took office. Though intended to be an independent corporation, the bank was forced to function as "proprietary organization of the government."[7] One former bank employee with whom I spoke referred to the thousand-industries era as a "laughing matter" that everyone, including the politicians and bureaucrats in charge, knew would fail.[8]

These stated policy shifts and the views of loan officers who were active in OSFC during the 1980s are corroborated by the bank's loan sanction data over time. In 1970–71, OSFC was small but well established. Thirty-six applications were pending from the previous year, and the bank received 71 new applications during that fiscal year. Of these, the bank sanctioned thirty-eight loans, a rate of 35 percent (OSFC 1970–71). By 1985–86, the number of loan applications had swelled to 2,301, only 195 of which were pending from the previous year, and the loan sanction rate had more than doubled to 73 percent (OSFC 1985–86).

Predictably, OSFC, which during its first decades had made small but steady profits in line with its conservative lending philosophy, started to show large losses by the middle of the 1980s.[9] The media gave this scant attention. One scholar of Odisha's media suggests a reason for the omission: once Patnaik declared printing to be an industry that could avail of OSFC loans, sixteen prominent regional newspapers were among OSFC's roster of loan recipients (Pattnaik 2014, 77). One of the few publishing houses that was critical of the government, Priadarshini Press, was denied a loan (Pattnaik 2014, 78). Like so many other small industries, all of the presses ultimately defaulted their loans and secured their debts to OSFC through one-time settlements. Not just with respect to the thousand-industries program and OSFC's role in it, but in general, the regional media were insufficiently critical of the government. Many of the papers were either run by or closely affiliated to prominent politicians, and as the largest regional advertiser, the government remained the principal source of newspaper revenue (Pattnaik 2014, 76–77).[10]

Lack of disciplined lending was not the sole reason for OSFC's failure; another barrier to success was the absence of working capital. OSFC was statutorily enabled to make term loans alone. These were enough for entrepreneurs to acquire capital assets—the land, machinery, electricity connections—to set up their businesses. The vast majority of entrepreneurs faced barriers to getting sufficient working capital, however. Commercial banks, which continued to operate with much more stringent rules, were often wary of the MSME sector.[11] Without access to working capital, entrepreneurs scrambled to start running their businesses. At the least hardship, without any financial cushion to fall back on, many of them declared bankruptcy and their loans joined the growing roster of OSFC's nonperforming assets.

Ultimately, the lack of discipline imposed on entrepreneurs, declining appraisal standards, and lack of working capital meant that while Patnaik's ambitious agenda of one thousand industries was useful enough to contribute to his election in 1980 and re-election in 1985, it was not able to catalyze Odisha's economic transformation via the MSME sector. This could be seen even in Patnaik's own constituency in the district of Cuttack, in an industrial estate that he had inaugurated in 1983 called Radha-Damodarpur. All ten small industrial plots, which at one time were occupied by young entrepreneurs who had received loans and favorable leases, were vacant by 1988 (Ahmed 1988). As one bureaucrat reflecting on that era put it, "MSME growth was equal to MSME death."[12] He was in a good position to know the difficulties of first-time entrepreneurship, having spent five years in the mid-1980s trying to set up a contracting business to carry out civil and mechanical projects for NALCO's smelter investment in Angul District. He added to the above remark by noting that another problem was that even those entrepreneurs as existed in Odisha were of "a half-mind. They would apply for a loan from OSFC but simultaneously be looking for a government job."[13] After his small business failed for a variety of reasons, including a near total absence of working capital, he himself turned to the safer haven of government employment and spent the subsequent thirty years as a bureaucrat charged with facilitating industrialization. Until today, the majority of the small parts and large machines that are required to keep NALCO's power plant and smelter functioning are purchased from outside the state. Although the state hosts India's largest integrated aluminum company, one local politician complains, the infusion of large-scale capital has spurred little ancillary and downstream activity in either the surrounding district or elsewhere in the state.[14]

Bringing to the forefront the hegemonic caste and class alliance that has characterized Odisha's political economy makes the transfer of wealth from the public OSFC to private entrepreneurs even more problematic (Mohanty 2014). It was a narrow stratum of the state's citizens who benefited from the public support for entrepreneurship. As one survey-based study of entrepreneurship has argued, the real beneficiaries were those who claimed alliances "through political patronage and articulation of caste and kinship ties with the influential state bureaucrats" (Meher and Sahoo 2008, 172). In the case of OSFC, for example, which had branch offices set up throughout the state to lend to rural enterprises as well, it was the urbanized districts that remained most significant in terms of number of enterprises and quantum of lending.

The JB Patnaik government's plan for small industries was undoubtedly a failure on many levels. One often-cited explanation for the failure is the dearth of entrepreneurs in the state, a fact that scholars of Odisha have long noted. According to a common narrative, the state's rich maritime history, with traders and merchants plying the indigenous textile and crafts of the state throughout Southeast Asia, faded into insignificance during the colonial period. The state's development efforts have struggled to revive this entrepreneurial past. According to the most critical assessments of Patnaik's thousand-industries effort, only 15 percent of enterprises forged during this decade survived past their first few years; even the most charitable estimate is still not higher than 25 percent. A great deal of public finance was disbursed to a coterie of young men with insufficient experience and assets to enable success. Those few entrepreneurs who survived the decade, though, acknowledge that credit provided by the public financial corporations was critical to launching their companies.[15] Both OSFC and IPICOL stopped lending in mid-2000s. IPICOL managed to reinvent itself as the institutional face of and vehicle for the state's single-window clearance system for new investments. As of 2016, OSFC faces more difficult circumstances. Without fresh capital infusions from the government, the bank has on its books almost exclusively nonperforming assets and is unable to repay its own loans to the Industrial Development Bank of India, which along with the government had been the primary source of capital for the bank.

The 1990s—: New Alliances of Business and State in a Greenfield Extractive Economy

In a trend that began in the 1980s but became more decisive in the early 1990s, private capital began to replace the public sector as the engine of extractive investment. Deregulation of key industrial and mineral sectors; cancellation of the freight equalization policy, which had weakened the comparative advantage of mineral-rich states; and rising global commodity prices led to a flurry of private interest in Odisha as a site for greenfield investments. The shift from public to private companies as the vehicles for new investment did not lead to the eclipse of the state, as an earlier generation of scholarship on neoliberalism had predicted, but instead has required a greater coordination between government agencies and private extractive firms. Rather than supplying credit, as in the past, the state's most pivotal role revolves around securing land and mineral leases, and providing environmental and social clearances. In many cases, though, businesses in the state coordinate with state agencies not through institution-alized channels and processes but through personal networks and connections.

The state's largest and most successful public and private industrial firms al-most exclusively occupy the extractive sectors of mining and metals. In the public sector, this small list of very profitable firms includes the central PSUs: Mahanadi Coal, currently among the most productive arms of Coal India Limited; NALCO, an aluminum producer that has maintained substantial profits even amid low commodity prices; NTPC's thermal power plants; and Rourkela, one of SAIL India's flagship steel plants set up after independence. While many of these PSUs recruited managerial talent from across India, they also provided important em-ployment opportunities for the dominant social groups within Odisha (Adduci 2009). Of the private companies, the majority have been set up in the last twenty years, although the private sector Hindalco, the aluminum company that is now part of the Aditya Birla group, has been operating since before independence. Odisha's iron ore and chromite mines in Keonjhar and Jajpur Districts have been integral to Tata Steel since the 1950s, but it was only since the mid-2000s that the company began investing in steel production in Odisha with the construction of what will eventually be a six-million-ton-capacity steel plant in Kalinganagar in Jajpur District. Unfortunately, this plant is being built at a time when automation in steel production means that the employment generation of Kalinganagar will be significantly less than in Tata's operations at Jamshedpur. Other large-scale private sector firms in the state include Jindal Stainless, Jindal Steel and Power, Vedanta Industries, and Paradeep Phosphates, all of them attracted to Odisha by subsoil resources.

The extractive industry remains Odisha's most dynamic economic sector, and within this the need for land is critical. Mining companies, mineral-based industries like steel and alumina refining, and power companies all re-quire large land parcels. The central government plays an important role in securing prospecting licenses and mining leases, but for access to land, state agencies are paramount, particularly the work of the Industrial Infrastructural Development Corporation, or IDCO. Formed in 1981 to create infrastruc-tural facilities for entrepreneurs, itself a sign of the move away from the public sector and toward private investments, IDCO continues to play the nodal role in land acquisition for new industries. Through IDCO, the government of Odisha hosts industrial estates throughout the state to cater to small- and medium-scale industries. In addition to several smaller industrial estates scattered throughout the state to house them, to attract larger-scale indus-trial investments IDCO began in the early 1990s to purchase large tracts of rural land, the most prominent of which is the Kalinganagar Industrial Estate in Jajpur District, a few hours north of Bhubaneswar. The state government originally acquired land for the estate in the early 1990s, when Biju Patnaik had returned to the chief minister's office reanimated by the goal of building Odisha's second steel plant.

During the period from the early 1990s to the present, 2006 stands as a turning point. Up until then, IDCO was engaged actively on behalf of private interests in securing land for industrial projects. In January 2006, a group of antidisplacement protestors had gathered in Kalinganagar to oppose land acquisition by Tata Steel. In the violence that ensued, the police opened fire on protestors, killing thirteen Adivasi protestors. Entrepreneurs and industrial developers argue that since that incident, although stated policies remained probusiness and proindustry, policy implementation has been weak, particularly for land acquisition. On paper, the government of Odisha has all of the facets of a proactive probusiness regime: the requisite single-window clearances, a land bank, ample power, and generous policies to allow energy-intensive industries to either produce their own power or purchase from the market. In practice, however, company officials argue that they are left doing much of the groundwork on their own, particularly so in the case of land acquisition. IDCO acquires land from agriculturalists and then turns this over to industrial users in long-term leases, in effect securing legal or de jure title to the land for industrialists. The crucial work of ensuring physical possession of the land is a secondary process in which company representatives argue that state agencies have played a negligible role.[16]

Large-scale land acquisition of land, as in Kalinganagar, was one of a number of policy changes intended to signal to private investors the state's probusiness stance. Particularly important for the energy-hungry extractives sector—for which lack of stable and ample power was a bottleneck in many parts of the country—was the state's precocious energy reform program. During the 1990s, well before the central government's own reform policies and preceding other states by several years, Odisha passed new electricity legislation, disbanded its vertically integrated utility, created an independent regulator, and signed on to a World Bank restructuring program that ended with the privatization of the entire distribution business (the segment that carries electricity from the power plant to the consumer). As in the case of other probusiness measures, Odisha had nearly uniform bipartisan support for electricity reform. The agenda was initially conceived during the Janata Dal administration, but much of the reform agenda was carried out when a Congress government came to power in 1995, which returned J.B. Patnaik to the chief minister's office.

The failure of Odisha's electricity reforms, and in particular privatization, is attested both by scholarly analyses as well as by the fact that all of the privatized entities had as of 2015 returned to government control. These failures only became evident over time, though. During the 1990s, Odisha's power reform agenda, along with its other probusiness positions, made the state an attractive site for investments in the mining and metal-processing industries. A flurry of MoUs was signed in the state. Though not all of these materialized into actual investments, enough of them did that Odisha gained substantially compared to other states: by the late 1990s, Odisha accounted for 12 percent of all investments in heavy industries in the country, a figure that includes mining and mineral-processing projects (Chakravorty 2003). Many of these investments were concentrated in the newly liberalized electricity sector itself, where new private thermal power plants surrounded the coalfields at Talcher and elsewhere in the state.

Among regional capitalists, the pattern of close relations between political elites and business worlds established in the decades just after independence has if anything become more pronounced in the current period, as deregulation of economic sectors has created even greater opportunities for those with capital. From tourism to education, many of the most successful businessmen in the state are also politicians. The same connection between politics and business is even more true of the extractives sector. One of the largest Odisha-based companies, IMFA, was set up in the early 1960s by Bansilal Panda, then a close associate of Biju Patnaik. Early on, the firm benefited from OSFC loans, and during the 1970s OSFC also owned preferential shares in the company, which was one of only five in which the bank invested directly.[17] While one of the founder's sons continues as head of the company, the other is a well-known BJD politician who currently serves as a member of parliament. Throughout IMFA's fifty-plus years of operating in the state, the media, civil society organizations, and rival political parties have censured the company and its subsidiaries for benefiting in myriad ways from political patronage, from the cancellation of electricity dues and generous debt restructuring to favorable court rulings (Srinivas 1992). In the case of other companies, even when owners have no direct relation to elected office, the growth and operations of successful firms can often be linked to close alliances between business owners, politicians, and bureaucrats. One prominent example from the past decade's rapid growth in the mining sector is Thriveni Earth Movers, which benefited from a close relationship to the local MLA in the mining district of Keonjhar. Commenting anonymously on how a company like Thriveni managed to secure the multifold licenses required to operate in the extractives sector, one former minister in Odisha remarked, "In Odisha, if you don't have any political background, your file won't move. . . . Look at any big-business owners in Odisha—they are either politicians [MPs or MLAs] or outsiders with some connections" (Rajashekhar 2015).

The importance of social networks that bind state and business is equally important in the nonextractives and MSME sectors, where the main challenge for new entrants is establishing sufficient bureaucratic and political networks. As one young entrepreneur who launched a dairy products business argued, whatever help businesses receive is due to the personal interventions of individual bureaucrats, the more senior the better.[18] Emphasizing the importance of high-level bureaucratic support, this entrepreneur recounted an episode from the first few years of operation, when the state-run dairy cooperative, Omfed, used a variety of tactics to prevent the new company's products from being carried in stores, including threatening to cancel retail and business licenses. It was only after a meeting convened at the highest bureaucratic levels, in this case by the state's chief secretary, that a detente was approached and the company was able to expand. For those who arrive without extensive networks in place in the state, building and tending to these connections becomes critical for success.

Given this political context, the importance of business lobbies has remained limited in Odisha. Certainly all of the major national business associations, like the Confederation of Indian Industry and the Federation of Indian Chambers of Commerce and Business, have branch chapters with headquarters in the state, and the largest regional business association, the Utkal Chamber of Commerce and Industry (UCCI), has active chapters throughout the state. On the face of it, UCCI has a strong relationship with various arms of the state, invited to participate in forty-two separate forums convened by the government of Odisha.[19] Likewise, UCCI and the national lobbies routinely organize conferences and seminars that bring corporate members together with bureaucrats and politicians around specific issues. But much of the interaction between business and the state remains heavily dependent on personal networks that connect these various worlds. One bureaucrat who facilitates land acquisition for industrial investments stated that "right now in Odisha, lobbies play maybe 20 percent of the role; the rest is direct contact" between agents of a company and the particular bureaucrats and politicians in charge. "Lobbies are not the major players."[20] He suggested that this is as true for the large companies, like Tata Steel, Jindal Steel and Power, and Bhushan, as it is for smaller companies.

Over the last two decades, Odisha's investment growth has been mostly concentrated in large-scale industries in the mining and metallurgy, with far less growth in the labor-intensive MSME sector. As in the 1970s and 1980s, the current government has established policies on paper to facilitate downstream manufacturing parks and support the MSME sector. Often these take a passive form, though, built on the expectation that investments in extraction and mineral-processing will naturally compel downstream investments.[21] The effects are seen in the overall size and growth rates of Odisha's MSME sector, which, in the last decade, accounted for less than 1 percent of all new proposals in the MSME sector in India. In 2007, Odisha could claim 0.8 percent of proposals in the MSME sector; in 2014–15 the figure was 0.7 percent (MSME 2016, 11).

Conclusion

Are relations between the state and business a type of benign collaboration that leads to economic growth or a detrimental collusion that preserves benefits for the very few? Scholars of the developmental state point to examples in East and Southeast Asia to argue that capital can be granted sufficient incentives to invest but simultaneously be disciplined enough by the state to produce economic growth that benefits the majority (Evans 1995; Kohli 2004). Far from being this kind of developmental success, though, the state in Odisha since independence has taken a "neopatrimonial" form, one marked by personalistic relations, single-party rule (particularly in the last four election cycles), and underinstitutionalization.

However, unlike other neopatrimonial states in India, such as Uttar Pradesh (Kohli 2012, 160–78), where overall economic growth rates are lower than all-India averages, Odisha's growth rates have increased markedly since the early 2000s (Nayak, Panda, and Pattanaik 2016). But even if state-capital relations are indeed leading to faster economic growth, it is still unclear whether higher growth will produce economic benefits for the majority. Not only do Odisha's state-business relations take a neo-patrimonial form, but its probusiness policies are concentrated in the extractives sector, now a capital-intensive sector with fewer prospects for employment generation than in the past. Without more concerted efforts toward public investments in agriculture, agro-industry, and employment-intensive manufacturing, the results of Odisha's higher growth rates will produce the kind of surplus populations about whom Sanyal (2007) writes, those who are able to socially reproduce but remain resolutely on the margins of economic development.

References

Adduci, Matilde. 2009. "Neoliberalism and Class Reproduction in India: The Political Economy of Privatization in the Mineral Sector in the Indian State of Orissa." *Forum for Social Economics* DOI:10.1007/s12143-011-9091-z.

Ahmed, Farzand. 1988. "Broken Promises: Patnaik Faces Opposition in His Constituency." *India Today*, October 31.

Alivelu, G., Avinash Samal, and Kunal Sen. N.d. "A Thousand Industries in a Thousand Days? State Business Relations and the Puzzle of Orissa's Industrial Performance." Unpublished manuscript.

Alivelu G., K. Srinivasulu, and M. Gopinath Reddy. 2013. "State-Business Relations and the Performance of the Manufacturing Sector in Andhra Pradesh." In *State-Business Relations and Economic Development in Africa and India*, ed. Kunal Sen, 198–214. New York: Routledge.

Amsden, Alice. 1989. *Asia's Next Giant: South Korea and Late Industrialization*. New York: Oxford University Press.

Banerjee, Partha Sarathi. 2014. "Orissa and West Bengal: The SEZ imbroglio." In *Power, Policy, and Protest: The Politics of India's Special Economic Zones*, ed. Rob Jenkins, Loraine Kennedy, and Partha Mukhopadhyay, 272–303. New Delhi: Oxford University Press.

Bailey, F. G. 1959. "The Ganatantra Parishad." *Economic Weekly*, October 24, 1469–76.

———. 1963. *Politics and Social Change: Orissa in 1959*. Berkeley: University of California Press.

Baral, J. K. 1987. "Congress Party of India." *Indian Journal of Political Science* 48 (4): 549–60.

Baral, J. K., and K. Banerjee. 1997. "Regional Political Parties in an Indian State: Growth and Decay." In *Indian Political System: Trends and Challenges*, ed. Verinder Grover, 440–66. New Delhi: Deep and Deep Publications.

BM. 1977. "SAIL Sinking?" *Economic and Political Weekly*, May 28, 865–66.

———. 1980. "Economic Salvation through Multinationals." *Economic and Political Weekly* 15 (12): 585.

Chakravorty, Sanjoy. 2003. "Industrial Location in Post-reform India: Patterns of Inter-Regional Divergence and Intra-regional Convergence." *Journal of Development Studies* 40 (2): 120–52.

Chibber, Vivek. 2003. *Locked in Place: State-Building and Late Industrialization in India*. Princeton, NJ: Princeton University Press.

Das, Keshabananda. 1997. "Politics of Industrial Location: Indian Federalism and Development Decisions." *Economic and Political Weekly* 32 (51): 3268–74.

Das, Prakash Chandra. 2007. *Mahtab's Government and Politics in Orissa*. Bhubanewar, Orissa: Athena Books.

Davis, Diane. 2004. *Discipline and Development: Middle Classes and Prosperity in East Asia and Latin America*. Cambridge: Cambridge University Press.

Dharmarajan, S. 1970. "Orissa's Stagnant Industry: Mixed Up Priorities." *Times of India*, September 26.

Evans, Peter. 1995. *Embedded Autonomy: States and Industrial Transformation*. Princeton, NJ: Princeton University Press.

Government of Odisha. 2014. *Report of the Comptroller and Auditor General of India, General and Social Sector for the Year Ended March 2014*. Report No. 7.

———. 2015. *Industrial Policy Resolution 2015*. August. http://investodisha.gov.in/download/IPR_BROCHURE.pdf.

Government of Orissa. 1991. *Economic Survey 1990–91*. Directorate of Economics and Statistics, Planning and Coordination Department.

———. 2006. "Orissa Resettlement and Rehabilitation Policy." In *Orissa Reference Annual*, 2009.

Guha, Ramachandra. 2007. *India after Gandhi: The History of the World's Largest Democracy*. New York: HarperCollins.

Harriss, John. 2006. "Institutions and State-Business Relations." IPPG Briefing Paper No. 2, June. http://r4d.dfid.gov.uk/PDF/Outputs/propoor_rpc/ippgbp2.pdf.

Kale, Sunila S. 2013. "Democracy and the State in Globalizing India: A Case Study of Odisha." *India Review* 12 (4): 245–59.

———. 2014. *Electrifying India: Regional Political Economies of Development*. Palo Alto, CA: Stanford University Press.

Khanna, H. R. 1969. *Report of the Commission of Inquiry*. Bhubaneshwar, Orissa: Government of Orissa, Home Department.

Kohli, Atul. 2004. *State-Directed Development: Political Power and Industrialization in the Global Periphery*. Princeton, NJ: Princeton University Press.

———. 2012. *Poverty amid Plenty in the New India*. New York: Cambridge University Press.

Mallik R. M., and S. P. Padhi. 1995. *Irrigation System in Orissa: Its Impact on Agricultural Development*. Bhubaneswar: Nabakrushna Choudhury Centre for Development Studies.

Meher, Rajkishor, and Renubala Sahoo. 2008. "Socio-economic Background of the Entrepreneurs and the Industrial Climate of the Small-Scale Sector Industries in Orissa." *Journal of Entrepreneurship* 17 (2): 169–88.

Mishra, Banikanta. 2010. "Agriculture, Industry, and Mining in Orissa in the Post-liberalisation Era: An Inter-district and Inter-state Panel Analysis." *Economic and Political Weekly* 45 (20): 49–68.

MSME (Ministry of Micro, Small and Medium Enterprises). 2016. *Annual Report, 2015–16*. New Delhi: Government of India.

Mohanty, Debabrata. 2015. "Odisha CM Naveen Patnaik Accuses Centre of 'Step-Motherly' Treatment." *Indian Express*, March 6. http://indianexpress.com/article/india/india-others/odisha-cm-naveen-patnaik-accuses-centre-of-step-motherly-treatment/.

Mohanty, Manoranjan. 1989. "Class, Caste and Dominance in a Backward State: Orissa." In *Dominance and State Power in Modern India*, vol. 2, ed. Francine R. Frankel and M. S. A. Rao, 321–66. Delhi: Oxford University Press.

———. 2014. "Persisting Dominance: Crisis of Democracy in a Resource-Rich Region." *Economic and Political Weekly* 49 (14): 39–47.

Nayak, Pulin B., Santosh C. Panda, and Prasanta K. Pattanaik. 2016. "Introduction." In *The Economy of Odisha: A Profile*, ed. Pulin B. Nayak, Santosh C. Panda, and Prasanta K. Pattanaik, 1–23. New Delhi: Oxford University Press.

Orissa State Finance Corporation. Various years. *Annual Report*.

Padel, Felix, and Samarendra Das. 2010. *Out of This Earth: East India Adivasis and the Aluminium Cartel*. Hyderabad: Orient Blackswan.

Parry, Jonathan. 2014. "Sex, Bricks and Mortar: Constructing Class in a Central Indian Steel Town." *Modern Asian Studies* 48 (5): 1242–75.

Panda, Manoj. 2008. "Economic Development in Orissa: Growth without Inclusion?" www.igidr.ac.in/pdf/publication/WP-2008-025.pdf.

Pattnaik, Sudhir. 2014. "Who Does the Media Serve in Odisha?" *Economic and Political Weekly* 49 (14): 74–81.

Rajashekhar, M. 2015. "How a Contractor from Tamil Nadu Carved Out an Enormous Mining Empire in Odisha." *Scroll*, November 5. http://scroll.in/article/760562/how-a-contractor-from-tamil-nadu-carved-out-an-enormous-mining-empire-in-odisha.

Sanchez, Andrew. 2012. "Deadwood and Paternalism: Rationalizing Casual Labour in an Indian Company Town." *Journal of the Royal Anthropological Institute* 18: 808–27.

Sanyal, Kalyan. 2007. *Rethinking Capitalist Development: Primitive Accumulation, Governmentality, and Postcolonial Capitalism*. New Delhi: Routledge.

Sarap, Kailas, and Partha P. Sahu. 2016. "Emerging Trends in Cropping Patterns, Crop Diversification, and Agricultural Productivity." In *The Economy of Odisha: A Profile*, ed. Pulin B. Nayak, Santosh C. Panda, and Prasanta K. Pattanaik, 27–53. New Delhi: Oxford University Press.

Simeon, Dillip. 1995. *The Politics of Labour under Late Colonialism: Workers, Unions, and the State in Chota Nagpur, 1928–1939*. New Delhi: Manohar.

Sinha, Aseema. 2005. *The Regional Roots of Developmental Politics in India: A Divided Leviathan*. Bloomington: Indiana University Press.

Srinivas, Alam. 1992. "Managing Indian Charge Chrome by 'Rule of Law.'" *Times of India*, August 18.

"Statenotes." 1990. *India Today*, November 30.

Strumpel, Christian. 2014. "The Politics of Dispossession in an Odishan Steel Town." *Contributions to Indian Sociology* 48 (1): 45–72.

Swami, N. K. 1968. "Trouble Brewing in Orissa Again? Sequel to Inquiry Report." *Times of India*, November 9.

Thapar, Romesh. 1977. "Economics, Dismal as Ever." *Economic and Political Weekly*, July 25, 1209.

Times of India, 1966. "Second Look into Contract to Patnaik's firm." August 30.

Times of India, 1970. "Dharna before P.M.'s House on Steel Plant Issue." November 10.

Times of India, 1980. "Industry Attracted to Orissa: CM." September 2.

Conclusion

CHRISTOPHE JAFFRELOT, ATUL KOHLI, AND KANTA MURALI

This volume has sought to analyze the growing power of business groups in Indian politics. The study is organized around three interrelated but overarching concerns. First, we have probed how the power of business is shaping political change in India. We know that social power molds state behavior via complex channels; these can vary from the political elite silently taking account of the growing power of private capital to business groups—especially big business—undertaking direct and deliberate actions to shape political outcomes. We have focused our attention on both structural and instrumental power of Indian business groups. Second, we have focused on some important policy areas that matter to business groups. We have analyzed how business seeks to influence labor and land policies, two critical factors of production. More diffuse but still important for business groups is the broader context within which they operate; how business shapes urban spaces and the role of media are two other issue areas that were probed in some detail in this volume. And finally, politics across Indian states varies quite a bit. The role of business in the politics of three Indian states—Gujarat, Tamil Nadu, and Odisha—then helps us take account of some of this regional variation.

This brief conclusion follows the three main concerns of the volume: the power of business in India, business influence across issue areas, and cross-state variations. The chapters that address these respective concerns and their main contributions were already summarized in the introduction to this volume. In this conclusion we will draw out some key themes that emerge when the chapters are either juxtaposed to each other or considered as a set. Toward the end we also raise some general considerations that situate the Indian materials in a global context.

Business and Politics in India

Business groups enjoy privileged access to the state in all capitalist democracies. That is not a new insight. The analytical issue really is how significant the power of business is in a specific polity—India, in the present volume—and how that influence operates as well as varies over time and across policy domains. To recall very briefly the variation over time in India: following independence, Nehru's power in India was relatively uncontested and the nationalist legitimacy gave the Indian state a degree of influence in society that even the economic elite were hesitant to challenge, at least openly. India, unlike many other developing countries, had a notable indigenous business class at the time of independence, but the role of private industry in the overall economy was modest during this early phase. The result was that the balance of power between the state and business during Nehru's India was uneasy, characterized by suspicious coexistence: though power was tilted to the state, businesses were not entirely passive observers and had a degree of veto power. Indira Gandhi first pushed state control of the economy in the name of a propoor agenda but then, later in her political career, moved India toward private-sector-led economic growth. Indira Gandhi of the *garibi hatao* vintage nationalized banks, put limits on the growth of private business houses, and chastised Indian business groups as enemies of progress. It would be fair to surmise that the 1970s were a low point of business influence in Indian politics.

This tide turned during the 1980s as leaders of India tilted toward private-sector-led economic growth. The power of business first grew slowly but steadily, but then took a quantum leap during the 1990s—and beyond—as the Indian state embraced economic "liberalization." In practice, liberalization in India has been rather calibrated: it has often led, not so much to state withdrawal from the economy, as to state support of private business groups in the name of rapid economic growth. Over time the balance of power between the state and business has shifted in favor of business groups. The Indian economy is now dominated by the private sector. India's major political parties, including the Communist parties, increasingly cater to private business in the hope of investment and growth. This enhanced business influence on politics operates via both indirect and direct channels. Business groups cannot always get their way; they cannot always coordinate their preferences, and democracy, particularly electoral imperatives in the midst of a relatively poor polity, remains a check. Nevertheless, political and economic elites are increasingly seeking pathways—including mobilizing religious nationalism to channel mass demands and adopting a discourse of aspiration and efficiency—that will maximize business interests while marginalizing the influence of excluded groups. The studies in this volume have sought to analyze the role of business in this new political context.

The Growing Power of Business

It is clear in the chapters above that the power of business in Indian politics is growing. Power, however, is difficult to study: not only is it difficult to measure but its exercise follows complex pathways. Our conclusions concerning the power of business groups in India thus necessarily take the form of "more" versus "less," or "great" versus "somewhat." Such assessments can readily be colored by personal judgments: critics of business, for example, might conclude that the power of business in India is by now overwhelming, while many businessmen and their supporters could readily point to all the constraints they face on a daily basis. Within the scope of this caveat, the studies in this volume suggest clearly that, over time, there has been a substantial growth in the power of business groups in Indian politics. If any one doubts this judgment, juxtapose the moment when Indira Gandhi nationalized India's private banks in 1969 to a more recent moment when such leading Indian business leaders as Anil Ambani, anointed Modi as "prime minister material" in 2009. Key drivers of this shift, moreover, have been the commitment of India's political elite—from the 1980s onward—to prioritize economic growth via the private sector, as well as the morphing of political and economic elites in India.

The chapters above document how this growing power of business groups is being exercised in India. The chapter by Murali clarifies that the growing significance of the private sector in the economy now inclines Indian politicians—of various hues—to pursue business-friendly policies that will attract investment and growth. Since the workings of such structural power are often hard to observe, it is important to keep the underlying mechanisms in mind. The legitimacy of politicians depends in part on economic growth. The more such growth depends on private investment, the more likely it becomes that political leaders will pursue business-friendly policies. Since factors other than economic performance also influence legitimacy, leaders are seldom only probusiness. However, all other things being equal, the growing role of the private sector in the economy inclines successful political leaders to pursue probusiness policies. As the role of the private sector in the Indian economy has grown, we should expect more and more politicians to pursue probusiness policies, even if silently.

At the national level in India, we thus notice important political developments that can be interpreted as the structural power of business at work. First, there is a noticeable convergence in the economic programs of India's major political parties, the BJP and the Congress. Key elements of a shared consensus are that economic growth is a priority, with redistribution a distant second, that the main engine of this growth is to be neither the public sector nor foreign investors, but national capital, and that the Indian state will remain an activist state that promotes private-sector-led growth. While there are shades of differences across the parties—in the emphasis on and strategies for redistribution, and on noneconomic issues, such as the position of minorities in India, the differences are even dramatic—the near-consensus on the economic goals in terms of priority accorded to growth and the means of achieving growth are notable. These could be interpreted as a function of direct pressure from business groups, say, in the form of electoral finance. Such an instrumental interpretation would not be wrong but complementary—and maybe even secondary—to the structural power of business. Notice, for example, the evolving role of the Communist Party of India (Marxist), or the CPI(M), when it was in power in West Bengal.[1] The dependence of the CPI(M) on corporate finance is a lot more limited than that of the Congress or the BJP (e.g., Sridharan 2006). And yet, while in power, the CPI(M) felt compelled to pursue probusiness policies; the example of the Tata Nano, with which Murali began her chapter, underlined this shift. Such evidence, then, supports the proposition that the leading position of the private sector in the economy increasingly pressures India's main political parties to pursue probusiness economic policies.

In addition to longer-term goals of sustained economic growth, the workings of capital markets increasingly condition political behavior. This too demonstrates structural power at work. For example, a dramatic instance followed the national election of 2004.[2] As soon as it became clear that the Congress Party would form only a minority government, India's stock market crashed, fearing that Congress would need the support of the Communists in order to govern. Sonia Gandhi immediately announced that key economic decisions would remain under the control of such probusiness leaders as Manmohan Singh, P. Chidambaram, and Montek Singh Ahluwalia. Capital markets calmed down. While such a demonstration of the power of capital markets is hardly unusual in more advanced capitalist countries, it was a relatively new development for India. The message was clear for all those willing to listen: any effort to move policies to the left will be punished by capital markets. By the turn of the new century, then, Indian capital had become quite capable of voting with its feet, announcing in the process to all and sundry that such votes matter more than popular verdicts.

We also notice the workings of structural power at the national level in a number of other essays in the volume. For example, Agarwala analyzes the changing position of labor in India's contemporary political economy. Since labor is a key factor of production, one would expect business groups to take advantage of a probusiness milieu to take aggressive actions to tame labor. We do notice in Agarwala's chapter that labor's position is increasingly under threat in India. However, the leading actors are not business groups, but the Indian state. She documents the efforts by India's state elite to help dilute labor laws, as well as to create a "flexible" labor force. We interpret such changes as structural power at work: since businesses have trouble coordinating actions around such policies, or cannot see far ahead into the future on their own, probusiness state elites take it upon themselves—often in conjunction with the well-organized chambers of commerce—to take the lead. The efforts of such leaders are eventually rewarded by business groups. The changing nature of the media—analyzed by Reddy—provides yet another instance of the growing structural power of business, though with a difference; this change is not mediated by the state. Instead, the growth of a commercial, capitalist economy is altering values of Indian society. The growing consumption ethos encourages advertising and advertising dominance of media in turn has diluted the news and analysis function of Indian media, encouraging instead values that support a growing economy, political stability and national security.

Below the national level, we observe structural power at work at the level of Indian states as well. As Murali observes, pressure on politicians to pursue probusiness policies is especially serious when investors can readily use the threat of capital flight, a threat that is rather serious in large federal political systems. Economic liberalization in India also intensified these pressures because of economic decentralization. A comparison of Gujarat and Punjab allows Murali to demonstrate structural power at work at the level of states; prior presence of a robust industrial and capitalist economy in Gujarat inclined Gujarati politicians to pursue more probusiness policies than in Punjab. The case of Tamil Nadu discussed by Harriss and Wyatt is also striking. Leaders of that state have enjoyed considerable autonomy from business classes, mainly because they have used ethnic nationalism, anti-dominant-caste politics, and appeals of charisma to capture power. And yet the leadership has stopped well short of turning state power against business groups. Sanguine about the important role of business in the economy, leaders of Tamil Nadu have not only let business groups flourish but have even supported their growth actively, again demonstrating the structural power of business at work.

How business groups exercise influence more directly—or, instrumental power—also becomes clear in a number of other essays. The use of such direct power is best viewed as a supplement to the influences that emanate from the growing structural power of business: wherever structural power is not sufficient to achieve desired ends, businessmen are increasingly in a position to achieve the policies they desire via direct control. This does not mean that businessmen will always get what they want. We will return below to a discussion of constraints on business power in India, including problems of collective action and pressures of electoral politics. However, it is the case that direct access to political institutions has enhanced business power to increasingly set the agenda of Indian politics. Sinha's chapter thus provides data to support the claim that businessmen now have more access to a variety of India's political institutions, including the Indian parliament, parliamentary committees where laws get written, regulatory agencies, and bodies that oversee public-private investment projects. Such access in a "porous state" marks a clear increase in the amount of power businessmen now have over India's political process. Moreover, the comingling of the political and economic elite may well be a harbinger of the emergence of a more durable power elite in India.[3]

Electoral finance is another pathway that provides direct influence to business groups over parties and politicians. Although none of the studies in this volume have discussed this issue in any detail, another recent volume has (see Kapur and Vaishnav forthcoming). Among its key findings are that the influence of money in politics is growing: if the national elections in 2009 cost some $2 billion, the price tag for the 2014 elections was closer to $5 billion.[4] While much is murky about the role of money in politics, money enters the political process both via large donations collected by national parties, and by numerous wealthy individuals who increasingly use their personal funds to run for office. Money is used both for ordinary election expenses and for "gift-giving" to sway votes. For our purposes, what is important is that the use of such money in politics both helps explain the phenomena Sinha documents, namely, more and more businessmen in leading political roles, and underlines the growing influence of the wealthy in politics.

Below the national level, the direct role of businessmen in state-level politics is pervasive. A number of chapters document such use of instrumental power across regions of India. Jenkins, for example, notes that businessmen—and business federations—are directly involved in helping politicians write land laws in select states. While legislation to free up land for business projects has been difficult to pass at the national level, businessmen are active in such probusiness states as Rajasthan and Gujarat to amend land laws in their favor. The case of Gujarat gets a full discussion in the chapter by Jaffrelot, as well as in several other chapters. The dominant role of businessmen in shaping politics and policy in Gujarat is evident even to casual observers. Sinha's data on Maharashtra underlines the near monopoly of direct representation that moneyed interests have achieved in the state legislature. While the direct role of business groups in the politics of such industrial states as Gujarat and Maharashtra is not all that surprising, the thick links that adjoin the political and economic elite in a relatively poor state like Odisha are. Kale's documentation of such links underlines how familial connections can help cement class and state collaboration.

Variations in the Power of Business

While the power of business in Indian politics—both structural and instrumental—has indeed grown over time, its exercise in contemporary India also varies, both across issue areas and across Indian states. The chapters above help us explore this variation. For example, a comparison of how labor and land policies are—or are not—changing in the current probusiness era is analytically rewarding. First, notice that national political elites have sought to modify both existing labor and land laws in a probusiness direction, but often face resistance. This struggle underlines the fact that interest groups other than business continue to retain some power to veto measures that go against their core interests, even though they are increasingly on the defensive and the power to set the agenda has now been grabbed by business interests and their political representatives. A second common pattern that emerges from a comparison of land and labor policy struggles is that, after these struggles reach a stalemate at the national level, they get played out at the level of regional states. Business interests then prevail more in some states than in others, potentially laying the groundwork for more significant long-term economic and political variation across Indian states.

And finally, it is worth underlining that national leaders seem to be making more headway in diluting India's labor regime than in facilitating ready access to agricultural land to industrialists. This contrast can be explained in terms of some combination of underlying electoral and class power. The main power resource of labor in the formal sector is their level of unionization. But the small size of the organized sector (almost 93 percent of the Indian labor force is employed in the informal sector), as well as the political fragmentation of organized labor in India across different party lines, limits the electoral strength of labor considerably. In contrast, landowners control land, another key means of production to confront urban capitalists. Moreover, when landownership of both small and large landholders is threatened, electoral consequences can be significant, as they were in West Bengal in defeating the ruling Communist Party in 2011; the lessons are there for anyone to see.

As already noted above, the focus on media leads to a different set of insights. The impact of business on the media is not directly mediated by the state. Instead, media as a commodity propagates values that further facilitate business interests in politics and society. While Reddy documents the changing nature of media in the probusiness era, other important sites of value creation in any society include educational and religious institutions. How is the growing significance of the private sector in the Indian economy altering changes in what is taught in schools and universities? Such influence may operate either through private funding of educational institutions or via strong-arm tactics by probusiness parties in power to modify curricula and limit free speech. BJP's efforts to impose its favored values—derived from its own understanding of Hindu nationalism—in India's educational institutions are well known.[5] In case there is any doubt about the relevance of promotion of such values to the probusiness political agenda of the BJP, it is worth recalling that this well-worn electoral formula has enabled right-wing leaders the world over to serve narrow class interests behind the cloak of ethnic nationalism.

The fourth issue area analyzed above concerned the impact of business groups on urban politics. The surprising insight that emerges from the chapter by Heller, Mukhopadhyay and Walton is the limited role business groups play in molding the political economies of cities, even the most important cities of India. An important underlying determinant of this pattern is the fact that most of the policies that businessmen care about are made at higher levels of government; the political energy of the economic elite is thus focused on state and national governments, not on city governments. What city governments do control, or can influence, however, is the pattern of land allocation within their jurisdictions. Much activity surrounding this issue occurs within metropolitan governments, though much of it also takes the form of rent-seeking by both the political and the economic elites. Unlike in other parts of the world, the ruling coalitions in Indian cities tend to promote neither growth nor social services. As to why this should be so, the answer is important but not readily evident; it requires further research. Elements of the answer would have to include both the incentives generated by the institutional context—for example, the limited power enjoyed by city governments inclines businessmen to focus their political energies elsewhere—as well as the ideological outlook of India's local political elite, who are seldom committed to the public good.

Variations across Indian States

A focus on variations across Indian states also leads to some new insights concerning state-business relations in India. These may be elaborated in two steps. First, it is instructive to focus on variations across India's more "advanced" states; two of which—Gujarat and Tamil Nadu—were discussed above, while a third—West Bengal—has been analyzed elsewhere (Bagchi 1998). The three regions of India where business classes emerged rather early were the old British presidencies of Bengal, Bombay, and Madras. Over time, politics in these three regions diverged, with significant consequences, both for the long-term developments of these regions and for any analysis of the power of capital in India. Business in Bengal, for example, was controlled either by the British or by other non-Bengalis, such as Marwaris. A communist party was thus able in West Bengal to combine class appeals with appeals of regional nationalism to create an antibusiness power bloc; the results included capital flight and sluggish industrial growth, though also some benefits for the poor. By contrast, business groups in the old Bombay were often indigenous, with roots in the local dominant castes. The political and economic elites in Gujarat, for example, shared similar caste backgrounds, paving the way for a probusiness regional politics from an early date.

Tamil Nadu is an in-between case, where regional politics was never as probusiness as in Gujarat but also never as antibusiness as in West Bengal. Mild radicals that they were, Tamil nationalists left the largely upper-caste businessmen of the region well alone. Business, in turn, took advantage of inherited advantages of an early start, including a good state-level bureaucracy, to develop regional commerce and industry. As noted above in the essay by Harriss and Wyatt, over time, state-business relations in the region have become quite complex. While business groups in Tamil Nadu are not powerful enough to shape the political process, it is also clear that state-business relations are by now a lot more cozy. The analytical message that emerges then from comparing three of India's states with early capitalist development is both simple and powerful. While business presence influenced the politics of all the three regions, politics also had its own life in these regions. This political variation, in turn, was consequential for shaping the development of regional economies and business groups, at least over the short to medium term. The general lesson, then, is this: any focus on how business molds politics needs to be complemented with an understanding of how politics shapes business.

A second set of insights emerge by comparing India's less developed states with more developed ones. In the chapter on Odisha above, Kale documents the personalistic relations of the political and economic elite in that state. This neopatrimonial tendency is also quite evident in other poor Indian states such as UP or Bihar. The intriguing analytical puzzle is this: why does probusiness politics in states like Gujarat help sustain economic growth, but degenerates into neopatrimonialism and crony capitalism in states such as Odisha? One part of the answer is that—as documented by Jaffrelot above—there is plenty of crony capitalism in Gujarat too. What is distinct is that state support for business groups in places like Gujarat is generating economic growth but not in states like Odisha. Why? The question is somewhat similar to the one raised above with reference to the rent-seeking collusion between the political and economic elites in India's major cities.

The answer to why elite collusion is productive in some instances but downright corrupt in other situations is likely to revolve around the nature of the political and economic elite on the one hand, and the nature of the institutional context within which the elite operates on the other hand. As one of us has proposed elsewhere, it may be helpful to think of probusiness strategies and crony capitalism as constituting a continuum (see Murali 2017). The degree of state arbitrariness and discretion is likely to be greater in the latter. As to why, the underlying institutional landscape is an obvious influence on all elite actions. In addition, it is likely that the internal structure of business groups helps set up the parameters of state actions: business concentration may well attract arbitrary state action and thus cronyism, while a more fragmented business community constrains state arbitrariness.

When comparing Odisha and Gujarat more concretely, it is likely that the ruling elite in a Gujarat has been more committed to economic growth all along. Such leaders, on balance, have supported a diverse business community who are likely to be productive. At the same time, capital in a place like Gujarat were already established at the onset of state intervention for deliberate development; government support led to the expansion of existing businesses and allowed new ones to enter. The fact that Gujarat is one of India's foremost exporting states also generates market pressure on firms to remain productive.[6] Moreover, political and economic elites in Gujarat are well embedded in institutions. By contrast, the business elite constituted a narrow group in Odisha, and the ruling elite there has from the outset viewed the economy as a source of personal aggrandizement.[7] Businessmen in such a context have also sought easy profits by gaining favors controlled by the state. The relations between the political and economic elites also tend to be personalistic. The analytical lesson that follows is that, depending on the context, close state-business relations can form the basis of both developmental dynamism and failure.

The Growing Power of Business: Some Final Implications

If the power of business in India is indeed growing, we conclude the volume by teasing out some more general and comparative implications: how do we assess the power of business in contemporary India? How is this power shift shaping democracy and development in India? Do insights from India travel to other countries? Each of these issues can now be finally discussed in turn.

Indian democracy has always been a fairly elitist democracy. Following independence, an anglicized political class ruled the country in collaboration with business and landowning groups. During the Indira Gandhi years there was a moment of hope, false hope, as it turned out, that India might evolve toward a social democracy. In the recent decades, power at the apex has again become more concentrated, but the character of the ruling coalition is undergoing a basic transformation. As the power of business groups has grown, landholding interests have failed to come together to counter that power, labor and other working-class groups remain fragmented, and political and bureaucratic leaders increasingly cater to business interests. Does that suggest that business power in India is now hegemonic?

Hegemonic power would involve a preponderance of power in the hands of business groups, on the one hand, and, on the other hand, an acceptance by citizens that such preponderance is both inevitable and desirable. The available evidence suggests that the power of business groups in India has grown, even grown sharply, but is not hegemonic. The business class is clearly the most powerful social class in India by now. However, their dominant position is hardly unquestioned, and they do not always get what they want. According to the World Values Survey, for example, only 31 percent of upper-class Indians in 2007 preferred that industry be owned by the private and not the public sector; the views of members of lower classes and the uneducated were even more negative. During the most recent Modi years, if one focused on mainstream Indian media, one might conclude that "India Incorporated" was the only going concern in India. However, politics of the dispossessed has a way to undermine such efforts to create hegemony at the apex. Notice, for example, the state election in Gujarat in 2017. While the BJP and its big-business supporters were clearly the winners, enough of the excluded groups—especially those in the countryside—voted against the BJP to suggest that challenges to probusiness hegemony remain.

The studies in this volume also documented some of the limits on the power of business groups. The chapter by Jenkins, for example, demonstrated the inability of business groups and of the probusiness political elite to push through favorable land policies. Resources and numbers of landowning groups were a major constraint on pushing through such policies, as were related electoral concerns of the political elite. The essay by Heller, Mukhopadhyay, and Walton also made it clear that businessmen are not even actively seeking to mold urban politics in India; instead, they remain focused on rent-seeking. Murali also notes some of the forces that limit the power of business groups: the importance of noneconomic electoral appeals, heterogeneous preferences of business groups, the diminished but still significant role of the public sector in the economy, and continued state intervention in certain sectors that encourages crony capitalism. As one looks to the future, a variety of new groups—such as informal labor, discussed in the chapter by Agarwala—are also organizing politically. And a large segment of Indian population is still rural and not fully incorporated into the market economy. The political preferences and behavior of the unincorporated masses will only become clear in the future, but this much is certain: the excluded groups in a democracy are not likely to fall in line with a close state-business collaboration.

If the power of business has grown but is not hegemonic, how best does one characterize the power of business in contemporary India? The power of business—especially the power of big business—has grown from veto power to agenda-setting power. Even in the heyday of "socialism," business groups in India had enough power to defend their core interests. For example, even if business groups could not prevent antibusiness legislation, say, during the 1970s, they could withhold investment. Over time, such an investment strike brought Indira Gandhi to her knees. Her antibusiness rhetoric and policies discouraged investors, leading to decline in economic growth. During the early 1980s, then, she quietly but surely moved away from redistributive politics and toward a more growth-friendly agenda. This was a classic demonstration of veto power at work.

By contrast, over the last three to four decades, the power of big business has grown so it increasingly sets India's political agenda. This does not mean that business gets all what it wants. However, policy focus is more on more on how to facilitate investment and growth. While examples of such policy efforts are interspersed throughout the chapters above, only a few examples need to be repeated in conclusion. Notice that major political parties in India now compete over who can be more business-friendly. Substantial redistribution of wealth or income is not even on the political agenda. When the issue of land is now discussed in politics, it is no longer land redistribution, but how to take the land away from agriculturalists to facilitate expansion of industry. The focus on labor is mainly about how to dilute labor laws even further so as to make labor more "flexible." Instead of focusing on how to improve the performance of the public sector, policies are tilted toward public-private cooperation or downright privatization. And major concerns behind tax reform are not so much its distributive implications but how new policies may impact revenue collection and ease of doing business across India.

Business influence on the political agenda operates both indirectly— structural power—and directly—instrumental power. These mechanisms of influence have also been demonstrated throughout the chapters above. To repeat in conclusion, it is best to conceptualize structural and instrumental power as complementary forms of power. The more important is the role of the private sector in the overall economy, the more politicians need to take account of what is good for business. This is not because politicians do not care about the votes of the poor—they care about that greatly—but they hope to mobilize support of the lower classes by other means: through noneconomic appeals, such as ethnic appeals; or by throwing policy crumbs at them, crumbs that high growth can facilitate; or by getting enough money from the corporate sector to distribute at the time of elections. Structural power then sets political limits; it bends the political process in a probusiness direction. Radical politicians can test these limits—and may even expand the room to maneuver—but that requires well-organized mass support to confront the power of wealth. Such social democratic power is currently missing in India. Instead, the instrumental power of business groups is also growing, further enhancing their capacity to pursue a probusiness agenda. As discussed above, such power in India now operates through direct control of political institutions, use of money in elections, lobbying, and molding of political values.

What are the political and economic implications of the growing power of business in India? Business dominance in Indian politics creates serious problems for Indian democracy, especially when political parties cater narrowly to the interests of business groups. Such is the case at present in India, with Narendra Modi and the BJP at the helm. Modi was the choice of business leaders, and he, in turn, caters to narrow business interests. Modi and the BJP may or may not last in power. The probusiness rule they offer nevertheless underlines the problems any rulers of India will face if they choose to cater to narrow interests; these are the problems of how to deal with all those who are excluded from the narrow ruling coalition (Jaffrelot 2017). Winning elections in such a context inclines leaders to shift the political discourse away from issues of economic inclusiveness, either toward a vapid discourse of anticorruption, good governance, and efficiency or, worse, toward manipulation of identity politics. The latter also encourages the politics of intolerance, the decline of institutional politics, and the rise of demagogues. Once in power, narrow, probusiness rulers face the problem of how to deal with the demands of the excluded groups. They can choose to do so by selectively co-opting the leaders of such groups; this is the most common strategy, but it does not always succeed. When demands for inclusion persist, state repression becomes a ready alternative. That narrow, probusiness rule regularly exhibits creeping authoritarianism is, then, a built-in tendency in such ruling arrangements, endangering democracy.

As to economic implications, both the prospect of a democratic developmental state in India and growing cronyism ought to be addressed. A case for probusiness rule in India could be made on the grounds that it offers the best opportunity for rapid economic growth and thus a pathway to a prosperous, modern society. Such an argument will not be without foundation, especially because the rapid economic growth in Japan, South Korea, Taiwan, and China was—or is being—led by probusiness, developmental states. However, any effort to extend the East Asian argument to India rests on thin historical parallels. While relatively obvious, a few important differences between India and East Asia ought to be kept in mind. First, India has never had successful land reforms. More important, land reforms in many countries of East Asia preceded the onset of rapid industrial development. Early land redistribution—along with spread of literacy—provided the base for inclusive economic growth in much of East Asia (e.g., Studwell 2013). Having missed these important set of historical developments, it is not surprising that India's recent economic growth has been accompanied by growing inequalities and a failure to spread the benefits of development widely. Related to this, economic growth in India does not rest on labor-intensive manufactured exports, a pattern of growth followed in much of East Asia that also contributed to job growth and inclusive development. And finally, the commitment of India's democratic state has always been to facilitate—and not to transform—economic change in India. In East Asia a variety of pressures, including corruption, control of labor, and repression of alternative political choices, were subdued by authoritarian governments that were deeply committed to both controlling and transforming economic change. It is our hope that thoughtful Indians will continue to believe that restricting democracy is not worth the prosperity of the few.

Cronyism and corruption is part and parcel of close cooperation between governments and business. The puzzle is when cronyism and growth go hand in hand—for example, in large parts of East Asia—and when, as in many parts of sub-Saharan Africa, personalism undermines the prospect of deliberate development.[8] What light do Indian materials shine on this issue? The evidence from India is mixed, somewhere in between East Asia and Africa. The comparison of Gujarat and Odisha discussed above suggests the following proposition: cronyism and growth can go hand in hand—as in Gujarat, but not in Odisha— when cronyism supports productive activities. Since such a proposition can readily become a tautology, we argued above that the deeper determinants of such processes have to be traced back to the context within which the political and economic elite operate, especially the developmental commitment of the political elite and the internal structure of business, particularly whether it is more or less concentrated. The chapter on urban governance also suggested the importance of the context: local governments in Indian cities facilitate easy rent-seeking, especially via land transactions, and thus discourage the emergence of growth-oriented coalitions.

Following economic liberalization in India, the level of state intervention in the economy did not shrink. Instead, state-business collaboration has continued to grow. Whether the balance of this collaboration will sustain productive growth in the future, or more cronyism that might undermine such growth, is hard to predict. To an extent, corruption in public affairs and economic growth are autonomous processes; for example, when commodity prices are booming, even corrupt resource-rich countries register good economic growth. However, once government-business collaboration is at the heart of the model of development, as it is in contemporary India, corruption can undermine economic growth. The Modi government in India seems to be aware of this conundrum. It is thus very much a pro-big-business government on the one hand, but it is also pursuing some actions to limit corrupt and unproductive practices on the other hand. For example, the demonetization policies in 2016 were aimed at reducing the scope of black money, though the results are not likely to meet the objectives (e.g., Reddy 2017). Even more recently, the newly established Insolvency and Bankruptcy Code in 2017 is aimed at reducing the role of "bad loans" that simultaneously benefit the likes of Vijay Mallya discussed earlier, and strain the capacity of government-owned banks to finance future development efforts.[9] Against these efforts to "rationalize" state support of big business are examples of cronyism spread throughout this volume. Contemporary India thus has plenty of growth and plenty of corruption; the best prediction is that both will continue, at least in the near future.

And finally, how well do insights generated by the Indian materials in this book travel beyond India? How the growing power of business groups shapes democratic—or even authoritarian—politics is a question of global significance. In any effort to develop cross-national generalizations, India will remain an important case. This is, in part, because of its sheer size: India will become the world's largest country in terms of population and the third largest economy in the very near future. The Indian case is also important because the processes of change are unfolding in front of our eyes. Many historical concepts and propositions concerning how the growth of capitalism shaped politics of Western countries can thus be examined against contemporary Indian materials. That is why we were able to readily adapt concepts developed in the context of Western countries—such as hegemony, and structural and instrumental power—to analyze Indian materials. An examination of Indian materials in turn enriches these concepts. Two observations about these concepts are in order.

First, the growing power of business notwithstanding, hegemony still seems like a distant goal in India. This could be because such an outcome will emerge only in the future. Or it could be that the concept of hegemony itself is somewhat problematic. Hegemony implies that the weaker groups in society come to believe that the powerful deserve to be powerful. Indian materials examined in this volume suggest instead that growing power of business groups and challenges to that power can readily coexist in a society. One wonders, then, if this is not the more general condition of emerging capitalism everywhere: beyond short periods here or there, does hegemony ever exist anywhere? If one sets aside the Marxist expectation that workers and peasants ought to embrace revolution, then weaker groups regularly protest their subjugation—using both democratic and nondemocratic pathways—in most societies.[10] Our suggestion, then, is that the study of power is best framed as a dynamic process between forces of domination and opposition. And second, unlike some scholarly debates, our study leads us to conclude that structural power and instrumental power are not alternate approaches to the study of power. Instead, both operate simultaneously and both have to be studied so as to understand how the power of business operates: the structural power of business often sets some basic limits on all politicians, and instrumental power in turn can further enhance the capacity of business groups to achieve their policy agenda.

As to substantive propositions, the most important claim to emerge from Western experience is that rising capitalism supported the emergence of democracy; in the famous words of Barrington Moore, "No bourgeoisie, no democracy" (Moore 1969). How does the Indian experience bear on this important proposition? Moore had suggested that India's nationalist movement could be interpreted as a "bourgeois revolution" of sorts, which in turn helped India emerge as a democracy. Viewed historically, then, a case can be made that capitalism supported the emergence of democracy in India.[11] However, the more recent trends examined in this study are more complex. As the state elite in India have sought higher rates of economic growth, they have privileged the interests of private investors over those of others. Business groups in turn have further pressured the Indian state to tilt the policy process in their favor. However, the emerging narrow coalition of the political and economic elites faces democratic challenges. The political strategies adopted by the ruling elite to cope with such challenges are often antidemocratic. In contemporary India then, probusiness politics seems to go hand in hand with creeping authoritarianism. It is not difficult to imagine that, if the contemporary Indian elite have their way, which one hopes they will not, they may well be satisfied with something less than a full democracy.[12]

A comparison of India with other developing countries is also likely to be fruitful. Given its size and economic dynamism, the most obvious comparative case is China. A Communist government and a much higher dependence on foreign capital obviously make class and power relations in China somewhat distinct from those in India. And yet, the commonalities across these cases suggest that a systematic comparative analysis can probe important questions. For example, China, even more than India, needs to keep "its house in order" so as to continue to attract foreign capital to sustain growth. How the structural power of capital conditions the political systems of India and China can thus be a useful line of comparative inquiry. Moreover, China in recent years has opened up membership in the Communist Party to business groups. One might then wonder how such growth in the instrumental power of business in China shapes the political agenda of that country. Again, a comparison with India is likely to yield important insights about government-business relations in the context of high growth.

Some of the larger developing and middle-income countries of today, such as Brazil, Turkey, and Indonesia, may also provide fruitful comparisons with India. These are capitalist economies with imperfect democracies, traits they share with India. Unlike India, however, the role of foreign capital in such countries is greater than that of indigenous capital. This contrast within the frame of shared traits can provide an important focus for comparative analysis. Given the perennial threat of capital flight, the structural power of foreign capital is likely to be greater than that of indigenous capital. How does this variation condition the political process? For example, when the leftist Lula came to power in Brazil, he immediately moderated his political message so as to persuade foreign capital that Brazil was still open for business. A comparative inquiry may then probe the question of whether heavy dependence on foreign capital rules out social democracy as a political alternative in developing countries (see Sandbrook et al. 2007). The issue of how instrumental power operates in such cases is also more complex than in India. For example, foreign business is a lot less legitimate actor in national politics than indigenous business groups. Foreign corporations cannot readily mobilize nationalist symbols in their support, or openly support political parties, or send their representatives to legislatures. Even lobbying has to be an act of stealth. A comparison with India may, then, enrich our understanding of the role of business in politics in developing countries.

Finally, what the Indian case offers beyond India is an approach to how to study the growing power of business in politics. We have sought to assess how much power business groups have in India: veto power, agenda-setting power, or hegemonic power. These concepts provide qualitative metrics of sorts to estimate variations in the power of business groups. We have also suggested that business groups influence politics along several pathways: values of a society, political institutions, direct lobbying, and eventually, if possible, by direct control of select state offices, if not the entire state. In order to assess the growing power of business in a variety of settings, it is important to study both the indirect and the direct pathways—structural and instrumental power—through which the power of business molds the politics of a society. If readers agree that it is important to study the role of business in politics—whatever the setting—we hope that the simple framework adopted in this volume helps others structure their own research.

References

Bagchi, A. K. 1998. "Studies on the Economy of West Bengal since Independence." *Economic and Political Weekly*, November 21–December 4, 2973–78.

Jaffrelot, Christophe. 2017. "Field of Despair." *Indian Express*. December 8.

Kapur, Devesh, and Milan Vaishnav, eds. Forthcoming. *Costs of Democracy: Political Finance in India*. Delhi: Oxford University Press.

Khan, Mushtaq, and Jomo Kwame Sundaram, eds. 2000. *Rents, Rent-Seeking, and Economic Development: Theory and Evidence from Asia*. Cambridge: Cambridge University Press.

Kohli, Atul. 2004. *State-Directed Development: Political Power and Industrialization in the Global Periphery*. Cambridge: Cambridge University Press.

———. 2012. *Poverty amid Plenty in the New India*. Cambridge: Cambridge University Press.

Mills, C. Wright 1956. *The Power Elite*. New York: Oxford University Press.

Moore, Barrington. 1969. *Social Origins of Dictatorship and Democracy: Lord and Peasant in the Making of the Modern World*. Harmondsworth: Penguin.

Murali, Kanta. 2017. *Caste, Class, and Capital: The Social and Political Origins of Economic Policy in India*. Cambridge: Cambridge University Press.

Reddy, C. Rammanohar. 2017. *Demonetization and Black Money*. Hyderabad, India: Orient Black Swan.

Rueschemeyer, Dietrich, Evelyne Huber Stephens, and John D. Stephens. 1992. *Capitalist Development and Democracy*. Chicago: University of Chicago Press.

Sandbrook, Richard, Marc Edelman, Patrick Heller, and Judith Teichman. 2007. *Social Democracy in the Global Periphery: Origins, Challenges, Prospects*. Cambridge: Cambridge University Press.

Scott, James C. 1990. *Domination and the Arts of Resistance: Hidden Transcripts*. New Haven: Yale University Press.

Sridharan, E. 2006. "Parties, the Party System and Collective Action for State Funding of Elections." In *India's Political Parties*, ed. P. R. de Souza and E. Sridharan, 311–40. New Delhi: Sage Publications.

Studwell, Joe. 2013. *How Asia Works: Success and Failure in the World's Most Dynamic Region*. New York: Grove Press.

NOTES

Chapter 1

1. While the terms "structural" and "instrumental" power are now used by many scholars, the original terms of the debate were set by Marxist scholars. See, for example, Miliband (1969); Poulantzas (1980); Gold, Lo, and Wright (1975). For more recent discussion, see Hacker and Pierson (2002) and Culpepper (2015).
2. On different conceptions of power, see Lukes (2005).
3. One dimension of power that we do not focus on is what some scholars might label "cultural hegemony." While the issue of cultural influence of business groups in India is touched upon here and there in this volume, especially in the chapter on media (by Ram Reddy), and to an extent in the chapter on labor (by Rina Agarwala), we leave it to others to pursue the study of this important dimension of power.
4. The British did eventually impose some protectionist tariffs during the 1920s, but the underlying pressures were not the demands of Indian industry but the need to keep Japanese and German goods out of the Indian market, as well as to increase public revenues.
5. Gandhi had close personal relations with such Indian industrialists as G. D. Birla and J. Bajaj. See, for example, Birla (1953) and Nanda (1990).
6. For a somewhat different argument about these early developments, see Chibber (2003).
7. For a critique along these lines, see Bhagwati and Desai (1970) A more nuanced assessment of India's import substitution strategy is in Jalan (1991).
8. A fine study of business and politics in India during this period that more or less adheres to this perspective is Kochanek (1974).
9. This is one reason why some businessmen supported the creation of a more probusiness Swatantra Party. See Erdman (1967).
10. In the words of a foremost student of the subject, Stanley Kochanek, written before the more recent sharp probusiness tilt: "The decade from 1956 to 1966 proved to be the golden age of private sector development based on close business-government cooperation" (Kochanek 1987, 1285).
11. An incomplete list of major studies might include Bhagwati and Panagariya (2013), Dreze and Sen (2013), Jenkins (1999), Kohli (2012), Murali (2017), Panagariya (2008), Ruparelia et al. (2011), and Sinha (2016).
12. The discussion below draws on Kohli (2012, 27–58).
13. To be precise, CII wasn't entirely a new chamber of commerce. Rajiv Gandhi suggested to the officers of what used to be the Association of Indian Engineering Industry that they should expand beyond engineering industries and become an apex chamber. The AIEI then renamed itself as CII and matured into the powerful organization that it is now.
14. For the role played by Narasimha Rao, see Sitapati (2016).

15. Studies of the rise of the BJP include Jaffrelot (1996) and Basu (2015).
16. To be fair, the percentage of poor population in Tamil Nadu is still greater than in Gujarat. The suggestion here is mainly to underline the rate of decline in poverty in Tamil Nadu over the recent period.

Chapter 2

1. This chapter draws substantially on Murali (2017). The introduction is drawn from pages 1–3 in that work.
2. Like other state governments, Gujarat chose not to publicly disclose full details of the package offered to the Tata group. However, media reports offer some information on benefits and concessions received.
3. This chapter treats the initiation of the economic liberalization process in India as a top-down and independent decision of policymakers. In other words, the chapter does not claim that structural power of business led to the initiation of market reforms. However, once initiated, market reforms since 1991 subsequently led to a steady increase of the structural power of business. In turn, there has been a feedback effect—by virtue of its increased power, capital has had significant influence on the policy process after 1991.
4. One caveat should be mentioned here. In this chapter, the term "business" refers to large, medium, and small enterprises. While the structural power of business can potentially vary within different categories of business, that aspect is not empirically examined here. The conclusion, however, briefly discusses the heterogeneity of business preferences as a limitation to capital's structural power.
5. Debates on the origins of business power exist in both strands of the scholarship. For example, see Vogel (1983) for a critique of pluralist structural power claims. On the Marxist side, Miliband (1969) offers a differing view to structural power claims.
6. Investment in this section refers to industrial investment by the private corporate sector and not portfolio investment. Empirical evidence on policies in this section draws on chapter 3 of Murali (2017).
7. By the provisions of the Indian constitution, state governments have jurisdiction in the area of industries, except those declared by parliament to be necessary for defense purposes or expedient to public interest. States also have significant responsibility in most policy areas relevant to investment promotion such as land, electricity, roads (excluding national highways), labor laws, certain taxes, special economic zones, and law and order. However, the presence of the industrial licensing system until 1991 allowed the center to control the location of investment.
8. Sinha (2005) suggests that even during the license-permit raj, some states, such as Gujarat, worked to attract investment despite constraints placed by the center. However, the situation after 1991 was markedly different, as noted by several authors (e.g., Ahluwalia 2000; Kohli 2006; Rudolph and Rudolph 2001). Formal policy control of industrial investment and its location prior to 1991 was in the hands of the central government through industrial licenses. With the elimination of licensing regulations in 1991, states went into open competition for industrial investment, and the center no longer controlled where industrial investments could be located. As such, the policymaking environment before and after 1991 was very different.
9. Data from Central Statistics Office, Ministry of Statistics and Program Implementation, Government of India (mospi.nic.in).
10. Captive ports are those where a particular company or companies have exclusive use of the facilities.
11. Under India's system of fiscal federalism, tax powers are exclusively assigned to the center or to the states. Prior to 2003, the tax on the sale and purchase of goods ("sales tax") was the main source of revenue for the states. States had complete power over the sales tax and used concessions as the primary tool of investment promotion.
12. In July 2017, India introduced the Good and Services Tax (GST). The GST subsumed several existing indirect taxes, including VAT. This book was already under review when the GST was implemented in 2017. The comparison of Gujarat and Punjab in this section, however, pertains to the time period 1991–2010 that preceded the introduction of the GST.

13. The center initially imposed a 2003 deadline for states to switch to the value-added tax system. However, political wrangling meant that only one state switched in 2003. A subsequent 2005 deadline saw most states switch to the system, with a few exceptions; those states where the opposition BJP was in power did not switch to the new system. By 2006, even these states had relented. Despite these different dates of adoption, the use of sales tax concessions by states effectively ended in 2003.

Chapter 3

1. Jenkins and Manor (2017, 13) also suggest that the Indian state is porous to social justice claims, as evident in the process that led to the enactment of the NREGA act.
2. The debate about the structural power of business goes back to the Marxist debates of the 1970s. Charles Lindblom (1977) and Fred Block (1980, 1987) renewed these ideas, but they again fell into disuse. Jeffrey Winters (2011) is a good example of the structural view. The literature on structural power was prone to static and rigid analysis, with some notable exceptions. A special issue of *Business and Politics* has revived the debate in an excellent set of papers (2015). The notion of structural power stresses the dependence of the state on holders of capital. Also see Fairfield (2015). Also see chapter 2, by Kanta Murali, in this volume.
3. A *developmental state* may be defined as a state that takes an active or proactive role in shaping economic development (Johnson 1982, 1999); this role is *not* merely to structure markets (neoclassical) but to "guide" them (Wade 2003) by creating nascent firms and industries and by "getting prices wrong" (Amsden 1989). A *new developmental state* is one that reduces state regulation in some domains but enhances it in others. It also relies on much greater private sector engagement and cooperation. See, for debates about the new developmental state, Block (2008); Trubek et al. (2013); Riain (2004, 2010); and Shaffer, Nedumpara, and Sinha (2015). For a discussion of whether India can be categorized as crony capitalist, see Mazumdar (2008).
4. Hector Schamis (2002) offered an innovative argument that economic reforms create the need to "re-form" the state. David Vogel (2012), Steven Vogel (1998), Weiss (2005), Shaffer (2014), and Snyder (1999) also demonstrate this idea for diverse contexts. Sinha (2016) and Shaffer, Nedumpara, and Sinha (2015) also argue that global trade rules create a refurbished state. Also see Nayar (2009). Recently, Chandra (2015) gave a slightly different version of the argument, arguing that patronage has been relocated to new parts of the Indian economy.
5. Akhil Gupta (1995) put forward the idea of blurred boundaries to talk about corruption. I use the same idea but modify it to apply to business-state interactions and the boundaries of state agencies.
6. An interesting story of business-politics nexus in cricket may also be worth telling but is beyond the scope of this chapter. See Dubey (2011). Other journalistic accounts of corrupt links are Bandyopadhyay (2015); Bhargava (2013); Anand (2014); Parakh (2014); and Thakurta (2014).
7. I don't delve into India's public sector companies, although they are an important component of the evolving Indian capitalism story. See Elizabeth Chatterjee for an analysis of India's public sector (2017).
8. The following categories were categorized as having business occupations: traders, business owners, oil industry oils, contractors, developers, builders, proprietors, and real estate.
9. This data can be found at myneta.com.
10. MP Track, Rajya Sabha, "Rajeev Chandrashekhar," http://www.prsindia.org/mptrack/rajeevchandrasekhar.
11. Government of India, "Who's Who," profile of R. Chandrashekhar, http://www.archive.india.gov.in/govt/rajyasabhampbiodata.php?mpcode=2010.
12. The names are Vectra, Jupiter Global Infrastructure Pvt. Ltd., Minsk Developers Pvt. Ltd, and Garden City Plantations Pvt. Ltd. See http://myneta.info/rajsab09aff/candidate.php?candidate_id=141&interest=true&year=2011.
13. Advisory Committee, Ministry of Information Technology, 1999–2002; chairman, Infrastructure Task Force, Government of Karnataka, 1999–2003; member, Prime Minister's Council on Trade and Development, April 2006; member, Committee on Information Technology, August 2010 onward; member, Parliamentary Forum on Youth, January

2010 onward; member, Consultative Committee, Ministry of Urban Development; president, Federation of Indian Chambers of Commerce and Industry (FICCI), 2009 onward; cochairman, Vigilance and Monitoring Committee, Bangalore Urban District, August 2009–August 2010; member, Committee on Finance, August 2009 onward; member, Consultative Committee for the Ministry of Finance, August 2012; member, Committee on Finance.

14. See web page of Parimal Nathwani at http://www.parimalnathwani.com/ Also see: http://www.vishwagujarat.com/politics/rajya-sabha-mp-parimal-nathwani-meets-pm-narendra-modi/.

15. Shruti Chaturvedi, "From a Disastrous Entrepreneurial Debut at Selling Soaps to Leading Reliance Industries, Here's the Story of Parimal Nathwani," https://chaaipani.com/parimal-nathwani-reliance/.

16. MP Track, Rajya Sabha, "Profile of Parimal Nathwani," http://www.prsindia.org/mptrack/parimalnathwani.

17. Andrew Wyatt's recent research notes the emergence of what he calls "entrepreneurial politicians" across India (Wyatt 2017).

18. Andrew Wyatt and John Harriss document this for Tamil Nadu. See their chapter in this volume.

19. I present data for about sixty-eight politicians of all parties drawn from Aman Malik's work in Livemint. Andrew Wyatt is collecting data on the same phenomena across many states. Also see Harriss and Wyatt's chapter on Tamil Nadu in this volume.

20. This section draws from Sinha (2016).

21. S. Venkitaramanan, "WTO and Its Implications," *Economic Times*, November 25, 1997, cited in Sinha (2016).

22. PM Manmohan Singh said in 2010: "I am told, in China an industrial establishment is visited by just six inspectors: one each for monitoring of adherence to laws pertaining to taxation, environment, labour, workers' health and working conditions, municipal laws and product quality. I believe in India many of you find your industrial establishments visited by over 30 inspectors. Therefore, the tyranny of over-regulation must end. I will be reconstituting the Prime Minister's Council of Trade and Industry. One of the areas of focus of this Council will be the reduction of the Inspector Raj. Through this forum, I will be seeking your ideas and suggestions to carry this idea far." http://www.pib.nic.in/newsite/erelcontent.aspx?relid=3417.

23. As Mathur (2014) notes: trade unions and NGOs go unrepresented in these new forums.

24. Securities and Exchange Board of India, *Annual Report*, 1992–93.

25. Vijay Mallya is supposed to have paid handsomely to get this Rajya Sabha nomination.

Chapter 4

1. For the remainder of the chapter I use the terms "formal" and "informal" worker, rather than "organized" and "unorganized" worker (which is more commonly used in India). The reason for this is, as I detail here, informal workers can and do organize. As well, informally-employed workers operate (at a growing rate) in formally registered and regulated, so-called "organized" enterprises.

2. These controls determined the areas and location of new investment, the scale of operations, and the technology to be used. The requirement that investments by large industrial houses needed a separate clearance under the Monopolies and Restrictive Trade Practices Act to discourage the concentration of economic power was abolished.

3. Privatization has been especially pronounced in power, telecommunications, road construction, metals, food, and transport. Some examples of privatized companies include Lagan Jute Machinery Company (LJMC), Videsh Sanchar Nigam Limited (VSNL), Hindustan Zinc Limited (HZL), Hotel Corporation Limited of India (HCL), and Bharat Aluminium Company (BALCO). For more on privatization and disinvestment in India, see *Economic Survey of India*, http://indiabudget.nic.in/es2008-09/chapt2009/chap32.pdf.

4. In recent years, there has been a growth in independent unions in India that are not politically affiliated to a party, because there is a growing sense that party affiliation weakens union powers. This argument is supported by early literature (Rudolph and Rudolph 1987). Recent

scholarship, however, has shown that political party affiliation is mutually beneficial for union and party power (Teitelbaum 2011). In my own research, I find support for this latter argument, which does not undermine the important role of independent unions.

5. Note the 2011–12 NSS (sixty-eighth round) was an unusual survey in that it was done just two years after the previous one in 2009–10. Normally the NSS is conducted every five years. The sixty-eighth round was conducted to re-examine the dismal results shown in the 2009–10 survey.

6. Due to space constraints, this chapter will focus only on government actions at the national level. Important variations exist at the state level.

7. Colonial-era labor laws that remain today include the 1926 Trade Union Act to enabled labor to organize and register unions free from harassment; the 1880 Factories Act set minimum conditions of hygiene, safety, and work hours; the 1923 Workman's Compensation Act provided for work-related injuries; the 1936 Payment of Wages Act regulated timely payment and overtime payments; and the 1929 Trade Disputes Act created an institutional framework to settle disputes.

8. For example, the 1948 Factories Act, which replaced the British act, calls for the registration of "factories" and regulates their work conditions to ensure workers adequate safety, sanitation, health, welfare measures, work hours, breaks, paid holidays, and a weekly day off. The 1948 Employees State Insurance (ESI) Act protects workers and their families against the risk of accidents and injury at work, sickness, maternity, and old age. Under ESI, workers receive medical care and cash benefits. Other welfare provisions for workers in certain establishments employing more than twenty workers are the 1952 Employees Provident Fund Act, the Maternity Act, and the 1923 Workmen's Compensation Act, designed for workers in occupations recognized as "hazardous" and not covered under the ESI.

9. For example, reporting requirements are waived for firms with less than twenty employees (ten if using power). The requirement to establish a pension fund is waived for firms with less than twenty employees. Mandatory health insurance under the ESI is waived for firms with less than fifty employees. Requirements for physical amenities such as child care, canteens, medical dispensaries, and even restrooms, increase with a firm's size.

10. The Payment of Wages Act ensures the timely and regular payment of wages.

11. In addition to labor, small-scale enterprises enjoyed other benefits, such as excise concessions, directed credit, exclusive rights to produce over eight hundred goods, and lighter reporting requirements.

12. Although it should also be noted that in addition to being excluded from labor legislations, there were several other incentives to remain small in India, as described in the preceding note.

13. For example, in 2001, contract labour was prohibited in handling of food grains, including loading and unloading, storing, and stacking in the godowns and depots of the Food Corporation of India (FCI).

14. Although this is the most contentious portion of the IDA, the IDA also provides a comprehensive measures to improve industrial relations. It stipulates an elaborate mechanism for the settlement of disputes through conciliation, arbitration, and adjudication and outlines procedures for changing employment conditions. The act introduced the concept of compulsory arbitration and prohibits strikes without notice in public utility services. The act entitles the government to intervene in industrial disputes, although it aims to further voluntary arbitration or collectively negotiated settlements.

15. The VRS began as part of the restructuring of unprofitable public-sector enterprises (assisted by the National Renewal Fund) and soon extended similar programs in the private sector.

16. This survey was conducted from July 1999 to June 2000, based on a sample of randomly selected households. The sample design was a stratified, multistage one, moving from rural villages or urban blocks to households. The 1991 census was used as the sampling frame for the selection of villages, and the latest NSSO lists of blocks were used as the sampling frame for the selection of blocks.

17. The survey spread across 6,208 villages and 4,176 urban blocks, covering 165,244 households and 819,011 persons. The raw data of the survey total 819,013 persons; however, two pairs of observations are duplicates. In the initial analysis below, I have dropped the duplicates of each pair, thereby totaling 819,011 individual observations.

18. Despite the relative advantages of the NSS compared to other national surveys in India, the NSS still suffers from an undercount of India's workers, especially of seasonal and female workers. Some Indian scholars have advocated time-use surveys as an alternative. For a comparison of the recent NSS to a pilot time-use survey, see Hirway (2002).

19. During this period, there are a corresponding decline in the share of regular-formal and casual workers in the public and private sectors. Data drawn from personal communication with Ajit Ghose, ICSSR national fellow and honorary professor, Institute for Human Development, New Delhi, February 2017.

20. Freedom of association and the right to form labor unions are part of the four fundamental standards recognized by the ILO. Convention 87, Freedom of Association and Protection of the Right to Organize Convention, guarantees that workers and employers, without distinction, shall have the right to establish and to join organizations of their own choosing without previous authorization. Convention 98, Right to Organize and Collective Bargaining Convention, protects all workers against acts of antiunion discrimination.

21. Interview reported by the ICLR delegation in their fact-finding report.

22. ICLR convened an international fact-finding delegation to investigate the workers' allegations. This delegation visited India May 25–31, 2013. The detailed report, titled *Merchants of Menace: Repressing workers in India's new industrial belt; Violations of workers' and trade union rights at MSIL,* is available online at http://laborcommission.org/reports. The breakdown of industrial relations at the MSIL plant came on the heels of other similar cases of autoworkers protests in Haryana's industrial belt in 2009. For example, in response to autoworkers' demands for recognition of their independent trade unions at Rico Auto Limited and Sunbeam Auto Limited, employers worked with local police to brutally suppress the workers and call for lockouts at both plants (Pratap 2011).

23. Several interviews conducted by author in 2014 including officials in state Labor Department and management in Honda and in Maruti Suzuki.

24. Infrastructure accounted for 49 percent of the market, housing and real estate 42 percent, and industrial projects 9 percent.

25. For example, construction workers are now eligible for the ESI to cover healthcare for the worker and family. The construction board also covers the workers' healthcare (although not his or her family's). When trying to defend their slow dispersal of benefits, government officials repeatedly noted this provision has increased procedures to confirm that beneficiaries are not "double dipping." Employers' associations are also starting to complain (for the first time) about the tax they pay into the welfare board as a duplicate tax.

26. Although it is worth noting that the unemployment that does exist is also gendered. Among the young and educated, unemployment was found to be much higher among women than men.

27. These include the Minimum Wages Act 1948, the Maternity Benefit Act 1961, Workmen's Compensation Act 1923, Inter State Migrant Workers Act 1979, Payment of Wages Act 1936, Equal Remuneration Act 1976, Employee's State Insurance Act 1948, Employees Provident Fund Act 1952, and the Payment of Gratuity Act 1972.

28. After a one-day solidarity strike in 1959 among domestic workers, two private member bills were introduced in parliament. The first was the Domestic Workers (Conditions of Service) Bill introduced in the upper house (Rajya Sabha) by P. N. Rajabhoja, and the second was the All India Domestic Servants Bill. Both bills included clauses for minimum wages, maximum hours of work, a weekly day of rest, fifteen days paid annual leave, casual leave, and maintenance of a register of domestic workers by the local police (Neetha and Palriwala 2011). Both bills were stalled during the parliamentary sessions, so they could lapse. In 1972 and in 1977, another private member bill was submitted to the lower house (Lok Sabha), called the Domestic Workers (Conditions of Service) Bill. This bill aimed to bring domestic workers under the purview of the Industrial Disputes Act. Both times, this too was allowed to lapse (Neetha and Palriwala 2011). In 1974, the Committee on the Status of Women in India noted the need to regulate the conditions of domestic workers, but this too was ignored by the government of India. During the 1980s, further attempts were made to legislate the working conditions of domestic workers, but all attempts failed to materialize into new laws. The 1988 National Commission on Self Employed Women

and Women in the Informal Sector recommended (to no avail) "a system of registration of domestic workers, a minimum wage, a legislation to regulate conditions of employment, social security and security of employment." Similarly, the 1989 House Workers (Conditions of Service) Bill, which proposed that every employer contribute to a House Workers' Welfare Fund, was ignored (Neetha and Palriwala 2011, 98–99). In 2007, the National Commission for Women drafted the Regulation of Employment Agencies Act. In 2008, the National Campaign Committee for Unorganised Workers and Nirmala Niketan drafted the Domestic Workers (Regulation of Employment, Conditions of Work, Social Security and Welfare) Bill. In 2009, Arjun Ram Meghwal introduced a private member bill, the Domestic Workers (Conditions of Service) Bill in parliament. IN 2010, the Domestic Workers Rights Campaign was launched.

29. For example: seven states have included domestic work in their minimum wages notifications; some states have recognized domestic work in the Rashtriya Swasthya Bima Yojana (RSBY), a health insurance scheme for those below the poverty line; and Delhi has passed the Delhi Private Placement Agencies (Regulation) Bill (2012), which requires compulsory registration of all placement agencies of domestic workers and at least one kin of the domestic worker.

Chapter 5

1. For highlighting this dynamic and suggesting this terminology, I am grateful to Vinay Sitapati, a participant in the workshop where the chapters for this volume were discussed, May 6, 2016, Princeton University.

2. Rajan later adapted this terminology to highlight the emergence of the "appellate raj," built around sector-specific dispute-settlement bodies ("RBI Governor" 2015).

3. The cases covered not only major industrial installations, but many kinds of civil engineering works as well ("HC Quashes Land Acquisition" 2016).

4. The relevant provision in LARRA is section 24(2). It was a sign of the state's complicated relationship with business that the central government, which under Modi is seeking to dismantle LARRA, is nevertheless arguing for the act's constitutionality in one of the country's most high-profile cases ("Centre Opposes Reliance Plea" 2016). For details on this and related cases, see "Why All Eyes Are on Reliance's Land Acquisition Case" 2016; "Two Acquisitions That Lapsed" 2016; "Gujarat: After RIL" 2016.

5. These views were shared on a not-for-attribution basis at a policy consultation hosted by the US-India Business Council, March 6, 2013, New York.

6. Vocal opponents included NAPM leader Medha Patkar. See "Repeal the Land Acquisition Act" 2011).

7. The debate over rights-based approaches are reflected in two competing assessments. A highly critical account is Bhagwati and Panagariya (2013). Far more sympathetic is Dreze and Sen (2013).

8. This included both the Swadeshi Jagran Manch, a group that called preserving India's "economic sovereignty," and the Bharatiya Kisan Sangh, the Sangh Parivar's official farmers' association ("RSS Affiliates" 2015).

9. States such as Kerala, ruled by a Congress-led coalition, focused on the part of LARRA that Kerala's business associations most complained about—the "cumbersome" SIA process ("State Moots Radical Changes" 2014).

10. Personal communication, retired IAS officer (Rajasthan cadre), December 12, 2015.

11. Personal communication with a Jaipur-based reporter for a national English-language daily, January 20, 2016.

12. Personal communication, retired IAS officer (Rajasthan cadre), December 12, 2015.

13. The Rajasthan material was presented at the New York University South Asia seminar series, February 2017. Many of the underlying ideas can be found in Levien (2015).

14. Rajasthan's rules on disposal compared favorably (from a business perspective) with the Maharashtra Land Revenue (Disposal of Government Lands) Rules, 1971. Maharashtra businesses were pressing for minor but crucial modifications to the way in which Maharashtra's rules were interpreted. Interview, business executive, November 19, 2014, Mumbai.

15. Interview with a senior journalist for a leading Marathi newspaper, November 18, 2014, Mumbai.
16. Accusations of purposeful evasion have been made against the Kerala government (e.g., "Pachalam ROB" 2016).
17. The instruction for the creation of a panel was NITI Aayog, Govt. of India, vide order No. Q11022/12/2015-Agri, dated September 7, 2015.
18. Business associations have sought to shape the process and standards to be used in carrying out SIAs ("India Inc Petitions Govt" 2015).

Chapter 6

1. Dobbs and Sankhe (2010) estimate India spent US$17 per capita on urban infrastructure, while China spent US$116.
2. For a review of the literature see Mossberger and Stoker (2001). The classic case study of a business-dominated regime is Stone's study of Atlanta (1989).
3. Hashim (2013) found that the urban consumption Gini rose from 0.27 in 1977–78 to 0.38 in 2009–10. In urban areas, the ratio of the top decile to the bottom decile rose from 8.4 to 10.1 over 2004–5 to 2009–10.
4. The ghetto stands as the obvious exception, but even race has not been an insurmountable barrier to inclusion. In the classic case that launched the "urban regime literature," Stone (1989) documents how an emergent black middle class was incorporated into city-level political settlement with downtown business interests so that "race would not get in the way of doing business."
5. Exceptions might be the two largest cities of Kerala—Thiruvananthapuram and Kochi—where the slum population is less than 1 percent and where water, sanitation, and transport services have excellent coverage. This high level of inclusion reflects that social-democratic history and profile of the state.
6. The relocation of industries in Delhi was subsequent to a court order, and recently in 2014 the parliament has legislated a Street Vendors (Protection of Livelihood and Regulation of Street Vending) Act, but the rules for this are yet to be notified.
7. In 2006 the courts ordered the enforcement of zoning rules in the Delhi Master Plan under which a large proportion of "formal" trading shops were illegal, with courts ordering them to be sealed. The traders responded with a vigorous agitation that eventually led to politically led changes in the zoning rules and the introduction of mixed-use zones in Delhi. Such changes in rules have been relatively few for less powerful constituencies than the traders.
8. This coordination role for the larger economy is not limited to the private sector with both cities accounting for 12 percent of national "government related services."
9. Manufacturing in NSS 2009–10 represented 29 percent of workers (12 percent in apparel), compared to 19 percent in modern services.
10. In New York it takes 47 years of average income to buy a 1,300-square-foot apartment. In Mumbai it takes 580 years.
11. The core in Mumbai is defined as the area of Greater Mumbai that is most of the peninsula and excludes the new developments across the bay Navi Mumbai and to the north (Thane), and in Delhi as the National Capital Territory, which is the city minus its new satellite cities (Faridabad, Gurgaon, etc.). These are highly populated areas, respectively 11.9 and 12.9 million.
12. The major exception to the absence of city-based political movements is the Shiv Sena, which is a major player in Mumbai. However, as this is an essentially nativist Maratha (and Hind) movement, it has not supported a programmatic approach to city development in Mumbai. In the 2014 elections to the Delhi State Legislature, a new political formation, the Aam Aadmi Party (common-man party) won a dramatic victory, securing sixty-seven of seventy seats. However, despite the Delhi base, the AAP is not really a city-based party, but rather the political expression of a national anticorruption movement that took root in the city-state. Its early behavior in power indicates it embodies an ambiguous mix of progovernance response to the rent-extracting system and an old-style populist and leader-focused party.
13. Officially, "planned colonies" and "regularized unauthorized colonies" represent 36 percent of Delhi (Delhi Development Report 2008).

14. See the plaint in *Relief Road Housing Societies v. State of Maharashtra* 2002 (1) BomCR 15, https://indiankanoon.org/doc/418767/. Similar sentiments are also seen in the media discussion around demolitions in Golibar in Mumbai and Ejipura in Bangalore, for example, http://www.dnaindia.com/analysis/column-middle-class-s-tailor-made-morals-can-collapse-against-bulldozers-1918837.

15. A possible historical exception is the Mumbai working class that had some organized clout in the 1960s but has since largely disappeared. It is otherwise difficult to identify any subordinate actor that has a citywide presence in any Indian city.

16. The National Housing Bank Residex records that in the most expensive parts of Bangalore (Zone C), the prices rose by 2.6 times over 2007 to 2012, a compound rate of 20 percent per annum, but less elsewhere. See http://www.nhb.org.in/Residex/BANGALOREres.php.

17. Goldman (2011 573) cites Infosys annual reports as listing a range of land bank investments. Similarly, the scandal in the Hyderabad-based Satyam, once the fourth-largest IT firm in India, revealed that its chairman had set up 275 real estate holding companies in the names of family members.

18. Joint Legislature Committee on Encroachment of Lands in Bangalore Urban District, 2006, cited in Goldman (2011, 571).

19. See also a companion paper by Chattaraj and Walton (2016).

20. See, for example, http://news.bbc.co.uk/2/hi/business/7676337.stm.

21. Since inception in 1996, the Mumbai Slum Rehabilitation Authority allotted 1,524 redevelopment projects, of which only 197 are complete. As many as 1,100 projects are being developed and 1.53 lakh families rehabilitated, while around 217 projects have stalled. http://www.mumbaimirror.com/mumbai/others/17-years-on-govt-realises-SRA-has-failed-Mumbai/articleshow/22271732.cms. http://www.sra.gov.in/Data/English%20ppt%20%2001.04.13%20short_files/frame.htm.

22. See http://dipp.nic.in/English/Publications/FDI_Statistics/2015/india_FDI_June2015.pdf. Maharashtra accounted for 29 percent; i.e., together these two urban centers accounted for half of all FDI. However, this can be more due to location of head offices than actual economic activity in the region.

23. Calculated from the NSS employment unemployment numbers for 1999–2000 to 2009–10.

24. Interview with DDA transport official.

Chapter 7

1. This a revised version of a paper presented at the conference "Business and Politics" at Princeton University, May 5 and 6, 2016. This chapter has benefited from comments made at the conference, by others including Aniket Alam, Krishna Ananth, Sashi Kumar, Sevanti Ninan, Y. V Reddy, Kalpana Sharma, and Padmaja Shaw, and also by two anonymous reviewers. I am grateful to all of them. The usual disclaimers apply.

2. There is a great deal of controversy about the circulation and readership numbers of newspapers in India. Different agencies collect different sets of numbers. The RNI expects publications to submit audited circulation numbers. Nonsubmission does take place and a monitoring of the audited numbers is not done regularly. Two private bodies (made up of publishers and advertisers)—the Media Research Users' Council and the Audit Bureau of Circulation (ABC) collect information on readership and circulation, respectively. The circulation numbers of the ABC are of a smaller universe than that of the RNI. The two sets of numbers have been hotly debated. The differences and disputes over circulation and readership are linked to advertising, a topic of discussion later in the paper. However, whatever the differences about the specific numbers of individual publications, the trend in aggregate circulation and readership has been moving in only one direction: up. For a discussion of the RNI and ABC see Jeffrey (2010b, 151–54).

3. All the statistics on circulation presented here are from Ministry of Information and Broadcasting, *Press in India (2016–17)*.

4. For a discussion of demonetization and its initial impact see chapter 1 in Reddy (2017).

5. The Indian Readership Survey 2017, released in early 2018, reported that readership of dailies had increased from 295 million in 2014 to 407 million in 2017, a growth of 39 percent. See Media Research Users Council (2018).

6. The same issues of reliability dog the TV viewership numbers and are at times more heated than those in print. TV channels frequently clash over viewership as measured by the "Television Audience Measurement," or TAM, yardstick; again this has to do with estimating the size of the market for attracting advertising.

7. TheHoot.org watchdog calls this "a conservative compilation" based on a monitoring of only English newspapers.

8. However, at some point digital access may soon pose a threat to print, what with a growing preference of Indians to access the internet via smartphones, thus circumventing the obstacle posed by the current low level of narrow or broadband subscriptions.

9. Jeffrey (2010a, 176) cites one estimate that by 1990, the share of English publications in advertising had fallen below 50 percent.

10. Total advertising spending in all media (including on radio, cinema, outdoor, and the internet) is placed at Rs. 16.9 billion in 1991 and growing to Rs. 330.4 billion in 2012. As with other numbers, these estimates, based on market research and industry group data, conflict with others. Jeffrey (2015, 34) has a very different set of figures, with advertising rising even more sharply from Rs. 9.3 billion in 1990–91 to Rs. 280.3 billion in 2012. These estimates are also based on market research and advertising agency sources.

11. In the 2010s, there has been a modest attempt to reversing the strategy of using the cover price to expand market share.

12. The KPMG-India report (2017, 121) placed the total print market at Rs. 303 billion in 2016, of which circulation income brought in only Rs. 102 billion.

13. News Laundry (2014) has painstakingly put together a very detailed presentation of the ownership structures and linkages in a select group of media houses.

14. See also Guha Thakurta (2013); and Kaushik (2015) for details of the Reliance group's financial arrangements with other media ventures.

15. There are yet to be systematic studies of the level of concentration in the Indian media, either in print or broadcast. Mehta (2015) argues that concentration in TV is less in India than in some of the major TV markets. His research also outlines the levels of concentration in different markets in India, but how this has been estimated and on the basis of what data is not clear.

16. There has been a great deal of discussion on this subject of cross-media holdings. See Telecom Regulatory Authority of India (2009 and 2013) for a consultation paper and report on the issue, and Muralidharan (2007 and 2014) for a discussion of the issues, the response of the press, and how the proposals were killed.

17. In the Indian-language media nothing can perhaps rival the spread and influence of the Sun TV group, even if the hold has waned a bit in recent years. The group traces its presence in the media to the 1960s, when the scion, Murosali Maran, was part of the then opposition Dravida Munnetra Kazhagam Party and editing a daily newspaper of the party. His sons, even as they have retained their political links to the DMK, entered the media business in the mid-1990s. Sun TV now holds the licenses for at least thirteen TV channels in all the four south Indian languages, two radio licenses and one cable distribution company in Tamil Nadu and publishes two newspapers. The apogee of its influence was during 2004–9, when a member of the family controlling the Sun Group, Dayanadhi Maran, was also the union minister for telecommunications—a direct conflict of interest with the family's business interests. It was also the first TV group to embark on the process of vertical integration when it began taking control of the cable TV distribution channel in Tamil Nadu in the middle to late 1990s. Its political influence, however, weakened with family feuds within the DMK (Parthasarathy 2013).

18. There is not only diversification into and across the media. At least some of the more financially successful media companies have used surpluses from their media businesses to enter other sectors. The most well-known is BCCL, which first established a bank, the Times Bank, in the mid-1990s; it merged with a larger bank in 1999. In 2016 the Times Group established a university of its own, Bennett University in Uttar Pradesh (see http://www.bennett.edu.in/overview).

19. See the section "Media Business" of TheHoot.org (2018b) for many detailed analyses during 2016 and 2017 of the financials of media companies. For an earlier picture see *Business Standard* (2016).

20. In the newspapers in the group, the dependence on advertising was much higher (see Auletta 2012, cited earlier).

21. The rest came from nonmedia businesses and investment income. See The Hoot's Analyst at Large (2017).

22. Over half of India's licensed news channels beam news, and in the aggregate they attract 7 percent of viewership, but 20 percent of total advertising (Mehta (2015, 27, based on a 2014 KPMG report).

23. The study has a lot of interesting information, but the problem is that all the interesting and new information is based on anonymous sources. So like much of data in the Indian media sector, this too needs to be validated.

24. As many as three dozen news channels were launched in the Indian-language media in the five months before the 2014 Lok Sabha elections. For a roll call of small and major political personalities who launched TV channels at the time, see news report by Shukla (2014).

25. The internet is potentially a disruptive influence that could counter the tendencies in traditional (print and TV) media. Indeed, a number of new digital publications such as The Wire, Scroll.in, and First Post with their immediate analysis threaten to disturb the monopoly of print and TV over news. However, the tendency among some of these digital publications (First Post, for example) to offer only opinion and that, too, of an extreme kind could make them guilty of the same practices as traditional media. (Disclosure: The author is currently readers' editor of Scroll.in.)

26. A well-known example in the national media was of the changes in the TV18 stable when the Reliance Industries took full control of the group. A number of senior journalists immediately left the TV channels they were working for.

27. See Pattnaik (2014) for the study of newspapers and TV channels in Odisha, where this phenomenon is analyzed in detail. Owners using their media outlets to push their business interests becomes common in the years after the mid-1990s when the economy was booming and there was much to capitalize on.

28. "Largely, there is a consensus among scholars that the media shapes the public's political knowledge, attitudes and behaviour" (Besley and Burgess 2002, Hamilton 2003, cited in Verma and Sardesai 2014, 86).

29. "At least three aspects of mediatization would be visible this time around: simplification and personalization of the contest; agenda setting by the media and political actors adapting themselves to the 'media logic'" (Palshikar 2014). Palshikar was using the framework of Stromback (2008).

30. For a brief overview of the many comments made on the media and Elections 2014 see Verma & Sardesai (2014).

31. See the editorial published in the week of the election, "Fourth Estate That Vanished," in *Economic and Political Weekly* (2014) where the journal commented, "[Modi] was cast not just as a challenger of the Congress and its corrupt rule, but as the messiah of a new order. Much of this was, of course, as the Modi spin doctors would have wanted. The media seemed to swallow the spin, hook, line and sinker."

32. The title of Ninan's 2011 lecture is "Indian Media's Dickensian Age."

33. In a significant attempt to counter the change in the practice of journalism, a number of philanthropists joined hands in 2015 to establish to establish the Independent and Public-Spirited Media Foundation to promote independent, public spirited, and socially impactful journalism. The foundation, established with a substantial corpus, is to fund and promote "excellence in journalism."

34. The Press Council of India, a statutory body dealing only with print, has no powers of enforcement. And TV broadcasters have the News Broadcasting Standards Authority and the Broadcast Content Complaints Council, self-regulatory bodies, which in their years of operation have exhibited no more than token after-the-event reprimands.

35. In its editorial "Anger, Aspiration and Apprehension" on the outcome of the 2014 Lok Sabha elections, the *Economic and Political Weekly* wrote: "If there is a message from Elections 2014

it is that India has been changing. It is becoming a society where those with a voice are becoming less tolerant, less compassionate and more aggressive to those without a voice."

Chapter 8

1. Besides industrialists, the business community comprised many small-scale enterprises, reflecting the strength of the urban economy, a development fostered by the shift of the Patidars
from villages to towns. See Rutten (1995), Dupont (1995) and Pathak (1982, 441–75). See
also Bondre (2013).
2. In 1991, Gujarat was clearly in a position to benefit fully from the new liberalization policy. It
then displayed a much more dynamic economy than most other states of the Indian Union.
Indeed, in the 1990s, it was ahead of other dynamic states like Maharashtra, Andhra Pradesh,
and Tamil Nadu by a margin of one to two percentage points in terms of annual growth rate.
3. Sanjay Gupta, the CEO of the Adani Group, uses the same words in an interview of 2003: The
industry-friendly, hassle-free, single-door clearance policy of the government has ensured
that the investment flow continues in the state. See "Industrial Policy to Usher Investment in
Gujarat" (2003, 11).
4. As Nikita Sud (2012, 63) herself says. The manner in which Gujarat's government related to
the corporate sector was illustrated by the way it retained control over the merging and acquisition of enterprises. For instance, when British Gas put up one of its subsidiaries, Gujarat
Gas, for sale, "Not only were Adani Gas and Torrent Power, two private companies interested
in the purchase . . . advised to keep away, but in the end the state company, GSPC, took over
Gujarat Gas at a cost of Rs. 2,694 crore: a heavy discount from the market price of Rs. 4,000
crore" (Nag 2013, 16).
5. Behavioural Science Centre (2012, 65). A Gujarati version of the text of the agreement is
available as appendix 7 of the document (100–101). When it leaked, Modi ordered an inquiry ("Did Modi Offer" 2008, 15). In December 2011, when he was about to retire, Ratan
Tata came to Gandhinagar in order to introduce his successor, Cyrus P. Mistry, to him ("Ratan
Tata Takes Mistry" 2011).
6. The unanswered CAG queries across departments, if quantified, pertain to suspected
regularities to the tune of Rs. 9,000 crore (Dave 2012, 1).
7. *Indian Express*, Ahmedabad edition, November 27, 2007.
8. Rathin Das (2013, 1). The day before, Mukesh Ambani had hailed in Narendra Modi a leader
with a grand vision ("India Inc" 2013). For more details, see "Vibrant Gujarat" (2013, 10).
9. Mukherjee (2011) and Statement on RBI's regional offices' year-wise (with state covered)
received FDI inflows from January 2000 to September 2012. http://dipp.nic.in/English/
Publications/SIA_Newsletter/2012/dec2012/index.htm.
10. See "Expansion Makes Jamnagar the World's Largest Oil-Refining Hub" (http://www.
bechtel.com/projects/jamnagar-oil-refinery/); "Reliance Industries Plans Major Expansion
at World's Largest Oil Refinery Complex," *Economic Times*, September 21, 2017, (https://
economictimes.indiatimes.com/industry/energy/oil-gas/reliance-industries-plans-major-
expansion-at-worlds-largest-oil-refinery-complex/articleshow/60764962.cms).
11. https://www.essaroil.co.in/about-us/operations/refining.aspx.
12. "Hazira: Steel Complex," http://www.essarsteel.com/section_level2.aspx?cont_id=FENytf
1sB94=&path=Operations_%3E_India_%3E_Hazira:_Steel_complex.
13. Planning Commission. Available at http://planningcommission.nic.in/data/datatable/
data_2110/table_57.pdf.
14. For more detail, see Parekh (2014, 198).
15. The Reliance refinery of Jamnagar, the largest in the world, has only 2,500 employees, for
instance.
16. For more detail, see Parekh (2014, 195 and 211).
17. One could read in the document presenting the 2009 industrial policy of Gujarat: "Though
the state has been witnessing very high levels of industrial activity, employment generation activities have not kept pace with the same" (Government of Gujarat 2009b, 10).
But the remedy proposed—"mega projects"—was a reflection of the "more of the same"
syndrome.

18. The state government officially recognized that there were "6.12 lakh educated-unemployed persons" in the state (Nair 2017). Among them, the engineers were well represented, according to the All India Council for Technical Education (Dave 2017).

19. For more detail and an analysis of the impact of the job problem on the Patel movement, see Jaffrelot (2016).

20. In 2009, the debt of Gujarat was only of Rs. 103,674 cr. against 188,197 for UP, 176,730 for Maharashtra, 146,563 for West Bengal, and 126,996 for Andhra (Shah 2009).

21. Archana Dholakia and Ravindra Dholakia, who attribute this policy to the economic "philosophy" of the Modi government, point out that it "led to a sharp decline in the total government expenditure to GDSP ratio from 17% to around 3%, one of the lowest in the country" (2015, 284).

22. Reserve Bank of India, "State Finances: A Study of Budgets," (http://rbidocs.rbi.org.in/rdocs/Publications/PDFs/41S_SF090113F.pdf), 173. Available at http://www.rbi.org.in/scripts/PublicationsView.aspx?id=14834.

23. Reserve Bank of India, "State Finances: A Study of Budgets."

24. In spite of this, the literacy rate increased significantly between 2001 and 2011. This achievement may be due to the fact that the educational system has become more effective, irrespective of the financial means at its disposal. But it may also result from growing number of families sending their children to private schools, which represent more than 18 percent of total primary education in Gujarat (National University of Educational Planning and Administration 2013, 2). This is especially true in urban areas. In rural Gujarat, the proportion of children from six to fourteen years old going to private schools is limited (11.8 percent), *Annual Status of Education Report (Rural) 2012*, 55. See http://img.asercentre.org/docs/Publications/ASER%20Reports/ASER_2012/fullaser2012report.pdf.

25. Reserve Bank of India, "State Finances: A Study of Budgets. See http://www.rbi.org.in/scripts/PublicationsView.aspx?id=14835.

26. D. Mavalankar and J. Satia, "Medical Scenario in Gujarat," http://ficci.in/events/20425/ISP/vibrant_gujarat_PwC.pdf, 6.

27. This goes well with the fact that, while Gujarat has the second largest number of Indian criminals on the list of Interpol (after Delhi—sixty-eight against seventy-three), a majority of them are involved in white-collar crime, including the creation of bogus companies. See John (2012).

28. Between September 2013 and May 2014, the wealth of Gautam Adani increased by Rs. 50,131 because of the market capitalization of his companies (it increased by Rs. 1,800 every day during the week that followed Modi's electoral success). Mukesh Ambani's wealth increased of "only" Rs. 30,503 during the same period ("Fortunes of Indian Promoters" 2014). Graphs published by *Business Today* help to visualize this surge that was mostly due to two major components of the Adani group: Adani Enterprises and Adani Ports and Economic Zone. By contrast, Adani Power followed an inverted-U curve in 2013–14 (Joseph 2015b, 48).

29. If Modi was relatively isolated in 2002–3, Gautam Adani was not part of the business establishment either, as evident from his marginal position in terms interlocking directorates (Naudet forthcoming).

30. In 2015, Sanjay Gupta was sent to judicial custody because of accusations of corruption ("Fall of Sanjay Gupta" 2015).

31. "Gujarat State Fertilizer & Chemicals (GSFC: Natl India)," (https://www.bloomberg.com/research/stocks/people/person.asp?personId=46242304&privcapId=874811).

32. For an account of the political protection Ambani enjoyed during the Indira Gandhi's years, see McDonald (2010).

33. This is obvious from the graph published in Naudet and Dubost (2016).

Chapter 9

1. These are all quotes from interviews with businessmen in Chennai, described in note 6. Interestingly, the substance of the first quote is also reported by Aseema Sinha from interviews she conducted in 1997. See Sinha (2005, 218).

2. For instance, Dreze and Khera (2015) have constructed a child development index, and according to this, Tamil Nadu was second only to Kerala in 2005–6, and slightly bested by

Himachal Pradesh, behind Kerala, in 2013–14. In both years Kerala and Tamil Nadu, with Himachal in 2013–14, were well ahead of all other states on this measure, while the index for Gujarat, in both years, is below the all-India average.

3. See Kalaiyarasan (2014). The Raghuram Rajan Committee Report 2013, which produced an underdevelopment index for India's states, placed Gujarat among the "less developed states," while Tamil Nadu ranked behind Kerala alone, among the top-ranking major states classified as "relatively developed."

4. For a fine account of how competition between the DMK and AIADMK has driven the delivery of programs benefiting informal workers, see Agarwala, chapter 4 in this volume. On the combination of policies, see Wyatt (2013).

5. John Harriss interviewed, late in 2015, in Chennai, seven senior businessmen (two of them CEOs of the Indian subsidiaries of major international companies; two managing directors and CEOs of major Indian companies; and three of them MDs and CEOs of Chennai-based majors); four business journalists; two former IAS officers, both still active in business and consultancy; two economic consultants; and two academics. He also had a meeting with nine members of the Chennai chapter of FICCI, among them the president of the Tamil Chamber of Commerce, and the secretary general of the Madras Chamber of Commerce. We have not usually attributed comments that are included in the chapter to any particular individual, in order to preserve the anonymity of interviewees—most of whom were remarkably open. The interviews were few in number, clearly, and were not based on a systematic sampling procedure. Most of those with whom Harriss spoke come from the forward castes, Brahmans and Chettiars. It is possible that different views would have been expressed by people from important corporate business groups elsewhere in the state, notably among Kamma Naidus and Gounders in western Tamil Nadu (Coimbatore and Tiruppur)—though from our own earlier research in that region, we strongly suspect not.

6. The MD of a very successful auto components company argued that the industrial culture of Tamil Nadu produces disciplined workers. "If German workers are rated 90," he said, "then Indian workers in general might be rated 30, but those of Tamil Nadu at 45."

7. The state has a comparatively good road network and had an international airport before the other major cities of the south. It also has high-bandwidth connectivity. The state is "blessed"—the word used by a businessman in the software industry—because the undersea cable from Singapore arrives in Chennai.

8. One of Harriss's interviewees wanted to distinguish very clearly between "enterprising" and "business" communities. None of the communities he listed, apart from the Nattukottai Chettiars, is what would usually be described as a "business community." See Damodaran (2008).

9. Srinivasan, interview in October 2015.

10. Reports published after J. Jayalalithaa's death on December 5, 2016, testified to her autocratic style. See, for example, Radhakrishnan (2016).

11. Another case in point is the backing that MGR gave to senior officials to bring about the effective implementation of the noon meals scheme when it was introduced in the 1980s, according to another former IAS officer who worked with MGR on the scheme; while research on the implementation of NREGA and other welfare schemes in Tamil Nadu draws attention to the importance of backing for the implementation of the scheme from the chief minister's office. See Jeyaranjan (2011).

12. Maran was elected to the Lok Sabha in 1996, when the DMK won most seats in Tamil Nadu in the general elections of that year and went on to become part of the United Front government at the center. Maran was minister for industry in the UF government and took the same portfolio (with the addition of commerce) when the DMK joined in the National Democratic Alliance government in 1999, until late 2002, shortly before his death.

13. In 2015, of the seventeen Tamil Nadu–based private companies in the *Economic Times'* top five hundred companies, seven belong to Brahmans (five of them in the TVS group), and three to Chettiars (two of them in the Murugappa group).

14. Myron Weiner's account of politics in early 1960s Madurai also hints at a rupture between business and state politicians in 1967. In contrast to the interviews reported here, Weiner says

that a number of large businesses in Madurai had well-developed connections with state-level Congress leaders (Weiner 1967, 414–16).

15. This is in line, of course, with Washbrook's argument about the Bonapartist character of the Tamil state, introduced earlier.

16. M. Vijayabaskar (2010, 39) has reported, too, that "there is a consensus among senior bureaucrats that the DMK has pursued this path [that of attracting private investment] more systematically than the AIADMK has by making appropriate institutional interventions."

17. *LiveMint* reported that the state government had offered four hundred acres to Kia, August 16, 2016.

18. Dutta argued the Tamil public paid a high price for the Nokia investment. The same author has reported on the price paid by labor with the closure of the plant in 2014 (2016).

19. SIPCOT has also established a number of IT parks, in addition to the TIDEL project, including the large Siruseri IT Park twenty miles south of Chennai. Many of the SEZ projects backed by the state government also attempted to promote further IT growth. See Kennedy (2014, 59).

20. The state exchequer may support business by other routes. Jaffrelot's chapter in this volume details how large companies with political connections in Gujarat have benefited from the sale of land at below-market rates and the nonpayment of taxes. In Tamil Nadu, loss to the exchequer has been tolerated in the minerals and alcohol sectors and as we detail below, the beneficiaries have been medium-sized companies and local entrepreneurs. The annual revenue reports of the CAG for Tamil Nadu since 2005 do not single out large companies as debtors of the government of Tamil Nadu. There are certainly problems with collecting tax, but the pattern is one of evasion of tax by small and medium-sized business. Similarly, irregularities in the control of public land tend to involve private individuals, private colleges, or other public sector bodies. Other earlier cases of some publicly owned land being passed to politically connected businesses occurred in the late 1980s. Again, these were not large corporates.

21. The associations claim influence, but it is likely that the views of one or two key officials were decisive.

22. The speed with which the Tata Nano plant was brought to Gujarat was made possible by such discretion (see Jaffrelot's chapter in this volume).

23. A scale of incentives, more generous toward larger projects, is set out in the Tamil Nadu Industrial Policy of 2014 with the caveat that further concessions can be offered to "deserving cases" (p. 23).

24. This was suggested by a leading business journalist but disputed by others with whom Harriss spoke, who reasoned that the decisions of transnational companies, such as their own, were explained by logistical factors—the "pull" of other locations in India, close to important markets, rather than by a "push" due to particular difficulties in Tamil Nadu.

25. Aside from the tax issue, there were reports that local politicians and contractors demanded favors from Nokia, which were rebuffed ("Death of Dream" 2014).

26. "World Bank Survey: India's Top 10 States on Ease of Doing Business Ranking," at www.economictimes.indiatimes.com.

27. Aseema Sinha reported a similar observation (2005, 229).

28. The case of the ET 500–listed Southern Petrochemical Industries Limited illustrates the risks of getting too close to one political party. The company, originally a joint venture between the industrialist M. A. Chidambaram and the government of Tamil Nadu, had public contracts to supply subsidised fertilizers. When the DMK returned to office in 1989, the joint venture was disrupted and a criminal investigation was launched against Chidambaram's son, A. C. Muthiah ("Industrialist A C Muthiah Relieved" 1991). The company was bought out of the joint venture when the AIADMK was in power, but "it was hurt adversely" after the DMK returned to office in 1996 ("Ashwin Muthiah" 2015). The experience of Sun TV also bears this out. The group, with its satellite television channels, is seen to be close to the leadership of the DMK, and when control of government passed to the AIADMK in 2011, pressure was put on its owners (Thakurtha 2015).

29. The text that follows draws very extensively on as yet unpublished research, focused on the DMK, by Andrew Wyatt (Wyatt 2015a, 2015b, 2015c).

30. This group of 150 politicians was defined as the holders of first- and second-rank posts in the party organization, members of parliament, and those selected as candidates in the 2011 election (Manikandan and Wyatt 2014, 34).

31. On liquor and revenues, see the following: Srinivasan (2015); "Tamil Nadu's "Corrupt" Cash Cow" (2015). On quarrying, see the following: "Sand Mining System" (2013); Rajasekharan (2015).

32. He is referring here to what he calls, after Marx—hence "classically"—"a form of Bonapartist or Caesarian democracy."

33. Feelings stirred through the appeal to the idea of the "Tamilian," the common man.

34. Work by Harriss (2003b) on the "industrial leaders of Madras," conducted almost forty years after Milton Singer's seminal 1964 work, showed the continuity in the ownership of the top corporations based in Tamil Nadu. See also Fuller and Narasimhan (2013, 96–98).

35. A number of politicians from wealthy Chettiar families have been active in politics, but mostly prior to 1967 or in national parties such as Congress since then. The Gounders with larger enterprises have tended to stay away from party politics. An exception to this was the trio of businessmen who formed a political party in 2009, the Kongu Nadu Munnetra Kazhagam, to defend Gounder interests (Vijayabaskar and Wyatt 2013). As the Gounders are a large and geographically concentrated caste group, the larger political parties make an effort to incorporate them. In the 2016 assembly election, the AIADMK selected twenty-eight Gounders among its 225 MLA candidates and the DMK 17 out of 172 candidates (C. Manikandan, personal communication, July 1, 2016).

36. On the orientation of the Dravidian movement, the anthropologist Nate Roberts has questioned whether the Dravidian movement was ever truly "radical" (personal communication with John Harriss, April 29, 2015). It eschewed communist leaders, and Dravidianists, including Periyar, never looked closely at the political-economic basis of caste. To have done so would have undermined their own leaders, and funders, who came from landed and merchant backgrounds. There is a sense in which the Brahman/non-Brahman distinction functions as an ideological dodge, diverting attention away from class contradictions and from the combined social and class antagonism between Dalits and all the others.

37. See the preceding note.

38. Prerna Singh's argument that it is "cohesive subnational solidarity" that has generated relatively high levels of social development in Tamil Nadu provides a complementary understanding (2015).

39. This contempt was frequently expressed in interviews with business leaders.

Chapter 10

1. The 2011 census gives the percentage of cultivators and agricultural laborers respectively among main workers as 23.4 percent and 38.4 percent. While the former figure decreased slightly from the previous decadal census figures, the latter increased. Census figures are cited in Government of Odisha, *Economic Survey 2015–16*, 8.

2. Not alone among interviewees to express this view, but perhaps the most noteworthy, was current MP and editor of Odiya and English dailies *Dharitri* and *Orissa Post* Tatagatha Satpathy. Satpathy is also the son of a former chief minister, Nandini Satpathy, who held the office from 1972 to 1976. His frank estimation was that "not more than two hundred families" control the wealth and power of the state. Author interview with Tathagata Satpathy, November 1, 2016, Bhubaneswar.

3. Thanks to reserved constituencies, plenty of SC and ST candidates are elected to legislative office. Their subordinate political position, though, is affirmed by a caste-wise analysis of contestants, MLAs, and Council of Ministers in Odisha governments from 1952 through 1986 that finds SC and ST candidates to be consistently underrepresented among cabinet-rank posts. Those cabinet positions that are occupied by SC and ST politicians are generally not the powerful ones, like home, revenue, and finance.

4. As Bailey notes, Ganatantra joined with local Socialist and Communist Party activists to support local movements opposing the Hirakud dam, a project that was essential for an economic development-model based on extractive industry.

5. Membership in UCCI includes over four hundred companies as of 2016. Interview with UCCI director general, September 2, 2016, UCCI offices, Bhubaneswar.
6. I heard broadly similar stories about the pressure to lend in the 1980s from one retired OSFC deputy general manager and two currently serving bank managers. Author interview with OSFC deputy general manager (retired), September 14, 2016, Cuttack, Odisha.
7. Interview with two current bank managers, OSFC head office, September 14, 2016, Cuttack, Odisha.
8. Interview with two current bank managers.
9. During the years 1983–84 and 1984–85, OSFC reported losses of 130 lakh and 126 lakh respectively (OSFC Annual Report 1985–86, 7). The cumulative losses of OSFC by the end of the 1990–91 stood at 731 lakh (OSFC Annual Report 1990–91, 4).
10. This would change only after the 1990s, when corporate interests in the extractives sector became the prime buyers of ad space (Pattnaik 2014, 78).
11. The problem of lack of access to working capital is something that I heard not only from OSFC managers but also from businessmen, including from several who were among the few who got their start in the "one thousand industries" days and survived the era.
12. Interview with a general manager at IPICOL, September 20, 2016, IPICOL House, Bhubaneswar.
13. Interview with a general manager at IPICOL.
14. Author interview with Tathagata Satpathy, Lok Sabha MP from Dhenkanal Constituency, which includes the sites of NALCO's power plant and smelter units; November 1, 2016, Bhubaneswar.
15. This viewpoint was expressed by two business owners who got their start as entrepreneurs in the 1980s with OSFC lending, as well as by two current managers of OFSC; all interviews took place in Bhubaneswar and Cuttack in September 2016.
16. This sentiment was repeated throughout interviews with senior managers at Jindal Steel and Power in Angul District as well as Tata Steel in Jajpur District, which has acquired several thousand acres in the Kalinganagar Industrial Estate. Author interviews carried out in July 2014, March 2016, and August to October 2016.
17. In 1975–76, for example, OSFC owned stock in IMFA valued at 9.8 lakhs, the largest amount out of the five companies in which it was then invested (OSFC Annual Report 1975–76, appendix V).
18. Author interview with Srikumar Misra, founder, managing director, and CEO of Milk Mantra, November 11, 2016, Milk Mantra main office, Bhubaneswar.
19. Author interview with Rajen Padhi, executive director, Utkal Chamber of Commerce and Industry, September 2, 2016, UCCI offices, Bhubaneswar.
20. Author interview with senior manager at Odisha Industrial Infrastructure Development Corporation, September 22, 2016, IDCO Tower, Bhubaneswar, Odisha.
21. This was the view of Jugal Kishore Mohapatra, who served as personal secretary to Chief Minister Naveen Patnaik from 2004 to 2009, finance secretary from 2009 to 2013, and chief secretary from 2013 to 2014. Author interview with Jugal Kishore Mohapatra, November 7, 2016, XIMB campus, Bhubaneswar.

Chapter 11

1. After a long stint in power, the CPM lost power in West Bengal during the 2011 state-assembly elections.
2. This paragraph is drawn from Kohli (2012, 47).
3. For a discussion of the concept of power elite in the American context, see Mills (1956).
4. See Kapur and Vaishnav (forthcoming, 5). Also see the concluding chapter for a summary of the main findings reported here.
5. Even the *Economist*—hardly a radical critic of the probusiness BJP—underlined this trend in its review of the "Modi juggernaut." See "The World in 2018" issue, p. 58.
6. Gujarat and Maharashtra account for nearly half of India's exports.

7. For a yet deeper analysis of why political leaders of Odisha had shallower commitment to the public good than, say, in Gujarat, one would have to study the political socialization of the respective political elite, probably within the preindependence nationalist movement.

8. Since many East Asian economies are export-oriented, one answer to this puzzle in the relevant literature is that the pressure to remain competitive in global markets limited the damaging impact of cronyism in such countries as South Korea of the recent past, or in China today. See, for example, Studwell (2013). Another answer focuses instead on the nature of East Asian states; see Kohli (2004). Also see Khan and Sundaram (2000).

9. We would like to acknowledge the help of Devesh Kapur in bringing this example to our attention.

10. For a similar conclusion see Scott (1990).

11. We are not necessarily endorsing this proposition. We are merely suggesting that such a scholarly case can be made.

12. In opposition to the claims of Moore, this was very much the point in Rueschemeyer, Stephens, and Stephens (1992). Their suggestion instead was that full democracy was eventually pushed forward, not by the bourgeoisie, but by the working class.

INDEX